The Social Encyclicals

and

Saint Thomas Aquinas

Donald G. Boland

En Route Books and Media, LLC

Saint Louis, MO

⊕ENROUTE

Make the time

En Route Books and Media, LLC

5705 Rhodes Avenue

St. Louis, MO 63109

Cover credit: Dr. Sebastian Mahfood, OP, from a section of
Dives and Lazarus, Luca Giordano (1634–1705)

ISBN-13: 979-8-88870-059-4

Library of Congress Control Number: 2023942060

To Venerable Eugenio Pacelli

Pope Pius XII

The pope of peace, whose pontifical motto was "Peace is the work of Justice" (*Opus Iustitiae Pax*)

Though he did not write a social encyclical, what he said in his two speeches commemorating *Rerum novarum* express in the most clear way the principles of distributive and commutative justice that are at the heart of the social doctrine of the Church.

He also penetrated most acutely into the modern politico-economic system of Capitalism and how its peculiar kind of social injustice was incorporated in its practice and seemingly justified by a nation's wealth being assessed according to the quantitative mea-sures of modern science.

Selected Quotes

On the place of Justice in the Social Doctrine of the Church and the position of Saint Thomas Aquinas as Common Doctor of the Church

Pope Blessed John Paul I

"… charity is the soul of justice". General Audience 6 September 1978.

Pope Benedict XVI

"Justice is the primary way of charity or, in Paul VI's words, "the minimum measure" of it". *Caritas in veritate* 2009.

"Politics must be a striving for justice, and hence it has to establish the fundamental preconditions for peace." Speech, Reichstag Building, Berlin 2011.

As for the regard St. Thomas is held in the Church, we recommend the reader read the encyclical of **Pope Benedict XV** *Fausto Appetente Die* published in 1921 in commemoration of the 700th anniversary of the death of St. Dominic from which we give only a couple of quotations.

n. 6 "… nothing is such a hindrance to eternal salvation as the ignorance of the truth and perversity of doctrine."

n. 7 "The very wisdom of God seemed to speak through the Dominicans when there rose up among them such heralds and defenders of Christian wisdom as Hyacinth Polonus, Peter the Martyr, Vincent Ferrer, and such miracles of genius and erudition as Albert the Great, Raymond de Penafort, Thomas Aquinas, in whom especially, a follower of Dominic, God 'deigned to enlighten his Church.' This Order, therefore, always in honor as the teacher of truth, acquired new luster when the Church declared the teaching of Thomas to be her own and that Doctor, honored with the special praises of the Pontiffs, the master and patron of Catholic schools."

Table of Contents

Foreword

We have completed after a fashion a treatment of human behavior from a practical moral philosophical point of view, taken from Aristotle as interpreted by Saint Thomas Aquinas. It was necessary to apply this knowledge to the modern condition of human life since the whole point of practical moral thought is to assess things in the concrete world that we live in.

There are a couple of things one needs to note in this exercise. Though we have given an overview of natural morality as a whole in our book "Ethics Today and Saint Thomas Aquinas", the focus of concern has been on Political Philosophy, and hence on the virtue of justice.

The reason for this concentration we hope has appeared in the books already written. But it comes from the major changes to the social nature of things human that have come to be constitutive of the modern world. It is here that the effects of the exclusion of wisdom (Metaphysics and Ethics) have most visibly determined the form of modern society.

This has meant the virtual official exclusion of Ethics altogether from modern thinking and acting, and therefore, were it not for the continued presence of Christ and the Church, the modern world would not have long lasted.

It is not strictly correct to refer to the post Christendom era as post Christian, because the beneficent influence of the Church on the lives of many individuals and civil societies, even at the natural level, has not failed and will not fail ("until the end of time").

It is not known, however, to what condition of iniquity human social life may descend.

But these are questions we must leave more principally to the study of sacred theology. Nevertheless, that does not mean that we cannot look at the social situation from the level of philosophy and reason. Indeed, the theologian is required to take the political life of the modern world into account.

So we can say that from the point of view of reason the nature of modern life has been defined by the exclusion of morality. Two new (value-free) "sciences" arose to dominate modern thinking about human behaviour, Politics and Economics, the latter (involving the worship of money) becoming in the end a sort of alternative to religion.

It will help therefore to understand the modern age if we examine what has happened to it from the point of reason and particularly moral philosophy, which Aquinas following Aristotle called Ethical Science, and within which is included domestic and political ethics, and within the latter comes what the modern mind calls Economics and Politics. This will be seen to have some relevance to the understanding of the social encyclicals.

We have noted that Ethics or natural morality is divided into three orders, Personal, Domestic and Political, according as we belong to three natural communities, as explained previously. These orders are distinguished by three common goods, the first being God, the second that of the family or household (*oikos*) and the third that of the civil society (*polis*). It is to be well noted that these three are knowable at the level of Moral Philosophy. In particular, religious worship is a necessary obligation in justice in natural morality.

But what is evident is that the natural order in each of these moral communities is and has been apparently from the beginning of history severely disordered. We may be able to account for this by putting it down to the failure of human will in particular cases. But the radical depth and universal extent of the disorder, affecting even our relation with things below us, defies rational comprehension. It is only by recourse to divine revelation that we can gain some insight into the causes and so also into the remedy.

This is where the social encyclicals enter the discussion. Nonetheless, there are certain peculiarities about this intervention that call for comment. Why was the intervention made as late as 1891? The pope indeed noted the desperate condition of the majority poor, represented mainly by workers, saying (RN, n. 3) "the hiring of labor and the conduct of trade are concentrated in the hands of comparatively few; so that a small number of very rich men have been able to lay upon the teeming masses of the laboring poor a yoke little better than that of slavery itself". Note the connection made between the use (or abuse) of labour as hired and the use (or abuse) of the market. Labour means human persons and the market means buying and selling of commodities.

But the civilisation with which the Church had lived within and dealt with at its beginning and for the subsequent 1500 years had been made up of a multitude of people who had labored under real slavery or serfdom. It seems that the existence of enslavement or lack of freedom in individual human beings unjustly dominated by others was not the flashpoint. Certainly, the re-appearance of chattel slavery in its modern form, and the widely used slave trade in non-Europeans by modern "civilised" nations, brought forth strong condemnation from the papacy.

But the modern social encyclicals were and are concerned with another problem that had arisen within the same civilised nations with respect to their own populations, upon whom a very rich few had imposed "a yoke little better that that of slavery". This was in a civilization that relatively recently had emerged from Catholic Christendom and still to some extent propounded itself to be Christian.

Indeed, we may say that there has to be some connection between the spirit of revolution that began to arise in the oppressed multitude and in those who took up their cause in the name of justice and the elevated Christian view of the dignity of every human person. As well, the prominence of references to the earlier history of the vicissitudes of the Jewish nation is not coincidental.

As the antipathy against the Catholic Church began to spread to Christianity and religion generally, however, reliance was placed rather on pagan myths to support the cause of justice and freedom, such as in the story of Prometheus, Thus, the intellectual support for the cause of the oppressed moved from being Judeo-Christian to humanist/atheist. The remedy then proposed took on an entirely different nature. Pope Leo XIII spells out the radical opposition between the remedies proposed right from the start in *Rerum novarum*.

The history of early modern society explains why the focus was first on the politico-economic level of the moral order within the modern nations of "Western" civilization itself. We have endeavoured to explain how it was that on the disappearance, at least in legal and political terms, of pagan chattel slavery and mediaeval serfdom, a new modern form of servitude came about within Christian/modern civilization. It prompts the question of whether the fact of unjust domination of some by others, or some socially systemic form of undue servitude, has a cause deep within fallen human nature (without forgetting that the injury does not strictly speaking touch the nature but the natural inclinations flowing therefrom).

The peculiar phenomenon of the modern form (for reasons we have given) was that, in the turmoil of a (supernaturally) religious revolution, it was able to be presented, politically and "legally", by the masters (the "fortunate" rich few), who had come to claim the right to property of the natural and inherited lands and wealth in the rising Western nations (best seen in the English speaking world) as making the workers free (a deceit shown up by Pope Leo XIII) and political rule (in fact oligarchical) as one controlled by the majority "free" working poor, and hence "democratic". Did they not get the right to elect who should rule them?

This new meaning that became attached to democracy is something we need to examine more closely as we go. It has even seemed to be adopted by the Catholic moral theologians and by the papacy. Pope Leo XIII's encyclical *Graves de commune re* (On Christian Democracy) needs to be looked at carefully in this regard. Our further discussion of the two basic dimensions of ethics, personal and social/political, will throw some light on what is a linguistic problem from an Aristotelian point of view.

However, the immediate needs and wants of the civil communities having to be supplied by the labour of the poor majority propertyless (proletariat), they having to make use of the "capital" of the capitalists (the increase in the value of which property was able to be claimed by the proprietors), the products (and services) so produced then "distributed" to all (first of all the rich) through the institution of the market (a significant part of which was that of "free labour"), made the majority working poor a necessary part of this whole system of production and exchange. From this modern economic system the workers "rightly" were entitled to receive only the wages agreed to with their employer, who was either the person who provided the capital (things/instruments) or his hired "steward" (overseer).

How the market came to provide a secondary means to enrichment for the already rich, and some others who were able to use money astutely, has been explained earlier. From this has come the confusion of wealth with money that distinguishes the modern use of the word "Capital".

Such a system of employment was so impersonal and profit driven in the way we have described, represented, by the way, as the modern ("Christian") politico-economic order of Liberal Capitalism, that it inevitably led to the subjection of the majority in the Western world to such a servile and inhuman condition that it made the institutions of servitude of old, as social systems, look rather mild by comparison. At least the average Roman slave owner did not fail to feed his slave. In principle, the modern employer did not need to worry about the welfare of an individual worker – there were plenty of others anxious to find employment, at a wage being driven down by the surplus ("pool") of labourers in the market.

It was into this desperate situation in Western modern social life that Pope Leo XIII felt the need to intervene as the Vicar of Christ. Yet what is noteworthy is that whilst he condemned the grave social injustice being perpetrated under the new politico-economic (dis) order (acquiring the name of "Liberal" Capitalism) he did not support any call to overthrow it. He recognised it as another kind of institutional enslavement worthy of condemnation as much as those of the pre-modern ages, found in all past societies, even civilized. But for reasons that may now be clear he applied Christ's dictum that the Church's kingdom is not of this world. Christ had the power to destroy the evildoers behind the temporal evil he and his followers were subjected to but he chose not to, and showed us another way.

Indeed, Leo XIII saw the attempts being made to destroy the modern system of servitude altogether as certain to produce a worse situation (he turned out to be prophetic in this regard). He saw too the connection of such attempts (generally going under the name of Socialism) with the radical modern attempts, dating from around the so-called Protestant Reformation, to destroy the Catholic Faith, together with the order of natural morality which it alone was capable of protecting (another truth proved historically in recent times).

This opposition expressed itself in various forms, some secret and others quite open, going by such names as Freemasons and Illuminati, the devilish influence of which the pope had discussed in other encyclicals. The use of notions such as light and freedom is significant when we remember that the most powerful of the fallen angels is given the name "Lucifer", and his choice is put in words intended to express freedom, *non serviam*.

More generally, such a modern mood against the Church and her divine authority in Faith and Morals, was already present in the view being publicly promoted that the modern era was a period of Enlightenment after a "Dark Age". This was fortified by the revolution in thinking and the radical change in meaning of science and reason that came to be identified with Isaac Newton's physico-mathematical explanation of the physical universe.

Though not essentially opposed to science and reason fully taken, this new truth (wisdom) and (moral) value free notion of science was soon taken up in the anti-Catholic cause of Protestantism and in the promotion of the anti-moral features of the new thinking in politics and economics. All this provided a convenient deceitful cover for the take-over at the politico-economic level we have discussed in our previous books. The multitude suffering a disguised servitude were further subjected to a system of compulsory education, "free and secular", wherein they were indoctrinated in the virtues of modern freedom and democratic rule under what is in Aristotle's political language a system of despotic/oligarchic rule.

We have gone into the details of this in our previous books, though we will say some more about this when the question of democracy comes up in the social encyclicals. The social encyclicals, however, simply focus on the fundamental fact of social injustice and, in a way, accept such as "natural" in the sense of not naturally eradicable. It is only able to be ameliorated under the light of Faith. Any attempt to remedy the social disorder by the efforts of reason alone will be futile and resort to violence, even in the spirit of vengeance (a proper moral virtue according to St. Thomas), will not only fail but will result in a worse condition even for the oppressed. Christ and his Church have the true and only answer.

The social encyclicals therefore shift our focus from the philosophical (natural) to the theological (supernatural) level of human life and association. However, they do not for that disconnect the two orders and, indeed, one may detect a certain parallelism between the two orders of Faith and Reason. This is most evident when we relate to each other the social political and the individual personal areas of concern.

At the level of nature and reason it is clear that though the individual person is part of the civil community (a fact that Aristotle is insistent upon) he is not so according to all that he is (as St. Thomas puts it). In the spiritual order, or as a person, the common good of the civil community is for his sake, not the other way around. The order of political morality is subordinated to that of personal morality. That is expressed most forcibly in the principle of subsidiarity. That is to say, though the common good of the civil community has rightful demands upon its members, the common good of the universal community, which is God, transcends that of the political community.

Put in other terms, at the level of reason, where the civil community or political order is concerned, the principle of subsidiarity is more fundamental than the principle of solidarity. This comes out in the social encyclicals in making the natural social order be ultimately for the sake of the person (which St. Thomas says is that which is most perfect in all nature).

When the notion of person is given its supernatural status this subsidiarity so far as any temporal or natural association is concerned is even clearer. The person as created by God is sacrosanct. But the relation between the Christian person and the Christian community of persons as a whole is not so clear, as it is difficult to distinguish the individual person in grace from the community of the faithful as the Body of Christ. The fact that the social encyclicals are moral theology also makes difficult the discussion in them of solidarity at a philosophical level. So, we can leave the fuller discussion of solidarity to theology.

However, to facilitate a reading of the social encyclicals, I will try to summarize the difference a theological perspective makes, not to the facts of the human condition, but to the assessment of their significance and the means of changing those conditions for the better. Despite the overwhelming evidence from history of the erroneousness and ineffectiveness of attempts to cure "the social problem" from reason alone what the Church proposes as the way to overcome the evident evils and injustices seems to some to be a capitulation.

It is only with Faith that we can understand that it is the only way, the way of the Cross, and indeed that it is also the secret of happiness here on earth and the means not only of one's own salvation but also, being joined to Christ's suffering and death, the salvation of others.

What we say here, of course, being to do with matters of Faith, is submitted to the judgment of the Church, as is whatever is said in all our books on natural morality, since it too comes under the authority of the Magisterium. But let us try. "Man" is used in the traditional sense to include woman.

From her beginning the Church's principal mission has been to preach the gospel. That is to say it is to tell the world of human persons "the good news". From the beginning of human existence in the first man and woman, in Adam and Eve, man sinned against God in effectively saying what Lucifer had said, *non serviam*. This was essentially to reject God's love, which was not only expressed naturally in his creating man but also insofar as man had been raised to a supernatural, divine, level by grace.

By this, man fell out of God's grace, by which was lost all that was good within the scope of his will, including his natural happiness, and seemingly irredeemably, as happened in Lucifer's case. But in the case of man God had a way for the human person to be forgiven and return to God's grace, and we know by Faith that God had that in mind from eternity.

Through his only Son, Jesus Christ, God thus provided a way back into God's "favour", or original grace. Each human person, male and female, could be born again, saved from the fate of Lucifer, because he or she had time to change his or her "mind" (repent). The original sin was thus forgiven by the free and sinless sacrifice of the Son of God made man. But this had to be applied to oneself by man's free will. This meant that one could fall out of grace, and back into grace (through a supplementary sacrament) over one's lifetime.

However, the essential message revealed through Christ and his Church was that we were all saved and bound for eternal happiness beyond our comprehension, if we but said in our hearts, *serviam*. This is also to recover true freedom – for it was by the first *non serviam* that man had fallen into the only real slavery, of sin.

But, as the Church warns us, man's redemption has not cured us of all the "natural" consequences of original sin, of which death, as St. Paul explains, is the last to be conquered in time. Mysteriously, however, the very pain, suffering and especially death that flowed radically from original sin could be turned, by association with Christ's, into the very means of contributing to not just our own salvation, but also that "of the whole world". So it is that the history of the Church is marked by a multitude of saints rejoicing in their embrace of suffering and death for the sake of the name of Christ.

Let that be enough to be said by way of preparation for the discussion of the individual social encyclicals to which we now turn, remembering that we are endeavouring to extract from them principles rather of a philosophical than theological nature.

Chapter One

Pope Leo XIII's *Rerum novarum* (1891)

When we move to consider the social encyclicals the popes are able to throw the light of Faith on the whole problem of disorder in all three areas of human conduct, political, domestic and personal, even though in modern times it has been the threat of social revolution at the political level by reason of the extremity of injustice in economic terms that has been the immediate cause of the Church's intervention.

At the heart of the problem at all levels is the issue of freedom. The root of this has been discussed above. The domination of others (despotic power) inevitably follows at the social level, both domestic and civil or political.

Certainly, changes in the personal and domestic order of things operate both as causes and effects of what occurs in the civic order. But our treatment is focused on the political, which includes the politico-economic. For this is where there is the most externally detectible contrast in the modern era with the era against which it revolted and, indeed, where the change to the modern era is propagated as good and necessary so far as humanity is concerned.

We can relate this concentration to the social doctrine of the Church in the papal encyclicals beginning with *Rerum novarum*. The initial focus there was per force on the extremely desperate socio-political condition the majority was driven to at the basic socio-economic level, so that it appeared that modern society, despite its gains in material terms, was about to collapse into a bitter warring conflict between its two "economic" parts, that of the propertied, who provided the necessary capital, and that of the propertyless, who provided the necessary labour, come to be described in the abstract terms of Capital and Labour.

What we wish to do is to bring together as best we can our treatment so far with what is contained in this first social encyclical and those that have built upon it. For, though it is clearly stated by the popes that the subject matter is one of moral theology, much of this series of documents of the Magisterium proceeds at the moral philosophical level, according as the relation between Faith and reason has been explained by St. Thomas.

We have noted, however, that a treatment exclusively at the level of reason or philosophy cannot provide the "cure" to what ills affect this condition. Indeed, many aspects of the problem, such as that of the relation between master and servant/slave, remain unresolved in our reading of Aristotle. It does not seem possible to reconcile his position in this regard with the essential connection of free will with every human person.

Still less can modern science and philosophy provide any solution to this and other kinds of despotic domination of some (usually many) by others (usually a few) also at the political level. Such necessarily related domination and servitude seem to be part of the very "nature" of human social relationships in every age.

The social encyclicals do provide the clue to the solution, but only if we take the study of the subject to the Christian, supernatural, level. The problem is not resolvable without taking into account the original condition of the fall from grace, i.e. the existential condition of original sin, and the redemption by Christ. With this the perfection of freedom in each human will is restored. But here enters the paradoxical problem of how we ourselves are to participate in the achievement of the perfect happiness originally intended by God for all, not only individually but also socially.

Before considering the encyclical in detail we will make some preliminary remarks regarding the nature of the problem to be dealt with. From the beginning of history of civilized human life, which Aristotle called *polis* (the city) it can be seen that political societies in fact were not one civil community but two, divided in politico-economic terms, as Plato observed, into the rich and the poor. Here we are talking not of the slaves, for they were not considered part of the citizenry.

Nor are we referring to those peoples who had not arrived at a civilized state, as the many tribal or village societies (Latin: *nationes*) of ancient and modern times. Aristotle regarded them as in an intermediate condition before the constitution of a city state, though their conditions, like those of the families of which they were associations, remained in some way as parts of the final perfect social state of the *polis*.

These parts still played an important role in the life of the civil community and many problems of the *polis* could and do arise from disorder at their level. So too do disorders in the political organization have repercussions in social life at the lower levels of ethnic association and family (particularly in the economic life of the *polis*). We mean to concentrate here on the political order, if involving economic considerations.

The basic disorders that come into play in this regard are to do with the two kinds of particular justice within a civil community, distributive and commutative, and the two basic social institutions which any deficiency in them bear upon, property and the market. How things have come about in modern times has been dealt with in our previous books.

Put shortly, the politico-economic changes the revolutionary times that put an end to the era of Christendom and led to the modern era brought about a new situation of the relation between the rich and the poor where, as Pope Leo points out, the old kinds of servitude, which excluded the slave/serf from the status of citizen gave way to an entirely new relation of master/servant, wherein servitude became a status that attached to the majority poor section within the *polis*.

These majority poor section remained regarded as having the rights and freedoms politically belonging to members of the civil community, but they were effectively without such rights (now regarded as privileges – hence they are called "underprivileged") because of their lack of "property". The work that formerly was performed by non-citizens slaves now had to be done by citizens/workers. A number of radical changes in social relations worked to effect this. We have seen how this new politico-economic system (come to be called Capitalism) was able to be accomplished through the application of the institution of the "free market" to the work of the hired labourer.

The very notion of worker came to be applied universally to a hired hand, because the modern worker/labourer had virtually no property of his own whereby to engage independently in production and exchange. The rich had successfully monopolized the "legal" ownership of "property", to which was able to be added the new system of "citizen" servitude by commandeering the labour of the working poor through a "labour market". One needs however to understand Aristotle's division of exchange into two (CMC and MCM) to understand how this came about, by labour being treated as a commodity. Unfortunately, despite St. Thomas's clear teaching on this aspect of exchange in II-II q. 77 very few, if any, modern moral theologians have paid any attention to St. Thomas in this regard.

From the point of view of the modern rich there was not only the satisfaction of economic dominance (of being oligarchs, if consciously or quasi-unconsciously letting the illusion of democracy prevail) but also of taking credit for the working poor "gaining" political freedom (democracy). The poor worker had no comeback. On the one hand, his poverty was his own fault; "why don't you work harder for those who provide you with employment and save up some property of your own" – just as we rich have done. On the other hand, "what are you complaining about", in the land of the free you are as able to become president as much as any other – just as you have equal opportunity of winning the lottery.

Pope Leo XIII showed up the deceit in this rosy politico-economic picture painted by the defenders of Capitalism, brazenly covered over by a diabolical stirring up of fear and hatred against the Catholic Church and "Catholic" nation states. The pope firstly described openly the enormity of the injustice of the servile condition into which the majority has been driven "legally" (n. 3); secondly, he exposed the hypocrisy of the "freedom" alleged to attend the wage contract (nn. 43-45).

In the early part of paragraphs 1 to 15 the pope sets out a short but telling description of the true picture of the modern relation between the rich and poor, which has come to be put in terms of those of property, or "capital", and those without, or of the propertied (capitalist/employing class) and the propertyless (proletarian/ employed class). The relation was clearly put in terms of a sharp divide between Capital and Labor within the modern civil community.

The pope put it in the starkest terms, that have been quoted over and over again and clearly warrant the strongest moral condemnation he gave it: " ... it has come to pass that working men have been surrendered, isolated and helpless, to the hardheartedness of employers and the greed of unchecked competition." To this he adds: " ... the hiring of labor and the conduct of trade are concentrated in the hands of comparatively few, so that a small number of very rich men have been able to lay upon the teeming masses of the laboring poor a yoke little better than slavery". All this flies in the face of the "official" defenders of Capitalism (Catholics among them) who are backed up by the "value-free" modern sciences of Economics and Politics. (Refer to Pope Pius XI's strong restatement of this in nn. 3 & 4 of *Quadragesimo anno*)

The Capitalist "West" of course did not like this. If one was not for Capitalism then one must be for Socialism. In the USA in particular, as Dickens noted on his visit there, there may be declared to be freedom of speech but there is no freedom of the expression of certain opinions critical of things. Dickens gives a graphic account of his experience in this regard. It is not permissible to say there is anything wrong with Western political or economic doctrine. The American idea of the right kind of political regime is the culmination of the march of history to freedom and prosperity realised in its own political and economic system of Capitalism. Many Catholics go along with this. In the case of Pope Leo XIII, one simply chooses to ignore what the pope says about the modern divide between the privileged ("fortunate few") and the unprivileged (the many "unfortunately") and focus on his critique of Socialism. A similar reaction may be noticed in relation to the present pope's social encyclicals.

Indeed, Pope Leo's devastating condemnation of Capitalism and its necessary deleterious effect on modern civilization is immediately followed by an even more powerful condemnation of the politico-economic ideology that had arisen to oppose it, Socialism. In the light of the history of modern civilization this seemed to be the only alternative and so attracted many dedicated adherents.

The pope saw things more even-mindedly and, whilst not denying the profound injustice to the working "class" (modern poor) in Capitalism, spent the rest of the first quarter of the encyclical (to para. 15) demonstrating the fundamental falsity of the (moral/ political) philosophical position of Socialism and the fateful consequences that would follow from its socio-political implementation.

His critique centered round the natural goodness and moral necessity of the institution of private property. The Socialists' argument was that property treated as a "legal" right was the root cause of the oppression of the working poor and hence urged its abolition.

The pope's response was that it was in truth a fundamental institution based on human nature, as the whole of human experience showed, and it could be rationally defended by the best of Christian wisdom, in Saint Thomas Aquinas, and indeed, by the best of pagan philosophy, in Aristotle.

It was a weakness in the understanding of the natural moral law that lay at the bottom of the problem in Socialism's political thinking. But, as is brought out in other parts of the encyclical and previous ones, it was a radical fault that was within modern Liberalism that underlay the mental and moral mistakes of both Capitalism and Socialism. Capitalism is, in politico-economic terms, but one expression of the liberalist ideology (favorable to the few rich oppressors). Socialism is but another expression of the same liberalist ideology (adopted deviously on behalf of the many oppressed poor).

The Socialists were of course hostile to the encyclical because of its condemnation of their ideology. The defenders of Capitalism did not know quite what to make of it. Obviously, they were pleased with the condemnation in principle of Socialism. But they would be uncomfortable with the baring of the gross injustice of Capitalism and the erroneousness of it as a theory justifying such structural injustice. They would have been relieved, however, at the pope not supporting a proposal to overthrow the existing politico-economic system.

They are also able to cleverly use the pope's argument for the naturalness of the institution of private property as a defence of their abuse of it on a grand scale. The positivist perversion of the understanding of law and politics that soon followed the change in the notion of science, together with the turn to oligarchical rule, enabled the institution of property (as well as all other natural institutions, such as marriage and government itself) to be presented, in the matter of government coming purely from an "original contract", and the institution of property as a matter of positive law or legality derived from the will of the rulers. These rulers were in fact the rich, an oligarchy, and the "people" in theory, a democracy. They are both perverse forms of constitutions in Aristotle's and Aquinas's political philosophy. For the notion of common good had long fallen out of the political picture.

As noted, the meaning of democracy has changed in modern times, being presented in a neutral way (the common good either ignored or taken for granted – it is something we should discuss further). The popes have come to use it in a good sense, but in the modern mind it mostly makes for despotic rule. Those in power, as understood in both kinds of political rule, oligarchy and democracy, can make what laws they like – to serve their own interests, though affecting to act in "the national interest".

However, we see how the Church has understood the two principal ideologies of modern times in Capitalism and Socialism, severely condemning both, but the pope goes on to finding a way that the world might "live with" Capitalism, as it has had to live with previous forms of domination by some of others reduced to a condition of widespread unjust servitude. The problem then became not so much to remedy "the condition of labour" in any complete way but to prevent the workers/poor from been driven into such a condition of misery as to provoke desperation and revolution.

This the pope turns to next where firstly he states the right and even duty of the Church to intervene and indeed that there can be no solution to the problem nor any significant amelioration without recourse to the precepts and guidance of "religion and the Church". (para. 16) Then he points out there are natural differences in the human condition, even with regard to working capacity, from which flow differences in possession of wealth, and these are not averse to the welfare of others. Indeed, properly used they work to the good of all. (para. 17)

It may be noted here that St. Thomas Aquinas and all great moralists explain the institution and right of property as applying to exclusive possession only (because the earth has to be worked individually) but that the use should remain "common". That way the more fundamental principle of the universal destination of goods is preserved and served. The right of property is derived from the natural law and therefore "sacrosanct" (before civil societies come into existence); but as St. Thomas explains it is not at the level of a primary principle of the Natural Law but belongs to the *Ius Gentium* (secondary principles necessarily flowing from the primary). Here the use of the distinction between natural and positive law has to be carefully applied. (cf. the excellent book by Santiago Ramirez, O. P. *El Derecho de Gentes*)

All of this, of course, went out the window with the rejection of the very notion of natural law and the substitution of positive law as the primary rule of social conduct. In modern political theory might (despotic power) replaces right (based on reality) and governments are pressured to create new ones. The notion of right itself becomes a "right" to use and abuse things at will. Think of the new right to marry in civil "law", where the same sex "couple" are given the right to abuse their own bodily organs. Refer to my book on Natural Law for a fuller treatment of this question.

However, then the pope refers to the condition of all because of the continued consequences of original sin. Do we hope by scientific means to abolish death someday? These consequences of sin we need to recognize "are bitter and hard to bear, and they must accompany man as long as life lasts." Those who promise an end to all human misery and troubles "delude the people and impose upon them, and their lying promises will only one day bring forth evils worse than the present." (para. 18) [how true]

Nor should the relations between individuals or groups within civil society be viewed as Thomas Hobbes did (as wolf is to wolf). This incidentally influenced the modern notion of Natural Law in such as Pufendorf. Not understanding that man is by nature political, if, like marriage, having to be constituted by human agreement, as explained by Aristotle, Locke went to the other extreme of basing the civil community, and so "natural" law, on pure "contract", or will, without reason, but put up as "rational".

But, as Pope Leo points out, even those who possess much wealth (if justly acquired) and those who possess little (or even none, for whatever reason) are naturally designed to live in harmony [as friend to friend, as Aristotle put it]. To present the relation in terms of perpetual conflict "necessarily produces confusion and savage brutality" [as is the history of Socialist countries]. (para. 19)

Then in the next paragraph (20) the pope sets out the basic duties each section of modern civil society, even existing as a "divide", are bound by. They are nothing but basic principles of justice (rendering to each his due). He deals first with the duties that pertain to "the proletarian and the worker" (*opifex*).

To render fully and faithfully what has freely and with equity been agreed upon. [note the pope's comments later on what is a free wage contract]

Never in any way to harm the things, or violate the person of the owner/ employer (*dominus*).

Never to resort to violence: "in defending one's own cause", says the English translation. It is a poor translation as English translations mostly are in my experience. The Latin is *rationibus tuis*. It evidently means "your reasons", i. e. not to come to blows in one's arguments. The translation suggests one should be a pacifist.

Not to engage in riot or disorder. To have nothing to do with men of evil principles who work upon the people with artful promises of great results, and excite foolish hopes which usually end in regrets and grievous loss.

Then the pope lists the duties of the capitalists [the rich as employers.] This list of duties is rather more lengthy, so the paragraph is quoted below from the encyclical. The Latin is given under so one who knows Latin may see how loose the translation is.

"The following duties bind the wealthy owner and the employer: not to look upon their work people as their bondsmen, but to respect in every man his dignity as a person ennobled by Christian character. They are reminded that, according to natural reason and Christian philosophy, working for gain is creditable, not shameful, to a man, since it enables him to earn an honorable livelihood; but to misuse men as though they were things in the pursuit of gain, or to value them solely for their physical powers - that is truly shameful and inhuman. Again justice demands that, in dealing with the working man, religion and the good of his soul must be kept in mind. Hence, the employer is bound to see that the worker has time for his religious duties; that he be not exposed to corrupting influences and dangerous occasions; and that he be not led away to neglect his home and family, or to squander his earnings. Furthermore, the employer must never tax his work people beyond their strength, or employ them in work unsuited to their sex and age.

His great and principal duty is to give everyone what is just. Doubtless, before deciding whether wages are fair, many things have to be considered; but wealthy owners and all masters of labor should be mindful of this - that to exercise pressure upon the indigent and the destitute for the sake of gain, and to gather one's profit out of the need of another, is condemned by all laws, human and divine. To defraud any one of wages that are his due is a great crime which cries to the avenging anger of Heaven. 'Behold, the hire of the laborers... which by fraud has been kept back by you, crieth; and the cry of them hath entered into the ears of the Lord of Sabaoth.' (6) Lastly, the rich must religiously refrain from cutting down the workmen's earnings, whether by force, by fraud, or by usurious dealing; and with all the greater reason because the laboring man is, as a rule, weak and unprotected, and because his slender means should in proportion to their scantiness be accounted sacred."

Ista vero ad divites spectant ac dominos :non habendos mancipiorum loco opifices: vereri in eis aequum esse dignitatem personae, utique nobilitatam ab eo, character christianus qui dicitur. Quaestuosas artes. si naturae ratio. si christiana philosophia audiatur, non pudori homini esse, sed decori, quia vitae sustentandae praebent honestam potestatem. Illud vere turpe et inhumanum, abuti hominibus pro rebus ad quaestum, nec facere eos pluris, quam quantum nervis polleant viribusque. Similiter praecipitur, religionis et bonorum animi haberi rationem in proletariis oportere. Quare dominorum partes esse, efficere ut idoneo temporis spatio pietati vacet opifex: non hominem dare obvium lenociniis corruptelarum illecebrisque peccandi: neque ullo pacto a cura domestica parcimoniaeque studio abducere. Item non plus imponere operis, quam vires ferre queant, nec id genus, quod cum aetate sexuque dissideat.

In maximis autem officiis dominorum illud eminet, iusta unicuique praebere. Profecto ut mercedis statuatur ex aequitate modus, caussae sunt considerandae plures: sed generatim locupletes atque heri meminerint, premere emolumenti sui caussa indigentes ac miseros, alienaque ex inopia captare quaestum, non divina, non humana iura sinere. Fraudare vero quemquam mercede debita grande piaculum est, quod iras e caelo ultrices clamore devocat. Ecce merces operariorum... quae fraudata est a vobis, clamat; et clamor eorum in aures Domini Sabaoth introivit [Jac. V, 4]. - Postremo religiose cavendum locupletibus ne proletariorum compendiis quicquam noceant nec vi, nec dolo, nec fenebribus artibus : idque eo vel magis quod non satis illi sunt contra iniurias atque impotentiam muniti, eorumque res, quo exilior, hoc sanctior habenda. His obtemperatio legibus nonne posset vim caussasque dissidii vel sola restinguere?

There is some difficulty inherent in the problem itself. That is in the language of master and servant, which in ancient times was associated with the status of master and slave, which signified the same as that of owner and thing owned, the slave being regarded as the property of the master. The Latin is *dominus* and *servus*, which could be rendered as master and slave, or lord and servant (serf). Pope Leo XIII tends to adopt the language of former times in trying to describe the modern relation of owner/ employer and worker/employee. As we have seen, this is a new relationship within the notion of a citizen, whereas previously the slave or serf was not regarded as having the "privileges" of citizenship at least in any full sense. This came through into modern times where even some not now regarded as slaves or serfs were excluded from participation in political rule because such was made dependent on property status.

So too the despotic character of the master/servant relationship carried over into St. Thomas's use of the terms. He contrasts this relationship with the political one of ruler and ruled. For instance, when asked whether any kind of subjection of one man to another would have existed in the state of original justice he makes a distinction saying that political rule would have, for it is natural and as a kind of self-rule does not take away from the subject's true freedom, whereas the master/servant relationship as traditionally understood would not have existed in the state of original justice. This is evidently because of its despotic and unnatural character in the subject/servant not having full self-control or true freedom. That must mean it is a consequence of original sin.

The modern relationship of master/servant is a peculiar one. For it is applied to a relationship between persons who are both politically equal in the classical sense, but, as Pope Leo XIII puts it, the majority subject because of unjust impoverishment in effect ("economically") to a yoke little better than slavery. Leo uses the term *dominus* to describe the status of the "master" in this situation, who is so dominant because of the (mis)appropriation of property (things – *rera*) that form the needed capital part of the productive process.

This change (brought into effect through the exchange process, as we have explained), complicates the understanding of the modern capitalist/worker (employer/ employee) relationship. It complicates as well the use of language in terms of master/servant. For in the modern era the despotic character is appropriate at the politico-economic level but not in theory at the purely political level (except when seen as in fact an oligarchical form of rule).

We must therefore do what we can to make sense of the matter in interpreting the social encyclicals, avoiding misunderstanding what is being said because of the difficulty of translation. Pope Leo is bringing out the servile character of the worker, whilst the modern mind, heavily influenced by a capitalist justifying "education", wants us to ignore the politico-economics relationship and focus on the purely political status (in theory).

The true lord and master of each human person is God and that is where the relationship of master/servant is able to be reconciled with the freedom of every human person. Where the subordination is natural and moral the subject does not lose his God given freedom of will.

Then the pope moves to the higher supernatural plane of eternal life without which one cannot judge aright our human situation. This is worth quoting in full but I first take out the passage that relates to what we are discussing and explains the Church's response to the social problem. "As for riches and the other things which men call good and desirable, whether we have them in abundance, or are lacking in them – so far as eternal happiness is concerned – it makes no difference; the only important thing is to use them aright."

"21. But the Church, with Jesus Christ as her Master and Guide, aims higher still. She lays down precepts yet more perfect, and tries to bind class to class in friendliness and good feeling. The things of earth cannot be understood or valued aright without taking into consideration the life to come, the life that will know no death. Exclude the idea of futurity, and forthwith the very notion of what is good and right would perish; nay, the whole scheme of the universe would become a dark and unfathomable mystery. The great truth which we learn from nature herself is also the grand Christian dogma on which religion rests as on its foundation - that, when we have given up this present life, then shall we really begin to live. God has not created us for the perishable and transitory things of earth, but for things heavenly and everlasting; He has given us this world as a place of exile, and not as our abiding place. As for riches and the other things which men call good and desirable, whether we have them in abundance, or are lacking in them - so far as eternal happiness is concerned - it makes no difference; the only important thing is to use them aright. Jesus Christ, when He redeemed us with plentiful redemption, took not away the pains and sorrows which in such large proportion are woven together in the web of our mortal life. He transformed them into motives of virtue and occasions of merit; and no man can hope for eternal reward unless he follow in the blood-stained footprints of his Saviour. 'If we suffer with Him, we shall also reign with Him.' (7) Christ's labors and sufferings, accepted of His own free will, have marvelously sweetened all suffering and all labor. And not only by His example, but by His grace and by the hope held forth of everlasting recompense, has He made pain and grief more easy to endure; 'for that which is at present momentary and light of our tribulation, worketh for us above measure exceedingly an eternal weight of glory.' (8)"

This might seem to imply that we ought not be concerned with the gulf in this world between the rich and the poor. Let those who have enjoy their good fortune and those who have not put their hope in the next world. But even apart from the question of injustice perpetrated on the part of those who have, this is to misread the Christian message. Certainly, to suffer and die was what Christ came to earth to do, to earn for us passage to heaven by paying the price of, making the sacrifice for, original sin and merit redemption for us. But that supreme act of love ("greater love than this no man has") did not cancel out the rest of God's great love for mankind, and God's desire to relieve our misery. One only has to look at what Christ did during his life on earth. So, we need to follow him in both respects, in our willingness to suffer evil (like St. Paul) for the sake of contributing to the salvation of ourselves and all others, including our "enemies", and to come to the aid of the afflicted (like the good Samaritan) when we find them on the way.

Nor does it mean that God overlooks not just the injury being done by some to others but also the failure of those who have to share their "good fortune" with their brothers and sisters in need. All are urged to do what they can in this regard both at the level of nature and justice and at the supernatural level of grace and charity. All this the pope explains in paragraph 22 warning the rich in the sternest terms. Throughout the encyclicals the parable of the rich man (*Dives*) and the poor man (Lazarus) is used to bring home this warning. What Christian, if offered the choice of lives here below, would choose to have that of Dives?

The Christian obligation to come to the aid of the poor applies not just in material terms but also in terms of what one has received of talents. "What have you got that you have not received?" Though she is the most famous in our time the history of the Church is replete with living martyrs of the likes of St. Teresa of Kolkata. Indeed, they live amongst us everywhere and inspire us every day. It is their love "that makes the world go round".

As for assuring the working poor, the example of Christ is again given in paragraph 23: "23. As for those who possess not the gifts of fortune, they are taught by the Church that in God's sight poverty is no disgrace, and that there is nothing to be ashamed of in earning their bread by labor. This is re-enforced by what we see in Christ Himself, who, 'whereas He was rich, for our sakes became poor'; (18) and who, being the Son of God, and God Himself, chose to be considered the son of a carpenter - nay, did not disdain to spend a great part of His life as a carpenter Himself. 'Is not this the carpenter, the son of Mary?'."

The beneficial effects even here below of adhering to Christian precepts of Faith and morals are summed up in paragraphs 24 & 25. The pope ends by saying: "Such is the scheme of duties and rights which is shown forth by the world of the Gospel. Would it not seem that, were society penetrated with ideas like these, strife must quickly cease?"

Paragraph 26 begins: "But the Church not content with pointing out the remedy also applies it." How this has been done, and continues to be done, despite many obstacles placed in the way in modern times, the pope outlines in the following paragraphs. In paragraph 27 he recounts briefly the marvellous history of human civilization from the beginning of Catholic Christian influence, being so bold to say, in the face of modern gainsayers, some maliciously motivated and many ignorantly falling into line, that civilization (called now "Western" but just as much Eastern) "was brought back from death to life, and to be so excellent in life that nothing more perfect had been known before, or will come to be known in the ages that have yet to be." [a prediction that seems surer than ever given the condition of the modern "culture of death"]

The pope, in paragraph 28, points out that this "renovation" is evident not just in spiritual or moral terms but also in material and temporal ones. People forget, to the frustration of their own disordered desires, that "Christian morality, when adequately and completely practised, leads of itself to temporal prosperity, for it merits the blessing of that God who is the source of all blessings …". He points, in paragraph 29, to the fact that such was the charity of the early Christians that: "neither was there anyone needy amongst them". (Acts 4: 34)

Pope Leo thus sums up the beneficial effect of religion and the Church, which reached its peak in the era of Christendom, but has continued to mighty effect despite the attempts in the modern age to denigrate and even destroy first Catholicism and then religion itself. This campaign has been gaining strength ever since the beginning of the modern era and has now become fully open and vitriolic. Even the good works and heroic charity of the past and present, so plain to see, are vilified now with a diabolic intensity.

This is how Pope Leo put it more than a hundred years ago: "At the present day many there are who, like the heathen of old, seek to blame and condemn the Church for such eminent charity. They would substitute in its stead a system of relief organized by the State. But no human expedients will ever make up for the devotedness and self sacrifice of Christian charity. Charity, as a virtue, pertains to the Church; for virtue it is not, unless it be drawn from the Most Sacred Heart of Jesus Christ; and whosoever turns his back on the Church cannot be near to Christ." (Para. 30)

At this point the pope indicates that it is not just a matter of relying upon the Church's aid, powerful as it is. The problem lies within the area of social affairs, within the natural and temporal order of things human, and therefore all human agencies must play their part. This is how he puts it in the next paragraph (31): "It cannot, however, be doubted that to attain the purpose we are treating of, not only the Church, but all human agencies, must concur. All who are concerned in the matter should be of one mind and according to their ability act together. It is with this, as with providence that governs the world; the results of causes do not usually take place save where all the causes cooperate. It is sufficient, therefore, to inquire what part the State should play in the work of remedy and relief."

The Latin is: 31. *At vero non potest esse dubium quin, ad id quod est propositum, ea quoque, quae in hominum potestate sunt, adiumenta requirantur. Omnino omnes, ad quos caussa pertinet, eodem intendant idemque laborent pro rata parte necesse est. Quod habet quamdam cum moderatrice mundi providentia similitudinem: fere enim videmus rerum exitus a quibus caussis pendent, ex earum omnium conspiratione procedure Iamvero quota pars remedii a republica expectanda sit, praestat exquirere.*

To this we need to connect what the pope said in the following paragraphs, which we set out in English and Latin:

"32. By the State we here understand, not the particular form of government prevailing in this or that nation, but the State as rightly apprehended; that is to say, any government conformable in its institutions to right reason and natural law, and to those dictates of the divine wisdom which we have expounded in the encyclical *On the Christian Constitution of the State*. (26) The foremost duty, therefore, of the rulers of the State should be to make sure that the laws and institutions, the general character and administration of the commonwealth, shall be such as of themselves to realize public well-being and private prosperity. This is the proper scope of wise statesmanship and is the work of the rulers. Now a State chiefly prospers and thrives through moral rule, well-regulated family life, respect for religion and justice, the moderation and fair imposing of public taxes, the progress of the arts and of trade, the abundant yield of the land - through everything, in fact, which makes the citizens better and happier. Hereby, then, it lies in the power of a ruler to benefit every class in the State, and amongst the rest to promote to the utmost the interests of the poor; and this in virtue of his office, and without being open to suspicion of undue interference - since it is the province of the commonwealth to serve the common good. And the more that is done for the benefit of the working classes by the general laws of the country, the less need will there be to seek for special means to relieve them."

32. *Rempublicam hoc loco intelligimus non quali populus utitur unus vel alter, sed qualem et vult recta ratio naturae congruens, et*

probant divinae documenta sapientiae, quae Nos ipsi nominatim in litteris Encyclicis de civitatum constitutione Christiana explicavimus.

Itaque per quos civitas regitur, primum conferre operam generatim atque universe debent tota ratione legum atque institutorum, scilicet efficiendo ut ex ipsa conformatione atque administratione reipublicae ultro prosperitas tam communitatis quam privatorum efflorescat. Id est enim civilis prudentiae munus, propriumque eorum qui praesunt officium. Nunc vero illa maxime efficiunt prosperas civitates, morum probitas, recte atque ordine constitutae familiae, custodia religionis ac iustitiae, onerum publicorum cum moderata irrogatio, tum aequa partitio, incrementa artium et mercatura, florens agrorum cultura, et si qua sunt alia generis eiusdem, quae pro maiore studio provehuntur, eo melius sunt victuri cives et beatius. - Harum igitur virtute rerum in potestate rectorum civitatis est, ut ceteris prodesse ordinibus, sic et proletariorum conditionem iuvare plurimum: idque iure suo optimo, neque ulla cum importunitatis suspicione: debet enim respublica ex lege muneris sui in commune consulere. Quo autem commodorum copia provenerit ex hac generali providentia maior, eo minus oportebit alias ad opificum salutem experiri vias.

"33. There is another and deeper consideration which must not be lost sight of. As regards the State, the interests of all, whether high or low, are equal. The members of the working classes are citizens by nature and by the same right as the rich; they are real parts, living the life which makes up, through the family, the body of the commonwealth; and it need hardly be said that they are in every city very largely in the majority. It would be irrational to neglect one portion of the citizens and favor another, and therefore the public administration must duly and solicitously provide for the welfare and the comfort of the working classes; otherwise, that law of justice will be violated which ordains that each man shall have his due. To cite the wise words of St. Thomas Aquinas: "As the part and the whole are in a certain sense identical, so that which belongs to the whole in a sense belongs to the part." (27) Among the many and grave duties of rulers who would do their best for the people, the first and chief is to act with strict justice - with that justice which is called *distributive* - toward each and every class alike."

(33) *Sed illud praeterea considerandum, quod rem altius attingit, unam civitatis esse rationem, communem summorum atque infimorum. Sunt nimirum proletarii pari iure cum locupletibus natura cives, hoc est partes vera vitamque viventes, unde constat, interiectis familiis, corpus reipublicae: ut ne illud adiungatur, in omni urbe eos esse numero longe maximo. Cum igitur illud sit perabsurdum, parti civium consulere, partem negligere, consequitur, in salute commodisque ordinis proletariorum tuendis curas debitas collocari publice oportere: ni fiat, violatum iri iustitiam suum cuique tribuere praecipientem. Qua de re sapienter, S. Thomas: sicut pars et totum quodammodo sunt idem, ita id, quod est totius quodammodo est partis [II-II, Quaest. LXI, a. I ad 2]. Proinde in officiis non paucis neque levibus populo bene consulentium principum, illud in primis eminet, ut unumquemque civium*

ordinem aequabiliter tueantur, ea nimirum, quae distributivaap-
pellatur iustitia inviolate servanda.

The English translation is not the best but we will not try to
correct all its misleading expressions, such as in blatantly not using the word "proletarian" where it appears clearly in the Latin.
This direct translation of "proletarian" is again avoided in the
paragraph 33. We do not know why but one educated in the
"West" does not like its negative connotation for the moral "values" of the economic system in place. For a western educated audience, it seems, we must be careful to avoid such communist-
type language, even if the pope uses it regularly.

What is most evident, however, is the failure to bring out the
important distinction between the two political meanings of
"State" or *respublica* (Aristotle's *polis*). It is equivalent of using
the same word for the human body as a whole and the head. In
calling for all to participate in the solution of the politico-
economic problem the pope is obviously referring to the political
or civil community as a whole, rulers and ruled. *Omnino omnes*
... laborent pro rata parte. That is plainly the intent of the use of
the word State in the last sentence of paragraph 32: "It is sufficient, therefore, to inquire what part the State should play in the
work of remedy and relief."

But, then the focus shifts to State meaning the government of
the civil community, which the translation itself notes in speaking of "the rulers of the State" [*per quos civitas* [*polis*] *regitur*]. I
grant that anyone ignorant of Aristotle's *Politics* would have difficulty making this distinction as well as the absolutely fundamental ones between the various forms of constitutional rule,

three of which are good because ordered to the common good and three of which are vicious because not so ruled, but instead ruled in the "interests" of the ruling "class". Pope Leo obviously uses the term *respublica* to refer to any of the three good forms, kingship, aristocracy and the rule by the many for the common good, for which last the word "democracy" is used today despite Aristotle classing it among the despotic ones. The pope explicitly says he is speaking of government in such general terms (provided it is ordered to the common good).

If the confusion here is not bad enough, we have the shift in the meaning of "democracy" in modern times to which the pope himself has felt it necessary to accommodate his language. To see what he intends by the use of this word one has to refer to his encyclical, *GRAVES DE COMMUNI RE, ON CHRISTIAN DE-MOCRACY, eighteenth day of January, 1901*. It is perhaps too much to expect the English translator of one encyclical to refer to another in order to properly understand the meaning of the words used by the pope. In the result the English readers tend to identify the meaning of democracy with that commonly adopted which abstracts from any relation to the common good, as explained above. That just opens the door to totalitarianism as is evident in what is happening in our times.

However, the confusion even amongst Catholics is today so deep rooted that it is practically beyond remedy in such a work as this. We would only ask moral philosophers and theologians in their study of political and economic matters to learn a bit of Latin and go back to the authoritative Latin texts of the social encyclicals. That way they may discover the moral and political philosophy of Saint Thomas Aquinas upon which they greatly draw.

So let us proceed to the next paragraphs concerned with the part "human agencies" must play in rescue of the proletarian part of civil society from their unjust exploitation under the modern politico-economic regime called Capitalism, posing, not without a great deal of success, on account of a compulsory system of secularist indoctrination/ education, as a political liberator.

In paragraph 33, which we have set out above in English and Latin, Pope Leo brings to the fore the fact already noted that the modern system of servitude is imposed by a few rich, not on people considered unworthy of citizen status, but on their fellow citizens, a truly remarkable phenomenon in the history of mankind. Moreover, at the start this system of oppression was carried out by "gentry" claiming to be the most respectable of Christians, a fact so much accepted by academia that modern sociologists proposed the theory that Capitalism was inspired by Protestant belief. (cf. "The Protestant Ethic and the Spirit of Capitalism" by Max Weber)

Here again we have noted the resort by the English translator to misleading expressions by avoiding using "proletarian" for the Latin *proletarii*, or by substituting a "genteel" or politically innocuous English word "commonwealth" (used mostly to refer to the collective of former colonies of the British Empire) for *respublica*. But we must say that by this stage this tendency is so deeply ingrained as to be unconscious.

One important thing to note here is the quote the pope uses from Saint Thomas Aquinas, about the nature of distributive justice. This is not the only place where the pope refers to distributive justice, which he puts as strict justice. But it is a form of justice that is unknown in modern political and economic science, and remains a puzzle for most Catholic moralists. Its explanation and profound significance in this context is fully dealt with in our book "Economic Science and Saint Thomas Aquinas" So foreign is it to modern Western ears (including most Catholics) that we can say that the phrase "social justice" has taken its place even in Church documents (ref. *Quadragesimo anno*).

In paragraph 34 Pope Leo develops what has been said and we do not need to comment further on it. So there is no need to set it out here.

In paragraph 35 the pope puts succinctly and clearly the nature and limits of the State, meaning political ruler of whatever legitimate form. It is sufficient to simply set out the paragraph: "We have said that the State must not absorb the individual or the family; both should be allowed free and untrammelled action so far as is consistent with the common good and the interest of others. Rulers should, nevertheless, anxiously safeguard the community and all its members; the community, because the conservation thereof is so emphatically the business of the supreme power, that the safety of the commonwealth is not only the first law, but it is a government's whole reason of existence; and the members, because both philosophy and the Gospel concur in laying down that the object of the government of the State should be, not the advantage of the ruler, but the benefit of those over whom he is placed. As the power to rule comes from God, and is, as it were, a participation in His, the highest of all sovereignties, it should be exercised as the power of God is exercised - with a fatherly solicitude which not only guides the whole, but reaches also individuals."

We might just note a couple of loose translations, the appearance of "commonwealth" as before commented upon, and the use of "individual" where the Latin says *civem,* another ignorant neutralizing of the political significance of the human person as a citizen.

In paragraph 36 the pope refers to the subsidiarity role of the Government (taken up by Pope Pius XI). This is an "interference" by the State which the liberalism in Capitalist politico-economic theory particularly rails against. Every individual within the community, it alleges, should be able to manage his own affairs, just as people of property do without disturbing the peace. All that is necessary is a police force to keep the peace. The Government should stick to protecting property rights and controlling the unruly tendencies of those like the pirate in St. Augustine's story who Alexander the Great reprimanded for disturbing the peace of his Empire (refer to quote in "Political Science and Saint Thomas Aquinas").

In paragraph 37 the pope points out that under modern conditions the "underprivileged" workers have a special claim on the assistance of the State.

However, in paragraph 38 Leo repeats the need for the law to ensure justice to all, acknowledging that there are some among the working "class" who are "imbued with evil principles" who should be restrained. This may best be gathered by setting out the paragraph in full:

"38. Here, however, it is expedient to bring under special notice certain matters of moment. First of all, there is the duty of safeguarding private property by legal enactment and protection. Most of all it is essential, where the passion of greed is so strong, to keep the populace within the line of duty; for, if all may justly strive to better their condition, neither justice nor the common good allows any individual to seize upon that which belongs to another, or, under the futile and shallow pretext of equality, to lay violent hands on other people's possessions. Most true it is that by far the larger part of the workers prefer to better themselves by honest labor rather than by doing any wrong to others. But there are not a few who are imbued with evil principles and eager for revolutionary change, whose main purpose is to stir up disorder and incite their fellows to acts of violence. The authority of the law should intervene to put restraint upon such firebrands, to save the working classes from being led astray by their maneuvers, and to protect lawful owners from spoliation."

In paragraph 39 the pope shows some sympathy for workers resorting to strike action "because the hours of labor are too long, or the work too hard, or because they consider their wages insufficient." But here he gives reasons against it and appeals to the authorities to remove the causes. The right to strike will however be affirmed in later encyclicals but under very strict conditions. We will deal with this issue where it is discussed.

In paragraph 40 the pope returns to the duty of the State [whether considered as the whole civil community or its principal ruling organ] to protect the worker. The translator translates the two Latin words used here, *plura* and *bona,* "several things" and "goods", as "interests". This may not be of any great significance except that it imports into the discussion the unfortunate tendency of the modern mind to subjectivize things, especially goods.

This becomes important when the first goods to be protected by the State are the workers' goods of the spiritual soul. How could the modern mind conceive of something so intangible – are they not a person's own private interests, of no concern to others, especially "in the public square"? Indeed, this fault, which is tied to materialism, has become so entrenched in the modern science of Economics that the notion of good or value being objective has been forever lost. The very mode of expression can show the probably unconscious bias of an English translator "educated" in a way of thinking that is subjectivist and materialist.

However, we will simply quote the general point the pope makes, which incidentally makes an important point about suicide or despair in one's state of servile misery, however imposed: "No man may with impunity outrage that human dignity which God Himself treats with great reverence, nor stand in the way of that higher life which is the preparation of the eternal life of heaven. Nay, more; no man has in this matter power over himself. To consent to any treatment which is calculated to defeat the end and purpose of his being is beyond his right; he cannot give up his soul to servitude, for it is not man's own rights which are here in question, but the rights of God, the most sacred and inviolable of rights".

In paragraph 41 the pope extends what he says to the right of the worker as a Christian to fulfil his obligations to rest and attend Church on Sundays, a right that, in a culture of contempt for religion even as natural, the State totally ignores today.

In paragraph 42 Pope Leo obviously turns his mind more directly to the shockingly unjust state of the "condition of labour" at the height (depth) of the dominance of Capitalism in the nineteenth century. The pope does not mince his words, saying at the start: "If we turn not to things external and material, the first thing of all to secure is to save unfortunate working people from the cruelty of men of greed, who use human beings as mere instruments for money-making. It is neither just nor human so to grind men down with excessive labor as to stupefy their minds and wear out their bodies."

He then outlines the conditions under which workers, men, women and children, ought to be expected to work, ending with this general principle: "In all agreements between masters and work people there is always the condition expressed or understood that there should be allowed proper rest for soul and body. To agree in any other sense would be against what is right and just; for it can never be just or right to require on the one side, or to promise on the other, the giving up of those duties which a man owes to his God and to himself."

Then in the next few paragraphs Pope Leo XIII comes to the issue of workers' wages. It is here that he famously demolishes the liberalist doctrine of free contract as the sole basis for judging the justice of the arrangement. In the case of the employer/employee relationship the pope does not need to appeal to the lack of full equality in the exchange of labour for money (fully expounded upon by Saint Thomas in II-II q. 77). It is clear that there is as much freedom on the part of the worker as if a gun were put to his head and he agreed to work at the rate and on the terms "offered".

The fact that the like injustice was being done to all other workers in the "market" simply creates the illusion that all have freely agreed to the market "price" of labour. The labour market is the capitalists' threatening instrument ('gun'): "hand over your labour at the driven-down market price or die" – it is your choice. The falsity of the argument is so blatant that only a people indoctrinated in a liberalist economic science defending such a notion of freedom are stupefied enough to swallow it. Despite the pope's clear refutation, the same freedom of contract doctrine continues to be taught in both modern Law and Economics.

The pope spells out his argument in paragraphs 43, 44 & 45. The key to the argument is put in these terms: "If through necessity or fear of a worse evil the workman accepts harder conditions because an employer or contractor will afford him no better, he is made the victim of force and injustice."

But Pope Leo has here referred to a degree of necessity that is most obvious. St. Thomas will base the justice of exchange, and hence of the wage contract, on a notion of necessity that is not so physical, namely that of equality of value that one is entitled to demand in any social exchange system.

So it is that the pope only argued for a wage that at least meets the basic needs for support of the worker and his family. This has come down in the notion of a minimum wage, or family wage. He did not even put it in terms of commutative justice but rather in terms of distributive justice. It could be put in terms of the right of all to access to external goods in accordance with the universal destination of goods below man.

But this does not necessarily equate with a wage that equals the value of the labour as objectively determined according to common estimation by the community, what should be the basis of a market price. Indeed, given the unequal bargaining power of the parties it is likely to be well below.

For some reason the popes have not gone into this aspect of the just price (and therefore wage) as so clearly expounded upon by St. Thomas in II-II q. 77, where incidentally he also makes the distinction between natural exchange (CMC) and non-natural exchange (MCM).

It has to be remembered though that the situation was dire and only the strongest of arguments had any chance of having an effect on those in power who were "men of greed, who use human beings as mere instruments for money-making". Indeed, his approach had some effect, not necessarily on those with the economic power but on those with political power, as we will see when we come to examine Pope Pius XI's encyclical. A minimum wage and family wage did become legislated in most countries and thus enabled the working poor to obtain a standard of living above that of subsistence, and at least for a time avoided the threat of revolution and possible demise of Western civilization.

In paragraph 46 Pope Leo says something that to some has seemed rather unrealistic, considering that the wages the workers can expect even with State assistance are only sufficient to support the basic needs of himself and his family. What he says is this: "If a workman's wages be sufficient to enable him comfortably to support himself, his wife, and his children, he will find it easy, if he be a sensible man, to practice thrift, and he will not fail, by cutting down expenses, to put by some little savings and thus secure a modest source of income. Nature itself would urge him to this. We have seen that this great labor question cannot be solved save by assuming as a principle that private ownership must be held sacred and inviolable. The law, therefore, should favor ownership, and its policy should be to induce as many as possible of the people to become owners."

How can a laborer expect to save much and acquire "capital" if he is on a minimum wage? He is lucky if he can borrow enough to buy a home for which it takes him practically a lifetime to pay off the mortgage. It would take him a high degree of "thrift" to get very far putting aside even "some little savings" (more likely nowadays to get even further into debt). Of course, once in the property market he might make some money in a rising price "market" by astutely using MCM, borrowing and buying and selling. But that is not the sort of business or (gambling) "hobby" that an ordinary person is attracted towards.

We will not go into what was behind the pope's thinking here. It may be part of a strategy of encouraging employers (or the State) to pay or supplement wages sufficient to make ownership a possibility for workers, in accord with the public interest in having property or ownership of capital more widespread, as argued for in the last sentence of paragraph 46.

Force is added in paragraph 47 to this argument, ironically based on the defence of the right of property. "Many excellent results will follow from this; and, first of all, property will certainly become more equitably divided. For, the result of civil change and revolution has been to divide cities into two classes separated by a wide chasm. On the one side there is the party which holds power because it holds wealth; which has in its grasp the whole of labor and trade; which manipulates for its own benefit and its own purposes all the sources of supply, and which is not without influence even in the administration of the commonwealth. On the other side there is the needy and powerless multitude, sick and sore in spirit and ever ready for disturbance. If working people can be encouraged to look forward to obtaining a share in the land, the consequence will be that the gulf between vast wealth and sheer poverty will be bridged over, and the respective classes will be brought nearer to one another."

The pontiff is no doubt proceeding most prudently in the pursuance of his object of restoring justice. Yet one finds it hard to see equally harsh words in subsequent statements on social justice in relation to those who still hold power because they obviously unjustly hold a disproportionate amount of wealth? With what has been achieved, and that held so tentatively, it is best not to upset the apple cart, I suppose.

The pope refers to other obvious benefits of the widespread diffusion of ownership, such as a greater increase in productivity, the "economy" would be able to support readily a comfortable standard of living for all (rather than the basic needs of an impecunious many and the luxuries of a moneyed few). There would also be a greater love of one's own country (and readiness, without conscription, to defend it).

The pope puts an interesting rider on the State's use of taxation which ought to be applied today not only to capital but also to income (see the chapter on public revenue in my book "Economic Science and Saint Thomas Aquinas"). These benefits, however, he says "can be reckoned on only provided that a man's means be not drained and exhausted by excessive taxation. The right to possess private property is derived from nature, not from man; and the State has the right to control its use in the interests of the public good alone, but by no means to absorb it altogether. The State would therefore be unjust and cruel if under the name of taxation it were to deprive the private owner of more than is fair." The current theory (and practice) of taxation puts no limit on the State's power in this regard. Indeed, in modern "democratic" political theory there is no limit on the will of a majority in parliament assembled to do whatever it sees fit.

The final quarter of the encyclical, paragraphs 48 to 61, is devoted to the human agency that has perhaps proved to be the most powerful in bringing back modern civilization from the brink. That is the power of association to be accorded as a right to all and especially to the (working) poor. This is something taken up vigorously in *Quadragesimo anno,* as based in the fundamental social principle of subsidiarity. But it is spelled out clearly here.

In paragraph 48 the pope refers to existing societies for mutual help and benevolent foundations already established to provide for the workers and the poor and vulnerable.

Then in paragraph 49 in respect of the matter in question he comes out frankly and says: "The most important of all are workers unions (the modern word is industrial) for these virtually include all the rest." These had long been stiffly resisted by the fortunate few and a compliant State. In order to provide examples of such the pope has to look to the past. Thus, he says: "History attests what excellent results were brought about by the artificers' guilds of olden times. They were the means of affording not only many advantages to the workmen, but in no small degree of promoting the advancement of art, as numerous monuments remain to bear witness. Such unions should be suited to the requirements of this our age - an age of wider education, of different habits, and of far more numerous requirements in daily life. It is gratifying to know that there are actually in existence not a few associations of this nature, consisting either of workmen alone, or of workmen and employers together, but it were greatly to be desired that they should become more numerous and more efficient. We have spoken of them more than once, yet it will be well to explain here how notably they are needed, to show that they exist of their own right, and what should be their organization and their mode of action."

In paragraph 50 he begins to argue for the naturalness of such intermediate associations referring particularly to their character of subsidiarity.

He further develops this in paragraph 51 pointing out their difference from civil society as a whole, and hence they are called private associations as opposed to the role of the State (as organs of government). They are natural and necessary parts of any civil community (polis). Thus, the pope adds: "Private societies, then, although they exist within the body politic, and are severally part of the commonwealth, cannot nevertheless be absolutely, and as such, prohibited by public authority. For, to enter into a 'society' of this kind is the natural right of man; and the State has for its office to protect natural rights, not to destroy them; and, if it forbid its citizens to form associations, it contradicts the very principle of its own existence, for both they and it exist in virtue of the like principle, namely, the natural tendency of man to dwell in society."

Then in paragraph 52 he acknowledges that these kinds of associations may need to have their activities curbed, and even be outlawed by public authority. "52. There are occasions, doubtless, when it is fitting that the law should intervene to prevent certain associations, as when men join together for purposes which are evidently bad, unlawful, or dangerous to the State. In such cases, public authority may justly forbid the formation of such associations, and may dissolve them if they already exist. But every precaution should be taken not to violate the rights of individuals and not to impose unreasonable regulations under pretence of public benefit. For laws only bind when they are in accordance with right reason, and, hence, with the eternal law of God."

This existence and threat of such abuse had long been used, by "the fortunate few", and compliant governments in power, as noted above, to stiffly resist the formation and/or continuance of such natural associations where proletarian workers were concerned. This is what happened to the long-established guilds the pope refers to.

Whereas the rich (greedy) few had used the arguments for the institution of property to justify their gross abuse of it, here they used the accusation of abuse of natural institutions of community aid to a section of the population, rendered helpless by the same few's gross injustice, to justify their objection to the many working poor section resorting to the use of natural institutions necessary for its welfare. The hypocrisy was blatant but generally not noticed, not even by many today.

Then in paragraph 53 Pope Leo refers to the treatment of religious associations in his times, with particular reference to the injustices heaped on Catholic associations, quite evidently out of a cultivated hatred of the Church. What he says needs to be set out in full; it is a history that the modern world wishes to "move on from". History, as the saying goes, if put out of mind, tends to "repeat itself".

"53. And here we are reminded of the confraternities, societies, and religious orders which have arisen by the Church's authority and the piety of Christian men. The annals of every nation down to our own days bear witness to what they have accomplished for the human race. It is indisputable that on grounds of reason alone such associations, being perfectly blameless in their objects, possess the sanction of the law of nature. In their religious aspect they claim rightly to be responsible to the Church alone. The rulers of the State accordingly have no rights over them, nor can they claim any share in their control; on the contrary, it is the duty of the State to respect and cherish them, and, if need be, to defend them from attack.

It is notorious that a very different course has been followed, more especially in our own times. In many places the State authorities have laid violent hands on these communities, and committed manifold injustice against them; it has placed them under control of the civil law, taken away their rights as corporate bodies, and despoiled them of their property, in such property the Church had her rights, each member of the body had his or her rights, and there were also the rights of those who had founded or endowed these communities for a definite purpose, and, furthermore, of those for whose benefit and assistance they had their being. Therefore, We cannot refrain from complaining of such spoliation as unjust and fraught with evil results; and with all the more reason do We complain because, at the very time when the law proclaims that association is free to all, We see that Catholic societies, however peaceful and useful, are hampered in every way, whereas the utmost liberty is conceded to individuals whose purposes are at once hurtful to religion and dangerous to the commonwealth."

The pope, ever alive to what was going on, then notes in paragraph 54 a disturbing phenomenon that had arisen in the latter part of the nineteenth century and that was the rapid rise to powerful influence of Communism. He was well aware of the social infiltration of anti-Catholic and hence anti-social associations, such as Freemasonry alluded to. But now, once the law had proclaimed that association was free to all, it became evident that workers' unions were being infiltrated, and even taken over, "by secret leaders", for evil and revolutionary purposes, so much so that "they do their utmost to get within their grasp the whole field of labor, and force working men either to join them or to starve". This posed an obvious problem for Catholic workers wishing to exercise their new found right to join a union. It is a problem that grew to great proportions after the turmoil of the Great Depression and World War Two, very familiar to those living during the early post-war period.

In Australia this was the era of B. A. Santamaria and "The Movement" which was a struggle by Catholics to counter the influence of Communism in the industrial unions. It famously led to a split within the Labor Party, one of the two major political parties. Though there was much contention even among Catholics about these efforts, the pope had this to say of them: "Those Catholics are worthy of all praise-and they are not a few-who, understanding what the times require, have striven, by various undertakings and endeavors, to better the condition of the working class by rightful means."

The last few paragraphs are taken up with the pope outlining the conditions needed to be adopted by associations for them to be effective. They do not call for any further comment. We move on then to the next encyclical which comes forty years later in Pope Pius XI's *Quadragesimo anno*.

Chapter Two

Pope Pius XI's *Quadragesimo anno* (1931)

We should first of all note that the second social encyclical comes forty years after *Rerum Novarum*, which those with a little Latin can discern from the very title. That is a long time and much had taken place in between. If we take into account that the encyclical came at a time just after the "Great War" ("the war to end all wars") and at the beginning of the Great Depression and the fact that this was immediately followed by the Second World War, during which there was one short speech and one shortly after on the subject by Pope Pius XII it is understandable that there was no further social encyclical issued till Saint Pope John XXIII's 1961 encyclical *Mater et Magistra*.

There have been a number of social encyclicals issued by popes since. What is noteworthy is that whereas there were only three in the first 70 years there have been seven in the last 60 and more (4) if we take into account documents dealing with the subject matter in some way. We will comment upon a possible reason for this.

Both Pius XI and John XXIII made special mention of the fact that the condition of modern society, involving necessarily the politico-economic level, had changed dramatically in the interim period before their encyclicals and had prompted the need to bring the fundamental doctrine of *Rerum Novarum* up to date, to be adapted to the changed conditions. In modern times conditions change constantly and at a deep level, seemingly with increasing rapidity. Were it not for the turbulence of the World Wars and the like, no doubt the popes before the Council would have had to bring up to date the social document more frequently. We can account for the increased frequency after 1960 to the almost galloping pace of the rate of social change in the last 50 years.

What is important to note is that almost immediately after the issue of *Mater et Magistra* (and the related *Pacem in terris*) the Second Vatical Council took place. In it there appeared the document *Gaudium et spes* which addressed the whole problem of the relation between the Catholic Church and the modern world, including from the politico-economic or economic perspective. Though this was not intended to provide an alternative basis of doctrine to that of *Rerum Novarum,* as is obvious from the continuance of the issue of further social encyclicals commemorating *Rerum Novarum* by Saint Pope John Paul II, it did put the economic problem into a wider perspective. A new line of social encyclicals was therefore begun by Saint Pope Paul VI shortly after the Council in 1967, a line continued by John Paul II (1987) and Benedict XVI (2009). Pope Francis is obviously concerned to address the same problem and has issued two social encyclicals, *Laudato Si* in 2015 and *Fratelli tutti* in 2019 (the only two encyclicals exclusively from his hand).

Things for the working poor after *Rerum Novarum* did improve in some respects, owing much to the influence of the encyclical, if mainly in the "developed" world, (i.e. in countries where the rich are richest and more powerful because the "economy" is more technologically advanced, as in USA. But, generally, the trend, taking the "developing" countries into account, was negative. This is with regard to economic conditions. But taking into account the overall moral/political condition of things the change has been towards deterioration of an alarming kind at a more alarming pace in all aspects of social life, from the lowest level of economics to the highest cultural level of religion. What is to be noted is the corruption in politics with the ideologies of capitalism and socialism descending to their extreme expressions and openly engaging in a war to the death.

But we are jumping ahead here. There were as noted by Pope Pius XI great social change in the 40 years between his encyclical of Leo XIII and his, particularly in politico-economic conditions to which had become tied the two now bitterly opposed ideologies of capitalism and socialism. We need to see what he had to say in this regard.

Pope Pius XI first of all refers to Pope Leo's description of "the condition of labour" at the time of *Rerum novarum*, "grieving that so large a portion of mankind should 'live undeservedly in miserable and wretched conditions,' took it upon himself with great courage to defend 'the cause of the workers whom the present age had handed over, each alone and defenseless, to the inhumanity of employers and the unbridled greed of competitors'." (n. 10)

He refers here to the prevailing ideologies of Liberalism and Socialism: "He sought no help from either Liberalism or Socialism, for the one had proved that it was utterly unable to solve the social problem aright, and the other, proposing a remedy far worse than the evil itself, would have plunged human society into great dangers." (n. 10)

He then indicates the three purposes of his encyclical:

a. to recall the great benefits this Encyclical has brought to the Catholic Church and to all human society;

b. to defend the illustrious Master's doctrine on the social and economic question against certain doubts and to develop it more fully as to some points;

c. and lastly, summoning to court the contemporary economic regime and passing judgment on Socialism, to lay bare the root of the existing social confusion and at the same time point the only way to sound restoration: namely, the Christian reform of morals. (n. 15)

We will basically leave aside the first, which, though important historically, does not add anything to the social doctrine. By way of preliminary Pope Pius XI confirms the role of the Church, indeed its "right and duty to pronounce with supreme authority upon social and economic matters." (41) Such a right relates to its role in pronouncing on matters of faith and morals. He distinguishes between the moral and "technical" aspects of economics. It is important, however, to clearly understand how this distinction is to be taken, for it is taken by some to distinguish the science of economics from moral science altogether.

Economic matters as referred to in the social encyclicals really come within Politics as an ethical study, which is where St. Thomas deals with them in his commentary on Aristotle's *Ethics* and *Politics*. So it is that when the pope speaks of the Church being concerned "not of course in matters of technique for which she is neither suitably equipped nor endowed by office, but in all things that are connected with the moral law" (n. 41), he is referring not to the formal aspect of politico-economic philosophy/science but to the material aspects, where there are many arts of production and technical matters regarding management, exchange etc. necessarily involved.

The moral aspect comes not from the multiplicity of particular occupations in regard to the conduct of economic affairs (including arts of government) but from the social order in which they occur. That is why the principal moral concern is that of justice. The social doctrine of the Church therefore is basically a doctrine of social justice from the viewpoint of morality, supplemented necessarily by an insertion into the doctrine of social charity (which "solidarity" has come to mean). It therefore comes within the scope of Moral Theology.

St. Thomas explains how Faith and Revelation include not only matters that are outside the range of reason (Trinity and Incarnation, Faith Hope and Charity) but also matters that come within the range of reason which in Moral Theology especially extends to all matters within the Natural Moral Law (e. g. natural justice, natural rights and political prudence), which are dealt with magisterially in the moral philosophy (science) of the *Ethics* and *Politics* of Aristotle.

The distinction between the moral and technical aspects of government in such matters can be gathered from the distinction St. Thomas makes between military prudence and the arts of war. The leader of the army, as a soldier, is primarily concerned with victory by the skilful management of the many and various arts of war by those under his command. But, as a citizen of the country waging the war, and especially as a part of the government, he needs to have military prudence, whereby he is primarily concerned with a just and honourable prosecution of the war. The Church has every right to hold him (and his government) to account in this regard.

Thus it is that the moral aspect is the most fundamental and highest in regard to all human affairs, including social, political, economic and military. The Church does not have the competence or technical expertise, nor the wish, to enter into the non-moral dimensions of these activities, though it is quite obvious that one cannot achieve any success without the necessary arts and skills required to prosecute them. The popes simply make the contrary point, practically forgotten by all those immersed in "the arts" of war, and in those of production, banking etc., that neither will a society or political economy achieve any real success, even material, without justice and morality. The disorder such organised brigandage necessarily engenders will turn against them, as it manifestly has done and continues to do.

The mistake that many, including Catholic writers on economics, such as Thomas E Woods Jnr, make is in accepting the liberalist ideological concept of Economics, as if it were a natural/physical, or mathematico-empirical, theoretical science, when it should be, as it is in Aristotle and St. Thomas's exposition, primarily and formally a study of human social behaviour, not of physical events or mathematical equations. Such a theoretical concept of economic science, especially cultivated by the Austrian school, plainly misreads the practical character of politico-economic affairs. It cannot accommodate even the notion of good or value, let alone moral value. (See my "Economic Science and St. Thomas Aquinas")

The liberalist approach in the modern science of Economics may be said to have begun as far back as the Physiocrats and Adam Smith. It was the first practical social science to adopt the new scientific method launched by Isaac Newton. It was empirically based but heavily influenced by the mathematical approach of Galileo and Descartes. Initially, the focus was on a naturalist /physicist interpretation of politico-economic laws, but over time the mathematical form began to dominate more and more, so much so that the name of the science was changed from Political Economy to Economics.

It was at this stage that there arose a distinction between classical and neo-classical economics. This was a turn in the science from a kind of pure natural science to one more mathematical (to which was connected the modern move to base mathematics on logic). This was a general turn involving people such as Alfred Marshall and W. S. Jevons in Britain, Leon Walras in France and Knut Wicksell in Sweden. However, it was the Austrian School founded by Carl Menger, Eugen Bohm von Bawerk and Friedrich von Wieser, enthusiastically taken up by Ludwig von Mises, Friedrich von Hayek, Lionel Robbins and others, that the Neo-Classical School is most associated with today.

The proponents of both the "classical" and "neo-classical" economics considered them true sciences to which morals had as much relevance as to the sciences of physics and mathematics. This was because of their false naturalistic and theoretical stances. We need to be careful not to interpret Pope Pius XI's distinction between the moral and technical aspects of politico-economic behaviour in these terms. The true basis of such a distinction has been given above.

Further developments in the theories of modern Economics, which seem to introduce a practical and technical aspect, also should be carefully separated from the distinction made by the pope. We refer here to politico-economic affairs as dealt with in the socialist ideology. It reduces the social organisation of such affairs to an art of management on the part of the government. This is to treat the social order with regard to external goods and services as an object of an art or technique (or business), one of management, rather like that of a household.

The first thing to note about this is that the reduction of the role of government in a civil community to that of a household is a distortion, something pointed up by Aristotle himself. The government, like any part of civil society has its own "household" concerns. But this is not to be confused with the "running" of the social economy as a whole, where the provisioning of the population comes about through free social exchange ruled by commutative justice, not by an allocation to everyone by a paternalistic government.

At best, this is to treat citizens as children; at worst, as servants/slaves. The civil government does have such a role, but it is subsidiary not primary. Adam Smith was right to regard the social system of exchange as a naturally ordered one; unfortunately, this came to be taken in the naturalistic sense referred to, when it needed to be taken in a moral sense, i.e. naturally effective provided the participants acted with justice.

This socialist conception has become entrenched in the modern practice of regarding the budget of the State, as a part, as if it were that of the State as the whole community, thereby sidelining the natural institution of the free market (as well as that of private property). So the second thing to note about this socialist concept of Economics is that it is a false view of the role of governmental art, usurping the moral role of political prudence and the particular, distributive and commutative, justices. It too excludes a proper moral appreciation of social economic life.

We should exclude here the pseudo-scientific conception of economic science in Communist politico-economic theory. Karl Marx called his theory scientific socialism. It is quite a convoluted concept, affecting to incorporate classical political economy (Capitalism), Socialism and Communism into a historical dialectic. We are not concerned to go into its details here. All we need to note is that it manages to combine the errors of both Liberalism and Socialism in a materialist view of history.

Neither liberalist nor socialist economic theory is to do with the "technical" aspects of politico-economic life referred to by Pope Pius XI and later popes. By way of completion, however, we should say something about Keynesian Economics.

Despite the growing socialist challenge, the dominant "science" of Economics up to the time of the Great Depression was the neo-classical. According to it the Depression could not happen. After that "shock" to scientific complacency with regard to the understanding of socio-economic affairs, J. M. Keynes developed an alternative "general theory" of the science, conceding some role to the State in managing the Economy after the socialist fashion of a purely paternalistic "management" of capital investment and labour, and money and exchange. This was in effect to mix a socialist theory with the liberalist one. Hence, thereafter the economic system was to be referred to not as a purely liberal capitalist one but as a "mixed economy". This mixture later was expressed in a division of the science into two parts, a liberalist microeconomics and a socialist macroeconomics.

Keynes, indeed, said that he had introduced his proposals in order to save "classical" (meaning neo-classical) economics. Keynesianism was thus enthusiastically embraced by the defenders of Liberal Capitalism as the only way to avoid a full attack from Socialism. This fear became intensified with the advance of Communism as Socialism in its most virulent form. However, in the event it was not pure Capitalism that became opposed to Communism but a half Capitalist/half Socialist State.

The inevitable result has been that in this "mixed economy" even so-called Liberal and Republican Parties, though resisting in differing ways the Communist push, have themselves moved more and more towards adopting a moderate sort of Socialism. To justify themselves in this regard these Liberal and Republican Parties have at times resorted to painting the opposition Labor and Democratic Parties as "communist", when the truth is that there is not much difference between any of the parties.

This common politico-economic trend in the anti-communist countries since the Second World War has brought with it the evils of both opposed ideologies. On the one hand, the Capitalist element has "evolved" to produce a greater and greater division between the rich and the poor, as the rich have exploited their dominance to extreme limits of monopoly of production ("Conglomerates") and money ("credit"). On the other hand, the Socialist element has "evolved" into the Welfare State, for those in the workforce not dependent directly upon the favour of multinational corporations. That is to say in the end the majority of the population are reduced to a state of servitude for the benefit of the powerful and wealthy few, but with an ever-increasing encroachment of the communist extreme of socialism.

To the extent that the capitalist "mode of production", as described above, has continued in the mixed economies these economies have continued to be subject to commercial and financial crises. However, the "classical" aftermath of these booms and busts cycles has become more and more "managed" by the State, with what eventual "success" we are yet to learn.

It is instructive to compare the recent economic history of the "West" with that which appertained at the time of *Quadragesimo anno*. Between the time of Pope Leo XIII and Pope Pius XI (1891–1931) there had been rapid and dramatic developments in both Capitalism and Socialism, in the former with regard to its practical hold on the politico-economic system and in the latter with regard to the theoretical basis of its ideology.

With regard to Capitalism let us let Pope Pius XI describe it: "In the first place, it is obvious that not only is wealth concentrated in our times but an immense power and despotic economic dictatorship is consolidated in the hands of a few, who often are not owners but only the trustees and managing directors of invested funds which they administer according to their own arbitrary will and pleasure." (n. 105)

That is to say the division between the few rich and powerful and the many poor and powerless had intensified to the point of being an economic "dictatorship". The pope continued: "This dictatorship is being most forcibly exercised by those who, since they hold the money and completely control it, control credit also and rule the lending of money. Hence they regulate the flow, so to speak, of the life-blood whereby the entire economic system lives, and have so firmly in their grasp the soul, as it were, of economic life that no one can breathe against their will." (n. 106)

The consequent power of those in control in such an economic system, even over the political system, is dramatically spelled out by the pope: "The ultimate consequences of the individualist spirit in economic life are those which you yourselves, Venerable Brethren and Beloved Children, see and deplore: Free competition has destroyed itself; economic dictatorship has supplanted the free market; unbridled ambition for power has likewise succeeded greed for gain; all economic life has become tragically hard, inexorable, and cruel. To these are to be added the grave evils that have resulted from an intermingling and shameful confusion of the functions and duties of public authority with those of the economic sphere - such as, one of the worst, the virtual degradation of the majesty of the State, which although it ought to sit on high like a queen and supreme arbitress, free from all partiality and intent upon the one common good and justice, is become a slave, surrendered and delivered to the passions and greed of men. And as to international relations, two different streams have issued from the one fountain-head: On the one hand, economic nationalism or even economic imperialism; on the other, a no less deadly and accursed internationalism of finance or international imperialism whose country is where profit is." (n. 109)

All this, note, without the input of socialist ideology in that part of the world then operating according to the capitalist economic system. Coming to our own day what we notice is, despite the good effect of reforms inspired by *Rerum novarum*, how much the socialist ideology has come to be mixed with the capitalist, yet, for the moment, without displacing its dominance. We might put it in politico-economic terms as the economic or real control of the economy continuing to be oligarchical, with the political or formal control becoming more and more democratic. Yet the communist ideology is fast gaining influence and power.

This social "contradiction" of itself results in revolutionary tensions within the civil communities concerned. The situation is of course enormously complicated by the rise to power of external forces, something that works both to exacerbate the internal difficulties and to enable "the powers that be" in such danger to deflect attention away from internal problems.

Socialism had "evolved" in the 40 years between Leo and Pius XI, as the pope himself observed. Indeed, there had risen to power as well forces external to Christian civilization in the pagan ideologies of Nazism and Fascism. The metamorphosis of Socialism, however, was into Communism.

Let us follow the story as told by Pope Pius XI: "Socialism, against which Our Predecessor, Leo XIII, had especially to inveigh, has since his time changed no less profoundly than the form of economic life. For Socialism, which could then be termed almost a single system and which maintained definite teachings reduced into one body of doctrine, has since then split chiefly into two sections, often opposing each other and even bitterly hostile, without either one however abandoning a position fundamentally contrary to Christian truth that was characteristic of Socialism." (n. 111)

The Pope draws a parallel with the transformation of Capitalism, with the "evolution" of its dominance over the economy to an extreme and absolutely inhuman form. "One section of Socialism has undergone almost the same change that the capitalistic economic system, as We have explained above, has undergone. It has sunk into Communism. Communism teaches and seeks two objectives: Unrelenting class warfare and absolute extermination of private ownership. Not secretly or by hidden methods does it do this, but publicly, openly, and by employing every and all means, even the most violent. To achieve these objectives there is nothing which it does not dare, nothing for which it has respect or reverence; and when it has come to power, it is incredible and portentlike in its cruelty and inhumanity. The horrible slaughter and destruction through which it has laid waste vast regions of eastern Europe and Asia are the evidence; how much an enemy and how openly hostile it is to Holy Church and to God Himself is, alas, too well proved by facts and fully known to all. Although We, therefore, deem it superfluous to warn upright and faithful children of the Church regarding the impious and iniquitous character of Communism, yet We cannot without deep sorrow contemplate the heedlessness of those who apparently make light of these impending dangers, and with sluggish inertia allow the widespread propagation of doctrine which seeks by violence and slaughter to destroy society altogether. All the more gravely to be condemned is the folly of those who neglect to remove or change the conditions that inflame the minds of peoples, and pave the way for the overthrow and destruction of society." (n. 112)

We should note the warning given at the end to those in power under Capitalism so conceived, and to those who seek to defend such a system. However, we know that the impending internal catastrophe was averted, in a way fortuitously (or mercifully), by a world war with a twofold external enemy, an enemy paradoxically common to the Christian countries then under Capitalist and Communist rule.

However, to complete what Pius XI had to say about Socialism, we need to attend to his assessment of the non-communist form of it. "The other section, which has kept the name Socialism, is surely more moderate. It not only professes the rejection of violence but modifies and tempers to some degree, if it does not reject entirely, the class struggle and the abolition of private ownership. One might say that, terrified by its own principles and by the conclusions drawn therefrom by Communism, Socialism inclines toward and in a certain measure approaches the truths which Christian tradition has always held sacred; for it cannot be denied that its demands at times come very near those that Christian reformers of society justly insist upon." (n. 113)

With regard to the development of Socialism, which was being proposed as a remedy to the system of social injustice that issued from the modern theory and practice of Capitalism, though condemning its ideology in equal terms as inimical to Christian faith and morals, Pope Pius XI made the distinction later emphasised by Saint John XXIII between the theory and the practice. In practice it may happen, the pope concedes, that with regard to "moderate socialism", "it can come even to the point that imperceptibly these ideas of the more moderate socialism will no longer differ from the desires and demands of those who are striving to remold human society on the basis of Christian principles." (n. 114)

It is not an easy matter then to assess the aims and motives of those who call themselves socialists and so to judge the extent to which a Catholic may join "forces" with them. So far as the institution of property is concerned, they may in fact be contending with the false notion of ownership (as an absolute right) that is proposed in justification of an unjust use of property. Nonetheless, the pope does not resile from passing judgment on Socialism as the politico-economic ideology that has arisen within Western society. "We make this pronouncement: Whether considered as a doctrine, or an historical fact, or a movement, Socialism, if it remains truly Socialism, even after it has yielded to truth and justice on the points which we have mentioned, cannot be reconciled with the teachings of the Catholic Church because its concept of society itself is utterly foreign to Christian truth." (n. 117)

For, at root it has in common with modern Liberalism an underlying materialist vision of reality, which leads to adopting an anti-religious and atheistic philosophy. "Socialism, on the other hand, wholly ignoring and indifferent to this sublime end of both man and society, affirms that human association has been instituted for the sake of material advantage alone." (n. 118) The secularist anti-religious character of modern politico-economic ideologies, Liberalist, Socialist and Communist has been present from the start in all, but most aggressively in the case of Communism. In recent days, however, for reasons that go beyond political morality into family and personal morality, the anti-moral and anti-religious position of all such ideologies has become intense to the point of open abuse, with the Catholic Church as the main target.

Looking ahead, from the end of the Second World War to date, the Liberalist ideological element and the modern Economic Science that it has engendered, though "corrected" to some extent by the efforts of genuine Christian and socialist reformers, nonetheless has "progressed" (as does a disease) to the extremity it had at the time of the Great Depression, so that it presents again its twofold evil effect, the extreme division within the social economy, between the "have all" of wealth and the "have nothing" but debt; and a crisis of instability within the monetary exchange system of unpredictable proportions.

The difference with the time of Pius XI is the way in which socialist theory (in macroeconomic theory) has been superimposed upon capitalist theory (in microeconomic theory), with regard to the "management" of the economy. Though Communism seems to have disappeared as a politico-economic threat the evil effects of socialism, an over-bearing State, and of capitalism indicated above, are at least as menacing as they were before the Second World War. What the issue this time will be one would be foolish to hazard a guess, except to say with confidence that the Catholic Church, which is so much under attack by all present forces, internal and external to Western civilization, is the only entity assured of surviving.

We should say that these observations are only from the politico-economic aspects of social life. We do not enter into the other more grave evils traceable to Liberalism and Socialism and Communism in regard to human life, religion and morals generally, and in regard to all other social institutions, such as marriage and the family.

Referring to the evils of social injustice in the modern era the pope connects their occurrence and growth to the failure of government to impose the necessary moral restraint (of just laws and institutions). Perceptively, he also relates them to the new "rationalism" applied to an "economic science" totally divorced from any moral concept of justice. Thus, he says: "Strict and watchful moral restraint enforced vigorously by governmental authority could have banished these enormous evils and even forestalled them; this restraint, however, has too often been sadly lacking. For since the seeds of a new form of economy were bursting forth just when the principles of rationalism had been implanted and rooted in many minds, there quickly developed a body of economic teaching far removed from the true moral law, and, as a result, completely free rein was given to human passions." (n. 133)

That new form of economy is precisely what is meant by Capitalism. Pope Pius XI was not afraid to name it and condemn it. However, because it is seen by many, including Catholics, as the only alternative "economic system" to that put forward by Social-ism and Communism, some commentators on the social doc-trine of the Church since then have, in an attempt to defend the theory of Capitalism as such, tended to make the same distinc-tion between "moderate Capitalism" and "unbridled Capitalism" as has been made between "moderate Socialism" and Com-munism. Some of the comments of the pope may be applied in parallel, but the commentators would do well to attend to the fi-nal conclusion about Socialism drawn by the Pope.

There is an important theoretical difference, though, between "Capitalism" and "Socialism", when taken in their "moderate" forms. Socialism specifically taken as a socio-economic philoso-phy denies the natural necessity for the institution of private property. This feature of it cannot be cured. Its political imple-mentation necessarily issues in worse social conditions than even the gravest abuse of the institution, as tends to happen under Capitalism, properly understood.

The problem with Capitalism is not in its championing of pri-vate property but of its taking advantage of its gross mal-distribution. To this may be added a perverse liberalist definition of it, as excluding any higher obligation to use it for the benefit of others. This virtual denial of its true nature can lead to a social condition that approaches the evils of Socialism. This has prompted both Chesterton and Saint John Paul II to describe So-cialism as State Capitalism.

However, it is possible to reform a capitalist economic system by restoring justice in the distribution of property and correcting the misunderstanding of its definition of the right of property.

The fault then is not so much in the economic system but in the liberalist ideology behind it.

Pope Pius XI indicated Pope Leo's intent on such a reform when he said: "With regard to civil authority, Leo XIII, boldly breaking through the confines imposed by Liberalism, fearlessly taught that government must not be thought a mere guardian of law and of good order, but rather must put forth every effort so that 'through the entire scheme of laws and institutions ... both public and individual well-being may develop spontaneously out of the very structure and administration of the State.' Just freedom of action must, of course, be left both to individual citizens and to families, yet only on condition that the common good be preserved and wrong to any individual be abolished." (n. 25)

The modern notion of Capitalism, however, as we have explained above, is tied to the misuse of the other main social institution of exchange, or the market, in the interaction between Capital and Labour. Socialism would do away with the "mechanism" of the market. That too is the denial of a natural social institution that is absolutely necessary to a civilised economy. The substitution of political planning in its stead must, as it inevitably did, result in a complete breakdown of the social order of production and distribution of goods, as well as in a system of forced labour.

True enough, the condition of labour under the system of Capitalism was described by Pope Leo in his time as under a "yoke little better than slavery". But under Socialism there is no way of reforming this abuse of workers. That is to say, Capitalism works with what is essentially good, the social institutions of property, market and hire of labour. The abuse, which is systematic, and tends to become dangerously extreme, is nonetheless curable if the State can be persuaded to carry out its responsibilities.

Essentially, that means the refutation of the dominant ideology of the modern era, Liberalism. Socialism and Communism cannot refute it, and ironically arise from it. The only effective answer to it is the social doctrine of the Church. See further discussion of the meaning of Capitalism below in comments on *Centesimus annus* 1991. There we see how some political scientists and economists, including some Catholics, have tried to tie the notion of modern Capitalism to the good social institutions it abuses, so that it means something necessarily good, as against Socialism that means something necessarily bad. It is clearly, however, the economic system that Pope Pius XI has called "to judgment" on account of its immoral form (of injustice). "There remains to Us, after again calling to judgment the economic system now in force and its most bitter accuser, Socialism, and passing explicit and just sentence upon them, to search out more thoroughly the root of these many evils and to point out that the first and most necessary remedy is a reform of morals." (n. 98)

The above long discussion has followed on the distinction Pope Pius XI made between the moral and "technical" aspects of politico-economic affairs. To make this clear we needed to clarify the use of many notions including those of theoretical and practical science, prudence and art, production and exchange and how the modern ideologies of Liberalism, Socialism, Capitalism and Communism relate to them.

We now come to the particular doubts expressed regarding Pope Leo's encyclical that Pius XI proposed to address. First of all, with regard to the right of private property he adds the following clarifications. The right of private property does not mean the right to use the thing exclusively for one's own benefit. As St. Thomas had pointed out possession needs to be proper in the individual but the use should remain common. That is already clear from the principle of the universal destination of all goods, but it also needs to be understood that private property must also serve the common good of the community.

Furthermore, it does not mean that the present distribution of property is necessarily a result of a just distribution. Indeed, the pope says the opposite: "To each, therefore, must be given his own share of goods, and the distribution of created goods, which, as every discerning person knows, is laboring today under the gravest evils due to the huge disparity between the few exceedingly rich and the unnumbered propertyless, must be effectively called back to and brought into conformity with the norms of the common good, that is, social justice." (n. 58)

The pope acknowledges that things have improved in some respects since Leo's time but not fundamentally: "The redemption of the non-owning workers - this is the goal that Our Predecessor declared must necessarily be sought. And the point is the more emphatically to be asserted and more insistently repeated because the commands of the Pontiff, salutary as they are, have not infrequently been consigned to oblivion either because they were deliberately suppressed by silence or thought impracticable although they both can and ought to be put into effect. And these commands have not lost their force and wisdom for our time because that 'pauperism' which Leo XIII beheld in all its horror is less widespread. Certainly, the condition of the workers has been improved and made more equitable especially in the more civilized and wealthy countries where the workers can no longer be considered universally overwhelmed with misery and lacking the necessities of life. But since manufacturing and industry have so rapidly pervaded and occupied countless regions, not only in the countries called new, but also in the realms of the Far East that have been civilized from antiquity, the number of the non-owning working poor has increased enormously and their groans cry to God from the earth. Added to them is the huge army of rural wage workers, pushed to the lowest level of existence and deprived of all hope of ever acquiring 'some property in land,' [43] and, therefore, permanently bound to the status of non-owning worker unless suitable and effective remedies are applied." (n. 59)

He reiterates the most serious charge of distributive injustice against modern governments: "Yet while it is true that the status of non-owning worker is to be carefully distinguished from pauperism, nevertheless the immense multitude of the non-owning workers on the one hand and the enormous riches of certain very wealthy men on the other establish an unanswerable argument that the riches which are so abundantly produced in our age of 'industrialism,' as it is called, are not rightly distributed and equitably made available to the various classes of the people." (n. 60)

Nor is private property in goods necessarily tied to labour (as some like John Locke asserted, giving rise to the labour theory of value used by Marx): "That ownership is originally acquired both by occupancy of a thing not owned by any one and by labor, or, as is said, by specification, the tradition of all ages as well as the teaching of Our Predecessor Leo clearly testifies. For, whatever some idly say to the contrary, no injury is done to any person when a thing is occupied that is available to all but belongs to no one; however, only that labor which a man performs in his own name and by virtue of which a new form or increase has been given to a thing grants him title to these fruits." (n. 52) "Occupancy" evidently means to take possession of in some physical way, not by building a fence around an area of land and putting up a "no trespassing" sign, or drawing lines on a map.

Thus, labour employed with the capital of another (or hired labour) does not give a person a right of ownership in the product. It does mean though that the worker is entitled to a fair share of the value of the product and the pope suggests an amendment to the wage contract (that has historically worked to the disadvantage of employees) so as to incorporate in current circumstances some kind of partnership arrangement, to give them an interest in what they produce from the things belonging to the employers, and no doubt as one way of restoring some level of commutative justice to modern employment agreements.

Though it is up to the State as government of a civil society to distribute common goods, like land, minerals, and other natural and commonly acquired resources, to all according to a proper proportion (which does not necessarily mean to all and sundry), as is evident from n. 52, the right of private property or exclusive possession is prior to any civil law or institution. Distributive justice supposes the right to common external goods, according to a due proportion, exists in individuals (as St. Thomas clearly points out). The role of the State is simply to allocate as fairly as possible what is in fact due to members of society, to fix more concretely the relation between individual persons/citizens and the goods to be distributed. It is a matter of what St. Thomas called "determining" by the concrete application the natural right of individuals (or particular groups) within the particular civil community concerned.

This is a duty on the part of the government, not a "right" to confer as it pleases. Where natural rights are concerned the State only defends rights; it does not create them, if it has a role in determining the right proportions. Accordingly, neither can the State define or redefine natural institutions. It can only apply them to the circumstances of the people and the particular resources and common goods existing in the community over which it has civil or political authority. As the popes insist again and again, natural rights exist prior to the State. That is forgotten in the positivistic legal mentality of our times.

We have not learnt from the communist political experiment to "redefine" (out of existence) the natural institutions of property and the market. The same consequences of totalitarianism, if not worse, will immediately follow the current plan of States to redefine marriage. It is a much more fundamental natural institution. Such a mindless experiment is not "a leap into the dark"; we know the danger; it is a leap into the abyss.

As is evident, in dealing with the right of property it is necessary to address the ideology of Socialism, for it directly attacks the natural institution of property. The ideology of Liberalism is also to be condemned in regard to its position on the right of property, but not so directly, for it appears to uphold the natural institution. Its error lies in an unstated false definition of it, in absolutizing it, and in preaching a "hands off" position by the State with regard to its duty to effect a just distribution of the common goods of the land. Compounding that wrong, the power of the State was then argued as reduced to having the minimal role of protecting the "property" of the privileged few, who had benefited from such colossal mal-distribution.

Pope Pius XI dispels any idea that Leo was only concerned to criticise Socialism and not Liberalism. Here are some of his comments in this regard: "… it happened that the teaching of Leo XIII, so noble and lofty and so utterly new to worldly ears, was held suspect by some, even among Catholics, and to certain ones it even gave offense. For it boldly attacked and overturned the idols of Liberalism, ignored long-standing prejudices, and was in advance of its time beyond all expectation, so that the slow of heart disdained to study this new social philosophy and the timid feared to scale so lofty a height." And again: "With regard to civil authority, Leo XIII, boldly breaking through the confines imposed by Liberalism, fearlessly taught that government must not be thought a mere guardian of law and of good order, but rather must put forth every effort so that 'through the entire scheme of laws and institutions … both public and individual well-being may develop spontaneously out of the very structure and administration of the State'." (25). And also: "And while the principles of Liberalism were tottering, which had long prevented effective action by those governing the State ..." (n. 27)

It will be seen that Socialism and Liberalism are relevant to all the particular issues addressed but in different ways. This is quite evident with regard to the role of the State. They have distinctive positions also in regard to Capital/Labour relations, and the market. Pope Pius XI refutes any argument against the private use of hired labour and as we have seen he refutes the notion that such workers are entitled to the whole value of the products in the production of which they are employed. In Marxism this latter position comes with a misunderstanding of the nature and use of capital, identifying it with the unnatural use of money in the process of exchange.

The main focus of political Liberalism is on the role of the State (as Government). It takes the other extreme position to that of Socialism, though Liberalism came first into modern political theory. Socialism gives the State exorbitant powers that deny the basic freedoms and rights of individual members of society. Effectively, it reduces them to being servants/slaves of the State. Liberalism, in an extreme reaction to the lawful authority of the State, which does tend to be abused, and historically making the authority of the Church (allied on occasion in the pre-modern era perhaps too closely with the State) the *bete noir* of any notion of political power or even moral authority over individuals, denies in theory any role to the State. As Pope Pius XI notes, pure Liberalism is pure Individualism.

Neither extreme is feasible in practice, so, except in Communism, the political theory tends to be "moderated" in Socialism and in Liberalism. The Pope has explained the former phenomenon; he has also said something about a similar distinction to be made in respect of Capitalism, which is Liberalism, as it were, in a politico-economic form. In practice then the Liberalists argue for a minimalist role of the State, as a sort of policeman enforcing "law and order", meaning the established disorder (of distributive and commutative injustice) in regard to the economic system.

It is important to note a distinction made in practice between Liberalism as a purely political philosophy and as a (politico) economic theory. Historically, the former seems to have followed upon the latter, which we have designated as the commercial revolution at the end of the Middle Ages. The religious and political revolutions seem to have occurred a little later. The importance of the distinction is that both are a rejection of moral restraints on individuals, the first on individuals' "freedom" to "trade" and the second on individual's freedom to live in modern society as they wish, with no moral restraint.

The economic liberalism, however, confines itself to commercial freedom. Its slogan became *laissez faire, laissez passer,* the freedom to do business and buy and sell in a free market. We have noticed the association of this with the rise to prominence of the second mode of exchange (MCM). There is therefore a sort of schizophrenia in modern liberalists; one side is intent on arguing for liberalism in its purely economic form only, taken to be Capitalism, but not wishing to go all the way in the dispensing with morality politically. The other side, sometimes called Libertarianism, takes the "logic" of liberalism all the way.

In Australia his division within liberals is epitomised in the Australian Liberal Party, causing a division between "conservative liberals", who wish to be conservative of traditional morality (excluding any notion of justice in commercial dealings) and "small l liberals" who wish to eradicate all moral "restraints" upon political and social life. It is perhaps of no great significance but in Australian politics at least there seems to be (or has been) a strong connection between "conservative liberals" (like Menzies) and Scottish/ Presbyterians. There was possibly a connection between Calvinism and the relaxing of moral "restraints" in commerce, yet retaining a strict rigorism of morals in personal life. For it, "success" in business or increase in wealth was seen as a sign of divine favour.

The extreme liberalism that excluded any moral or religious constraints was something that Marx inherited and it became a defining characteristic of Communism. Indeed, what is implicit in pure liberalism in modern political theory became explicit in Communism so that in more recent times the name of liberal is generally associated with the extreme of Socialism.

The popular division of modern political parties into "Right" and "Left" is thus fundamentally based on the attitude to traditional morality but confused with an inverse division between the parties of the rich (Liberal/Republican) and the poor (Socialist/Democratic). Thus, the rich (oligarchy) is associated with the maintenance of the "Establishment", meaning, that is, the *status quo* so far as social injustice is concerned, whilst the poor ("democracy") is associated with overturning established morals, equating the natural moral code with a system of injustice serving the interests of those in power, whether politically or economically.

Pope Leo XIII, expanded on by Pope Pius XI, set out the proper assessment of the authority of the State in relation to the individual person. Liberalism and Socialism are extreme errors, the former in excluding the State from any authority over individuals, the latter going to the other extreme of subjecting individual persons to the total control of the State. But each extreme is held by many (if not most) in a "moderate" form. "Conservative" liberals (capital "L" liberals) restrict their theory to the politico-economic field, subscribing to modern liberal microeconomic theory; small "l" liberals extend the theory (logically) to the whole field of political life.

"Moderate" socialists similarly view the State as needing to take over all politico-economic affairs, subscribing to modern macroeconomic theory, but generally are not concerned to "reform" the other aspects of morality. The Communists, however, allow to the State the "implementation", by socialist measures, of the destruction of established morality and religion to achieve the same end as pure liberalism, a state of human nature absolutely free from all moral restraint (*non serviam*).

The social doctrine of the Church avoids both extremes (both of which it condemns severely). In the first place, however, it declares the fundamental priority of the God given freedom of the individual person within any civil community. The State, whether taken as the community as a whole, or as its principal organ, the government, is for the sake of the good of the human person. Yet, on the other hand, civil society (and the family) is a natural institution necessary for individual persons to meet their natural needs and to attain their ultimate end or happiness. Thus, Aristotle says, man is by nature political. The way to natural happiness determined by the author of nature is to be had in natural association with others. This end is what primarily constitutes the common good of the community.

What then is the role or function of the State as government? It is primarily to administer the natural laws and institutions and pass the positive laws required to do this. They are all ordered to the common good. Thereby is preserved the order of peace and justice from which will "naturally" flow (by a moral necessity) all the benefits of civilization to all the citizens, from the economic level (production and distribution of material wealth) to the highest cultural level (education in science, philosophy, arts, religion and spiritual life). All this, the (adult) individual persons will be able to achieve by themselves, freely and co-operatively, provided the State does its work of preventing any injustice and exploitation by others.

The role of the State is not confined to this primary role of protecting the unity of the community and ensuring the common goods that are related to this. For, it has the care of the whole community including every part of it, i. e. each individual person. As noted, it exists for the sake of every human person/citizen within the particular community concerned. So, as Pope Leo XIII, refuting the tenets of Liberalism in this regard, clearly showed, the State has also the grave duty and right to come to the aid of those who without fault, for one reason or another, find themselves unable to obtain what rightfully belongs to all members of a civilized community, namely, not only life and freedom from want, but also the level of well-being that it is in the capacity of a civilized community to provide.

In the case where such deprivation is the result of systemic or other injustice perpetrated upon the individuals or groups concerned, the task of the State will be twofold; firstly, to provide immediate and urgent assistance and, secondly, to correct the injustices that have been allowed to develop. It is not enough to attend only to the first. There will be less need for the State to act on the first score if it ensures justice.

In the modern capitalist "new" economy Pope Leo XIII saw the first issue of injustice as to do with the wage contract. He thus made his argument for a living wage. Pope Pius XI explicitly included the workers' family in the notion of a living wage. Thus, he said: "In the first place, the worker must be paid a wage sufficient to support him and his family ... It is an intolerable abuse, and to be abolished at all cost, for mothers on account of the father's low wage to be forced to engage in gainful occupations outside the home to the neglect of their proper cares and duties, especially the training of children. Every effort must therefore be made that fathers of families receive a wage large enough to meet ordinary family needs adequately. But, if this cannot always be done under existing circumstances, social justice demands that changes be introduced as soon as possible whereby such a wage will be assured to every adult workingman." (n. 71)

More generally, Pope Pius XI re-affirmed the "grave evil" involved in the treatment of workers in their search for employment as mere commodities to be bought in the market for the purpose of the sale of their contribution to production. Thus, he said: "Labor, as Our Predecessor explained well in his Encyclical, [48] is not a mere commodity. On the contrary, the worker's human dignity in it must be recognized. It therefore cannot be bought and sold like a commodity. Nevertheless, as the situation now stands, hiring and offering for hire in the so-called labor market separate men into two divisions, as into battle lines, and the contest between these divisions turns the labor market itself almost into a battlefield where, face to face, the opposing lines struggle bitterly. Everyone understands that this grave evil, which is plunging all human society to destruction, must be remedied as soon as possible." (n. 83)

The most noteworthy clarification of the social doctrine of the Church made by Pope Pius XI was, however, to do with private associations. Pope Leo XIII had pointed up the natural right of all to form associations: it is the very basis of the making of civil communities. The State had the right to regulate their use in light of the common good but it could by no means prohibit or inhibit unreasonably their formation and conduct. This was especially applied to the right of workers to form trades' unions. Both popes lamented the disappearance of "the rich social life" of former times, which Pope Pius XI specially notes proved to be of so great advantage not only to the individuals concerned but also to the State itself.

"When we speak of the reform of institutions, the State comes chiefly to mind, not as if universal well-being were to be expected from its activity, but because things have come to such a pass through the evil of what we have termed 'individualism' that, following upon the overthrow and near extinction of that rich social life which was once highly developed through associations of various kinds, there remain virtually only individuals and the State. This is to the great harm of the State itself; for, with a structure of social governance lost, and with the taking over of all the burdens which the wrecked associations once bore, the State has been overwhelmed and crushed by almost infinite tasks and duties." (n. 78)

Earlier the pope had referred to the efforts of the State, plainly influenced by the capitalist motive to keep workers isolated and defenceless, to oppose workers' unions: "These teachings [of Pope Leo XIII] were issued indeed most opportunely. For at that time in many nations those at the helm of State, plainly imbued with Liberalism, were showing little favor to workers' associations of this type; nay, rather they openly opposed them, and while going out of their way to recognize similar organizations of other classes and show favor to them, they were with criminal injustice denying the natural right to form associations to those who needed it most to defend themselves from ill treatment at the hands of the powerful. There were even some Catholics who looked askance at the efforts of workers to form associations of this type as if they smacked of a socialistic or revolutionary spirit." (n. 30)

Such associations, however, are a valuable means to individual persons being able to achieve the ends of satisfying their natural needs and rational wants. On no account should these associations be allowed to so act as to subject their members to ends alien to their personal nature, especially in regard to their moral and religious duties. Pope Pius XI extended this principle that associations should only provide such aid as was necessary to enhance the individual person's free initiative. This has become known as the principle of subsidiarity:

"As history abundantly proves, it is true that on account of changed conditions many things which were done by small associations in former times cannot be done now save by large associations. Still, that most weighty principle, which cannot be set aside or changed, remains fixed and unshaken in social philosophy: Just as it is gravely wrong to take from individuals what they can accomplish by their own initiative and industry and give it to the community, so also it is an injustice and at the same time a grave evil and disturbance of right order to assign to a greater and higher association what lesser and subordinate organizations can do. For every social activity ought of its very nature to furnish help to the members of the body social, and never destroy and absorb them." (n. 79)

That simply reiterates the fundamental principle of the priority of the individual human person over every other power under God. Social organisations, even though natural and necessary, such as the family and civil society, exist for the sake of their members and not vice versa. That is the natural truth, only understood in full within Christian Revelation, that Liberalism tries to express but, unfortunately, turns into a lie: that man can have such freedom without God and the moral law.

Thus, having added a number of clarifications in view of doubts expressed upon certain aspects of *Rerum novarum*, Pope Pius XI finishes with the two most important things needed, "the reform of institutions and the correction of morals": "Still, in order that what he so happily initiated may be solidly established, that what remains to be done may be accomplished, and that even more copious and richer benefits may accrue to the family of mankind, two things are especially necessary: reform of institutions and correction of morals." (n. 77) The two are closely connected, the principal institution concerned being the State and the principal moral virtue concerned being that of social justice.

What needs to be clearly understood, however, is that an erroneous political and economic theory is one thing, the condition of injustice in the actual society and economy is another. The ideology of Liberalism/Capitalism misreads (or misrepresents) the actual social condition, so as not to see any injustice in the use of the social institutions of government, property, market and labour service. The truth is that these institutions of the economic system are good and natural in themselves but have been allowed (by governmental neglect and even connivance) to be distorted to serve the interests of a few against the rest of the citizens.

This is made clear by Pope Pius XI: "With all his energy Leo XIII sought to adjust this economic system according to the norms of right order; hence, it is evident that this system is not to be condemned in itself. And surely it is not of its own nature vicious. But it does violate right order when capital hires workers, that is, the non-owning working class, with a view to and under such terms that it directs business and even the whole economic system according to its own will and advantage, scorning the human dignity of the workers, the social character of economic activity and social justice itself, and the common good." (n. 101)

Thus, Pope Pius XI added a powerful adaptation of the social doctrine of the Church outlined by Pope Leo XIII. Subsequent popes will continue to use the anniversaries of *Rerum novarum* to do the same thing for the remainder of the twentieth century, with additional encyclicals following the pastoral constitution of the Vatican Council of *Gaudium et spes*. We deal next then with what Pope Pius XII had to say in his radio message of 1941 and address of 1951.

Chapter Three

Pope Pius XII's Radio messages of 1941 and 1951

Though Pius XII did not write a social encyclical he did give two short speeches, the first in 1941 and the second in 1951 in which he commented on *Rerum Novarum,* on its 50th and 60th anniversaries. The first was of course early in World War Two given to Italian workers, the second shortly after the end of the war to Spanish workers.

The War of course brought about huge changes not only in political and economic conditions but also in thinking, rationally and ideologically, in those two levels of modern social life. As regards the first it accelerated even more the rapid advances in technology that had been taking place already in the nineteenth century. To some extent these advances were spread more widely after the war than they had been in the nineteenth century when Capitalism was at its unquestioned height of dominance both in terms of power and influence and "Capital" seemed able to claim nearly all the benefits and "Labour" hardly any. Indeed, prior to *Rerum Novarum* the condition of labour had worsened with the improvements in machinery and manufacturing. Not only were adult men "employed" working the machines but also women and even children. One only has to read Charles Dickens to gain a picture of what this phase of the Industrial Revolution was like for an even greater majority of the population in the "rich" Capitalist nations, of which England with its British Empire was the richest and most powerful.

In 1941 Pope Pius XII simply treated of three fundamental values, the use of material goods, labour and the family". In Italian: *l'uso dei beni materiali, il lavoro, la famiglia.* The last becomes relevant because it is the natural institution through which individuals mostly exercise their rights to property in goods and, through their labour, make use of the goods of the earth.

One can read what the pope had to say about the family directly. We will comment only on the other two fundamental values. With regard to the first value, the pontiff simply repeats what he had said in an earlier encyclical (*Sertum laetitiae*, directed significantly/ pointedly to the bishops of the United States): the unquestionable exigency of the fact that "the goods created by God for all men flow equally to all, according to the principles of justice and charity": *"che i beni, da Dio creati per tutti gli uomini, equamente affluiscano a tutti, secondo i principi della giustizia e della carità".* This is the clearest possible statement of the universal destination of external goods. Yet Pope Francis had to repeat it in 2015 and point out that for Christians it was not just a natural moral obligation but a divinely revealed Commandment (See leading quote in my book "Economic Science and Saint Thomas Aquinas").

Pope Pius could not be more emphatic about this right under the natural moral law, binding prior to any government's fulfilment of its obligation in distributive justice to distribute common things justly. *"Ogni uomo, quale vivente dotato di ragione, ha infatti dalla natura il diritto fondamentale di usare dei beni materiali della terra, pur essendo lasciato alla volontà umana e alle forme giuridiche dei popoli di regolarne più particolarmente la pratica attuazione. Tale diritto individuale non può essere in nessun modo soppresso, neppure da altri diritti certi e pacifici sui beni material."*

"Every man, a living being endowed with reason, has in fact the fundamental right of making use of the material goods of the earth, it being left to human will and the laws of peoples to regulate more particularly the practical actuation of this right. Such individual right can in no way be suppressed, not even by reason of certain and peaceful rights to one's material goods."

It is only then that he brings in the right of property, and of exchange significantly, in view of our treatment of the market, calling them institutions. *"Senza dubbio l'ordine naturale, derivante da Dio, richiede anche la proprietà privata e il libero reciproco commercio dei beni con scambi e donazioni, come pure la funzione regolatrice del potere pubblico su entrambi questi istituti. Tutto ciò nondimeno rimane subordinato allo scopo naturale dei beni materiali, e non potrebbe rendersi indipendente dal diritto primo e fondamentale, che a tutti ne concede l'uso; ma piuttosto deve servire a farne possibile l'attuazione in conformità con il suo scopo. Così solo si potrà e si dovrà ottenere che proprietà e uso dei beni materiali portino alla società pace feconda e consistenza vitale, non già costituiscano condizioni precarie, generatrici di lotte e gelosie, e abbandonate in balia dello spietato giuoco della forza e della debolezza."*

"Without doubt the natural order derived from God requires also private property and the free reciprocal interchange of goods by exchange and gift, with the regulatory function of public over both these institutions. Nonetheless, all this remains subordinate to the natural scope of material goods; and cannot be rendered independent of the primary and fundamental right whose use is conceded to all. Rather it should serve to make possible actuation in conformity with its scope. Thus only will and should property and the use of material goods be able to bring about a peaceful, fruitful and stable living society; not one constituted of precarious conditions, producing conflicts and jealousy, and abandoned to cruel games of force and weaknesses."

What this says is what St. Thomas makes plain; that the universal destination of goods below man for man's benefit is primary, and the other "values", right of private property in material goods, and to free exchange according to equal value in exchange, are natural in the sense of rationally necessary. But they are secondary – according to *ius gentium*. Read the *Summa* in the relevant parts, but in Latin not in English. The institutions of property and exchange (free market) are not playthings for individuals or corporations, or the State, as they have become under the oligarchical political arrangements and within the capitalist economic systems of modern times. The modern "sciences" of Politics and Economics have been set up (almost unconsciously) to try and justify this perverse regime as "democratic" and "free market".

Pope Pius XI had already noted that private property may be based on claims made prior to the institution of a civil community (*polis*) and its government. "That ownership is originally acquired both by occupancy of a thing not owned by any one and by labor, or, as is said, by specification, the tradition of all ages as well as the teaching of Our Predecessor Leo clearly testifies. For, whatever some idly say to the contrary, no injury is done to any person when a thing is occupied that is available to all but belongs to no one; however, only that labor which a man performs in his own name and by virtue of which a new form or increase has been given to a thing grants him title to these fruits." (n. 52)

These titles to property are not created by the civil community and the State (as government) has no right to negate them or regulate their use except according to the demands of the common good.

One extremely important point that Pope Pius XII makes is totally neglected today; indeed, one has to suspect that it is explicitly excluded so as to hide the profound injustice that is in place: that it is possible for a civil community to be put forward as wealthy, or a rich nation, when the majority of the population is poor and it is only a minority who are rich, and excessively so. But this is a debased concept of national well-being for "economic richness of a people does not properly consist in an abundance of goods, measured according to a pure and simple material computation of their value, but rather in that such abundance represents and holds out really and efficiently the sufficient material base for the due personal development of its members."

"Dal che, diletti figli, vi tornerà agevole scorgere che la ricchezza economica di un popolo non consiste propriamente nell'abbondanza dei beni, misurata secondo un computo puro e pretto mate-

riale del loro valore, bensì in ciò che tale abbondanza rappresenti e porga realmente ed efficacemente la base materiale bastevole al debito sviluppo personale dei suoi membri."

"If a similar just distribution of goods is not made actual or comes to be procured imperfectly, the true scope of the national economy would not be achieved; on the contrary in so far as it should occur that a people is not called to participate in a fortunate abundance of disposable goods it would not be economically rich but poor. Should it happen on the other hand that such a just distribution be effected in real terms and in a lasting manner, you would see a people only having at its disposal fewer goods to make itself and be economically healthy."

"Se una simile giusta distribuzione dei beni non fosse attuata o venisse procurata solo imperfettamente, non si raggiungerebbe il vero scopo dell'economia nazionale; giacché, per quanto soccorresse una fortunata abbondanza di beni disponibili, il popolo, non chiamato a parteciparne, non sarebbe economicamente ricco, ma povero. Fate invece che tale giusta distribuzione sia effettuata realmente e in maniera durevole, e vedrete un popolo, anche disponendo di minori beni, farsi ed essere economicamente sano."

The words following should be engraved in the pavement of every Catholic educational institution in which modern "science", especially if called "Economics" is a subject. It identifies the modern worship of mathematical measurement of things ("phenomena"), and even goods, as if the secret to the deep understanding of "reality" (meaning material things sensibly perceived) lay, as the pope says, with criteria simply quantitative, whether of space, or of excess of goods. In Italian: *con criteri semplicemente quantitativi, sia dello spazio, sia della ridondanza dei beni.*

"*Questi concetti fondamentali, riguardanti la ricchezza e la povertà dei popoli, Ci sembra particolamente opportuno porre innanzi alla vostra considerazione oggi, quando si è inclinati a misurare e giudicare tale ricchezza e povertà con bilance e con criteri semplicemente quantitativi, sia dello spazio, sia della ridondanza dei beni. Se invece si pondera rettamente lo scopo dell'economia nazionale, allora esso diverrà luce per gli sforzi degli uomini di Stato e dei popoli e li illuminerà a incamminarsi spontaneamente per una via, che non esigerà continui gravami in beni e in sangue, ma donerà frutti di pace e di benessere generale.*"

"These fundamental concepts regarding riches and poverty of the people seem to us particularly opportune to put before your consideration today. When one is inclined to measure and judge such riches and poverty by balances and criteria simply quantitative be it of space be it of excess of goods. If instead one weighs rightly the scope of the national economy then it will come into light through the forces of men of the State and of the people and illuminate them to travel spontaneously on one way that will not exact continuous harm in goods and blood but will bear fruit in peace and general well being."

The true basis of a civil community's wealth is thus described by the pope: "*Anche l'economia nazionale, com'è frutto dell'attività di uomini che lavorano uniti nella comunità statale, così ad altro non mira che ad assicurare senza interrompimento le con-*

*dizioni materiali, in cui possa svilupparsi pienamente la vita indi-
viduale dei cittadini. Dove ciò, e in modo duraturo si ottenga, un
popolo sarà, a vero dire, economicamente ricco, perché il benessere
generale e, per conseguenza, il diritto personale di tutti all'uso dei
beni terreni viene in tal modo attuato conformemente all'intento
voluto dal Creatore."*

"Also the national economy, as the fruit of the activity of men
who labour united in the civil community so that, it is not to be
wondered at, to secure without interruption the material conditions in which the individual life of citizens can fully develop.
Whence, and in a lasting manner there is effected that a people
will be truly economically rich because the general well being, as
a consequence, is the personal right of all, coming to be in such a
way actual in conformity with the intended will of the Creator."

That it is an insight completely foreign to practically all modern academics including Catholic can be seen from the state of
the universities and colleges in modern times, even more so 60
years after the truth was brought into broad daylight by the great
pope. Economic science continues to be ruled by mathematics
whereby the modern mind is captivated by measuring everything
in quantitative terms, such as by numbers, which an Australian
Treasurer at one time famously (and ignorantly) called "beautiful". Everyone goes to worship in the temple of Statistics (which
is a word derived from State arithmetic, a most useful tool of
despotic government).

The pontiff sees through this narrow and distorting prism of
scientific knowledge, which we have pointed up again and again
in our reference to the modern science of Economics. Unfortu-

nately, few Catholic "economists" and even moral theologians seem able to free themselves of this distorted view of science and scientific method as applied to the social order. Incidentally, on Pius XII's criterion the USA is an exceedingly poor nation. Pius XII noted perceptively the falsity in equating a nation where the majority are in a state of poverty and impotence and an oligarchical few are in possession of excessive wealth and great power as a nation or empire. One should refer back to the quote from St. Augustine regarding Alexander the Great given at the front of my "Political Science and Saint Thomas Aquinas". How close are modern super powers to the comparison there made to a band of robbers?

This deceptive representation affects the discussion where blame is put on a "rich nation" as a whole for environmental degradation, when it is only a few excessively rich who are responsible not only for the exploitation of people of other nations but also for that of a majority in their own. Was it the majority poor working population in Britain (the modern Lazaruses) who were responsible for the exploitation of the "poor nations" in the British Empire? For that matter to put the blame for the degradation of the earth and its natural wealth on Humanity as a whole is hardly more than a sick joke. Talking in such simplistic terms bedevils the whole discussion of environmental degradation of "the planet", and for that matter enables the true culprits to escape unnoticed in the cultivated anger against the "developed" world – which must be made "to pay". But that is par for the course in the hopeless confusion of modern discourse generally.

Having dealt with the use of material goods Pope Pius XII takes up Leo XIII's important distinction between the free and necessary aspects of hired labour. This is another aspect of the capitalist economic system where a profound deception is in play. As dealt with already the liberalist argument in this regard is that workers are free to accept offers of employment or not, no employer is forcing them to accept a subsistence wage. The wage contract is but one aspect of the operations of a "free market". You and your family do not have to starve. You can go on the dole. Such is the power of modern education /indoctrination in a liberalist based economic pseudo-science. Who knows to what extent many Catholics take it in, even when the sophistic leger-demain is pointed out by a succession of popes?

This is what Pope Pius XII says (the Italian hardly needs trans-lating) – it is simply repeating what Leo XII has said:

"Con l'uso dei beni materiali voi stessi, diletti figli, comprendete come viene a congiungersi il lavoro. La <u>Rerum novarum</u> insegna che due sono le proprietà del lavoro umano: esso è personale ed è necessario. E' personale, perché si compie con l'esercizio delle parti-colari forze dell'uomo: è necessario, perché senza di esso non si può procurare ciò che è indispensabile alla vita, mantenere la quale è un dovere naturale, grave, individuale.

Al dovere personale del lavoro imposto dalla natura cor-risponde e consegue il diritto naturale di ciascun individuo a fare del lavoro il mezzo per provvedere alla vita propria e dei figli: tan-to altamente è ordinato per la conservazione dell'uomo l'impero della natura.

Ma notate che tale dovere e il relativo diritto al lavoro viene imposto e concesso all'individuo in primo appello dalla natura, e non già dalla società, come se l'uomo altro non fosse che un semplice servo o funzionario della comunità. Dal che segue che il dovere e il diritto a organizzare il lavoro del popolo appartengono innanzi tutto agli immediati interessati: datori di lavoro e operai. Che se poi essi non adempiano il loro compito o ciò non possano fare per speciali straordinarie contingenze, allora rientra nell'ufficio dello Stato l'intervento nel campo e nella divisione e nella distribuzione del lavoro, secondo la forma e la misura che richiede il bene comune rettamente inteso."

"With the use of material goods you yourselves, dear sons, understand how it comes about that labour is conjoined with them. Rerum novarum teaches that there are two properties of human labour, that it is personal and necessary. It is personal because it exercises the particular forces of man: it is necessary because without it one cannot procure what is indispensable to life, to maintain which is a natural grave and individual duty.

To the personal duty to labour imposed by nature corresponds and follows the natural right of each individual to make of labour the means for providing for one's own life and that of one's children as much food as is required by the demand of nature for the conservation of man.

But note that such duty and the relative right to labour comes imposed and conceded to the individual in the first appeal of nature and not already from society as if man were simply a servant and functionary of the community. From this it follows that the duty and the right to organise the labour of people pertains initially to all those immediately interested, the employers and workers. If then that they cannot accomplish their task or that which they cannot do through special extraordinary contingencies, then the office of the State reenters the field and the division and distribution of labour according to the form and measure the common good rightly understood requires."

In 1951 Pope Pius XII took up the same themes but focused on the defence of the right property. Here however, he brought out the urgency of the need for a more just distribution of property and denounced what is contrary to nature in a social situation where in the face of a small group of the privileged and rich there is an enormous mass of impoverished people. He laments the fact that there will always be economic inequality. In Spanish: *lo que hay de contrario a la naturaleza en una situación social donde, frente a un pequeño grupo de privilegiados y riquísimos, hay una enorme masa popular empobrecida. Siempre habrá desigualdades económicas.*

"What is contrary to nature in a social situation where opposed to a small group of the privileged and rich there is an enormous mass of impoverished people. Always there will be had economic [inordinate] inequalities."

Here again we can put the full paragraph in Spanish since it too hardly needs translating. I would not trust standard English translations by those well "educated" in modern economic science.

"*2. En su historia, dos veces milenaria, la Iglesia ha tenido que vivir en medio de las más diversas estructuras sociales, desde aquella antigua con su esclavitud, hasta el moderno sistema económico, caracterizado por las palabras capitalismo y proletariado. La Iglesia nunca ha predicado la revolución social; pero siempre y en todas partes, desde la Epístola de S. Pablo a Filemón hasta las enseñanzas sociales de los Papas en los siglos diez y nueve y veinte, se ha esforzado tenazmente por conseguir que se tenga más cuenta del hombre que de las ventajas económicas y técnicas, y para que cuantos hacen de su parte lo que pueden, vivan una vida cristiana y digna de un ser humano.*

Por eso la Iglesia defiende el derecho a la propiedad privada, derecho que ella considera fundamentalmente intangible. Pero también insiste en la necesidad de una distribución más justa de la propiedad y denuncia lo que hay de contrario a la naturaleza en una situación social donde, frente a un pequeño grupo de privilegiados y riquísimos, hay una enorme masa popular empobrecida. Siempre habrá desigualdades económicas. Pero, todos los que de algún modo pueden influir en la marcha de la sociedad deben tender siempre a conseguir una situación tal, que permita a cuantos hacen lo que está en su mano, no sólo el vivir, sino aun el ahorrar.

Son muchos los factores que deben contribuir a una mayor difusión de la propiedad. Pero el principal será siempre el justo salario. Vosotros sabéis muy bien, queridos hijos, que el justo salario y una mejor distribución de los bienes naturales constituyen dos de las exigencias más apremiantes en el programa social de la Iglesia.

Ella ve con buenos ojos y aun fomenta todo aquello que, dentro de lo que permiten las circunstancias, tiende a introducir ele-

mentos del contrato de sociedad en el contrato de trabajo y mejora la condición general del trabajador. La Iglesia exhorta igualmente a todo que contribuye a que las relaciones entre patronos y obreros sean más humanas, más cristianas y estén animadas de mutua confianza. La lucha de clases nunca puede ser un fin social. Las discusiones entre patronos y obreros deben tener como fin principal la concordia y la colaboración."

"In her history of two millennia the Church has had to live in the midst of the most diverse social structures, from that of antiquity with its chattel slavery to the modern economic system characterised by the words capitalism and proletariat.

The Church has never preached social revolution, but always and everywhere from the Epistle of St. Paul to Philemon to the social teachings of the popes in the nineteenth and twentieth centuries she has insisted on tenaciously to follow out that which takes more account of man than do economic and technical advantages, so that for their part as many as can live a christian life and one worthy of a human being.

For that the Church defends the right of private property, a right that she considers fundamentally untouchable. But she also insists on the necessity of a more just distribution of property and denounces what is contrary to nature in a social situation where opposed to a small group of the privileged and rich there is an enormous mass of impoverished people. There will always be economic [inordinate] inequalities but all that which in any way can influence the advance of society ought to be held always so that there follows a situation such that permits as many as can be had what is in man's hand not only in order to live but also to save. There are many factors that ought to contribute to a greater diffusion of property but the principal one will always be a just wage. You know very well dear sons that a just wage and a better distribution of natural goods constitute the two most urgent exigencies in the social program of the Church. She sees with clear eyesight and even forcefully all which within what circumstances permit tends to introduce elements of the contract of society in the contract for work and ameliorates the general condition of the worker. The Church exhorts equally to all that contributes to the relations between employers and workers be more human, more christian and animated by mutual trust. The conflict of classes can never be a social end. Discussions between employers and workers ought to have as their principal end concord and collaboration."

There is one interesting, and equally important, aspect of the matter that the good pope brings out that is not generally brought out. That is something we have already alluded to: the historical fact that "the Church has had to live in the midst of the most diverse social structures, from the ancient one with its system of [chattel] slavery to the modern economic system characterised by the words capitalism and proletariat." "*La iglesia ha tenido que vivir en medio de las más diversas estructuras sociales, desde aquella antigua con su esclavitud, hasta el moderno sistema económico, caracterizado por las palabras capitalismo y proletariado.*"

There is that word "proletariat" again and so closely linked with capitalism as to appear to be somehow connected. If you do find an "official" English-speaking translation look to see what alternative expression is employed. However, Pius XII is simply employing the same word as Leo XIII, and it is no coincidence that the plight of the workers under the capitalist system as "little better than slavery" is a social structure put together with the ancient social structure.

Yet as the pope goes on to say: the Church has never preached social revolution *La Iglesia nunca ha predicado la revolución social.* Leo XIII has given the reason and Pius XII puts it in his own terms: refer to *pero siempre ... digna de un ser humano* above.

We will not elaborate on this but simply note that, like the Jews were with the Messiah, some Catholics are disappointed that the Church, given its clear diagnosis of the social evil and its gravity, is not more militant. Those outside the Church, such as Nietzsche, will naturally not understand and charge the Church with being weak.

Before coming to the next social encyclical of Pope St. John XXIII, *Mater et Magistra,* we should say something about the great social changes, at all levels including cultural, but particularly at the politico-economic and purely political levels, that took place between the time of Leo XIII and that of John XXIII, which pretty well coincides with the period leading up to the Second Vatican Council.

The changes in the first forty years have been well covered by Pope Pius XI in his encyclical. We do not need to add much to what he has outlined, except to note how profound these changes were in many ways not just to material but also to mental conditions. Capitalism for instance was developing, to a sort of terminal stage of its pure ("unbridled") state, to a politico-economic dictatorship, as the pope put it. The era of "free competition" was growing, like a cancer, into huge monopoly "Trusts".

"Trust" was a word taken from law that distanced the details of personal ownership from public awareness, something that a *polis* of oligarchical nature, wanting to have people believe the political constitution was really not oligarchical but "democratic", found congenial. This difficulty of identifying who were the "established" super-rich hard to find (as opposed to the Vanderbilts and other "new rich" moguls) had already been achieved by the (positive) legal extension of the notion of corporation (body) to groups or companies formed for commercial and financial purposes.

Such pooling (shareholding or "stock" holding) of "assets" or "capital" (money) had its rational justification in giving an association, or "body corporate," the status of a "legal person", but conveniently covered up the "personalities" of the real persons involved behind the "corporate veil". The games of Monopoly and Money Making could then be carried on with great abandon by "managers" of "funds", ending as we know in the Great Depression. This was a "natural" outcome unable to be explained by the "classical" ("neo-classical") economic science of the time; hence the "adjustment" found necessary by J. M. Keynes (a clever politico-economic mathematician).

Though there was only a worsening of economic conditions during \the Depression immediately preceding the war it itself was the occasion of a great change in politico-economic thinking. We need only cite the work of J. M. Keynes. Paradoxically, if one were dealing with anything socially normal, the war 'cured", at least for the time being, the ailing economic condition, particularly the problem of unemployment.

In a way it was the death of both pure ("unbridled") Capitalism in theory and practice. Pope Pius XI had described how "liberal" Capitalism, as all extremes do, transformed itself from a politico-economic movement espousing a form of extreme individualism, "free competition", into the harshest form of economic dictatorship, generating the study of a new part of economic science, "monopolistic competition.". As Keynes saw, the State had to come to the rescue of Capitalism. Keynes's inventive imagination produced the theory behind it. It was a kind of artificial respiration to be applied if "the Economy" was to survive in any shape.

So, Capitalism did manage to emerge again after World War II, much emasculated, in the form of a "mixed economy", accommodated to socialism., but of the moderate kind as Pope Pius XI had described it. The condition of Labour benefited from the change but only insofar as the influence of *Rerum Novarum* penetrated the social and political mind. Otherwise, it was the ideology of Socialism, especially in the extreme form of Communism, that gained strength. As we shall see the post Second World War era, especially in the 1950's and 1960's was a battle against the rise of Communist influence in the "West", which was simplistically put as between Socialism in the USSR and Capitalism in the USA.

There are too many aspects of change for us to deal with in this book whose principal object remains politico-economic or "economic" for short. But we need to say something about the changes taking place at the purely political level since the political and economic in this discussion are so closely intertwined.

Here, then, we wish to focus on a change at the level of the purely political order (or disorder) of things, which comes out as a push towards "Democracy" as the only legitimate form of political constitution or regime. Notice that the word "regime" is obviously from the kind of constitution that Aristotle (and Aquinas) called kingship, a rule that he regarded as a good form, indeed an excellent kind of political government in so far as it was ordered to the common good. Its opposite was called tyranny, a "regime" which served not the common good but the good of the ruler. Today we have invented a new term "totalitarian" with the same pejorative significance (as is the wont with the modern coining of new words – usually long equivalents of Latin words). This makes Aristotle's distinctions rather meaningless. For "democratic" means good rule and "totalitarian" bad.

In modern times the relations between the purely political and politico-economic aspects of the *polis* became quite complicated and confused, as might be expected when the real regime is oligarchical, whose object, as Aristotle observed, was not to serve the good of all (*totum* in Latin, by the way – it is individualism that is linguistically opposed to totalitarianism) but to enrich the rulers. Modern political terminology is designed to support the underlying ideology of Liberalism. This comes out in the use of the word "democracy" which Aristotle used to describe the rule by the majority (not all) for the sake of themselves but more pointedly motivated by their desire for unlimited freedom.

Thus, we have it applied to whatever rule, moral or immoral, just or unjust, even rational or irrational, that the majority, through their "representatives' in Parliament assembled, will to impose by law on "the people" (all). That Aristotle and Aquinas show is a classic form of bad government. The political Party with the majority in the government have carte blanche; for it is simply assumed that they are expressing the "will of the people" (the ones who have voted for them) and considerations of justice or the common good are irrelevant. We have before our own eyes to what extreme depths of depravity that method of rule can descend.

The use of the word "'democratic" however has changed its meaning in modern times since the French Revolution. This is when the other kinds of political arrangements by one or a few came to be disparaged so as to be called pejoratively the old or anti-modern kinds of rule (*Ancien Regime*). Aristocracy and Kingship were equated with Oligarchy and Tyranny and the notion of "for the common good" was replaced by "for the people". We can see how that phrase can be manipulated by a liberalist ideologist.

But it is simply that the distinctions came to be expressed purely quantitatively without the qualifications put on them by Aristotle. For Aristotle, rule by one few or many can be good or bad. "Good" dropped out of the picture and was replaced by "interests" or desires. "Values" then was able to be used in a merely subjective sense. "Western values" became whatever life style people in the "West" (USA, UK, Australia, Canada especially) found to their liking and "the people" desired to adopt, be it free love, abortion, same sex marriage, euthanasia, or American football.

The "national interest" is whatever the government in place wishes to pursue, purporting to "represent" the will of the people. Even Abraham Lincoln was taken in by this sleight of hand: Democracy came to mean government "of the people, by the people for the people". The first part is simply a tautology, every political government is of people. "By the people" and "for the people" have all the ambiguities we have referred to.

All that needs to be said is government by whom and for whom. The modern classification then comes down to (1) Democracy - by majority of representatives in a "free" election (presumed to be by all) for the sake of the majority (presumed falsely to be all) and (2) Totalitarianism - by a minority in their own interests, presumed to be "totally" focused on themselves. How "total" gets into the expression no one can explain, but it sounds oppressive.

However, historically, after the French Revolution got rid of the idea of any good in old type regimes, there arose in Europe, spreading throughout the "West", movements wherein "the people", that is the working poor, or their champions, came to insist more and more that all should be able to participate in the field of government. This was not contrary to what Aquinas proposed, for he argued with Aristotle that the rule of a civil community (polis) had to be a form of self-rule, by the free for the free. The order to the common good ensured that, but St. Thomas said that all governments should also provide for all adults in some way to have a role in government if it were only by electing the one or few or many to rule them.

It was not the form of previous rule by one or few that was the problem but the inevitable tendency for rulers (like St. Augustine's robber gangs taking over whole communities) to abuse their God given authority. Given original sin, man is just as prone to abuse the institution of civil government as any other good natural institution such as property (and the market). Moreover, an era of misrule had to follow immediately upon the rejection of the divine authority of the Church in matters of Faith and Morals.

So the reaction to the past was a mixture of the recovery of something defensible and the assertion (somewhat stronger) of something indefensible. Universal suffrage, not carefully distinguished from Socialism, came to be insisted upon – the feminist movement was also gathering strength. These popular movements acquired the name "democratic". The political phenomenon had however been growing in Europe in the nineteenth century, much influenced by the French Revolution, despite the horrific violence it generated. Pope Leo was well aware of all this. We are concerned here however only with the use of the political word "democracy" as the political scene changed. Political movements and even parties began to use in their names "democratic", such as "social democratic" and "democratic socialism" and even "Christian democracy". Conrad Adenauer who lived long enough to become German Chancellor after World War Two called his party the "Christian Democratic Union".

The use of the word "democratic" became a problem that caused bitter debate among Catholics not just because it was linked to Socialism but because it seemed to exclude the legitimacy of other forms of regime. This is what Pope Leo XII addressed in *Graves de communi re*. His resolution of the problem, if known at all, is not well understood today.

Speaking of the reception of *Rerum novarum* the pope had this to say: "Hence it happened that the differences of opinion which prevailed among them [Catholics involved in social work] were either removed or lessened. In the order of action, much has been done in favor of the proletariat, especially in those places where poverty was at its worst. Many new institutions were set on foot, those which were already established were increased, and all reaped the benefit of a greater stability. Such are, for instance, the popular bureaus which supply information to the uneducated; the rural banks which make loans to small farmers; the societies for mutual help or relief; the unions of working men and other associations or institutions of the same kind. Thus, under the auspices of the Church, a measure of united action among Catholics was secured, as well as some planning in the setting up of agencies for the protection of the masses which, in fact, are as often oppressed by guile and exploitation of their necessities as by their own indigence and toil." (n. 3)

As yet there was no mention of involvement in Politics. The pope goes on: "This work of popular aid had, at first, no name of its own. The name of Christian Socialism, with its derivatives, which was adopted by some was very properly allowed to fall into disuse. Afterwards, some asked to have it called the popular

Christian Movement. In the countries most concerned with this matter, there are some who are known as Social Christians. Elsewhere, the movement is described as Christian Democracy and its partisans as Christian Democrats, in opposition to what the socialists call Social Democracy. Not much exception is taken to the first of these two names, i.e., Social Christians, but many excellent men find the term Christian Democracy objectionable. They hold it to be very ambiguous and for this reason open to two objections. It seems by implication covertly to favor popular government and to disparage other methods of political administration. Secondly, it appears to belittle religion by restricting its scope to the care of the poor, as if the other sections of society were not of its concern. More than that, under the shadow of its name there might easily lurk a design to attack all legitimate power, either civil or sacred. Wherefore, since this discussion is now so widespread, and so bitter, the consciousness of duty warns Us to put a check on this controversy and to define what Catholics are to think on this matter. We also propose to describe how the movement may extend its scope and be made more useful to the commonwealth." (n. 4)

The pope then resolves the basic problem so far as the use of the name "democratic" in a Christian social context is concerned in the next two paragraphs:

"5. What Social Democracy is and what Christian Democracy ought to be, assuredly no one can doubt. The first, with due consideration to the greater or less intemperance of its utterance, is carried to such an excess by many as to maintain that there is really nothing existing above the natural order of things, and that the acquirement and enjoyment of corporal and external goods constitute man's happiness. It aims at putting all government in the hands of the masses, reducing all ranks to the same level, abolishing all distinction of class, and finally introducing community of goods. Hence, the right to own private property is to be abrogated, and whatever property a man possesses, or whatever means of livelihood he has, is to be common to all.

6. As against this, Christian Democracy, by the fact that it is Christian, is built, and necessarily so, on the basic principles of divine faith, and it must provide better conditions for the masses, with the ulterior object of promoting the perfection of souls made for things eternal. Hence, for Christian Democracy, justice is sacred; it must maintain that the right of acquiring and possessing property cannot be impugned, and it must safeguard the various distinctions and degrees which are indispensable in every well-ordered commonwealth. Finally, it must endeavor to preserve in every human society the form and the character which God ever impresses on it. It is clear, therefore, that there in nothing in common between Social and Christian Democracy. They differ from each other as much as the sect of socialism differs from the profession of Christianity."

The use of the expression "Christian democracy" is made allowable then if "democracy" is freed of any connection with anti-Christian or anti-religious associations that often go with it and necessarily do so in the expression "Democratic Socialism". But one has to be careful not to make too much of this in the party political nature of modern politics. This is brought out in what follows in the next paragraph 7: "Moreover, it would be a crime to distort this name of Christian Democracy to politics, for, although democracy, both in its philological and philosophical significations, implies popular government, yet in its present application it must be employed without any political significance, so as to mean nothing else than this beneficent Christian action in behalf of the people. For, the laws of nature and of the Gospel, which by right are superior to all human contingencies, are necessarily independent of all particular forms of civil government, while at the same time they are in harmony with everything that is not repugnant to morality and justice. They are, therefore, and they must remain absolutely free from the passions and the vicissitudes of parties, so that, under whatever political constitution, the citizens may and ought to abide by those laws which command them to love God above all things, and their neighbors as themselves. This has always been the policy of the Church. The Roman Pontiffs acted upon this principle, whenever they dealt with different countries, no matter what might be the character of their governments. Hence, the mind and the action of Catholics devoted to promoting the welfare of the working classes can never be actuated with the purpose of favoring and introducing one government in place of another." [this obviously means good form of government]

This is perhaps where what the pope has said has not always been understood properly so that Catholics have thought that the use of the name "Christian Democratic" by a political party is OK. Unfortunately, what happens then is that the name "democratic" comes to be customarily associated with "Socialist". That is not helped by holding to the secularist doctrine to keep one's religion out of one's politics, a common enough position taken, mostly in ignorance one would hope, by many Catholics.

Let that be enough to say here about the changes in purely political terms that impinges on the economic, especially in respect of the ideology of Socialism. But the terms in politics such as democratic and republican are used in such a confused way in modern times that it is almost impossible to put any fixed meaning on them. "Republic" is but the Latin equivalent term ("public thing") for the Greek *politea,* which simply means a political constitution. How Plato's dialogue came to be given this Latin name is a bit of a mystery.

Aristotle used the general term to refer to the good rule by the many, according to the linguistic custom of using general terms to refer to the most basic of the specific kinds. Accordingly, "constitutional rule" is used for one species of the three kinds of good government rule by the many for the common good. Republic can be used in the same way. Democracy, which for Aristotle was the opposite to this good kind of rule for the common good, has lost its pejorative sense. But this is evidently because the notion of common good has dropped out of political discourse. In such a mixed-up state of mind it is easy for parties to manipulate their use of such terms to suit their own purposes.

But let us return to the "economic" changes, meaning political at the level of social intercourse at the basic material level in the use and exchange of external goods and services. As noted, the theory and practice of Capitalism underwent a transformation post war of contradictory mix with semi-socialism. The support of the State for the victims of Capitalist exploitation, even when moderated by a multiplication of State regulations, involving increase in taxation, with the need to invent all sorts of new methods of raising taxes, so that the Taxation Office grew to enormous proportions, along with the Social Welfare (called "security") Department.

However, we do not want to do more here than provide an indication of the continuous process of change in the social situation from 1931 to 1961 much of which time obviously was taken up with the Great Depression and the Second World War. We will leave further discussion of the periods of the 1950's to what Pope St. John XXIII had to say in *Mater et Magistra*. So we move to Chapter Four.

Chapter Four

Pope Saint John XXIII's *Mater et magistra* (1961)

Pope John issued his own commemorative social encyclical 70 years after *Rerum novarum*. He did what the popes before him did, confirming the perennial validity of the social doctrine contained therein and "updating" it. For, the social situation is constantly changing and in our times it appears to be at an ever-increasing rapid rate. Thus, even though Pope Pius XII's major message of 1941 was only 20 years before, Pope John put out a quite lengthy document. He explained himself this way: "As We pass all this in review, We are aware of Our responsibility to take up this torch which Our great predecessors lighted, and hand it on with undiminished flame. It is a torch to lighten the pathways of all who would seek appropriate solutions to the many social problems of our times. Our purpose, therefore, is not merely to commemorate in a fitting manner the Leonine encyclical, but also to confirm and make more specific the teaching of Our predecessors, and to determine clearly the mind of the Church on the new and important problems of the day." (50)

Such was the pope's concern with the social conditions of the times, the same pope who called for an ecumenical council (Vatican II) within a hundred years of the previous one, when there had been three hundred years between it (Vatican I) and the one before (Trent). Many have noted that the reason for the calling of the council was not doctrinal but pastoral. That is to say it was social conditions that had changed so much that it was necessary to clarify the application of the Church's position in regard to doctrine, worship and government, with particular emphasis on the last.

Pope John's mind on the matter may be described as one wishing to "hold the fort", not by shutting the gates, as had been the first defensive tendency after the Protestant Reformation, but by opening them "to the modern world". The Catholic Church, being the work of God, and the bastion of Truth, had no reason to fear the world (and its devil) but indeed had an obligation to show forth its goodness, beauty and truth (of Christ) to all men and women so that all might be one (*ut unum sint*) in the Kingdom of God.

The reaction within the Church was mixed. Some thought the move too rash. Some of these now see their fears realised in subsequent events, which seem to have left a church in turmoil. Others, including three popes, all canonized, counselled the faithful "be not afraid", the Lord will uphold us in the stormy waters into which the Church must venture on her journey of salvation for all in the world.

The world is indeed in a sorry state. Pope John observed: "As is well known, the outlook that prevailed on economic matters was for the most part a purely naturalistic one, which denied any correlation between economics and morality. Personal gain was considered the only valid motive for economic activity. In business the main operative principle was that of free and unrestricted competition. Interest on capital, prices - whether of goods or of services - profits and wages, were to be determined by the purely mechanical application of the laws of the market place. Every precaution was to be taken to prevent the civil authority from intervening in any way in economic matters. The status of trade unions varied in different countries. They were either forbidden, tolerated, or recognized as having private legal personality only." (11)

And he added: "In an economic world of this character, it was the might of the strongest which not only arrogated to itself the force of law, but also dominated the ordinary business relationships between individuals, and thereby undermined the whole economic structure." (12) "Enormous riches ac-cumulated in the hands of a few, while large numbers of workingmen found themselves in conditions of ever - increasing hardship. Wages were insufficient even to the point of reaching starvation level, and working conditions were often of such a nature as to be injurious alike to health, morality and religious faith. Especially inhuman were the working conditions to which women and children were sometimes subjected. There was also the constant spectre of unemployment and the progressive disruption of family life." (13) And finally: "The natural consequence of all this was a spirit of indignation and open protest on the part of the workingman, and a widespread tendency to subscribe to extremist theories far worse in their effects than the evils they purported to remedy." (14)

Then, coming to the encyclical *Rerum novarum* itself Pope John made the extraordinary claim: "... here for the first time was a complete synthesis of social principles, formulated with such historical insight as to be of permanent value to Christendom. It is rightly regarded as a compendium of Catholic social and economic teaching." Not wishing to be seen as words of empty praise the pope went on to list these principles in his following paragraphs under the headings highlighted:

"*Work - a Specifically Human Activity - Private Property and Its Social Aspect - The State's Role - Right to Enter into Associations - Human Solidarity and Christian Brotherhood*

"18. They concern first of all the question of work, which must be regarded not merely as a commodity, but as a specifically human activity. In the majority of cases a man's work is his sole means of livelihood. Its remuneration, therefore, cannot be made to depend on the state of the market. It must be determined by the laws of justice and equity. Any other procedure would be a clear violation of justice, even supposing the contract of work to have been freely entered into by both parties.

19. Secondly, private ownership of property, including that of productive goods, is a natural right, which the State cannot suppress. But it naturally entails a social obligation as well. It is a right, which must be exercised not only for one's own personal benefit but also for the benefit of others.

20. As for the State, its whole *raison d'etre* is the realization of the common good in the temporal order. It cannot, therefore, hold aloof from economic matters. On the contrary, it must do all in its power to promote the production of a sufficient supply of material goods, 'the use of which is necessary for the practice of virtue.' (7) It has also the duty to protect the rights of all its

people, and particularly of its weaker members, the workers, women and children. It can never be right for the State to shirk its obligation of working actively for the betterment of the condition of the workingman.

21. It is furthermore the duty of the State to ensure that terms of employment are regulated in accordance with justice and equity, and to safeguard the human dignity of workers by making sure that they are not required to work in an environment, which may prove harmful to their material and spiritual interests. It was for this reason that the Leonine encyclical enunciated those general principles of rightness and equity which have been assimilated into the social legislation of many a modern State, and which, as Pope Pius XI declared in the encyclical *Quadragesimo Anno*, (8) have made no small contribution to the rise and development of that new branch of jurisprudence called labor law.

22. Pope Leo XIII also defended the worker's natural right to enter into association with his fellows. Such associations may consist either of workers alone or of workers and employers, and should be structured in a way best calculated to safeguard the workers' legitimate professional interest. And it is the natural right of the workers to work without hindrance, freely, and on their own initiative within these associations for the achievement of these ends.

23. Finally, both workers and employers should regulate their mutual relations in accordance with the principle of human solidarity and Christian brotherhood. Unrestricted competition in the liberal sense, and the Marxist creed of class warfare are clearly contrary to Christian teaching and the nature of man.

24. These, Venerable Brethren, are the basic principles upon which a genuine social and economic order must be built."

Pope John then moved to consider *Quadragesimo anno* (1931) and shortly listed three matters addressed in it where there had been difficulties even amongst Catholics in accepting the teaching of *Rerum novarum*. These difficulties principally concerned the Catholic attitude to private property, the wage system, and moderate Socialism. (MM 29) Pope Pius XI's clarifications in this regard were to emphasise the social aspect of private property, to point out that the wage system was not itself unjust but that it was often implemented in an unjust and inhuman way, and to emphasise that Communism and Socialism were fundamentally opposed to Christianity, making it clear that no Catholic could subscribe even to moderate Socialism in view of its materialist ideology and its fundamental error with regard to the nature of the authority of the State.

Pope John himself was to make a further clarification in regard to this last matter, pointing out that over time an ideology may be adhered to in such a qualified way that those who described themselves as socialists may really be subscribing only to the part that was true or good in it, as every error contains some truth, and so opening up to Christians the way to co-operation with such others in certain respects. In the present fight between the two politico-economic extremes of Socialism and Liberalism, for instance, a person may think he is a socialist because he does not go to the Liberalist extreme of excluding the State altogether from "management" of the economy. Moreover, each extreme will tend to paint anyone who criticises it as belonging to the other extreme, thereby hoping to diminish any rational opposition to itself.

However, Pope John then highlighted the marked change that had come over the political and economic structure of society in the forty years since 1891. The "free market" of Liberal Capitalism's economic theory, somewhat illusory at the best of times, had virtually disappeared. It had become a free-for-all clash of the "forces" of self-interest of those few rich and powerful who profited most from the lack of just governmental restraint. Good Pope John put bluntly the state of affairs faced by Pope Pius XI:

"35. Pius XI was not unaware of the fact that in the forty years that had supervened since the publication of the Leonine encyclical the historical scene had altered considerably. It was clear, for example, that unregulated competition had succumbed to its own inherent tendencies to the point of practically destroying itself. It had given rise to a great accumulation of wealth, and, in the process, concentrated a despotic economic power in the hands of a few 'who for the most part are not the owners, but only the trustees and directors of invested funds, which they administer at their own good pleasure.' (14)

36. Hence, as the Pope remarked so discerningly, 'economic domination has taken the place of the open market. Unbridled ambition for domination has succeeded the desire for gain; the whole economic regime has become hard, cruel and relentless in frightful measure.' (15) As a consequence, even the public authority was becoming the tool of plutocracy, which was thus gaining a stranglehold on the entire world."

Can we not see a parallel with recent times here; where a period of oppressive government regulation (approaching a state of Socialism) gave way to a resurgence of "deregulation" at the end of the last century, only to see again the return of that economic despotism inherent in unbridled Capitalism – for where freedom is not restrained by right it will become might.

Pope Pius XI therefore urged (begged) for a restoration of social authority to bring these unruly marauders of humanity, now grown to global proportions, back within the social order. "This, he taught, necessitated an orderly reconstruction of society, with the establishment of economic and vocational bodies which would be autonomous and independent of the State. Public authority should resume its duty of promoting the common good of all. Finally, there should be co-operation on a world scale for the economic welfare of all nations." It took a worldwide depression and a second world war to break this stranglehold of plutocracy and enable the States to re-assert some sort of public authority.

Pope Saint John sums up his predecessor's teaching as a rejection of the errors of the ideologies of both Liberalism/Capitalism and Socialism/Communism:

"38. Thus Pius XI's teaching in this encyclical can be summed up under two heads. First he taught what the supreme criterion in economic matters ought not to be. It must not be the special interests of individuals or groups, nor unregulated competition, economic despotism, national prestige or imperialism, nor any other aim of this sort (39). On the contrary, all forms of economic enterprise must be governed by the principles of social justice and charity (40). The second point which We consider basic in the encyclical is his teaching that man's aim must be to achieve in social justice a national and international juridical order, with its network of public and private institutions, in which all economic activity can be conducted not merely for private gain but also in the interests of the common good."

We may note that just as the teachings and criticisms contained in Leo's encyclical were adopted to some extent afterwards, thereby greatly moderating the evils of the time, so it would seem that Pius's were also influential to some extent, as in the attempts after the end of the World War to at least rein in the economic despotism and political imperialism of pre-war times and to institute some sort of national and international juridical order. The seeds (ideologies) of the modern evils, however, were not expunged from the modern mind and again we face similar, if not the same, conditions.

Pope Pius XII did not write a social encyclical. This is a great pity, for, as on every other subject on which he spoke and wrote, this great pope showed in the brief speeches he did make on the subject such a profound wisdom and prudence that it would have been a great document. Pope Saint John acknowledged this and shortly recounted the basic points on what Pope Pius XII had to say on the use of material goods, work and the family that we have already outlined.

Pope Saint John then highlights the great social political and economic changes that had taken place even in the short period after the war leading up to his pontificate, applying the principles of *Rerum novarum* to these new circumstances.

In this process he draws upon the wisdom of Pope Pius XII on two matters of major importance. Firstly, for political leaders not to be drawn into the modern obsession with measuring social wealth or economic prosperity (not for all, but rather for the privileged few creditors, for the rest a measuring of increasing debt) by crass quantitative calculations of "growth" according to an accountancy mentality, but to attend to how a sufficiency of wealth might be able to be enjoyed by the whole population: "... the economic prosperity of a nation is not so much its total assets in terms of wealth and property, as the equitable division and distribution of this wealth." (MM 74)

Secondly, to attend to fostering the work of all in the community, especially those in small and average sized undertakings, encouraging them in forming co-operatives and associations and as well countering the lack of the ability of workers in large organisations to participate by introducing some kind of partnership arrangement, according to what Pope Pius XII had said: "The small and average sized undertakings in agriculture, in the arts and crafts, in commerce and industry, should be safeguarded and fostered. Moreover, they should join together in co-operative associations to gain for themselves the benefits and advantages that usually can be gained only from large organizations. In the large concerns themselves there should be the possibility of moderating the contract of work by one of partnership." (MM 84)

Then again, Pope Saint John reiterates what Pope Pius XII had said about the gross modern mal-distribution of property. "[The Church] also insists on the need for a fairer distribution of property and denounces what is contrary to nature in a social situation where, faced with a small group of privileged and rich, there is a huge impoverished mass." In the words of Pope Saint John: "But it is not enough to assert that the right to own private property and the means of production is inherent in human nature. We must also insist on the extension of this right in practice to all classes of citizens." (MM 113)

The pope immediately repeats the further words of Pius XII: "As Our Predecessor Pius XII so rightly affirmed: 'The dignity of the human person normally demands the right to the use of the goods of the earth, to which corresponds the fundamental obligation of granting an opportunity to possess property to all if possible.' This demand arises from the moral dignity of work. It also guarantees 'the conservation and perfection of a social order which makes possible a secure, even if modest, property to all classes of people.'" (MM 114) The sternness of the two popes' moral demands directed at the rich and powerful in this regard could not be clearer.

Sadly, if anything, this civilization-saving measure of distributive justice has been largely ignored by modern States, so that, adapting the very words of Pope Pius XI, once again "the public authority [is] becoming the tool of plutocracy, which [is] thus gaining a stranglehold on the entire world."

Pope Saint John then moves on to consider new aspects of the social question. He notes an aspect that has perhaps not been greatly noticed before, that systems of social injustice affect not only relations between workers and employers, as individuals and groups, but also between the various sectors of the social economy, extending not only within countries but also between them. Thus, he says: "History shows with ever-increasing clarity that it is not only the relations between workers and managers that need to be re-established on the basis of justice and equity, but also those between the various branches of the economy, between areas of varying productivity within the same political community, and between countries with a different degree of social and economic development." (MM 122)

He notes this social phenomenon with particular regard to the situation in agriculture (a sector close to his heart, being of peasant stock), where there is a decided trend for a continuous shift of population into towns and cities. To a certain extent this is a natural trend as an economy develops. Improvements in methods of production and in technology only go to accelerate this trend. However, the pope is more concerned with an accompanying trend, a worrying imbalance in the way the benefits of such economic progress are distributed not just between owners/employers and workers but also between the various sectors of production and exchange, with agriculture becoming the most depressed – providing an additional reason for people, especially the young, to leave the farm.

Here we may note a curious fact that points to something contrary to nature, but will become intelligible if we consider its unnatural cause. In economic terms, so far as our reliance on material wealth is concerned, agriculture is the most basic order of production without which a society could not live. After that, come the various manufacturing occupations that provide us with all sorts of needs such as housing, clothing, transport etc. After these, come the occupations specially concerned with the exchange system whereby all these occupations and orders of production are socially co-ordinated so that what is produced meets the needs of each (consumer) in society and the producers receive a just return for their efforts. This last level we call commerce. The natural order economically considered, or from the point of view of material wealth, therefore, is to place in order of social importance first agriculture, then manufacturing and last commerce. So far as rationality is concerned commerce serves production, not vice versa.

However, commerce or the exchange system holds a very powerful position in the socio-economic order of things. It produces nothing, yet it socially controls the production of everything. The individual producer cannot gain access to what he needs except through exchange (fairly) of what he produces. He is therefore at the mercy of the market in that his productivity cannot be realised to his benefit unless he can sell his products.

If anyone therefore can get into a position of control over the market they are in a very powerful position; they can control to a lesser or greater extent the whole production process of a community. In general terms that is the secret of the modern system of social injustice. It is one thing to have obtained a disproportionate share in the common wealth or natural resources of the community; it is another thing to have also a disproportionate control over the capital (tools) of industry; but it is the greatest kind of economic domination of all to control the exchange capital (money) of the market of a community.

In the order of nature and reason the exchange system is meant to serve the ends of production. The function of the market is to allow producers and consumers to meet. These are not two sets of people, but two aspects of the same people who go to market in order to sell what they produce or possess and buy from other producers what they need or desire.

Money creates the illusion that they are separate sections of the populace. This is what deceives the modern economists (and politicians). The exchange system works properly if there is equivalence of value between the goods sold and purchased, which is naturally effected through a just price system. This is not understood in modern economic theory because the "market" price is thought to be determined by "supply and demand", with the two, especially the latter, able to be conceived as separate economic "forces". But they can only influence the price if they have been somehow monopolised – which is indeed the modern situation owing to the huge disparity of bargaining power in any given exchange situation. This disparity (inequity/injustice) comes from a failure of distributive justice at all levels, of land, capital and labour.

The tendency in the modern economic system is for the sectors of production to become more and more impoverished (and burdened by debt), for people to move out of agriculture into manufacturing in search for more money, and then out of manufacturing into "service" industries such as advertising, media, insurance, banking and finance, in order to get closer to where money is made. All this has been explained in more detail in my book "Economic Science and St. Thomas Aquinas".

One further thing that needs to be noticed, however, is that it is not commerce itself that is the root of the problem but the way the exchange system has come to be dominated by a process of unnatural exchange, which takes two forms, called "moneymaking" and "moneylending". Commerce has come to stand for the former and finance for the latter. Social injustice in more modern times therefore tends to emanate from the more sophisticated levels of economic life. This is reflected in the political sphere where the government tends to become aligned with the powerful and rich sections of society, corrupted increasingly by the love of money. We tend to develop then a regime called Cacocracy (from Gk. *kakos* for bad), described by a wit as that form of political system where the scum rises to the top.

The social encyclicals do not go into these details. However, they clearly recognise the deep "imbalances" in the modern economic order (or disorder). Pope Saint John concludes after reviewing all the great social changes of his era: "After all this scientific and technical progress, and even because of it, the problem remains: how to build up a new order of society based on a more balanced human relationship between political communities on a national and international level?" (MM 212)

The Church looks to the more fundamental causes of this disorientation of human social relations: "Let men make all the technical and economic progress they can, there will be no peace nor justice in the world until they return to a sense of their dignity as creatures and sons of God, who is the first and final cause of all created being. Separated from God a man is but a monster, in himself and toward others; for the right ordering of human society presupposes the right ordering of man's conscience with God, who is Himself the source of all justice, truth and love." (MM 215)

He continues: "Here is a spectacle for all the world to see: thousands of Our sons and brothers, whom We love so dearly, suffering years of bitter persecution in many lands, even those of an ancient Christian culture." He asks: "will not men who see clearly and compare the superior dignity of the persecuted with that refined barbarity of their oppressors soon return to their senses, if indeed they have not already done so? (MM 216)

Indeed, the Church's teaching "rests on one basic principle: individual human beings are the foundation, the cause and the end of every social institution. That is necessarily so, for men are by nature social beings. This fact must be recognized, as also the fact that they are raised in the plan of Providence to an order of reality which is above nature." (MM 219)

His Holiness elaborates: "On this basic principle, which guarantees the sacred dignity of the individual, the Church constructs her social teaching. She has formulated, particularly over the past hundred years, and through the efforts of a very well informed body of priests and laymen, a social doctrine, which points out with clarity the sure way to social reconstruction. The principles she gives are of universal application, for they take human nature into account, and the varying conditions in which man's life is lived. They also take into account the principal characteristics of contemporary society, and are thus acceptable to all." (MM 220)

He ends with this stress upon the importance of this doctrine in the Catholic conception of life and an urgent appeal for its study: "First, We must reaffirm most strongly that this Catholic social doctrine is an integral part of the Christian conception of life. (MM 222) It is therefore Our urgent desire that this doctrine be studied more and more. First of all it should be taught as part of the daily curriculum in Catholic schools of every kind, particularly seminaries, although We are not unaware that in some of these latter institutions, this has been done for a long time now and in an outstanding way. We would also like to see it added to the religious instruction programs of parishes and of Association of the Lay Apostolate. It must be spread by every modern means at our disposal: daily newspapers, periodicals, popular and scientific publications, radio and television." (MM 223)

Pacem in terris (1963)

Two years later just a few months before his death the saintly pope published another encyclical that relates to the social order at its most fundamental level, namely, that of recognising all the natural rights of human beings as a necessary condition for peace on earth. The respect for the natural order in relation to human individual and social life is the foundation of the whole order of law and justice. It really extends to safeguarding all that is necessary for human beings to reach their goal of happiness, from liberty, life itself and all the benefits of civilized co-operation and communication, not merely at the basic level of material or economic goods but also at the highest level of spiritual and cultural goods.

This is possible for all, however, only if the order of natural law, natural justice and natural rights is put in place. The first two take their objects from the third. Thus the institution of private property and the obligation in others to render what is due in this regard depends on the right to exclusive possession of particular external goods had by the owners. More obviously the law making physical assault a crime and the duty to refrain from such depends upon a person's right to his bodily integrity.

The encyclical, from paragraphs 11 to 27 then lists the full range of natural rights (sometimes referred to as personal or human rights) according to their main or major categories:

"Man has the right to live.

He has the right to bodily integrity.

He has the right to the means necessary for the proper development of life, particularly food, clothing, shelter, medical care, rest, and, finally, the necessary social services.

He has the right to be looked after in the event of ill health; disability stemming from his work; widowhood; old age; enforced unemployment; or whenever through no fault of his own he is deprived of the means of livelihood.

Man has a natural right to be respected.

He has a right to his good name.

He has a right to freedom in investigating the truth, and - within the limits of the moral order and the common good - to freedom of speech and publication, and to freedom to pursue whatever profession he may choose.

He has the right, also, to be accurately informed about public events.

He has the natural right to share in the benefits of culture, and hence to receive a good general education, and a technical or professional training consistent with the degree of educational development in his own country.

He has the right to worship God in accordance with the right dictates of his own conscience, and to profess his religion both in private and in public.

Human beings have also the right to choose for themselves the kind of life which appeals to them: whether it is to found a family - in the founding of which both the man and the woman enjoy equal rights and duties - or to embrace the priesthood or the religious life.

The support and education of children is a right, which belongs primarily to the parents.

Man has the inherent right not only to be given the opportunity to work, but also to be allowed the exercise of personal initiative in the work he does.

The conditions in which a man works form a necessary corollary to these rights.

He has the right to engage in economic activities suited to his degree of responsibility.

The worker is likewise entitled to a wage that is determined in accordance with the precepts of justice. The amount a worker receives must be sufficient, in proportion to available funds, to allow him and his family a standard of living consistent with human dignity.

He has the right to the private ownership of property, including that of productive goods. The right to own private property entails a social obligation as well.

Men have the right to meet together and to form associations with their fellows. They have the right to confer on such associations the type of organization, which they consider best calculated to achieve their objectives. They have also the right to exercise their own initiative and act on their own responsibility within these associations for the attainment of the desired results (24). As We insisted in Our encyclical *Mater et Magistra*, the founding of a great many such intermediate groups or societies for the pursuit of aims which it is not within the competence of the individual to achieve efficiently, is a matter of great urgency. Such groups and societies must be considered absolutely essential for the safeguarding of man's personal freedom and dignity, while leaving intact a sense of responsibility.

Every human being has the right to freedom of movement and of residence within the confines of his own State.

When there are just reasons in favor of it, he must be permitted to emigrate to other countries and take up residence there.(22) The fact that he is a citizen of a particular State does not deprive him of membership in the human family, nor of citizenship in that universal society, the common, world-wide fellowship of men.

He has the right to take an active part in public life, and to make his own contribution to the common welfare of his fellow citizens.

As a human person he is entitled to the legal protection of his rights, and such protection must be effective, unbiased, and strictly just."

This is a clear and comprehensive statement of the rights of human beings. It applies to all human beings regardless of their condition whether within society or outside it. We could add some others to the list, such as the right to benefit equally from trade, or the right to benefit according to a just proportion from the common wealth or natural resources available within a particular community, but all such will be found to be included in some or other of the ones mentioned.

The right to benefit equally from trade within one's particular social economy may be included under the right to engage in economic activities. It is worth special mention, however, under modern conditions where this right is effectively negated by the great disparity of bargaining power of the property-less majority relative to that of the privileged propertied few.

So too the right to benefit according to a just proportion from the common wealth or natural resources available within a particular community, may be included under the right to the means necessary for the proper development of life. This, however, is worth a special mention in view of the enormous maldistribution in modern times in this regard, noted particularly by Pope Pius XII: "[The Church] also insists on the need for a fairer distribution of property and denounces what is contrary to nature in a social situation where, faced with a small group of privileged and rich, there is a huge impoverished mass."

It is worth mentioning also that there is a general right based in the inherent freedom of will in human nature, to exercise all these rights freely. That is why all rights can also be called freedoms. Rights generally entail an obligation on the possessor to act according to them.

However, though it is always wrong to do evil it is not always wrong to suffer it. There is a hierarchy of rights and duties and one may legitimately suffer death or injury for the sake of a higher good. The same applies to other cases of relinquishment of rights, such as that of property. In some particular cases the right need not be exercised for any reason because the obligation to which it is tied does not bind all individually, such as that of marriage. St. Thomas points out that it is for the sake of the perpetuation of the human race and therefore only imposes an obligation on individuals if it were necessary in their particular case for the continuance of human kind.

The encyclical goes on to deal with the rights of States both in relation to their subjects and other States. In regard to the first it is important to note that civil society (and political government) exists for the benefit of its individual members and not vice versa. The reason for this lies in the fact that it is only individual human beings that are persons and accordingly they cannot be subjected totally to any other creature let alone other human beings. Each person is made for personal happiness, which is to be achieved (freely) in the possession of God alone. All other relationships, including the family and civil society, are ordered to this end. It is necessary for individual persons to belong to such societies only to the extent that they work for the ultimate good of each person.

Thus, Pope Saint John states: "The attainment of the common good is the sole reason for the existence of civil authorities. In working for the common good, therefore, the authorities must obviously respect its nature, and at the same time adjust their legislation to meet the requirements of the given situation." (54) Further: "These principles are clearly contained in that passage in Our encyclical *Mater et Magistra* where We emphasized that the common good 'must take account of all those social conditions which favor the full development of human personality.'" (58)

The intimate connection between the common good and individual rights is then expressed: "It is generally accepted today that the common good is best safeguarded when personal rights and duties are guaranteed. The chief concern of civil authorities must therefore be to ensure that these rights are recognized, respected, co-ordinated, defended and promoted, and that each individual is enabled to perform his duties more easily. For 'to safeguard the inviolable rights of the human person, and to facilitate the performance of his duties, is the principal duty of every public authority.'"(60)

The encyclical then refers to relations between States. Here the Pope notices two things. Firstly, there is the need for an authority of international or global standing to ensure the order of justice at world level. This has to be based upon agreement between States. The universal common good of this world order has too to be founded upon the natural moral law. "But one of the principal imperatives of the common good is the recognition of the moral order and the unfailing observance of its precepts. 'A firmly established order between political communities must be founded on the unshakable and unmoving rock of the moral law, that law which is revealed in the order of nature by the Creator Himself, and engraved indelibly on men's hearts .... Its principles are beacon lights to guide the policies of men and nations. They are also warning lights - providential signs - which men must heed if their laborious efforts to establish a new order are not to encounter perilous storms and shipwreck.'" (PT 85)

Here again Pope Saint John refers to the teaching of Pope Pius XII (Pius XII's broadcast message, Christmas 1941). Indeed, the encyclical that first addresses the new emerging problems of the whole world is peppered with quotations from the immediate predecessor of Pope John.

At the end the encyclical the intimate connection between the universal common good and the rights of the human person is highlighted. "The common good of individual States is something that cannot be determined without reference to the human person, and the same is true of the common good of all States taken together. Hence the public authority of the world community must likewise have as its special aim the recognition, respect, safeguarding and promotion of the rights of the human person. This can be done by direct action, if need be, or by the creation throughout the world of the sort of conditions in which rulers of individual States can more easily carry out their specific functions." (MM139)

Finally, we might note the early hint of the theme of development of all peoples to be taken up by Pope Saint Paul VI immediately after Vatican II. "In Our encyclical *Mater et Magistra*, therefore, We appealed to the more wealthy nations to render every kind of assistance to those States which are still in the process of economic development ... The result We look for is that the poorer States shall in as short a time as possible attain to a degree of economic development that enables their citizens to live in conditions more in keeping with their human dignity." (MM 122, 123)

Chapter Five

Part I

Pope Saint Paul VI's *Octogesima adveniens* (1971)

At this point we come to an event that though it did not change the basic teaching of the social encyclicals from *Rerum Novarum* to *Pacem et terris* introduced something new in the Church's relation to the modern world, though it was the world that was new. It is difficult to put it in natural terms, as for instance saying that it was a move from a more defensive attitude to a more "understanding" one. Pope John referred to the Church as Mother and Teacher. Both roles are necessary at all times. It is a mistake to oppose one to the other. But there may be a call for a different emphasis at different times.

Pope Saint Pius X alluded to this in *Pascendi Dominici gregis* (though he was speaking internally and making a contrary point). "Wherefore We may no longer be silent, lest We should seem to fail in Our most sacred duty, and lest the kindness that, in the hope of wiser counsels, We have hitherto shown them, should be attributed to forgetfulness of Our office." ["namely, to guard with the greatest vigilance the deposit of the faith delivered to the saints"] The pope spoke with the utmost severity and sternness of doctrinal errors, objectively heretical of the most serious kind. Interestingly, he puts what he says in a pastoral framework. It is a mother's love that prompts her to warn her children of known dangers.

By the time of Pope John's pontificate, short as it was, it was clear that many things in the world were changing dramatically. History can be read from multiple angles and we do not presume to be able to do justice to all or any particular one. But for our purposes here we need to give some "reading" in politico-economic terms that ties together as best we can the threads of thought and action we are concerned with. As well, it is clear that the Holy Spirit is at work and we do not want to enter into any debates over the wisdom of any particular matters of ecclesiastical "policy" since the Council. It obviously involves a delicate balance requiring supernatural prudence. We will try to remain as best we can at the rational level of the discussion in natural moral and politico-economic terms.

Of course, the modern mind is more interested in the state of the world from a naturalistic or secularist political point of view. Unfortunately, when so taken, without original sin being in the picture, one necessarily falls into one moral error or other or, to put it into political (or politico-economic) language, into one ideology or another. Such political arrangements will involve the relation of master and servant, which, as we have seen, generally comes across in practice as some sort of domination by some human beings over others, that is in some form of servitude occurring at both the domestic (or ethnic) and political levels of association.

This division in societies seems to be derived from a basic division from an economic point of view of societies into two parts, as Plato put it, into that of the rich and the poor. Generally speaking, the rich are few, as are the masters or lords, or "capitalists", and the poor are many, as are the slaves or serfs, or "workers". But these proportions are affected by various factors. Such are family connections, inter-tribal relations, and in modern times, international relations. So it was in ancient Rome that many slaves were quite well off and in modern times many in a servile condition are able to live comfortably provided they serve well in some way their rich "patrons" and defend the politico-economic system "in force". Think of the modern media about whom Chesterton quipped: "We do not need freedom of the Press but freedom from the Press", and Marshall McLuhan is reported to have said is "a Luciferian conspiracy against the truth".

There are other extrinsic factors that affect the picture, such as being able to live off the government not just by pensions and "welfare", but also by political corruption on a grand scale, getting privileged access to natural resources, gaining government "contracts" to supply services and equipment (including much in demand weapons of war) and by a host of other "ways and means" discoverable by the inventive imagination of man. Astute individuals have the ready means of making money by the secondary mode of exchange described by Aristotle and Aquinas, much engaged in the buying and selling not just of "personal estate" (such as cars) but also of "real estate". There is also the possibility of working harder than most to obtain an advantage in some craft or "trade". We do not exclude these "exceptions" to the general "mode of production" that defines the politico-economic system as ideological, which like a drug has the tendency to absorb many of these exceptional activities into its "system".

After Vatican II, though the popes insist on preserving the truth of the doctrine as a fundamental part of the social magisterium it is more difficult to connect the treatment of social changes to *Rerum Novarum*. For the notion of the social problem has widened to take in the division not only between the rich and poor in terms of Capitalism and Proletarianism that had arisen out of the European/ Christian zone of influence but also this division into rich and poor as manifested worldwide, taking in countries with radically different ways of life and government to that of Europe and its offshoots.

Of course, in a way this globalization of the problem had a connection with the spread of domination by "Western" powers and so the social problem was simply extended into the rest of the world as it became "westernized", and thus subject politico-economically to the same capitalist system. Indeed, this domination by mainly the British Empire in the nineteenth century and the USA in the twentieth worked by the same principles of domination and virtual enslavement of the subject populations as it went "global".

Nonetheless, this process of domination was not complete and so there remained even civilizations, such as the Chinese, retaining their own cultures and systems of government to a large extent - till mid twentieth century. The Indian and Japanese civilizations were differently affected again by "Western" intrusion. Moreover, even within the Capitalist part of the world not just its roots in Christianity were being disconnected but religion itself.

It was not only the Socialist/Communist totalitarian part of the world that was turning atheist but also the Liberalist/Capitalist "free world". Might have something to do with the modern liberalist doctrine that puts Man (i.e. Me) before God (i.e. my Maker).

But there seemed to be no connection retained with the Christian religion in much of the world, officially that is. In any case the world situation which the Church turned to face in the 1960's was quite mixed and rapidly becoming more so. For instance, how does one fit Russia after the fall of the USSR and with the revival of Orthodox Christianity there into this picture? What are we to make of the opposite process in China where Communism, really a European/ Christian aberration of Liberalism, with its "dialectical" relation to Capitalism, has come to be the dominant politico-economic system?

The Leonine analysis of the question of social justice was in what was basically a Christian context if become somewhat contorted and this began to seem rather outmoded. The modern world seemed to be better analysed in more purely political terms, seeing the conflicts of systems rather as between democratic regimes and totalitarian, if the immediate contrast was between Capitalist and Communist. But the vast Muslim world could be fitted into the picture of the non-democratic (theocratic) and therefore analogously totalitarian. More disconnected from Christianity, the Chinese regime could be similarly characterised even before it became Communist. The Indian/Asian world could be fitted somewhere in between. But the disconnect with the world of Leo XIII and more so of Aquinas was beginning to look like a real rupture.

On top of that there were clear signs that even if the old capitalist domination was still strong in the USA and its allies in the "free world" their social and political framework was starting to fall apart, noticeable particularly in a rapid moral decline – corruption was coming to the surface and becoming almost resigned to: "that's Politics". Even in terms of Western political philosophy Hobbes and Machiavelli seemed to have finally vanquished Aristotle and Aquinas. To some even within the Catholic Church it seemed as if it was time for the Church authorities to wake up and deal with the world as it really is.

What is relevant here is that to a certain extent this is reflected in the Church documents on the "social justice question" in and following the Vatican Council. Whereas from Leo XIII to Pope John XXIII the documents are peppered with quotes from Aquinas, afterwards they trickle to almost a halt. This is despite the continuance of the issue of a commemorative letter and two social encyclicals for three decades until the hundredth anniversary in 1991 and the insistence that Leo's document is still the *Magna Carta* as well as Pope Benedict XVI's strong statements that the Council documents were in perfect continuity with all that had gone before.

This apparent disconnect is something that affects our own reliance on Aristotle and Saint Thomas Aquinas in our books on the subject. So we will have to deal with this modern shift of attention on the part of the Church. But we only mean here to signal the problem so as to have some better understanding of the social encyclicals after Vatican II. Hopefully we can tie all things together by the end. We need only to acknowledge that after Vatican II the problem comes to be discussed at a level that is more elevated and general, bringing out more clearly the dignity of the human person in whatever condition of servitude.

After Vatican II it became a broader social issue, meant to move from within national boundaries or that group of nations of European "heritage" (inheriting the politico-economic ideology of Capitalism/Proletarianism) to the whole world (as a "globe"). This was a true shift of object of concern which had many non-ideological causes that brought peoples together as never before, with developments of a technological nature following the Second World War being a major factor. In a negative way weapons of destruction, such as the atomic/nuclear bomb, could be used by the "developed" nations (still European in origin in some way such as USA and USSR) to terrorise other nations and even other civilizations. These "Christian" and anti-Christian nations sub-scribing to the connected ideologies of Liberalism, Capitalism or Communism now had the capacity, and the evident intent, to dominate the world.

This focus on geographical and demographic shift, with its genuine causes of "development", such as in the means of communication, brought in its train many benefits to those nations and even whole cultures considered "undeveloped" in these ways. The other civilizations and cultures (even if considered "primitive") had naturally many positive goods to offer to others including to the cultures that had had the benefit of Christian civilization.

It still needs to be acknowledged, however, that the era of Christendom, which gave to the world not only a high civilization in spiritual, religious and moral terms, higher as Pope Leo XIII pointed out than any before and since, but also much, as many would resist admitting, in temporal and material terms. This is where you will find the roots of all that is good in modern science and Western culture. However, Vatican II, whilst conscious of the negative, wished to focus on the positive.

A full history of the modern age in respect of the true civilizing elements we might put, at least in large part, at the risk of being accused of triumphalism, somewhat like the story of Robinson Crusoe (by Daniel Defoe) where he could only survive by retrieving what he needed from the ship that had been wrecked. Christendom is the wreck whose contents modern Europe has survived on in terms of capital, both intellectual and moral, but as well the scientific and technological inventiveness it and its descendant nations have inherited. As is all too evident at the present time "Europe" and its former colonies have stripped bare the metaphorical wreck. Apart from divine intervention it is plain that like the "old" pagan world the modern one is doomed to fall and sooner than we think.

It is not a strange thing that the modern world (named appropriately from a word meaning a passing fashion) should have risen to great heights of material wealth and temporal power after it rejected its Catholic Faith. For then it was able to use such an advantage, even greater than that of Alexander and Augustus, over the rest of the world without scruple. Indeed, the other parts of the world that had become known or better known around that time were "sitting ducks" precisely because of their lack of the material benefits of Christian civilization.

It is not a strange thing then that the triumph of the competing modern nations, or rather their robber barons, who rejected the moral leadership of the Catholic Church (including the so called modern Catholic nations that profited from robbing the material wealth and profiting from the cultural knowledge of the Church) were able to dominate others, including the majority of their own people (as Capitalists) for a time, owing to their command of such superior wealth and power, conferred on them by their "Christian" heritage. But now that this heritage is all but exhausted this powerful part of the world (the USA representing less than 5% of the world population, and we are only talking about 5% of their population) is being overtaken by rival nations or blocs (also ruled by dictators) that have been able to acquire the benefit of that heritage so far as it is materially scientific and technological. It is more of a level playing field and those who have enjoyed their temporary superiority do not like it.

It is this mix of changes, both rational and irrational, with which the Church has to deal, in a time of almost unfathomable turmoil. Indeed, one may see the decision of the Council to "enter the fray" as but a repeat on a much larger scale of that of Leo XIII seventy years before to try to stave off catastrophe. But the agents of the Evil One, who will resort to murder and deceit without restraint, do not give up without a fight to the death.

We should note however that though persecuted grievously in the process the Church did benefit from the geographical and demographic expansion that went with the rise of modern empires, just as Christianity was able to spread with the expansion by arms of the Roman Empire. No doubt providentially missionaries travelled to foreign lands with the armies and with the explorers that were able to make use of modern technology; and so the gospel was able to be preached to a greater and greater portion of the human race.

However, we cannot go further into these deep matters of world history. We hope only to provide some insight into the reading of the social encyclicals post Vatican II and in particular into the meaning to be put on "development" which plays such a central role in them.

But before taking this up we must take note of the two social encyclicals (and letter) commemorative of *Rerum novarum* which commemoration continues for the eightieth, ninetieth and centenary anniversaries. This line then stops and is taken over by a new line begun just after the end of the Council with Pope Saint Paul VI's 1967 encyclical *Populorum progressio*, whose twentieth anniversary is commemorated by Pope Saint John Paul II in 1987 and fortieth by Pope Benedict XVI in 2009 (delayed by the GFC). Indeed, Pope Benedict XVI describes *Populorum Progressio* as the *Rerum Novarum* for our times.

So here we propose to complete the first line even though it continues for a time after the Council and will be affected by its documents particularly *Gaudium et spes*. We can then return to the Council document and the social encyclicals following it.

We can see from the start the right way to read the Church documents on social justice following the Council. The initial focus of Pope Leo was prompted by a social situation within the modern world that was a successor to Christendom, which was based in Europe including the British Isles the colonies founded by the countries that made it up (especially the USA), which we may identify in politico-economic terms as Capitalist in the sense we have been discussing. In 1891 Pope Leo felt the need to intervene (not in a political way as now understood but in a religious moral way) believing that the politico-economic order (or disorder) had reached such a point that the modern civilization that had succeeded Christendom was in danger of catastrophic collapse owing to the clash of the two parts of it that we may shortly call Capital and Labour if it did not result in any essential change of the structural injustice that he described as "little better than slavery". As Pope Pius XII said:

The Church must condemn what offends the natural moral law, whether applying personally, domestically or politically, and warn against the danger, most importantly spiritual, but also bodily, for human nature is one. But it belongs to human free will to fix things under its control, even spiritual and eternally consequential, let alone material and of temporal consequence, no matter how dire. The danger to Western/Capitalist civilization was and is significant. But to some extent the temporal catastrophe has been averted and it is a much wider catastrophe that looms. However, the popes have warned that the spiritual and temporal danger addressed in *Rerum Novarum* is still present.

Note what Pope Saint Paul VI has said later in this letter: "44. Under the driving force of new systems of production, national frontiers are breaking down, and we can see new economic powers emerging, the multinational enterprise, which by the concentration and flexibility of their means can conduct autonomous strategies which are largely independent of the national political powers and therefore not subject to control from the point of view of the common good. By extending their activities, these private organizations can lead to a new and abusive form of economic domination on the social, cultural and even political level. **The excessive concentration of means and powers that Pope Pius XI already condemned** on the fortieth anniversary of Rerum Novarum is taking on a new and very real image." (bold added).

Note also what Pope Saint John Paul II said in *Centesimus annus*: "I also mean to show that the *vital energies* rising from that root have not been spent with the passing of the years, but rather *have increased even more.*" (1) And later: "In this sense, it is right to speak of a struggle against an economic system, if the latter is understood as a method of upholding the absolute predominance of capital, the possession of the means of production and of the land, in contrast to the free and personal nature of human work. (73) In the struggle against such a system, what is being proposed as an alternative is not the socialist system, which in fact turns out to be State capitalism, but rather *a society of free work, of enterprise and of participation.* Such a society is not directed against the market, but demands that the market be appropriately controlled by the forces of society and by the State, so as to guarantee that the basic needs of the whole of society are satisfied." (35)

But first we have to deal with the letter of Pope Saint Paul VI. Even in this letter of Pope Saint Paul VI commemorating *Rerum novarum* we begin to see the change of focus that was taken in the Council.

Thus, he begins saying quite early in the document: "Since the period in which the encyclical *Rerum Novarum* denounced in a forceful and imperative manner the scandal of the condition of the workers in the nascent industrial society, historical evolution has led to an awareness of other dimensions and other applications of social justice. The encyclicals *Quadragesimo Anno* (2) and *Mater et Magistra* (3) already noted this fact. The recent Council for its part took care to point them out, in particular in the Pastoral Constitution *Gaudium et Spes*. We ourself have already continued these lines of thought in our encyclical *Populorum Progressio*. 'Today', we said, 'the principal fact that we must all recognize is that the social question has become worldwide' (4). 'A renewed consciousness of the demands of the Gospel makes it the Church's duty to put herself at the service of all, to help them grasp their serious problem in all its dimensions, and to convince them that solidarity in action at this turning point in human history is a matter of urgency'." (5)

Ex quo tempore per Encyclicas Litteras, a verbis "Rerum Novarum" incipientes, vivaciter impenseque pronuntiata est indigna probrosaque opificum condicio in societate, quae oriebatur, quaestuosae industriae dedita, progressio rerum alia capita et alias rationes iustitiae socialis mentibus insinuavit, quemadmodum etiam per Litteras, a verbis "Quadragesimo Anno" (AAS 23 (1931), p. 209 sq.) et "Mater et Magistra" (AAS 53 (1961), p. 429) appellatas, iam est declaratum. Recens autem Concilium Oecumenicum operam navavit hisce quaestionibus expediendis, praesertim in Constitutione Pastorali, quae a verbis "Gaudium et Spes" initium sumit. Ac Nosmet ipsi per Encyclicas Litteras,

"Populorum Progressio" inscriptas, hasce agendi normas iam amplificavimus: *Illud hodie maxime interest omnes pro certo habere ac veluti sentire, socialem quaestionem nunc ad universam coniunctionem inter homines hominum magnopere pertinere* (3: AAS (1967), p. 258). *Cum enim Ecclesia clarius etiam altiusque iudicavisset, et expendisset quid hac de re Christi Iesu Evangelium flagitaret, suum esse duxit hominibus magis etiam egregiam navare operam, ut non modo gravissimae huius quaestionis ii momenta omnibus vestigiis indagarent, sed etiam sibi persuaderent, hac summa discri,minas hora, communi omnium actione vehementer opus esse* (*Ibidem*, 1: p. 257)

Yet the pope had opened his letter by saying: "1. The eightieth anniversary of the publication of the encyclical *Rerum Novarum*, the message of which continues to inspire action for social justice, prompts us to take up again and to extend the teaching of our predecessors, in response to the new needs of a changing world."

That is to say, he is but extending the teaching of the pre-Vatican popes to an even greater range of change, worldwide. The praise of *Rerum Novarum* continues in the documents of the social doctrine of the Church after Vatican II. So too does this apply to the evident reliance on the teaching of St. Thomas Aquinas, not just in expounding upon the social doctrine of the Church, but also generally, as may be seen in a multitude of documents of popes from Saint Pius X, Benedict XV, Pius XI, Pius XII, Saint John XXIII through Saint Paul VI to Saint John Paul II.

How is it then that after Vatican II the citations of the works of Aquinas, so pronounced before, seem to fade away and may be found only here and there? Does that not look as if the Church has taken a "new direction" and has abandoned a narrow reliance on one mediaeval theologian? Not a few apparently would like to think so.

But there is another explanation. Though Leo's social doctrine, drawing upon St. Thomas's genial expression of its principles, was directed at a particular social situation that had arisen within the part of the world that had come to be called "Christian" - spoiled by the modern political ideology of Liberalism, from which had sprung two politico-economic sub-ideologies of Capitalism and Socialism - his encyclical expressed the fundamental principles of natural morality (justice, as elaborated upon in my previous books) under the light of Faith. Accordingly, it could be extended to all human life and behaviour, and so to the relations between men and women of all nations, still retaining where relevant the focus on the relations between master and servant, rich and poor.

The change in the citations from Aquinas can therefore be put with the less direct reliance on *Rerum Novarum* in the change in the object of concern. Pope Saint Paul VI's attention is directed at the same question of social justice but now in a worldwide context, but he is careful to note that it is the same kind of question dealt with by his predecessors. Thus, he says: "7. In so doing, our purpose - without however forgetting the <u>permanent</u> problems already dealt with by our predecessors - is to draw attention to a number of questions. These are questions which because of their urgency, extent and complexity must in the years to come take first place among the preoccupations of Christians, so that with other men the latter may dedicate themselves to solving the new difficulties which put the very future of man in jeopardy. It is necessary to situate the problems created by the modern economy in the wider context of a new civilization. These problems include human conditions of production, fairness in the exchange of goods and in the division of wealth, the significance of the increased needs of consumption and the sharing of responsibility."

Notice it is not the future of "Christian"/Western civilization that is in danger but "the future of man". The two dangers are evidently related and it would take a deal of analysis to spell this out. But the focus now has to be on the worldwide social situation. That is one reason why the Church's appeal is to the deepest and most personal considerations of human nature common to all, to the urgency of peace and to common fraternity more directly than to liberty and equality, without continuing to insist that peace will is not possible without respect for human dignity in freedom and justice. It is the social situation that has changed, not the doctrine.

I pause to make a comment here, however, about the translation of the above underlined word; the Latin is *perennium*. "Permanent", though not quite exact (why not perennial?), may be allowed to pass. But as noted before the study of the social encyclicals is dogged by bad translation that misleads in important parts of the documents. I advert here in this document to its treatment of "democracy"

How does one cope with this way of translating "democracy" in paragraphs 37 and 47? (bold added)

(47) *Ut vero gliscenti technicorum potestati obsistatur, novae* **popularis imperii formae** *inveniendae sunt, hodiernae vitae consentaneae, ita ut non modo cuique homini tribuatur facultas res cognoscendi suamque de iis opinionem exprimendi, verum etiam is communi munerum et officiorum susceptione obstringatur.* "In order to counterbalance increasing technocracy, modern forms of **democracy** must be devised, not only making it possible for each man to become informed and to express himself, but also by involving him in a shared responsibility."

37. *His ceteroqui temporibus darius deprehenditur doctrinarum debilitas per ipsa scilicet systemata, quibus ad effectum deduci nituntur. Etenim graphiocraticus socialismus, capitalismus, qui dicitur, technocraticus,* **imperiosum democratiae** *genus plane declarant, quam aegre ac difficulter magna illa hominum quaestio una simul vivendi solvi possit secundum iustitiam et aequalitatem. Quonam pacto poterunt illi revera effugere materialismum, nimium suarum utilitatum studium, vel crudelem etiam oppressionem, quam ea secum necessario inferunt?* "Today moreover the weaknesses of the ideologies are better perceived through the concrete systems in which they are trying to affirm themselves. Bureaucratic socialism, technocratic capitalism and **authoritarian democracy** are showing how difficult it is to solve the great human problem of living together in justice and equality. How in fact could they escape the materialism, egoism or constraint which inevitably go with them?"

An Aristotelian would have no difficulty taking *imperiosum* as signifying a bad form of popular rule, *popularis imperii formae,* which ought to be replaced by a good form, by being ordered to the common good. The modern form of "democracy" (without qualification), with political theorists not knowing the difference between rule by the many for the common good and rule for the good of the rulers (even if they were a true majority, which Aristotle would still class a democracy in the bad sense) inevitably think "democracy" refers to a good form of rule (indeed the only good form).

The translator quite evidently also does not know the difference, the only political science he or she knows most likely being the modern. This is only one further example of the misleading translation from Latin to English even of official magisterial documents, not to speak of the atrocious examples we have cited in the case of the works of Aquinas.

However, let us turn to what the pope had to say in his letter. The first of the problems he addresses according to their worldwide significance is urbanization. This is how he puts it: "8. A major phenomenon draws our attention, as much in the industrialized countries as in those which are developing: urbanization. After long centuries, agrarian civilization is weakening. Is sufficient attention being devoted to the arrangement and improvement of the life of the country people, whose inferior and at times miserable economic situation provokes the flight to the unhappy crowded conditions of the city outskirts, where neither employment nor housing awaits them?" *Maioris vero ponderis res eaque singularis hodie Nostrum animum tangit, id est nimis den-*

satus urbium incolatus; quae res in cunctis accidit regionibus, sive in iis, quae quaestuosa industria iam sunt instructae, sive in iis, quae ad humani cultos progressum adhuc nituntur. Post longum cursum saeculorum civilis cultus agrarius iam imminuitur. Ceterum, num sufficiens cura intenditur in recte disponendam melioremque reddendam vitam agrestium, quorum condicio, quoad rem oeconomicam minor et interdum misera, causa est, cur in suburbia, tristes hominum coacervationes, illi commigrent, ubi neque opus faciendum inveniunt neque habitationem?

The terminology here is obviously affected by the modern meaning of industrialization, which described the movement off the land of small landholders (yeomen) into the town in search of more economically rewarding work, soon to become factory workers, which as we have seen happened in the context of the division of modern societies into two parts under the titles of Capital and Labour. Industrialization thus came to mean much the same as urbanization.

But this process, if accelerated in the case of Capitalism/Proletarianism, would have been seen by Aristotle as a natural one where the dependence on the land was a mark of an intermediate stage of tribal or village life that led on to the city or fully civil life (*polis*). What complicates things in this regard is that in whatever form of "progress", which should take place at all levels of human social existence, from economic to high cultural, there necessarily intrudes an unnatural element (original sin) that has the effects we see in every politico-economic social arrangement.

Indeed, it may be said that in some respects the "progress" of the modern post-Christendom form has been more deranged than in the pagan, whether ancient or not. Thus, Chesterton remarks that the moral degeneration (in regard to the love of sexual pleasure) is much worse, infinitely more so, in the so-called Western civilization, than in the ancient pagan. At least he says the ancient sexual degeneracy did not deny the fruitfulness of sex. A similar verdict might be given on the modern love of money. (cf. Essay on Sex and Property in his book "The Well and the Shallows"). I have an article entitled "A Taste of Sweet Decay" inspired by Chesterton's essay – see Appendix A.

Pope Saint Paul VI relates the impact of the phenomenon of "industrialization" now worldwide upon various sectors of a modern civil society, focusing mainly on the ill-effects, even though he admits the phenomenon (movement towards "the city") is to some extent natural. The victims are especially the youth, women, workers, migrants. There is much misery that is generated by this "disordered" growth (productive as he notes of delinquency, criminality, abuse of drugs and eroticism). How is the Christian to meet this phenomenon now existing on a global scale. It presents new and great challenges. This is his plea:

"12. To build up the city, the place where men and their expanded communities exist, to create new modes of neighborliness and relationships, to perceive an original application of social justice and to undertake responsibility for this collective future, which is foreseen as difficult, is a task in which Christians must share. To those who are heaped up in an urban promiscuity which becomes intolerable it is necessary to bring a message of hope. This can be done by brotherhood which is lived and by concrete justice. Let Christians, conscious of this new responsibility, not lose heart in view of the vast and faceless society; let them recall Jonah who traversed Niniveh, the great city, to proclaim therein the good news of God's mercy and was upheld in his weakness by the sole strength of the word of Almighty God. In the Bible, the city is in fact often the place of sin and pride - the pride of man who feels secure enough to be able to build his life without God and even to affirm that he is powerful against God. But there is also the example of Jerusalem, the Holy City, the place where God is encountered, the promise of the city which comes from on high."

One can see how the problem of social justice has been broadened beyond the confines of Western capitalism/proletarianism. But one can still see how this European generated "Christian" social situation has impacted, for good and ill, upon the worldwide situation. Many good measures have been taken to rescue society from the catastrophe that threatened in Leo's time, but it has to be conceded that the gains have been limited and the fundamental structural injustice of the maldistribution of property rights and unnatural treatment of labour as a commodity has not gone away. Indeed, it has been extended with the extension of the domination of the rest of the world by the politico-economic systems of Capitalism and its political system of "Democracy", of which Communism and its brand of "authoritarian democracy" is a kind of more violent tribal rival.

The pope observes: "15. In short, progress has already been made in introducing, in the area of human relationships, greater justice and greater sharing of responsibilities. But in this immense field much remains to be done. Further reflection, research and experimentation must be actively pursued, unless one is to be late in meeting the legitimate aspirations of the workers - aspirations which are being increasingly asserted according as their education, their consciousness of their dignity and the strength of their organizations increase."

Indicating how deep rooted is the sinfulness against which man has to contend, he continues: "Egoism and domination are permanent temptations for men. Likewise, an ever finer discernment is needed, in order to strike at the roots of newly arising situations of injustice and to establish progressively a justice which will be less and less imperfect. In industrial change, which demands speedy and constant adaptation, those who will find themselves injured will be more numerous and at a greater disadvantage from the point of view of making their voices heard. The Church directs her attention to those new "poor" - the handicapped and the maladjusted, the old, different groups of those on the fringe of society, and so on - in order to recognize them, help them; defend their place and dignity in a society hardened by competition and the attraction of success."

Having noted the many causes of injustice, from unjust treatment of those within a nation to those between nations, and even civilizations, the pope looks at other phenomena that both draw all men and women together but also constitute a worldwide threat. Thus, he notes the spectacular improvement in the means of communication, for good and bad, for it is but a means. "20. Among the major changes of our times, we do not wish to forget to emphasize the growing role being assumed by the media of social communication and their influence on the transformation of mentalities of knowledge, of organizations and of society itself. Certainly they have many positive aspects. Thanks to them news from the entire world reaches us practically in an instant, establishing contacts which supersede distances and creating elements of unity among all men. A greater spread of education and culture is becoming possible. Nevertheless, by their very action the media of social communication are reaching the point of representing as it were a new power."

So too with the right of man "to subdue the earth", which command is taken without the corresponding duty to take care of it. The temptation to domination that leads to unjust treatment of one's fellow man has led with the advance of man's technical power to an uncontrolled appetite to overuse natural resources which even national governments would find difficult to restrain, even if they had the will.

The pope's words are prophetic: "21. While the horizon of man is thus being modified according to the images that are chosen for him, another transformation is making itself felt, one which is the dramatic and unexpected consequence of human activity. Man is suddenly becoming aware that by an ill-considered exploitation of nature he risks destroying it and becoming in his turn the victim of this degradation. Not only is the material environment becoming a permanent menace - pollution and refuse, new illness and absolute destructive capacity - but the human framework is no longer under man's control, thus creating an environment for tomorrow which may well be intolerable.

This is a wide-ranging social problem which concerns the entire human family."

One only needs to be careful not to include the poor Lazaruses of the world in blaming "man" for the exploitation of nature (as has already been noted in regard to "man's inhumanity to man"). Unfortunately, the generalized impression that it is the fault of all men comes through in the English translation. A careful reading of the Latin will not necessarily give such an impression. As noted before, there is a convenient shift of attention away from the real culprits (a relatively small portion of humanity) who are quite happy to join in the general condemnation of Man for their sins.

The Latin is put below but we will only point to two phrases where the translation is loose to say the least. *rerum conspectus, in quo homo ponitur*, which literally means "the situation in which man is placed", is given as "the horizon of man", suggesting some human determination of the scene.

For *Cuius rei fere repentino conscii homines hodie fiunt: se scilicet ex rebus naturae tam inconsiderate lucra fecisse, ut periculum sit,* the translation given is: "Man is suddenly becoming aware that by an ill-considered exploitation of nature he risks destroying it and becoming in his turn the victim of this degradation." More literally, it could be put: "of which thing men today are quite suddenly made conscious that in making profits inconsiderately from the things of nature there may be a danger that they destroy it [nature] and the harm from this kind of perverse use on the contrary falls back upon themselves."

Why does the translator not bother to translate *lucra*? We have dealt with the meaning of *lucrum* in our discussion of it in II-II 1. 77 in our book "Economic Science and Saint Thomas Aquinas" where St. Thomas puts it within a species of profit making that has "a certain turpitude". It is probable that Pope Saint Paul VI was aware of this usage. One cannot expect a person whose only knowledge of Economics is devoid of any moral import to know this. So he falls back on a nothing word in this context like "exploitation" which of course is perpetrated by "Man", rather than the profiteers.

21. *Dum rerum conspectus, in quo homo ponitur, ita secundum imagines convertitur, quae selectae ei exhibentur, alia quoque animadvertitur immutatio, quae modo sane calamitoso et inopinato humanam consequitur navitatem.*

Cuius rei fere repentino conscii homines hodie fiunt: se scilicet ex rebus naturae tam inconsiderate lucra fecisse, ut periculum sit, ne eam destruant damnumque huiusmodi pravi usus in ipsos vicissim recidat.

At non modo ea, quae circa hominem sunt, huic continenter infesta redduntur, cuius generis sunt naturae contaminations, purgamenta, novi morbi, absoluta delendi potentia; verum etiam ipsi humanae consortioni homo amplius non moderatur, ita ut vitae condiciones, in quibus in posterum conversabitur, sibi prorsus intolerabiles inducere possit.

Agitur de quaestione sociali, quae tam late patet, ut universam humanam familiam attingat.

"21. While the horizon of man is thus being modified according to the images that are chosen for him, another transformation is making itself felt, one which is the dramatic and unexpected consequence of human activity.

Man is suddenly becoming aware that by an ill-considered exploitation of nature he risks destroying it and becoming in his turn the victim of this degradation.

Not only is the material environment becoming a permanent menace - pollution and refuse, new illness and absolute destructive capacity - but the human framework is no longer under man's control, thus creating an environment for tomorrow which may well be intolerable."

The pope ends the paragraph with: "This is a wide-ranging social problem which concerns the entire human family. The Christian must turn to these new perceptions in order to take on responsibility, together with the rest of men, for a destiny which from now on is shared by all." Regardless of the cause of the degradation, all men, especially Christians, must work to remediate it for it affects "the entire human family".

There is also the fact that the divide between the rich and the poor is not only within nations but also between nations. The divide has not disappeared from within Christian/Western civilization but in terms of economic welfare it has been greatly ameliorated by all sorts of measures at the fully political level and at the lower levels of intermediate associations. At the political level there has developed what has been called Labour or Industrial Law. But much assistance has been provided by what has come to be criticised as the Welfare State. However, the spread of capitalist domination to other nations has also contributed to the virtual disappearance of the proletarian status of workers in the "developed" nations.

This does not mean the disappearance of a virtual condition of servitude but it does mean that the threat of revolution no longer hangs over these nations. Extreme poverty, barring accidents, disability and illness of one kind of another, has been eliminated. But the basic condition of dependency and tendency to greater dependency (e. g. in the form of debt) remains. So "the social question" (of justice and freedom) is still quite complex within national boundaries and even more complicated when considered worldwide.

Pope Saint Paul VI next moves to consider the political situation. He begins by saying: "24. The two aspirations, to equality and to participation, seek to promote a democratic type of society." But here again we come up against a misuse of the word "democratic". The Latin, the relevant part we have placed in bold, which translates as "a certain kind of popular society" is: *Duplex, quod diximus, studium assequendae aequalitatis et munerum participationis ad promovendum sane **quoddam popularis societatis genus** spectat.* The translator cannot help himself, not discriminating between the good and bad forms of such rule of the many, and so almost inevitably leading the reader to assume it is the modern (bad) form that is meant.

What follows is: "Various models are proposed, some are tried out, none of them gives complete satisfaction, and the search goes on between ideological and pragmatic tendencies. The Christian has the duty to take part in this search and in the organization and life of political society. As a social being, man builds his destiny within a series of particular groupings which demand, as their completion and as a necessary condition for their development, a vaster society, one of a universal character, the political society. All particular activity must be placed within that wider society, and thereby it takes on the dimension of the common good." Tell me where order to the common good fits into the modern meaning of democracy. Or is not the modern form leading to this conclusion warned of by the pope? "It is not for the State or even for political parties, which would be closed unto themselves, to try to impose an ideology by means that would lead to a dictatorship over minds, the worst kind of all." (25)

That leads the pope on to discuss political ideologies, which is summed up in the next paragraph 26: "Therefore the Christian who wishes to live his faith in a political activity which he thinks of as service cannot without contradicting himself adhere to ideological systems which radically or substantially go against his faith and his concept of man. He cannot adhere to the Marxist ideology, to its atheistic materialism, to its dialectic of violence and to the way it absorbs individual freedom in the collectivity, at the same time denying all transcendence to man and his personal and collective history; nor can be adhere to the liberal ideology which believes it exalts individual freedom by withdrawing it from every limitation, by stimulating it through exclusive seeking of interest and power, and by considering social solidarities as more or less automatic consequences of individual initiatives, not as an aim and a major criterion of the value of the social organization."

Now tell us that the Church condemns Socialism/ Communism only and not Liberalism/ Capitalism as well, or that it regards only "unbridled" Capitalism as a politico-economic ideology.

There is of course more to be said about a person's espousal of an ideology in the abstract and his carrying out of its theory into practice. So the pope makes reference to what Pope Saint John XXIII said in this regard. Thus, he adds, in para. 30: "Because the teachings, once they are drawn up and defined, remain always the same, while the movements, being concerned with historical situations in constant evolution, cannot but be influenced by these latter and cannot avoid, therefore, being subject to changes, even of a profound nature. Besides, who can deny that those movements, in so far as they conform to the dictates of right reason and are interpreters of the lawful aspirations of the human person, contain elements that are positive and deserving of approval?" (30) One has to try to understand what a person who says he is a Communist is really advocating.

With regard to Marxism the pope makes this wise observation: "34. While, through the concrete existing form of Marxism, one can distinguish these various aspects and the questions they pose for the reflection and activity of Christians, it would be illusory and dangerous to reach a point of forgetting the intimate link which radically binds them together, to accept the elements of Marxist analysis without recognizing their relationships with ideology, and to enter into the practice of class struggle and its

Marxist interpretations, while failing to note the kind of totalitarian and violent society to which this process leads."

No less perceptive is his assessment of Liberalism: "35. On another side, we are witnessing a renewal of the liberal ideology. This current asserts itself both in the name of economic efficiency, and for the defense of the individual against the increasingly overwhelming hold of organizations, and as a reaction against the totalitarian tendencies of political powers. Certainly, personal initiative must be maintained and developed. But do not Christians who take this path tend to idealize liberalism in their turn, making it a proclamation in favor of freedom? They would like a new model, more adapted to present-day conditions, while easily forgetting that at the very root of philosophical liberalism is an erroneous affirmation of the autonomy of the individual in his activity, his motivation and the exercise of his liberty. Hence, the liberal ideology likewise calls for careful discernment on their part."

The task of the Christian in the complexity of these competing ideologies is spelt out at the end of his treatment of these dominant ideologies in the political thought and action of our time. "The dynamism of Christian faith here triumphs over the narrow calculations of egoism. Animated by the power of the Spirit of Jesus Christ, the Savior of mankind, and upheld by hope, the Christian involves himself in the building up of the human city, one that is to be peaceful, just and fraternal and acceptable as an offering to God. In fact, 'the expectation of a new earth must not weaken but rather stimulate our concern for cultivating this one. For here grows the body of a new human family, a body which even now is able to give some kind of foreshadowing of the new age.'" (37)

The pope continues: "38. In this world dominated by scientific and technological change, which threatens to drag it towards a new positivism, another more fundamental doubt is raised. Having subdued nature by using his reason, man now finds that he himself is as it were imprisoned within his own rationality; he in turn becomes the object of science. The "human sciences" are today enjoying a significant flowering. On the one hand they are subjecting to critical and radical examination the hitherto accepted knowledge about man, on the grounds that this knowledge seems either too empirical or too theoretical. On the other hand, methodological necessity and ideological presuppositions too often lead the human sciences to isolate, in the various situations, certain aspects of man, and yet to give these an explanation which claims to be complete or at least an interpretation which is meant to be all-embracing from a purely quantitative or phenomenological point of view. This scientific reduction betrays a dangerous presupposition. To give a privileged position in this way to such an aspect of analysis is to mutilate man and, under the pretext of a scientific procedure, to make it impossible to understand man in his totality.

39. One must be no less attentive to the action which the human sciences can instigate, giving rise to the elaboration of models of society to be subsequently imposed on men as scientifically tested types of behavior. Man can then become the object of manipulations directing his desires and needs and modifying his behavior and even his system of values. There is no doubt that

there exists here a grave danger for the societies of tomorrow and for man himself. For even if all agree to build a new society at the service of men, it is still essential to know what sort of man is in question."

That should be enough to make evident the nature of the change of focus after Vatican II from an examination of Pope Saint Paul VI's letter of 1971. But we will say more about this in our comments on the two social encyclicals of Pope Saint John Paul II in 1981 and 1991. However, there is one other subject addressed in the letter in which there are significant comments about modern science that are worth noting.

We have made extensive reference to the application of modern science and its scientific method to the sciences of Economics and Politics. In Aristotle and Aquinas these are practical moral sciences but are treated in modern science as theoretical ones and indeed at the level of natural or physical science and mathematics. The subject of human life, individual and social, can be studied theoretically, but one has to realise that human nature exists on two levels, spiritual and bodily. That means its study has to involve not only physical or natural science but also Metaphysics. This is all explained masterfully by Aristotle in his *Peri psyche*.

The theoretical study of human nature is already distorted then by limiting it to the physical (or physico-mathematical as can be clearly seen in modern Economics). As such, provided one admits the higher level of study as necessary, the lower level can give useful information. But as the pope points out it is partial and as engaged "betrays a dangerous presupposition". Most Catholic scientists (in the modern mode) and many Catholic philosophers and theologians seem blissfully unaware of the dangers the pope points out in the modern studies in the "human sciences".

There is much more that could be said here. But most of it could be gathered from what we have already said in our previous books. The balance of the letter is mainly concerned with a "call to action" especially on the part of Christians/Catholics. So we can pass on to dealing with the two social encyclicals of Pope Saint John Paul II, *Laborem exercens* and *Centesimus annus*.

Part II

Pope Saint John Paul II's *Laborem exercens* (1981)

We quote first from section 8 of the encyclical.

8. Worker Solidarity: third paragraph

"Following the lines laid drawn by the Encyclical *Rerum Novarum* and many later documents of the Church's Magisterium, it must be frankly recognized that the reaction against the system of injustice and harm that cried to heaven for vengeance and that weighed heavily upon workers in that period of rapid industrialization was justified *from the point of view of social morality*. This state of affairs was favoured by the liberal socio-political system, which, in accordance with its "economistic" premises, strengthened and safeguarded economic initiative by the possessors of capital alone, but did not pay sufficient attention to the rights of the workers, on the grounds that human work is solely an instrument of production, and that capital is the basis, efficient factor and purpose of production."

This enables us to see the pope's mind as to the meaning of "the condition of labour" that was addressed in *Rerum Novarum*. It also shows the proper meaning to be put on the political philosophy and economic science of modern times, Liberalism as a political ideology and Capitalism which we have put as a politico-economic ideology, both of which can be seen as expressive of deep and widespread structures of social injustice, and which can be understood best in terms of the Aristotelian division of general justice into the particular justices, distributive and commutative.

Throughout this encyclical and his other two social encyclicals the pope uses a variety of phrases by which he tries to accommodate this basic system of social injustice to changing circumstances. Thus, he refers to "early capitalism", "rigid capitalism" and later in *Centesimus annus* makes a distinction between capitalism as referring to a naturally (morally/ politically) functionally politico-economic order, which is good, and to one functioning without moral/juridical restraint, which is bad.

It can be seen from the quote above that it is the latter that is the "real" capitalism in question. Unfortunately, as we have noted elsewhere, the use of the distinction is jumped upon by Catholics who may wish to defend the established economic system, to argue that the pope was at least confused about the injustice of the capitalist system that has come to dominate politico-economic affairs in the West, and particularly in the USA. A similar case of a variation in terminology, but perhaps more relevant to the Continent, may be seen in the pope's use of the phrase "real socialism".

To some extent, then, this variation in terminology, no doubt prompted by the pope's desire to employ a language more attuned to modern ears, can tend to obscure the fundamental clarity of the original Aristotelian meanings of the terms. However, if read carefully (with due deference to the official Latin), the clear picture of the structure of injustice of the modern capital-ist/worker relationship may be gained.

But Pope Saint John Paul II does widen the notion of labour in this encyclical, to bring the meaning of "work" back to its root sense. Pope Leo XIII had already in *Rerum Novarum* noted that work in the most general sense would have been natural in the state of original justice, but without what is now attached to the idea of labour as toil. After the Fall this notion of difficulty neces-sarily became connected with human work, "in the sweat of one's brow". But this is not quite the notion of labour that Pope Leo was concerned with in the phrase "the condition of labour". For worker and labourer had already acquired the connotation of be-ing hired labour from the very nature of the division between Capital and Labour.

As indicated in the quote above, capital in this context is property that is needed to be used by the worker in production, as material ("land"/resources) or instrument ("tools"/ equip-ment), and it comes to be appropriated (with arbitrary "legal" warrant) by the "fortunate" few (rich) in a situation where the worker/labourer necessarily has to obtain "employment" from the one who effectively possesses all property, the capitalist. The modern worker (as proletarian) is bereft of both materials and tools, so that he is put into a position of dependence more abso-lute than that of a brute animal, which has at least access to the needed "land".

What is more, the brute animal has natural equipment to make use of the earth and its fruits (e.g. claws), whilst the human hand of itself is rather useless in this regard. That is because the worker can use his intelligence to make suitable tools (technology). But he cannot even do this without natural materials (land). "No trespassing" is the sign of his absolute "economic" enslavement. Yet Pope Leo described his condition not as slavery but as "a yoke little better than slavery". For there was one respect in which the workers were not the same as chattel slaves, or even serfs. They could "sell" their labour in a market within a political system in which they were regarded as free citizens. A more devilish system of servitude could hardly have been devised, economic servitude in a nominal democracy.

That is the theory of Capitalism. Its realisation in practice is another thing, which is the reason for the variation in terminology in discussing it and assessing the degree of its socially evil effect. As for Socialism, Pope Leo could see that to deny the natural moral worth of the institution of property necessarily put the workers into a worse condition, of servitude both economically and politically, totally at the mercy of those in power and effective rulers of the State. That is "real" Socialism, which is motivated by a hatred not of injustice but of those they identified as Capitalists. The inevitably of the evil being identified with the evildoers attaches itself to the agents of the one who was a murderer from the beginning and the father of lies. The Church, and the person of reason, as agents of God, can make the distinction, to hate the evil but continue to love the evil-doer and work for his repentance and salvation, as one might love one's drunkard father but work to free him of his drunkard condition. One who dispenses with the natural moral law in any respect will be bent on destruction of the whole social order.

The pope gives a definition of work in its widest sense. "And work means any activity by man, whether manual or intellectual, whatever its nature or circumstances; it means any human activity that can and must be recognized as work, in the midst of all the many activities of which man is capable and to which he is predisposed by his very nature, by virtue of humanity itself." It is simply human activity as freely done under the direction of reason. It may be equated with the notion of art although most properly it should be restricted to what the scholastics called the mechanical arts, that is the operation on things external to human nature as rational, external goods or wealth.

This definition, as noted, goes beyond hired labour, or the worker as an "employee", which is a common condition, and which in the modern Capitalist politico-economic system had been reduced to one "little better than slavery". It might also be noted that Leo was not endorsing a revolt against this condition, as the Church has never approved of revolution against any social system of servitude. He was simply warning the few rich and those in power not only of the injustice of the system but more urgently that the modern conflict between capitalist/master and proletarian/"worker" had reached such a point of extremity as to threaten the very existence of "Christian"/Western civilization.

The poor and workers/victims of injustice he, as a father, counselled to resist the temptation to return evil for evil, as besides being unchristian it would bring on even worse evil, but rather to return good for evil. This would not only serve for salvation but also for amelioration of evil suffered in this life. This Christ-inspired message was not only valid for the particular situation faced by Leo but also for the whole situation of humanity worldwide. The lesson of Leo with regard to social justice was thus able to be extended as became clearer before and during the Council deliberations. We will take up this more directly when we come to consider the line of documents on the social doctrine of the Church following the Council. In the meantime, we need to complete our consideration of the two documents commemorative of *Rerum Novarum* by Pope Saint John Paul II.

The pope is quite clear about the continuity of what he teaches with the teaching of Leo. But there is a noticeable difference of language which perhaps points to him introducing terminology more in line with modern thinking (such as Phenomenology) and not all that classically Aristotelian/ Thomist. Thus, he makes a distinction between work as objective and subjective, meaning the many ways in which the mechanical arts may be employed and the one agent or person employing those arts (even as an "employee") who is a being of spiritual form. That is not exactly the language of Aristotle, or Aquinas for that matter. The "objects" of the art or technique, even though material, are also subjects, as things. But the idea meant to be conveyed is much the same. The Thomist should not quibble about the terminology.

So too with the distinction between direct and indirect employer. This means to convey the making up by social means, both public and private (intermediate associations, if acting "for profit"), of what is lacking in the wages of the workers. This may constitute what is sufficient for him and his family to live on. The just wage, however, given the gross maldistribution to the Capitalists, may very well be more than that and most likely will be in a "developed" economy. But the social assistance does make for alleviating the condition of labour where the accidents of life put him at risk of falling below subsistence level. So, to that extent such indirect employer is a necessity from the point of view of social justice.

All these advantages attach to the capitalist system in the "West" since its near collapse in the first half of the twentieth century. On this account it is reasonable to regard the countries in this part of the world as rich or "developed" (though many are the poor in them still). As nations they are certainly much more "fortunate" than the rest of the world. It ought to be acknowledged however that the poverty and misery of the undeveloped or "developing" nations may not only be attributed to their lack of belonging within Western civilization but also to the capitalist exploitation of their inferior political and economic situation by the advantaged or Western "developed" nations.

This puts the obligation of helping those in such conditions of suffering and impoverishment upon those not so desperately affected not just at an individual level but also at a national level. This is what is taken up in earnest by the Church in the Council and afterwards.

Taking these things into account we may regard the encyclical *Laborem exercens* as not introducing any new teaching but as presenting it in a new way, especially from the point of view of the labourer as a human person, whether he be a victim of the capitalist system or in another condition of impoverishment.

We will however look a bit more closely at what the pope had to say in *Laborem exercens*. Pope John Paul II notes the amelioration of the capitalist kind of thinking since the last part of the nineteenth century, owing in large part to the influence of Leo's encyclical. But he warns: "Nevertheless, the *danger* of treating work as a special kind of 'merchandise', or as an impersonal 'force' needed for production (the expression 'workforce' is in fact in common use) *always exists,* especially when the whole way of looking at the question of economics is marked by the premises of materialistic economism." (7) We might note also the more modern expression of "human resources", likening human beings to non-human natural resources. As well, human persons' acquired knowledge, arts and skills are called "human capital" – with a view to be put to good use by their purchase or hire in the making of a profit.

Referring to the period in which the modern presentation of the social doctrine of the Church has taken shape, the pope says: "Throughout this period, which is by no means yet over, the issue of work has of course been posed on the basis of the great *conflict* that in the age of, and together with, industrial development emerged *between 'capital' and 'labour',* that is to say between the small but highly influential group of entrepreneurs, owners or holders of the means of production, and the broader multitude of people who lacked these means and who shared in the process of production solely by their labour. The conflict originated in the fact that the workers put their powers at the disposal of the entrepreneurs, and these, following the principle of maximum profit, tried to establish the lowest possible wages for the work done by the employees. In addition, there were other elements of exploitation, connected with the lack of safety at work and of safeguards regarding the health and living conditions of the workers and their families."

He continues: "This conflict, interpreted by some as a socio-economic *class conflict,* found expression in the *ideological conflict* between liberalism, understood as the ideology of capitalism, and Marxism, understood as the ideology of scientific socialism and communism, which professes to act as the spokesman for the working class and the worldwide proletariat. Thus the real conflict between labour and capital was transformed into *a systematic class struggle,* conducted not only by ideological means but also and chiefly by political means. We are familiar with the history of this conflict and with the demands of both sides. The Marxist programme, based on the philosophy of Marx and Engels, sees in class struggle the only way to eliminate class injustices in society and to eliminate the classes themselves. Putting this programme into practice presupposes *the collectivization of the means of production* so that, through the transfer of these means from private hands to the collectivity, human labour will be preserved from exploitation."

That is a fair summary of the two dominant political ideologies and their corresponding economic systems (both affecting the title of "science"). We know what has happened to the ideology of Marxism, as radical Socialism, and the economic system of collectivism it was concreted in, which the pope refers to at a later time as "real socialism". It has suffered a severe reversal in the collapse of the USSR, its first great political experiment. But, what is not noticed so much in those countries that subscribe to the Liberalist ideology of Capitalism, is that the pope clearly draws attention to "liberalism as the ideology of Capitalism" as the other extreme politico-economic error.

In the USA, the principal model for this politico-economic system, and the countries subscribing to the same ideology and economic system (referred to as "the West", or "the free world"), one is encouraged to concentrate on the greater evils of "scientific" socialism or communism and to be a defender of politico-economic "liberal values", such as freedom of enterprise, meaning employment of one's money (owned or borrowed) in a most profitable way, free competition, meaning lack of any political restraint upon one's monopoly power, free trade, meaning liberty to exploit one's possession of greater bargaining power in the market; to which are added the related "Enlightenment values" of political freedom of speech, the press and so on, all intent on excluding any notion of socially moral restraint upon those in positions of power by reason of natural advantage or, more particularly, by reason of the abuse of political and economic advantage.

The relevant moral restraint is, of course, that of the social virtue of justice, whose maintenance in any civil society is principally the responsibility of the civil government. The liberalist, however, poses as the champion of the "enterprising" individual and the opponent of government constraints on free enterprise etc., when it is precisely through the abuse of political power by the propertied (capitalised, monied) few that the mighty constraint of "a yoke little better than slavery" was imposed, and is continued to be imposed (if moderated by labour legislation, and changes in national and global conditions) upon the unjustly dispossessed majority, leaving those in effective power free to exploit their advantage in the "open market".

There continues, then, in the countries ruled by governments subscribing to the liberal capitalist ideology, "the great conflict between capital and labour". For it is only in established totalitarian regimes that such conflict is violently suppressed by the government. A good number in each new generation in "the free world" do see through the deception. However, many of these are further deceived into joining the opposite ideological camp, whether by "conversion" to its tenets or simply out of aversion to the liberalist's.

Such is the depth of the deception able to be engineered by the rich and powerful few, however, that all sorts of manipulations of the population may be contrived, not excluding possible connivance in the urging of the disaffected and disillusioned youth, especially the more "intelligent" who go to university, to senseless rampage and violent revolt, whereupon the legal authority of the government may be presented as justified in curtailing not only their unruly behaviour, but also discrediting in the eyes of the "people" ("lucky" to be living in a free democracy) their criticisms of the "established" status quo.

Having particularised the problem of the condition of labour in his (and our) times, the pope returns to more general considerations of the true relation between capital and labour, whereby we are able to judge the justice or injustice of the modern economic production and exchange system and the politico-economic philosophies (ideologies) that purport to defend it, or purpose to destroy it. Pope John Paul II reiterates the Church's traditional insistence on the priority of labour, which is not especially a religious position but one of plain common sense, and which only the cleverest of sophistries can and does succeed in obscuring for many, rich and poor.

The priority of labour over capital is the same as the priority of human nature over all that is evidently below it. The pope sums it up: "Man, as the subject of work, and independently of the work that he does – man alone is a person." Never then, even in the lowest level of activity, as a hired hand, must a human person be treated as a non-person, a chattel, a useful tool, as the word "hand" suggests, or as a piece of merchandise or "commodity" to be bought in the market.

How was it then that this obvious relationship was, as it were, turned upside down? The pope explains: "This *consistent image,* in which the principle of the primacy of person over things is strictly preserved, *was broken up in human thought,* sometimes after a long period of incubation in practical living. The break occurred in such a way that labour was separated from capital and set in opposition to it, and capital was set in opposition to labour, as though they were two impersonal forces, two production factors juxtaposed in the same 'economistic' perspective." (13)

The pope relates this distortion to the more general modern philosophical error of materialism. "This way of stating the issue contained a fundamental error, what we can call *the error of economism,* that of considering human labour solely according to its economic purpose. This fundamental error of thought can and must be called *an error of materialism,* in that economism directly or indirectly includes a conviction of the primacy and superiority of the material, and directly or indirectly places the spiritual and the personal (man's activity, moral values and such matters) in a position of subordination to material reality."

The error is one of practical philosophy, one that rather comes out of bad conduct than comes before it. "This is still not *theoretical materialism* in the full sense of the term, but it is certainly *practical materialism,* a materialism judged capable of satisfying man's needs, not so much on the grounds of premises derived from materialist theory, as on the grounds of a particular way of evaluating things, and so on the grounds of a certain hierarchy of goods based on the greater immediate attractiveness of what is material." (13)

Materialism, both theoretical or scientific and practical or political, developed in the modern era, as it did in ancient times as an alternative mental position to that of religion. In ancient times it took the part of reason against religious superstition, which tended to be cultivated by the poets and the general populace, though there was also an official religion of the State. The first scientists were investigators of nature. At that early stage there was no distinction made between science and philosophy. Accordingly, the early natural scientists were called natural philosophers. However, these considerations belong more to a separate discussion.

The most persistent opponent of religion in modern times, taking it in the widest sense to refer to all belief in a world above and beyond the material, is the materialist vision of reality, which retains something of reason but loses more than it retains. As a modern author has lamented: "I wonder not at what men lose, but at what they throw away". When applied to human behaviour, the proper object of ethical and political philosophy (practical science, in the Aristotelian sense) this materialism takes the form of practical materialism, as the pope noted. Since the most material dimension of social affairs is the economic, the pope coined the term "economism" for this practical materialism as evidenced in modern thinking in social and political affairs.

The undeniable material success of modern science in both theoretical and practical matters is to be attributed to the truth of its conclusions and the goodness of its method that, if partial, are nonetheless powerful within their limited range. Such power, however, is a double-edged sword, especially when applied to the practical world of human and social life and behaviour. For, lacking any acknowledgement of the spiritual dignity of the human person and any moral direction, it is, like the quality of physical strength, a good thing, but a power for evil as much as for good. So it is that the marvels of scientific progress in modern times have not brought fewer wars, let alone peace, but, on the contrary, a terrifying increase in human aggressiveness and conflict, with the actuality of wholesale human slaughter and possible disaster to the point of extinction of the human race.

Economism, then, is a basic explanation of the materialist philosophical principle underlying both politico-economic ideological errors in modern times, the liberalist and the socialist. They are opposed only on the score of individualism and collectivism as "solutions" to the evident extreme poverty and oppressed condition of the modern worker. The liberalist's, however, is not so much a solution as a warning not to try to solve it. For, it is "natural", and any attempt to alter the course of human affairs would be as foolish as an attempt to alter the course of the stars. That a privileged few should seem to prosper whilst the many languish is due to the inexorable laws of Economics. Human (governmental) "interference" can only make things worse than they are.

The liberal capitalists gain much satisfaction in their ideological stance from the recent history of socialist regimes. For, the proposals of the opposite ideology of radical socialism are also no solution, but, from one point of view, as we have noted, a case of jumping out of the frying pan into the fire, or, as the Greeks would put it, of avoiding the rocks of Scylla to be sucked into the whirlpool of Charybdis.

The Catholic solution, which is also that of rational ethico-politics, is to avoid both dangers, to sail cautiously well clear of Scylla (Liberal Capitalism) and Charybdis (Radical Socialism). That involves being careful to understand the first principles and necessary conclusions of the natural moral law as it applies to politico-economic affairs, which in the divine dispensation involves necessarily the illumination of Faith and the inspiration of Charity.

Before finishing we should however note what the pope had to say about the institution of private property as it relates to labour. The two most relevant social institutions in regard to the problem of Capital and Labour, are those of private property and hired work or employment. The pope proceeds to outline the Church's position in regard to these in paragraph 14, under the heading "Work and Ownership". He observes: "Behind both concepts [Capital and Labour] there are people, living, actual people: on the one side are those who do the work without being the owners of the means of production, and on the other side those who act as entrepreneurs and who own these means or represent the owners. Thus *the issue of ownership or property* enters from the beginning into the whole of this difficult historical process."

However, we should first note that whilst property and employment, as well as the market, are social institutions and in principle natural and necessary for social well being generally, as concretely realised in history they have been abused (by the rich and powerful) rather than used properly. The liberalist understanding of the right of property, like that of freedom, is thus given an absoluteness that turns it into an instrument of oppression. This comes out in the following statement of the pope: "The above principle [of property], as it was then stated and as it is still taught by the Church, *diverges* radically from the programme of **collectivism as proclaimed by Marxism** and put into practice in various countries in the decades following the time of Leo XIII's Encyclical. At the same time it differs from the programme of **capitalism practised by liberalism** and by the political systems inspired by it. In the latter case, the difference consists in the way the right to ownership or property is understood. Christian tradition has never upheld this right as absolute and untouchable. On the contrary, it has always understood this right within the broader context of the right common to all to use the goods of the whole of creation: *the right to private property is subordinated* *to the right to common use,* to the fact that goods are meant for everyone." (bold added)

The original Latin of the part applying to Liberalism and Capitalism is set out here: *Verum simul etiam discrepat a consiliis capitalismi, quemadmodum is revera exercetur in consuetudine liberalismi necnon in rei politicae tractandae formis inde manantibus. Hoc altero in casu discrimen in eo consistit quod aliter ius possessionis ipsum intellegitur. Numquam traditio christiana ius illud affirmavit veluti absolutum et inviolabile. Contra vera id accepit semper latiore in ambitu communis omnium iuris ad bona totius creationis adhibenda: videlicet ius privati dominii, quatenus iuri usus communis destinationique bonorum universali subicitur.*

Just a note on the word "untouchable" (*inviolabile*) used here by the pope with "absolute" (*absolutum*). Previous popes have used "untouchable" with reference to the institution of property. But there they were referring to the rational necessity of the right, to be respected by all including the State. Here the pope (also Pope Francis) is evidently associating it with being unconditioned by anything else including the universal destination of goods and the common good, which the previous popes clearly understood in their statements about the right of property. The liberal capitalist takes the right as inviolable absolutely, which suits the unjust possessors, for they do not want their possession to be "touched", especially by the custodians of justice in society, the civil government.

In a system of government effectively oligarchical the "government" (even if democratic in superficial form) will see its role as protecting the fundamental institution of property and the right of property as it exists (no questions asked as to how it was acquired – law and politics, is concerned here with economic facts, not moral values). The association of grand robbery with regard to property went out with the "religious" Ten Commandments. In modern legal and political "theory" possession on such a scale is ten tenths of the law. It punishes the opportunistic minor thieves but turns a blind eye to historical dispossession that continues to be legally based.

That is sufficient for us to appreciate what the pope has had to say in *Laborem exercens*. He also confirms the social doctrine regarding basic workers' rights such as the right to association. He finishes dealing with "the spirituality of work in the Christian sense". This requires no further comment on our part. We can therefore move on to an examination of the last encyclical in the line of social documents from *Rerum Novarum*, which is *Centesimus annus*.

Part III

Pope St John Paul II's *Centesimus annus* (1991)

Only four years after he had issued a social encyclical, follow-ing upon one six years previously, and only half way through the period of his long pontificate, Pope John Paul II put out his third and last social encyclical. Naturally enough, he did not go over in detail what he had covered in his two previous social encyclicals and this explains why there are only two parts devoted to dealing more fully with specific social issues of the half dozen or so dealt with in the development of the social doctrine of the Church over the one hundred years since *Rerum novarum*. They are part IV. PRIVATE PROPERTY AND THE UNIVERSAL DESTINA-TION OF MATERIAL GOODS, from paragraphs 30 to 43, and part V. STATE AND CULTURE, from paragraphs 44 to 52. There are only 62 paragraphs in the encyclical, with these two special subjects making up a good third of the whole document.

The other two thirds of the document (about 40 paragraphs), apart from the introduction (paragraphs 1 to 3), are divided into four parts of roughly the same length; Part I. CHARACT-ERISTICS OF "RERUM NOVARUM" (paragraphs 4 to 11); Part II TOWARDS THE "NEW THINGS" OF TODAY (paragraphs 12 to 21); Part III THE YEAR 1989 (paragraphs 22 to 29); and Part VI. MAN IS THE WAY OF THE CHURCH (paragraphs 53 to 62).

Part I is taken up with a brief run through of the main issues dealt with in *Rerum Novarum* which show John Paul II's appreciation of Pope Leo XIII's position on the various matters involved. He says: "The Pope and the Church with him were confronted, as was the civil community, by a society which was torn by a conflict all the more harsh and inhumane because it knew no rule or regulation. It was *the conflict between capital and labour,* or - as the Encyclical puts it - the worker question." The politico-economic basis of the conflict is brought out: "In the face of a conflict which set man against man, almost as if they were 'wolves', a conflict between the extremes of mere physical survival on the one side and opulence on the other."

The absence of fundamental justice (the primary responsibility of the State) is clearly seen: "The Pope's intention was certainly to restore peace, and the present-day reader cannot fail to note his severe condemnation, in no uncertain terms, of the class struggle. However, the Pope was very much aware that *peace is built on the foundation of justice:* what was essential to the Encyclical was precisely its proclamation of the fundamental conditions for justice in the economic and social situation of the time." (5)

Pope John Paul II further commented: "Another important aspect, which has many applications to our own day, is the concept of the relationship between the State and its citizens. *Rerum novarum* criticizes two social and economic systems: socialism and liberalism. The opening section, in which the right to private property is reaffirmed, is devoted to socialism. Liberalism is not the subject of a special section, but it is worth noting that criti-

cisms of it are raised in the treatment of the duties of the State."
(10)

The two opposing ideologies, Liberalism and Socialism, can be
defined through their positions on the institution of private
property, the one for, the other against. Pope John Paul II had
clearly explained in his previous social encyclical how each erred,
Socialism in its denial of the right; Liberalism in its absolutizing
of it, so as effectively to deny it to the many (indigent) in favour
of the few (opulent). But, an important point of difference was
the position of each ideology in regard to the role of the State;
here the Liberalist denying any, the Socialist absolutizing it, so as
to effectively destroy its true role of protection of the rights of
citizens and the promotion of their common good.

The two fundamental social institutions, private property and
civil government, are natural and good; but they are not without
subordination to higher principles, the universal destination of
goods in the first case, and the personal good and ultimate end of
the individual human person in the second. Both ideologies err
fundamentally in regard to both, if it might appear that Socialism
saves the first and Liberalism the second. But Socialism blocks
the free access of individuals to the property in goods ("capital")
they need in order to work in the first case and Liberalism, whilst
also blocking the majority from free access to goods needed to
work with, blocks the necessary communitarian "support" for
each person even in his or her work. Apart from that they both
suffer from the limited vision of a materialistic and mechanistic
philosophy, thus distorting the very understanding of human na-

ture and human happiness, which is formally and finally spiritual and divine. That makes them both atheistic.

The State has the grave duty of ensuring that every person within its care can achieve the true common good of all in the community. Both ideologies clearly neglect or reject this duty. Pope John Paul II explains: "If Pope Leo XIII calls upon the State to remedy the condition of the poor in accordance with justice, he does so because of his timely awareness that the State has the duty of watching over the common good and of ensuring that every sector of social life, not excluding the economic one, contributes to achieving that good, while respecting the rightful autonomy of each sector. This should not however lead us to think that Pope Leo expected the State to solve every social problem. On the contrary, he frequently insists on necessary limits to the State's intervention and on its instrumental character, inasmuch as the individual, the family and society are prior to the State, and inasmuch as the State exists in order to protect their rights and not stifle them." (11)

In Part II Pope John Paul II, according to his statement of the purpose of his encyclical at the start begins to apply "the principles enunciated by Leo XIII" to the current social situation. The statement of purpose is put this way: "The present Encyclical seeks to show the fruitfulness of the principles enunciated by Leo XIII, which belong to the Church's doctrinal patrimony and, as such, involve the exercise of her teaching authority." It is clear from this that the social doctrine of the Church is not changed in the Council or in the magisterial documents issued subsequently. It is but a case of extending and applying that teaching to new circumstances. This applies to the use made of the contents of the works of Aquinas.

The pope goes on: "But pastoral solicitude also prompts me to propose *an analysis of some events of recent history*. It goes without saying that part of the responsibility of Pastors is to give careful consideration to current events in order to discern the new requirements of evangelization. However, such an analysis is not meant to pass definitive judgments since this does not fall *per se* within the Magisterium's specific domain." (3)

This application is in two parts, the first taken up in Part II and the second being taken up in Part III. The "events of recent history" that the pope alludes to are particularly those dealt with in Part III.

In Part II the pope discusses the positive influence of Pope Leo XIII's encyclical. "The Encyclical and the related social teaching of the Church had far-reaching influence in the years bridging the nineteenth and twentieth centuries. This influence is evident in the numerous reforms which were introduced in the areas of social security, pensions, health insurance and compensation in the case of accidents, within the framework of greater respect for the rights of workers." (15) However, these reforms were only in the countries that did not fall into the hands of those revolutionaries committed to making the ideology of radical Socialism/Communism.

The Communism of those that did so fall spread to half the world, and suffered the fate that Leo XIII had predicted. though socialism had hardly progressed beyond a theory at the time of Leo. Pope John Paul continues: "He correctly judged the danger posed to the masses by the attractive presentation of this simple and radical solution to the 'question of the working class' of the time — all the more so when one considers the terrible situation of injustice in which the working classes of the recently industrialized nations found themselves." Further: "His words deserve to be re-read attentively: 'To remedy these wrongs (the unjust distribution of wealth and the undeserved poverty of the workers), the Socialists encourage the poor man's envy of the rich and strive to do away with private property, contending that individual possessions should become the common property of all … ; but their contentions are so clearly powerless to end the controversy that, were they carried into effect, the working man himself would be among the first to suffer. They are moreover emphatically unjust, for they would rob the lawful possessor, distort the functions of the State, and create utter confusion in the community'. The evils caused by the setting up of this type of socialism as a State system — what would later be called 'Real Socialism' — could not be better expressed." (12)

Pope John Paul recalls Pope Leo's judgment on Socialism: "*Rerum novarum* is opposed to State control of the means of production, which would reduce every citizen to being a 'cog' in the State machine." (15) This does not mean that the Capitalist attitude to the State is correct: "It [*Rerum novarum*] is no less forceful in criticizing a concept of the State which completely excludes the economic sector from the State's range of interest and action. There is certainly a legitimate sphere of autonomy in economic life, which the State should not enter. The State, however, has the task of determining the juridical framework within which economic affairs are to be conducted, and thus of safeguarding the prerequisites of a free economy, which presumes a certain equality between the parties, such that one party would not be so powerful as practically to reduce the other to subservience." (15)

We should note well the problem with liberalist capitalism: its assumption that justice is not a prerequisite of freedom. In principle this is evidently absurd, for it would mean that the government should let bands of robbers roam free. But, it was conceded, against all liberalist reasoning, as a sort of secondary political theory, that the State was indeed necessary to maintain "law and order" with respect to thieves and robbers, in order to protect the right of property, come to be regarded as almost sacred. So, in practice, the role of the State was rather seen as limited more or less to that of the modern policeman, to protect the property of the people of property against the predations of the people without any.

The pope had traced the error of Socialism back to its root in atheism. "If we then inquire as to the source of this mistaken concept of the nature of the person and the 'subjectivity' of society, we must reply that its first cause is atheism. It is by responding to the call of God contained in the being of things that man becomes aware of his transcendent dignity. Every individual must give this response, which constitutes the apex of his humanity, and no social mechanism or collective subject can substitute for it. The denial of God deprives the person of his foundation, and consequently leads to a reorganization of the social order without reference to the person's dignity and responsibility." (13)

A more severe judgment on Liberalism is referred to later. "Reading the Encyclical within the context of Pope Leo's whole magisterium, we see how it points essentially to the socio-economic consequences of an error which has even greater implications. As has been mentioned, this error consists in an understanding of human freedom which detaches it from obedience to the truth, and consequently from the duty to respect the rights of others. The essence of freedom then becomes self-love carried to the point of contempt for God and neighbour, a self-love which leads to an unbridled affirmation of self-interest and which refuses to be limited by any demand of justice." (17)

We might simply add that justice is but truth in action and so obedience to the truth here equates with what the pope meant by the need for the State to determine that economic affairs be conducted within a "juridical framework". This will become relevant to his discussion of the two meanings of capitalism later in the encyclical. It belongs to liberalism and capitalism as preached in modern times to be a conscious and absolute detachment of freedom from justice, and accordingly a denial of any role of the State in the distribution of property or the exchange of goods and services.

The "structures of sin", the unjust distribution of wealth and the quasi-servitude of the workers, which were the excuse used by the revolutionary communists, did not indeed go away. The ideology of liberalist capitalism still dominated the political and economic thinking of the West, if somewhat "bridled" However, the reforms, after much struggle, did have an effect in moderating the evils that all could see (but few understood the causes of).

The victory in the Second World War also gave rise to a feeling of optimism for the future of "democracy". This led to a period of optimism. The acceptance of reforms led to a belief that a "third way" could be had between the extremes of radical Socialism and unbridled Capitalism, a sort of mixed economy, with the State "managing" an economy that was basically operating according to "free market principles". J. M. Keynes provided the theoretical adjustment of the "classical economics" that was needed.

We need to remember that the "free market" is still dominated by the unnatural exchange process, with particular application to the employment of labour, which we find clearly explained in Aristotle and St. Thomas and which I have dealt with in my previous books. No one, not even the moral theologians who profess to be followers of St. Thomas, seems to have picked this up. This oversight has badly affected the discussion of justice in exchange (just price and just wage) and the notion of profit in regard to modern "businesses" (the Latin for business, *negotiatio*, was precisely the word used by St. Thomas for the non-natural exchange, to which was attached a kind of turpitude).

Even in the encyclicals the ambiguities attaching to some of these matters are not completely overcome if one relies on the defective translations, especially the English ones. Would that the modern theologians studied more closely what St. Thomas has to say in his *Summa Theologiae* (II-II qq.77 & 78) about the distinction between natural and unnatural exchange, and "profit" (*lucrum*), as applying specifically to such secondary mode of exchange, as moneymaking!

But, we should follow the pope in his sober and measured assessment of the long period that followed the publication of Pope Leo's encyclical through to his own times. The early reforms were interrupted by two world wars and a great depression. But, having survived those, the West did take to heart the reforms demanded and with spirits lifted by the victory in the Second World War, a new era of prosperity and peace was envisaged. Genuine efforts were made to change the world for the better. The pope lists some of these.

The condition of labour itself was a central focus of reform, in which both governments and workers themselves participated. "These reforms were carried out in part by States, but in the struggle to achieve them *the role of the workers' movement* was an important one. This movement, which began as a response of moral conscience to unjust and harmful situations, conducted a widespread campaign for reform, far removed from vague ideology and closer to the daily needs of workers. In this context its efforts were often joined to those of Christians in order to improve workers' living conditions." Unfortunately, as the pope remarks, "Later on, this movement was dominated to a certain extent by the Marxist ideology against which *Rerum novarum* had spoken."(16) It was a continuing battle to achieve the improvement of workers' wages and conditions in a situation brought about by one ideology, without falling into the opposed ideology and suffering the same socialist fate.

This effort of reform was also carried out at the more general social level of intermediate associations, for once given some freedom of action individuals will naturally form such important instruments of socialization to their great benefit. It was the expropriation carried out in the early period of the modern capitalist system that had destroyed these initiatives. The pope points to these post-war efforts at reform: "These same reforms were also partly the result of *an open process by which society organized itself* through the establishment of effective instruments of solidarity, which were capable of sustaining an economic growth more respectful of the values of the person. Here we should remember the numerous efforts to which Christians made a notable contribution in establishing producers', consumers' and credit cooperatives, in promoting general education and professional training, in experimenting with various forms of participation in the life of the work-place and in the life of society in general."

These reforms themselves had a great beneficial effect and we have in large part to thank Pope Leo, and God, as the pope says, for the amelioration of the condition of workers in particular. "Thus, as we look at the past, there is good reason to thank God that the great Encyclical was not without an echo in human hearts and indeed led to a generous response on the practical level. Still, we must acknowledge that its prophetic message was not fully accepted by people at the time. Precisely for this reason there ensued some very serious tragedies."

One of these tragedies, of course, was the rise of Socialism in the violent form of Communism and its alarming spread. This conditioned the efforts being made to rebuild society as one of freedom inspired by social justice. The pope explains: "Following the destruction caused by the war, we see in some countries and under certain aspects a positive effort to rebuild a **democratic** society inspired by social justice, so as to deprive Communism of the revolutionary potential represented by masses of people subjected to exploitation and oppression." (bold added)

Here however we come up against the appalling ignorance of the English translator. The Latin is: *Quibusdam in Nationibus et quibusdam sub modis nisus conatusque conspiciuntur* **societatem popularem** *resarciendi post belli calamitates; quae societas iustitia sociali perfundatur et ipsum communismum vi cupiditateque rerum novarum exuat, quas hominum multitudines demonstrant vexatae et oppressati.* (19)

Again and again, we see this misuse of the word "democracy" as an automatic translation for a civil society by the many which can be taken as good or bad depending on whether it is ordered to the common good of all or to the good of the ruling "majority". Quite obviously in modern times the notion of "democracy" can only be what Aristotle regarded as bad because not ruling for the common good but dictatorially ruling as it liked. How anyone, especially a Catholic, could regard a government that legislated to protect murder of the unborn on a grand scale, to promote sexual depravity and "assisted suicide" as a good form of government beggars belief.

A "democratic society ruled by social justice" in the context of the meaning of democracy as used today is simply a contradiction in terms. Only an indoctrination to the point of invincible ignorance can excuse this. But what we have here is a translator insinuating that belief in a democratic society which most would take for "American democracy" - that a belligerent US Government wants to impose on the rest of the world - is being promoted by the popes. And no theologian protests!

The positive efforts of reform took on the character of a competition between the West and the East. It is to be remembered, though, that the war that was won was only over Nazism and Fascism, virulent outbreaks of the totalitarianism that is latent in modern liberalism (the worship of human liberty as absolute). These outbreaks, indeed, have their philosophical seeds in modern political voluntarism and legal positivism (so that they are ever present as latent threats). What is peculiar to them is not the liberalist/positivist or socialist/totalitarian political theory, which they have in common with Liberalism and Socialism at their common root, but their nationalist or racialist "spirit" (*volkgeist*). This seems to have come also from the roots of modern thinking, but survives as a sort of underground emotional/romantic counterpart to "pure" reason. It is evident in Schopenhauer and in the will to power of Nietzsche. It is also evident in the dialectical philosophies of Hegel and Marx. It has surfaced in more recent times as Postmodernism.

However, this is too big a subject to pursue here. The pope is concerned here with socialism/ communism as the post-war rival to liberal capitalism. This rivalry shaped many of the efforts in the West to overcome the problems of the past. In the result such an effort to counter communism risked causing self-harm. Let the pope explain: "Then there are the other social forces and ideological movements which oppose Marxism by setting up systems of 'national security', aimed at controlling the whole of society in a systematic way, in order to make Marxist infiltration impossible. By emphasizing and increasing the power of the State, they wish to protect their people from Communism, but in doing so they run the grave risk of destroying the freedom and values of the person, the very things for whose sake it is necessary to oppose Communism." (19) Prophetic words considering how things have developed recently, with terrorism being an additional spur to the Statist control of the whole of society.

Then, there was the effort to show that the West was economically superior in terms of general affluence. "Another kind of response, practical in nature, is represented by the affluent society or the consumer society. It seeks to defeat Marxism on the level of pure materialism by showing how a free-market society can achieve a greater satisfaction of material human needs than Communism, while equally excluding spiritual values. In reality, while on the one hand it is true that this social model shows the failure of Marxism to contribute to a humane and better society, on the other hand, insofar as it denies an autonomous existence and value to morality, law, culture and religion, it agrees with Marxism, in the sense that it totally reduces man to the sphere of economics and the satisfaction of material needs." (19) Here liberal Capitalism shows its materialistic basis, which it has in common with radical Socialism. We have noted what goes with this, namely, atheism, the supreme irrationalism that comes out of "enlightened" human reason.

The pope makes other perceptive comments in his survey of how Pope Leo's encyclical influenced the course of history in the twentieth century. His comments on the end of colonialism deserve mention, in so far as they bring out the spread of the Western economic/political hegemony into the affairs of the newly formed nations: "During the same period a widespread process of 'decolonization' occurred, by which many countries gained or regained their independence and the right freely to determine their own destiny. With the formal re-acquisition of State sovereignty, however, these countries often find themselves merely at the beginning of the journey towards the construction of genuine independence. Decisive sectors of the economy still remain *de facto* in the hands of large foreign companies, which are unwilling to commit themselves to the long-term development of the host country. Political life itself is controlled by foreign powers, while within the national boundaries there are tribal groups not yet amalgamated into a genuine national community. Also lacking is a class of competent professional people capable of running the State apparatus in an honest and just way, nor are there qualified personnel for managing the economy in an efficient and responsible manner."

Finally, he refers to the strongly positive effort after the war to provide international guarantees of the basic rights of all individual human beings, and individual nations as well, an effort that had undoubtedly been influenced by the Church's social doctrine. "Lastly, it should be remembered that after the Second World War, and in reaction to its horrors, there arose a more lively sense of human rights, which found recognition in a number of *International Documents* and, one might say, in the drawing up of a new 'right of nations', to which the Holy See has constantly contributed." (21)

However, for reasons that perhaps can be appreciated, the efforts even at this international level have issued in results that have "not always been positive". "While noting this process with satisfaction, nevertheless one cannot ignore the fact that the overall balance of the various policies of aid for development has not always been positive. The United Nations, moreover, has not yet succeeded in establishing, as alternatives to war, effective means for the resolution of international conflicts. This seems to be the most urgent problem which the international community has yet to resolve." (21)

Part III is basically an examination of the implications of the end of communism in the USSR, provoked by the uprising of workers in a Polish Labour union, going by the name *Solidarność (Solidarity)*, that was founded on 17 September 1980 at the Lenin Shipyard under the leadership of Lech Walesa. The year 1989, as the pope says, marks the climax of a process of events in the 1980's, particularly in Latin America, Asia and Africa, with the fall of dictatorships and other events that raised hopes of "a transition towards more participatory and more just political structures." The pope thus remarked: "From this historical process new forms of democracy have emerged which offer a hope for change in fragile political and social structures weighed down by a painful series of injustices and resentments, as well as by a heavily damaged economy and serious social conflicts." (22)

The pope asserts that: "An important, even decisive, contribution was made by *the Church's commitment to defend and promote human rights.*" He further maintained that: "Often, the vast majority of people identified themselves with this kind of affirmation, and this led to a search for forms of protest and for political solutions more respectful of the dignity of the person."(23) Thus, we may connect to the influence of the social encyclicals at least in part this change in people's social political and economic attitudes away from passive subjection to ideological regimes.

The pope then listed the more significant factors in the fall of oppressive regimes, making special mention of "the violation of the rights of workers". Another factor is put by the pope in this way: "The second factor in the crisis was certainly the inefficiency of the economic system, which is not to be considered simply as a technical problem, but rather a consequence of the violation of the human rights to private initiative, to ownership of property and to freedom in the economic sector." (24)

Another factor, however, the pope identifies as the decisive one. "But the true cause of the new developments was the spiritual void brought about by atheism, which deprived the younger generations of a sense of direction and in many cases led them, in the irrepressible search for personal identity and for the meaning of life, to rediscover the religious roots of their national cultures, and to rediscover the person of Christ himself as the existentially adequate response to the desire in every human heart for goodness, truth and life." (24)

Then, the pope reflects upon the implications of the fall of the Soviet regime. First of all, from the manner in which it collapsed, not by violent overthrow but "by means of peaceful protest, using only the weapons of truth and justice. While Marxism held that only by exacerbating social conflicts was it possible to resolve them through violent confrontation, the protests which led to the collapse of Marxism tenaciously insisted on trying every avenue of negotiation, dialogue, and witness to the truth, appealing to the conscience of the adversary and seeking to reawaken in him a sense of shared human dignity."

From this the pope draws an interesting conclusion and warning for all modern oppressive regimes: "The events of 1989 are an example of the success of willingness to negotiate and of the Gospel spirit in the face of an adversary determined not to be bound by moral principles. These events are a warning to those who, in the name of political realism, wish to banish law and morality from the political arena." (25)

The warning is drawn from a consideration of the nature of humanity itself: "Not only is it wrong from the ethical point of view to disregard human nature, which is made for freedom, but in practice it is impossible to do so. Where society is so organized as to reduce arbitrarily or even suppress the sphere in which freedom is legitimately exercised, the result is that the life of society becomes progressively disorganized and goes into decline." (25)

This philosophical perception applies also to liberal capitalism as an ideology, which has its own kind of oppressive domination of the many by the few. The pope makes this point: "The crisis of Marxism does not rid the world of the situations of injustice and oppression which Marxism itself exploited and on which it fed." (25) Signs of grave disorganization and accelerating decline in the West are already to be seen. The radical socialists should by now begin to realise that the Marxist method of violence is a profound mistake even in their efforts to destroy Capitalism. The pope warns against any theological flirting with Marxism.

There are lessons here also for the instigators of radical change of any fundamental social institution. The pope perceptively pinpoints what is behind these "progressive" political manoeuvres. "When people think they possess the secret of a perfect social organization which makes evil impossible, they also think that they can use any means, including violence and deceit, in order to bring that organization into being. Politics then becomes a 'secular religion' which operates under the illusion of creating paradise in this world." (26)

The pope foresaw the possibility of the revival of old enmities between national and regional groups under the previous Soviet domination. "Many individual, social, regional and national injustices were committed during and prior to the years in which Communism dominated; much hatred and ill-will have accumulated. There is a real danger that these will re-explode after the collapse of dictatorship, provoking serious conflicts and casualties, should there be a lessening of the moral commitment and conscious striving to bear witness to the truth which were the inspiration for past efforts." (27) Recent history attests to his foresight in this regard.

It behoved all other countries to come to the aid of those previously under the heel of the USSR. Thus, the pope said: "Assistance from other countries, especially the countries of Europe which were part of that history and which bear responsibility for it, represents a debt in justice. But it also corresponds to the interest and welfare of Europe as a whole, since Europe cannot live in peace if the various conflicts which have arisen as a result of the past are to become more acute because of a situation of economic disorder, spiritual dissatisfaction and desperation." (28)

In the last paragraph of this Part, Pope John Paul II sets out the conclusions that must be drawn for all concerned from the fall of communism in the former USSR. They extend not just to fully totalitarian regimes but to all political systems based on an ideology that subjects the many to the will and interests of a few, in the name of freedom and democracy. "In the totalitarian and authoritarian regimes, the principle that force predominates over reason was carried to the extreme. Man was compelled to submit to a conception of reality imposed on him by coercion, and not reached by virtue of his own reason and the exercise of his own freedom. This principle must be overturned and total recognition must be given to *the rights of the human conscience,* which is bound only to the truth, both natural and revealed. The recognition of these rights represents the primary foundation of every authentically free political order." (29)

We are already seeing how the rights of conscience, i.e. to refuse to approve or co-operate in what one regards not just as against one's religious beliefs, but even as against natural morality (something professed atheists claim to adhere to), are being eroded in the West under the rapidly rising dominance of the new secularist religion. It is sad to see professed Catholic political leaders in the forefront of this decline. If I am not mistaken, the Governor General of Australia who signed the Same Sex Marriage Bill into law is a Catholic, and the two politicians who attended on the signing into law, the Prime Minister and the Attorney General are also Catholics! None of them seems to be aware of what their Catholic catechism has to say on the matter.

In **Part IV** Pope John Paul II turns to the specific task of updating the Church's social doctrine to take into account more recent changes in the economic and political situation of modern nations and in the global politico-economic scene. In doing this he begins by introducing nuances, necessary in themselves, in regard to the relation between work and property, or in modern terms between labour and capital. In paragraph 30 he merely repeats the Church's doctrine regarding the natural character of the right of private property and of its subordination to the original common destination of created goods, to which he adds "as well as to the will of Christ as expressed in the Gospel.

In regard to the last aspect of the use of the right he says: "Pope Leo wrote: 'those whom fortune favours are admonished ... that they should tremble at the warnings of Jesus Christ ... and that a most strict account must be given to the Supreme Judge for the use of all they possess'; Pope John Paul II points out that this affirmation was repeated by the successors of Leo XIII and clearly restated in the Second Vatican Council. He himself had repeated it in his two previous social encyclicals. It has been repeated, most forcefully in regard to its subordination to the universal destination of goods for the benefit of all, by the present Pope Francis. There can be no mistaking the message and the warning.

Then the pope relates the right of property to work. "The original source of all that is good is the very act of God, who created both the earth and man, and who gave the earth to man so that he might have dominion over it by his work and enjoy its fruits

(Gen 1:28)" (31) This necessary connection between the right of property and work (or between Capital and Labour) has been wrenched apart in the modern notion of the right of property, making it something that a person claims absolute dominance over goods, to use or abuse as he wills, with no obligation to use it for the good of others. This divorces the subordination of the right to the common good of all. The separation of property or capital from work or labour is a defining characteristic of the modern ideology of Capitalism. The distortion of the notion of freedom, making it something absolute, is but the intellectual root of such an attitude to wealth. So it is that the ideology is named Liberalism/ Capitalism.

The pope then goes on to note a change, not in the notion of property as a right, but in the object of the right as civilization has developed. "In our time, in particular, there exists another form of ownership which is becoming no less important than land: *the possession of know-how, technology and skill.* The wealth of the industrialized nations is based much more on this kind of ownership than on natural resources." (32) This is to do with the notion of capital includes instruments used by man in production, the rational science behind which is made by law "intellectual property". With the progress of civilization a most amazing fact in economic life is the development from men (and women) working with primitive tools to having human production almost taken over by the tools they make, what we call technology (the science of making). There is even talk of robots replacing human beings; and, fancifully, of computers replacing human intelligence.

When to property in land is added property in the tools necessary for man to work the mastery as previously pointed out is
complete. With civilization technical science, treated as property.
Gives such a command that it by itself can seem to be all powerful. With this what is felt more important is a greater degree of
intellectual input, not of a metaphysical /wisdom kind, but of a
mathematical/scientific kind. The new style "workforce" needs to
be skilled in the new technology, requiring a time of training
much more sophisticated than that for manual labour of agricultural or factory workers. Moreover, fewer workers are required,
for the science can produce tools that seem to have artificial intelligence", especially powerful as weapons of war.

What this means in terms of the relation between capital and
labour, however, is a great increase in the power of property in
capital over labour as such, which latter (still human beings)
come to be more and more dispensable. For the new "property"
is in the knowledge necessary to use the new kind of capital, giv-
en the name "intellectual property". When misappropriated (not
properly ordered to the universal destination of goods; in many
cases produced by the inventiveness of individuals who profit
little from their inventions), this is simply added as more power
to the people of property. This does nothing to improve the situation of those without property; it rather exacerbates their poverty, and widens the gap between "capital" and "labour".

As the popes have noted, this imbalance works not just within
nations but also between nations, so that the gap between the
propertied rich and the propertyless poor only widens, at the individual and national levels. The human beings, and nations,

who miss out are discarded like waste, if prompted by a humanitarian sense of shame paid state aid (pension) or foreign aid. This is something particularly noted by Pope Francis, when he speaks about the more than marginalized, the excluded in modern economic systems.

This quite significant change, which brings within the use of the right of property aspects of human nature itself, specialized knowledge, though by reason of the structures of injustice already in place it often results in an exacerbation of injustice, is not of itself to be viewed negatively. To do so would be to act like the Luddites in the early period of the use of machinery in place of men. The serious social problems the change engenders need to be carefully attended to by the societies concerned, but they are not necessary effects of the change as such.

At this point the pope makes an observation about the modern economy that has been seized upon by defenders of Liberalism/Capitalism, as identified with the actual economic system in the West (particularly in the USA). He observes: "The modern *business economy* has positive aspects. Its basis is human freedom exercised in the economic field, just as it is exercised in many other fields. Economic activity is indeed but one sector in a great variety of human activities, and like every other sector, it includes the right to freedom, as well as the duty of making responsible use of freedom."

But, the freedom he is talking about is not the freedom preached within the ideology, no more than its concept of property, as we have noted above. Economic freedom, or initiative, is a positive aspect of a natural and just economy. It is not the freedom presented as absolute as in Liberalism, nor is it the same as "free enterprise" as conceived within the context of an economy dominated by a few who have misappropriated all or most of the property or capital within a social economy.

Therefore ,what the pope says is not really any endorsement of the liberalist capitalist or "free market" economy. The difficulty is in the ambiguity that he will address in paragraph 42 below. Liberal capitalism as an ideology uses the language of freedom and initiative, and property, the natural social character of which the Church is anxious to defend. It is to be remembered that here the pope is discussing matters in the context of the fall of socialist economies. He is anxious to highlight the values of freedom and initiative against the backdrop of their denial under socialist/totalitarian regimes. But, we must be very careful to avoid the equivocations that abound in the liberalist/capitalists' defence of their ideololgy.

The description of the modern economy as a business economy does make it appear that the pope is referring to the "real" economy of the West precisely as it is capitalist. This impression is strengthened when he says: "It would appear that, on the level of individual nations and of international relations, the *free market* is the most efficient instrument for utilizing resources and effectively responding to needs." (34) Even more so with the statement: "The Church acknowledges the legitimate *role of profit* as an indication that a business is functioning well. When a firm makes a profit, this means that productive factors have been properly employed and corresponding human needs have been duly satisfied." (35)

But, these are all concepts that within the context of the social doctrine of the Church need to be interpreted in a way that refers to an economy of free production and exchange operating under laws ensuring natural justice. The concepts of freedom and also profit within modern economic science are given an absoluteness that perverts them. "The modern business economy" suggests a market in which moneymaking is the principal motivation. Indeed, St. Thomas associates "business", *negotiatio*, with this secondary mode of exchange (MCM). The English word is used here to translate *administrationis*, which has no such connotation. This mistranslation is a problem that we will deal with more fully below. Profit (*lucrum*) also suggests something connected with the use of the market for moneymaking, rather than with the simple exchange of goods at equivalent value (CMC; no gain). The word in the original Latin translated as "profit", moreover, is *quaestus*. We will discuss further the translation of this word below.

The distinctions that need to be made are alluded to by the pope where he says: "In this sense, it is right to speak of a struggle against an economic system, if the latter is understood as a method of upholding the absolute predominance of capital, the possession of the means of production and of the land, in contrast to the free and personal nature of human work. In the struggle against such a system, what is being proposed as an alternative is not the socialist system, which in fact turns out to be State capitalism, but rather *a society of free work, of enterprise and of participation.* Such a society is not directed against the market, but demands that the market be appropriately controlled by the forces of society and by the State, so as to guarantee that the basic needs of the whole of society are satisfied." (35)

The Latin for the last sentence is: *Ea scilicet mercatui non opponitur sed convenienter est Reipublicae auctoritatibus temperanda ut totius societatis expleat necessitates;* "controlled by the forces of society and the State" would be better translated as "regulated by the authorities of civil society"; legal authority is basically moral authority; though it may use physical force, it is not to be reduced to such, nor is it necessary to double the notion of "Republic" with State as government and society; it simply means society politically considered, i.e. civil society.

It is clear that here the pope is not talking about "freedom" and "enterprise" as usually understood in the West, which is that system of economic domination that when merged politically with the State is to be called State Capitalism. It is true that the pope here refers to the legitimate role of profit and makes observations that would make it appear that he is using it in a sense that would cover the secondary mode of exchange – "an indication that the business is functioning well" indeed suggests such an interpretation - but here again the English translation is defective. What the Latin says is: *Ecclesia probat iustas quaestus partes, tamquam administrationis prosperae indicem.*

Note the word translated as "profit" is *quaestus*, and as "business" is *administrationis*. Thus the pope is primarily speaking about the meaning of profit in the case of natural exchange, where the shoemaker can only continue in his "business" if his profit exceeds his costs. There is no question here that he is engaging in a merchant-style exchange process of buying shoes and selling them "at a profit" (in modern times achieving the dimensions of a giant monopoly). He is just providing goods for money that he then uses to purchase, at equal value, the goods he needs to live on. He is not driven by a desire to make more money.

We do not say that this looseness in translation is easy to avoid. For, as noted above, the moral theologians do not make use of St. Thomas's distinction in this regard, and it seems too that the encyclicals themselves do not make explicit use of it (it does appear there implicitly, however). The points that the pope makes here about there being more to operating a business than to make a profit can be applied generally to the natural and unnatural modes of exchange.

Perhaps the force of his points suffers somewhat from lack of the necessary distinction, and it might be a thought to reserve, say, *quaestus* for the natural meaning of profit and *lucrum* for the non-natural. But, then again, we have to remember that strictly limited and directed (voluntarily) to natural needs or rational wants the secondary kind of profit can be legitimate. A real problem in this discussion is that the "normal" meaning of profit in the liberalist/capitalist economic system is the money-profit from buying and selling again "at a profit". That is the kind of "business" that tends to dominate the modern economy and, left to operate within the economy without restraint, leads to speculative booms and busts. It is quite important therefore that the real nature of the difference between natural and unnatural exchange, clearly delineated in Aristotle and St. Thomas, be brought out.

Other problems, such as the increase in indebtedness on the part of those who lack property or capital, both at the individual and national level, would become more intelligible if the above distinctions were well understood. The pope proceeds to discuss "specific problems and threats" (36) which are the consequences of the "structures of sin" referred to in his earlier encyclical, evidently unjust structures belonging to the liberalist/capitalist systems of economy.

One is the shift of focus in production to quantity away from quality. Substituting machines for human beings means a loss of the fine quality of art, involving a shift of attention from the fineness of products to their mere usefulness. So it is that modern cities are the soulless ant heaps constructed either by giant corporations bent upon making money, or governments bent upon saving money – this is what is meant by "efficiency" - whose operations are directed by university graduates fitting the description of the perceptive Catholic historian Christopher Dawson.

We should remember, of course, that what we are discussing is something like a parasite. Generally civil society, as something healthy in itself, is always resisting it and attempting, with varying degrees of success, to throw it off. That is the struggle against the system that the pope speaks of. Marxist Communism is the taking the extreme step of cutting off one's head to cure the headache. Pope John Paul II devotes a long paragraph (41) at the end of this part criticising along these lines Marxism's attack on Capitalism. The headache may be severe; but living with it, and treating its symptoms, is much to be preferred to the alternative offered.

The pope spends some space on other significant consequences that ravage modern society that can be looked upon as emerging from the economic conditions of modern society, such as the drug problem. But an important development is what he calls "the ecological question". This he argues "accompanies the problem of consumerism and is closely connected to it." The modern world has developed an appetite to have more and more with less and less satisfaction of the desires so stimulated – rather a mimic of the desire for more money, which tends to infinity. Refer to Appendix A: "A Taste for Sweet Decay."

This spills over into "the senseless destruction of the environment". Along with this comsumerist mentality goes what we may call a "producerist" complete lack of sensitivity to the delicate balances in the natural world down even to the mineral resources. Spurred on by the prospect of huge profits, the industrial giants, like savage animals, rip and tear at their prey, the natural environment.

What is to be noted here is how early the popes drew notice to the problem of environmental damage of the earth upon which we live and upon which we depend. So obvious has the damage become that the two opposed politico-economic ideologies have been drawn into the debate, typically taking two extreme positions. The capitalist defenders of the system that is largely responsible for the destruction tends to downplay the connection between man and modern society and any deleterious consequences; whilst the socialist attackers of capitalism tend to make man and human society totally responsible. We will leave further discussion of this aspect of the Church's social doctrine until we have to comment upon the encyclical of Pope Francis, *Laudato si'*, that deals with it directly.

The pope comes now to a consideration of the meaning of the word "Capitalism" in paragraph 42. This paragraph has been much commented upon, being used by some, including Catholics, to suggest a turn in the Church's social doctrine, more favourable than in the past, towards Capitalism, traditionally understood as Liberalism/Capitalism as "realised" particularly in the USA.

We should therefore give some close attention to what he says (it has already been discussed in our book "Thomist Tradition: avoiding Scylla and Charybdis") and so will first quote the entire paragraph. "42. Returning now to the initial question: can it perhaps be said that, after the failure of Communism, capitalism is the victorious social system, and that capitalism should be the goal of the countries now making efforts to rebuild their economy and society? Is this the model which ought to be proposed to the countries of the Third World which are searching for the path to true economic and civil progress?

The answer is obviously complex. If by 'capitalism' is meant an economic system which recognizes the fundamental and positive role of **business** (*administrationis* = care of affairs with regard to production and exchange of goods), the **market** (*mercatus* = to do with wealth and its natural exchange or trade), private property and the resulting responsibility for the means of production, as well as free human creativity (exertions) in the economic sector, then the answer is certainly in the affirmative, even though it would perhaps be more appropriate to speak of a '**business** economy', '**market** economy' or simply 'free economy'. But if by 'capitalism' is meant a system in which freedom in the economic sector is not circumscribed within a strong juridical framework which places it at the service of human freedom in its totality, and which sees it as a particular aspect of that freedom, the core of which is ethical and religious, then the reply is certainly negative.

The Marxist solution has failed, but the realities of marginalization and exploitation remain in the world, especially the Third World, as does the reality of human alienation, especially in the more advanced countries. Against these phenomena the Church strongly raises her voice. Vast multitudes are still living in conditions of great material and moral poverty. The collapse of the Communist system in so many countries certainly removes an obstacle to facing these problems in an appropriate and realistic way, but it is not enough to bring about their solution. Indeed, there is a risk that a radical capitalistic ideology could spread which refuses even to consider these problems, in the *a priori* belief that any attempt to solve them is doomed to failure, and which blindly entrusts their solution to the free development of market forces."

We should first note that here we have at its most egregious the presence of mistranslations of the original Latin, particularly with regard to words that we have highlighted in the text. Next, let us note a couple of preliminary points. The English word "complex" does not quite give the precise meaning of *implicata*. The answer is not so much complex as if difficult to unravel, but entangled as needing to be unravelled, though not all that difficult.

Indeed, in the instant case, it is only necessary to separate out two meanings that are clearly distinguishable, as is the case with related words such as "freedom" and "property" that are used in opposed ways according to the two meanings being dealt with. As explained by the pope, the difference depends upon the word "Capitalism" signifying, on the one hand, an economy ruled by justice, enforced by the State, and on the other hand, an economic system understood without reference to any "restraints" of justice, or State "control".

There is no problem with recognising which one is the "real" Capitalism, and which is the one that the ideologues would have us believe it is. It is an elementary exercise in equivocation that is all too familiar in modern politico-economic "scientific" discourse. The pope is raising it in the context of new nations freed from the Soviet stranglehold and being enticed by political and economic advisers that they should now adopt liberalism/capitalism as naturally the only real alternative to socialism/communism. Many if most did. The pope was trying to warn them not to.

The words highlighted have been translated in a way that is almost reprehensible, so slanted are they to interpretation according to the modern unnatural mode of exchange. For a start, and most blatantly, "of business", is a translation of the Latin *administrationis*. This means simply of administration, which is a general term for carrying out some work or operation. In an economic context, then, it simply signifies working or being productive, or engaging in the exchange process. In fact, in St. Thomas, in the classical moral theological text for this matter, *negotiatio,* which is not the word *(administrationis)* tried to be translated, has the special meaning of business as it refers to trading in the non-natural or unnatural mode ("wheeling and dealing" is the nearest English translation), which he describes as associated with a kind of turpitude. (cf. II-II, 77, 4 c)

The mistranslations are grounded in ignorance of the moral context of the subject, but it is clear that the translator is captured by the modern perversion of the meaning of trade. The translator of the *Summa Theologiae* itself is also profoundly ignorant of the meaning in Latin of the words he is attempting to translate when we look at how *negotiator* is translated in the fourth article in the seventy-seventh question of II-II. There the translation given of *negotiator* is "tradesman", which has nothing essentially to do with trade meaning exchange, which comes from the Latin root of *traditio*. Trade, as in tradesman, comes from the Old English *tredan* which means to tread, as an accustomed path, thus to follow an occupation.

The trader in the first sense refers simply to one engaged in the exchange of goods, or selling and buying. *Negotiator* St. Thomas clearly uses to mean someone engaged in the business of buying and selling again (at a money profit, MCM), a merchant, not even one engaged in natural exchange (CMC), let alone a plumber! This last kind of tradesman is then, wait for it, because he is not a trader, made to come within the meaning of what is translated as householder. In translating St. Thomas's *economos vel politicos,* what is intended are those who have to engage in natural exchange (CMC) to supply their needs as an ordinary citizen, or as a government official.

Most ordinary citizens gain the money they need to make the purchases for their households from a trade; the government gets it from some sort of taxation. Neither is necessarily thus engaged in the "business" of making money by buying "commodities" (especially shares and "stock") cheap and selling the same "at a profit". It can be seen also that an equivalent distorted meaning will automatically be put on the word "market", used in the same context. Instead of being taken as natural exchange (CMC), to which attaches no profit (for it is ruled by a just or equal price; fair bargain, no gain), it will be taken in the second sense of artificial or unnatural exchange (MCM) in which case St. Thomas uses the meaning of profit (*lucrum*) specific to "wheeling and dealing", meaning the monetary gain from the "deal".

The standard English translation of this question 77 is absolutely hopeless. It is no wonder that English-speaking moral theologians, and clerical and lay commentators on the social encyclicals, are so at sea in dealing with questions of economics. They are fair game for shooting down by liberalist modern economists, who infest the universities with their Departments of Economics, and are hired by ignorant politicians to advise on fiscal and monetary policies - a classic case of the blind leading the blind. **Note:** The Latin for business is *negotiatio*, literally the opposite of *otium*, not doing anything, which in an economic context would signify not working, by being productive, or engaging in the exchange process.

In the final paragraph of Part IV the saying of the pope "The Church has no models to present" is latched upon to insinuate that the Church has no alternative to propose to "real" Capitalism (or "real Socialism" for that matter – but this implication is suppressed). The Latin word is *exempla*. But the pope is simply saying that it is not within its role (or competence) to "design" an actual social economy. That is precisely the role of each community itself and its government, which have to take into account all the circumstances of the time and place. Nonetheless, the Church can offer its social doctrine not "as an indispensible and ideal orientation" but a necessary optimal direction", *tamquam necessariam directionem optimam, suam doctrinam socialem,* (not ideal in the modern sense but real in the moral sense) as a true alternative to the two "suboptimal", because false, directions of the opposed politico-economic ideologies. "Models" surreptitiously slips into referring to the two perverse systems as they are realised. It would help if the English translators did not attempt to use the language of modern "scientific" (heavily mathematicized) economics in interpreting the popes' thought.

At the very end of this last paragraph of Part IV the pope returns to the precise matter signified in the heading, private property and the universal destination of goods, connecting them both to work or labour. Thus, he says: "Ownership of the means of production, whether in industry or agriculture, is just and legitimate if it serves useful work. It becomes illegitimate, however, when it is not utilized or when it serves to impede the work of others, in an effort to gain a profit which is not the result of the overall expansion of work and the wealth of society, but rather is the result of curbing them or of illicit exploitation, speculation or the breaking of solidarity among working people. Ownership of this kind has no justification, and represents an abuse in the sight of God and man."

Both Socialism and Capitalism as practised today are prime examples of such abuse. Nor for that very reason can those societies "attain social peace".

Part V: STATE AND CULTURE

The heading in Latin is *CIVITAS ET ANIMI CULTUS*. The English translation is ambiguous and affected by modern connotations that border on the gross. In the first place *Civitas* is Latin for City (Gk. *Polis*), which is best translated as civil community. It signifies the whole civil community at all levels of life. "State" in English, on the other hand, can be used for that but it more commonly stands for the civil or political organ of government, which is a part of the whole community, considered only according to its self-governing aspect. Like the head, it is meant to direct all social functions material and spiritual to the good of the whole, but it can and often does take the whole body in the wrong direction. It is probable that that is the way "State" will be taken here.

Under modern conditions, the tendency is to look upon this political head as somehow disconnected from the rest of the body, over which it rules somewhat like a master over servants. That notion of State is what comes to be most associated with the use of the word. This is a sign of the fact that modern government generally corresponds to Aristotle's oligarchical rule, even when superficially it is presented as a "democracy". Modern politicians certainly act as if they can do what they like, once in power, with a passive people, sick of political wrangling anyway.

However, the point we wish to draw out here is that the word State, in its modern context, misses altogether the wholeness and beauty of the notion of *Civitas* as the whole civil community. St. Thomas following Aristotle's concept of the *polis*, stated that the civil society is the greatest thing that human nature can know **and constitute**. <u>Hence its "artificial/ moral form" of government is called a constitution</u>. Though natural in the sense of a moral necessity it is also man-made, and if made according to the requirements of the natural moral law a work of art of the highest (moral) order.

The modern notion of State carries with it the idea a heartless and bureaucratic organisation with its own agenda and serving interests of those in power, only corresponding accidentally and occasionally to the common good of the whole community. The people submit to its rule sullenly and silently in case they get on "the wrong side of the law".

That is the political aspect of the heading. The cultural aspect is similarly affected by the divided character of modern social life. "Culture" as a word does not ordinarily conjure up today a vision of a whole society enjoying the benefits of civilized life (as at the height of Christendom). It is generally associated with the preserve of a privileged few, going to the opera and enjoying the best of art and culture that money can buy. The language of the heading harks back to the healthier notion of culture as simply cultivation of human social life to the fullest, the best of civilized living meant to be made available to every citizen and indeed to everyone as human.

This is more the sense of *animi cultus,* the cultivation of the human soul, spirit and mind (*animi cultus ei erat humanitatis cibus* – Cicero) It is the relation between the whole community and its culture at all levels from the lowest bodily to the highest spiritually that the heading signifies, if this is placed in the modern context of a disordered political organisation and a culture the best of which the majority is deprived of, having to be content with a debased "mass culture" (not for that necessarily negative – some goodness of human social nature will come out under the most extreme conditions of oppression and deprivation).

However, though this is the intent of this part from the heading, the pope wishing to use these words according to their full traditional meaning, it is clear that he intends to focus on the nature of political rule within a community. For, he focuses from the start on contrasting a sound teaching on society with the totalitarian kind of regime put forward in Marxist-Leninist theory and put into practice in the USSR. If one's political theory is not based upon objective truth "then there is no sure principle for guaranteeing just relations between people". Political power and "law" then become nothing but an expression of will only and "then the force of power takes over and each person tends to make full use of the means at his disposal in order to impose his own interests, or his own opinion, with no regard to the rights of others". That is what plainly occurred in the Soviet Communist regime.

It necessarily involves a rejection of the Church, and not just the Church but also any objective morality. For, it "cannot tolerate the affirmation of an objective criterion of good and evil beyond the will of those in power". Furthermore, it "tends to absorb within itself the nation (i.e. all aspects of the whole community, *civitas*), the family (supporters of same sex marriage take note), religious groups and individuals themselves." (45)

By contrast with such a repressive regime, which attempted to put into permanent effect the political and economic theory of Socialism – thereby labelled "Real Socialism" - the pope then details the features of a political constitution (the kind of State) that the Church would approve. Since the language that applies to the principles and values so favoured is used also by the opposite ideology of Liberalism/Capitalism, but with meanings already adverted to that are opposed to those intended by the Church's social doctrine (and indeed by the political philosophy of Aristotle), we have to be very careful to avoid the distinct danger of equivocation present.

It is here that the English translation tends to let us down again, as we have seen happen in Part IV. For, the translator struggles to avoid translating words used by the pope with words in English that are generally taken in a liberalist sense. But here it is not freedom, property and the like, that are applicable even outside a social and political context. We have noted the distortions given by liberalism to these notions. Here, however, we are mainly concerned with words that have a direct political significance, such as apply to the types of constitutions, governments, regimes etc.; words like republic, democracy, monarchy, tyranny, despotism, aristocracy and oligarchy, to which we may add the more modern terms such as totalitarian, authoritarian, autocratic and so on.

The principal mistranslation in this regard concerns again the word "democracy". This word does not appear in the original Latin of the encyclical, even though there is a Latin equivalent for the English word, *democratia* (fr. Gk. *demokratia*). The Latin words the pope uses that are translated as democracy are *populare regimen, Reipublicae populari,* and *popularis gubernii,* all of which simply mean government by the many as opposed to government by one or the few. The classical Aristotelian classification of political constitutions is into three kinds, by one, few or many, each of which has an opposite according to a division into good or bad, determined by whether they govern for the common good or their own good. This therefore gave the kinds of political constitutions as six, to which the names given by Aristotle seem to have been kingship and tyranny, aristocracy and oligarchy, constitutional government and democracy.

Notice that democracy is regarded as a bad form of government, precisely for the reason that it is a government by the majority in the interests of the majority and not for the common good of all (including the minority). Even on this criterion the modern notion of democracy is no different from that within Aristotle's classification. The modern use, however, has been affected by the fundamental change of attitude to government brought about by the French Revolution. This overthrew existing monarchical and aristocratic systems of government in France (thereafter referred to as *ancien regime*) in the name of a republic, seen as a popular kind of government, more or less equivalent to Aristotle's rule of the many.

Thereafter, monarchy and aristocracy were regarded as unacceptable forms of government, no different in essence from tyranny or despotism, oligarchy or plutocracy. (They might be allowed to continue to exist without real power, as in the U.K.) Government "by the people" became by definition the only good kind of government. It became unnecessary to enquire whether popular government was good or bad. We may equate the word republic with Aristotle's constitutional government. But the word democracy came to be used in the same way. Both simply signify government "by the people", or the majority. What the majority of representatives of the people ("in Parliament assembled") decide is law, without any possible demur – that is democracy.

Rather, however, it is an irrational and irresponsible form of government; for it is pure voluntarism, a mere counting of individual wills agreeing upon a certain course of action. As Pope John Paul II has put it about the Soviet political system, "the force of power takes over" from reason, truth and justice. Such a notion of democracy has within it the seeds of totalitarianism. The ease with which fundamental social institutions can be "reformed" is a telling sign.

The two political ideologies use the terms "republic" and "democracy" indiscriminately to claim that they are realized in regimes "of the people", "by the people" Both the former USSR and the USA described and describe themselves as republics and democracies. This is so despite the fact that the former was clearly totalitarian in either being ruled by a tyrant or a despotic few;

and the latter is clearly a divided nation effectively plutocratic in that the great proportion of wealth and property is in the control of a small minority, the welfare of the majority basically depending upon finding employment "provided" by capital (money) of the rich and powerful. This is what is commonly known as a capitalist system.

The big difference is that the evil of the second (Liberalist / Capitalist) in regard to its economic system, and to some extent in regard to political freedom, can be alleviated, and has been in the past in the way we have described. The evil of the former (Socialist/Communist), however, is ineluctable and completely enslaving. Both, however, are in the end self-destructive.

However, let us resume what the pope said about democracy, according to the English translation: "The Church values the democratic system inasmuch as it ensures the participation of citizens in making political choices, guarantees to the governed the possibility both of electing and holding accountable those who govern them, and of replacing them through peaceful means when appropriate. Thus she cannot encourage the formation of narrow ruling groups which usurp the power of the State for individual interests or for ideological ends." (46)

The language that the pope in fact uses - "popular government". "popular political constitution" and "popular regime" - points rather to what Aristotle termed "constitutional government". That is to say it points to a regime that supposes rule by the many for the common good. However, the modern word "democracy" is most often used today in the same bad sense given by Aristotle; but this is obscured by leaving out altogether any such moral judgment. Politics in modern thinking is all about power, not moral considerations, such as justice. After all, justice and morality are generally preached by liberal thinkers as only a matter of opinion.

Thus, no doubt unwittingly, the translator has fortified the belief (even among some Catholic commentators on the social encyclicals, especially in the USA) that the pope is favouring "democracy" as it is taken for the constitutional arrangement existing, "enlightened" by the liberalist ideology that inspires it. There is no "third way" between Socialism and Liberalism. The Socialist/Communist "model" having been entirely discredited, not just by Church doctrine but also by history, the Liberalist/Capitalist "model" stands justified.

But what was the pope saying? He was asserting what Aristotle had said in his *Politics* about all constitutional government having to be self-government. The *Polis (Civitas)* is an association of human beings come together freely to further their own common good, adopting one or other of the three possible genera of political constitutions or forms of civil government, by one, few or many. According to St. Thomas all citizens must be given a role in the government precisely because they are free agents. Thus, the preferred political arrangement is where there is a principle of unity, an equivalent of a king, assisted by the best counsel, or senior advisers, an equivalent to an aristocracy or senate, and a way of ensuring the consent of the governed, an equivalent of popular government, which in a large civil society is generally feasible only through elected representatives.

That is what the pope is saying is what the Church favours – it is the fundamental popular basis of all civilized government. It presupposes that all such government, of whatever combination or permutation, is ordered to the common good of all. The translator renders it as "the democratic system", making it seem as an endorsement of the political system realised in the West, of which the USA is the "model". But the liberalist ideology which it purports to base itself on excludes the very concept of common good, would, if it could, dispense with all political authority, and leave the rich and powerful few "free" (with the neglect and connivance of the shadow of government left) to press home their superior power and influence upon an economically servile multitude.

The "real" democratic system in place, then, is as much like the "popular political constitution" as Aristotle's "democracy" is like his "constitutional government", or his "oligarchy" his "aristocracy", or even his "tyranny" is like his "kingship".

All this analysis, however, is at the level of theory or "principle". As we have noted, in fact since the Second World War the liberalist/capitalist system is much ameliorated by political and social reforms, particularly at the economic level where the most serious evils are most manifest. This moderation may delay and even avoid indefinitely the end built into the system, which is so entrenched now that it is hard to conceive of modern civilization recovering full normality. Perhaps the best we can hope for is a "bridled" capitalism. That may perhaps be read into the popes' pleas.

One important way to "reform" the system is to educate people as to the true meaning of freedom and its dependence on truth and justice. Drawing attention to human rights is another way of ensuring "authentic democracy", though we can see before our very eyes how this can be twisted to destroy natural human rights (to life) and construct unnatural "human rights" (to death).

The pope ends his general observations at this point: "The Church respects *the legitimate autonomy of the democratic order* and is not entitled to express preferences for this or that institutional or constitutional solution. Her contribution to the political order is precisely her vision of the dignity of the person revealed in all its fullness in the mystery of the Incarnate Word." (47) Hopefully, the English-speaking reader can now interpret this correctly.

Pope John Paul II then turns to the role of the State "in the economic sector". He begins by saying: "Economic activity, especially the activity of a market economy, cannot be conducted in an institutional, juridical or political vacuum." (48) We have seen what this means. The State has the duty to ensure individual freedom and protect private initiative but will only do so if it performs its primary function of ensuring justice in individuals' economic relations with one another and protecting the common good. The pope goes on to say: "The absence of stability, together with the corruption of public officials and the spread of improper sources of growing rich and of easy profits deriving from illegal or purely speculative activities, constitutes one of the chief obstacles to development and to the economic order." Sound familiar in the land of "free enterprise"?

The State has the further role, right and duty "to intervene when particular monopolies create delays or obstacles to development." This however is part of its duty to maintain justice in the economic order. It also has the role, right and urgent duty, as a last resort, to come to the aid of those who through injustice or even weakness cannot provide for themselves or their families. This it does in the exercise of its subsidiary function, which as we have noted, is strictly limited by the principle of subsidiarity. In this regard the pope notes the rise of the "Social Assistance State" (Welfare State) and the socialist implications of this. What we have seen, however, is not the right correction of this social evil but the use of it as an excuse to revert to "unbridled Capitalism" (in political deregulation).

The pope then refers to the Church's active involvement among the needy "offering them material assistance in ways that neither humiliate nor reduce them to mere objects of assistance, but which help them to escape their precarious situation by promoting their dignity as persons." For, far more serious is spiritual and moral poverty than material and bodily, which latter the secularist State alleviates, in an unjust politico-economic system in which the hand that accepts curses the hand that offers.

To counter this sentiment of envy and hurt the pope counsels all to have a concrete commitment to solidarity and charity, as ultimately the only true way to overcome the evils dealt on the one hand and suffered on the other. This is the fundamental way to restoring the culture of a community, which derives its character from what has been handed down from generation to generation. It is a matter of eliminating what is evil and rescuing what is good, and despite appearances there is much that is good always in any particular civil society.

The young have the problem of sifting the good from the bad, but are ready targets for the ideologues, who are committed to persuading them to evil and violence in the cause of defeating each's ideological opponents. The Church is anxious to convince each new generation of the great (divinely given) goodness that naturally belongs to each particular civilized society. That is how the Church interacts with diverse cultures. Thus, the pope says: "The way in which he [man] is involved in building his own future depends on the understanding he has of himself and of his own destiny. It is on this level that *the Church's specific and decisive contribution to true culture* is to be found. The Church promotes those aspects of human behaviour which favour a true culture of peace, as opposed to models in which the individual is lost in the crowd, in which the role of his initiative and freedom is neglected, and in which his greatness is posited in the arts of conflict and war." (51)

The alternative to listening to the Church's message is only conflict and war, to which the pope links the continuance of structures of sin and injustice. Thus, he observes: "Furthermore, it must not be forgotten that at the root of war there are usually real and serious grievances: injustices suffered, legitimate aspirations frustrated, poverty, and the exploitation of multitudes of desperate people who see no real possibility of improving their lot by peaceful means." (52)

For this reason, the way to peace must be through States not continuing to neglect their fundamental duty to ensure justice in all aspects of social life, legal, distributive and commutative; they must restore just laws and natural institutions; and promote the good of all and not just that of the privileged few and those to whom they are often beholden. The pope puts it this way: "For this reason, another name for peace is *development*. Just as there is a collective respon-sibility for avoiding war, so too there is a collective responsibility for promoting development. Just as within individual societies it is possible and right to organize a solid economy which will direct the functioning of the market to the common good, so too there is a similar need for adequate interventions on the international level." And he ends: "This is the culture which is hoped for, one which fosters trust in the human potential of the poor, and consequently in their ability to improve their condition through work or to make a positive contribution to economic prosperity." (52)

Part VI - Man the Way of the Church

There is no need for us to comment of this part which brings in directly the order of grace and charity. But there is one matter that we must advert to. One would not expect any great problem of translation in this last section of the encyclical. However, the very first word in Latin is *Proletariatus*, which is translated as "the working class". It would almost seem that the translator felt that the exact translation "proletariat", with its communist associations, might make his liberalist readers in the West uncomfortable. But Pope Leo XIII used it freely and that was before Socialism and Communism gained a foothold in modern times.

The class that works, as such, is not necessarily oppressed with injustice, but referring to it as the proletariat does imply it is. This is a word that the Church's social doctrine and Marxism had in common in Leo's time. Hence Pope John Paul II is not loathe to use it when recalling the condition of the worker in Capitalism at the close of the nineteenth century.

The pope, however, in this final part is concerned to place the social doctrine of the Church squarely within the work of evangelization. It is there too that the real solution of all man's ills is to be sought, including political and economics ones. Evangelization is not a merely clerical concern; it involves all. "On the hundredth anniversary of that Encyclical I wish to thank all those who have devoted themselves to studying, expounding and making better known Christian social teaching. To this end, the co-operation of the local Churches is indispensable, and I would hope that the present anniversary will be a source of fresh enthusiasm for studying, spreading and applying that teaching in various contexts." (56)

The pope reveals the special concern he has for those countries, including his own, which "following the collapse of "Real Socialism", are experiencing a serious lack of direction in the work of rebuilding." Nonetheless, the pope warns the Western countries not to congratulate themselves too smugly, for they "run the risk of seeing this collapse as a one-sided victory of their own economic system, and thereby failing to make necessary corrections in that system."

They should in particular look to their responsibilities in relation to that huge part of the world that is "underdeveloped". "Meanwhile, the countries of the Third World are experiencing more than ever the tragedy of underdevelopment, which is becoming more serious with each passing day."

Catholics, too, should evangelize more by example than by theological argument. "the Church's love for the poor, which is essential for her and a part of her constant tradition, impels her to give attention to a world in which poverty is threatening to assume massive proportions in spite of technological and economic progress." This does not exclude working tirelessly for justice. "Love for others, and in the first place love for the poor, in whom the Church sees Christ himself, is made concrete in the *promotion of justice.*" (58) Again justice is not enough, "what is needed is *the gift of grace, a gift* which comes from God. Grace, in cooperation with human freedom, constitutes that mysterious presence of God in history which is Providence." (59)

Though proclamation of the Gospel is the primary task, there is a need to have the courage to denounce the systems of oppression and virtual slavery under which too many or our fellow men women and children continue to suffer. "Furthermore, as she [the Church] has become more aware of the fact that too many people live, not in the prosperity of the Western world, but in the poverty of the developing countries amid conditions which are still 'a yoke little better than that of slavery itself', she has felt and continues to feel obliged to denounce this fact with absolute clarity and frankness, although she knows that her call will not always win favour with everyone." (61)

Thus, the pope brings in the worldwide scope of the question of social justice, which we now must take up with a consideration of the document of the Council and subsequent social encyclicals.

Chapter Six

Gaudium et spes (1965)

Preface and Introduction

The document has a Preface and Introduction and then divides into two parts. We will cover what is said in the first few paragraphs and then take up what is said in Part I dealing with only two chapters, and Part II dealing mainly with the two chapters most pertinent to our purposes. Subheadings will indicate the divisions we use.

Firstly, then, with regard to the Council document's scope we need to outline as best we can the aim of the Council. The Council document is directed to Man (*Homo*). It wishes to explain to the whole world of man how the Church "conceives of the presence and activity of the Church in the world of today." It is really a restatement of the message of salvation which was meant from the start for all mankind but which, being placed in time, had a small beginning and took time to spread literally "to the ends of the earth". The Church therefore has seen itself as missionary from the beginning, travelling to the end of the world as it was known, spreading "the good news".

Over time this world has expanded and kept expanding until almost the present day. In a way, the time had come for the Church to proclaim its message afresh to the whole world (this came also to mean a new evangelisation to parts of the world that had been evangelised, had indeed been Christian, but had lost the Faith). This meant reaching by readily accessible means of modern communication beyond those belonging "visibly" to the Church as the Body of Christ, beyond those who called themselves Christians, beyond those who regarded themselves as religious, even to those who claimed to be atheists, as the document states. It did not exclude those who thought of the Church as a power for evil, even the work of the devil. Its message was not meant primarily as a work of conversion, but of evangelisation, hopefully of course to correct misunderstandings and lead to a change of heart in relation to it, or rather to its Lord and God.

This proclamation has two aspects. Firstly, it is addressing what is most common, both good and bad, that pertains to human nature, which is rational and free. Man has been made in the image of God and is capable therefore of the best and most noble things. But, on the other hand being free, man is capable of the worst and most ignoble things. Thus, even considered at the level of nature and reason, as Aristotle noted the bad man is worse than the most savage animal.

But we know from Revelation that man was created for higher things than what is within the range of his nature, even for things divine. This meant however that he could use his (and her) free will to commit an even graver sin (of pride), that would lead to the fall from grace, to something like a devilish level of being and behaving – *corruptio optimi* – a seemingly impossibly hopeless condition beyond ordinary slavery to sin, to the pit of the "absurdity" of rejection of divine grace.

But, again by Revelation, we know that the human story has a happy ending. That is the message of salvation, wrought by the Son of God becoming man and freely offering himself as the price of our redemption. This is the meaning of human existence that the Church wished to get across, of joy and hope.

What this meant however, so far as the nature of the document with which we are concerned is, is that it is not addressing particularly any section of mankind, whether considered in terms of its power or influence at the present time, no matter how great, or its extension geographically. Indeed, if it has any preferential object, it can be expressed in its option for the poor.

The Church wished to reach into the depths of human misery which in material and temporal terms seemed to be the lot of mankind apart from a privileged few. Its message to all was that we needed to look beyond this passing world of time, where joy and hope tended to be put in terms of material wealth and sensual pleasure and cast our eyes heavenward, to the more real part of our human nature that is spiritual, "a little lower than the angels", and pay heed to what the Creator God had in mind for us – a life of unending bliss in the company of God as Triune and those who had proved their love of the Father Son and Holy Spirit, and of us, by being willing to suffer and die like Christ.

This sublime message was intended for all, but for the many "unfortunate", poor in the eyes of the world it was a special comfort and joy to be able to see their suffering and even death as working for their own good and that of their fellowman. For the fortunate few, rich, enjoying the good life of wealth and pleasure, to the message was added a warning, more severe if the "good" life was based in a lack of justice and charity.

Now this gospel was essentially the same as what had been proclaimed to the world that was the civilisation that had succeeded that of Christendom and was at least to some extent still Christian, if greatly diminished as we have seen. Its political and economic structures had already come to dominate most of the rest of the world. But it was its internal state of conflict that prompted Leo XIII to speak out. He was reminding this (First) world that unless it returned to Christian values (of morals) as a matter of urgency it would inevitably "implode". As it turned out, though there was an economic collapse and military conflicts on a massive scale, this world did take to heart the words of Leo and there was a recovery of sorts in that part of the world that did not succumb to Socialism.

The end of the Second World War, however, was the beginning of the rise of Communism as a real threat to the capitalist part of modern civilisation. It was a period of "cold war" during which the rest of the world became virtually absorbed into one or other of two "blocs" defined by the two opposed politico-economic ideologies described within the social encyclicals. It was in the middle of this situation of the modern world that the Second Vatican Council was held.

What is remarkable about the document, which purports to discuss the relation of the Church to the modern world, is that though there is general mention of this kind of ideological conflict there is no naming of Communism or Capitalism, let alone its principal protagonists, the USSR and the USA, remembering that it was at the very time when the whole world of mankind was as close as it ever has been before or since to total destruction. Some might think that the detachment of the Fathers of the Council from mentioning the actual players in this drama bordered on a mental state of unreality. What world did they think they were describing?

The Council had certainly detached itself from what seemed to many to be "the world of today" in its most concrete situation. From the point of view of those within that world it was the whole world, just as those living in the Roman Empire would have seen it as the whole world. The two ideologies were after all but (heretical) offshoots of the world that had been evangelised and still called itself Christian. Indeed, the extent of the reach of these two ideologies was enormous. China had turned Communist before the Council. India had been subjected to Capitalism under the British. Much of Asia had been colonised by European nations riding the capitalist wave. Even the nations of the Middle East and Africa had been subjected to European or British or other European rule. What was left?

But, for one thing, the Council had declared that the Church has already much to say in this regard, referring no doubt particularly in the social encyclicals from Leo XIII onwards. Moreover, the Church was not looking at man as capitalist or communist, important as these characterisations are in the modern world. They remain the dominant politico-economic ideologies and Liberalism continues as the dominant purely political ideology. But they are but manifestations or symptoms of a deeper social condition that the Church is more interested in addressing.

Moreover, it was most concerned with the spiritual and religious dimension of human nature which to the modern mind tended to lie hidden in the individual souls of human persons engaged in temporal conflicts and material concerns at a superficial level.

Closer to this deeper aspect of human nature were the intellectual and philosophical changes that had occurred in the minds of modern men and women, movements which underlay the practical political conflicts, and therefore were common to people of either politico-economic ideology, Capitalist or Communist. So, the Council notes: "5. Today's spiritual agitation and the changing conditions of life are part of a broader and deeper revolution. As a result of the latter, intellectual formation is ever increasingly based on the mathematical and natural sciences and on those dealing with man himself, while in the practical order the technology which stems from these sciences takes on mounting importance."

That is something we have made special note of previously in this book and in previous books. It is a critical shift in the notion of science that ties its practical side to technology rather than morality, and accounts for the rise of many modern practical, considered neutral but effectively amoral, sciences from Economics to Sociology. Disconnected from Metaphysics and Morals they are engines of error and social destruction. But if subordinated to these higher sciences, of wisdom as the document notes, and calls for, they have their contribution to make to particular truth and useful goodness for mankind. The Council acknowledges the value of their real contribution to human knowledge and welfare in modern times. We have particularly noted the power of this kind of science when empirical knowledge is combined with mathematical (as able to be understood in Aristotelian and Thomist terms).

But the Council goes deeper still referring to questions that stir in the modern soul at the most basic level of science as it is wisdom, metaphysical and moral. Thus, it says: "Nevertheless, in the face of the modern development of the world, the number constantly swells of the people who raise the most basic questions or recognize them with a new sharpness: what is man? What is this sense of sorrow, of evil, of death, which continues to exist despite so much progress? What purpose have these victories purchased at so high a cost? What can man offer to society, what can he expect from it? What follows this earthly life?" (10)

Chapter I of Part I THE DIGNITY OF THE HUMAN PERSON

After briefly outlining the revealed truth about man his origin and how he came to be in his present sinful condition the Council acknowledges the natural pride that man has in his dominant position in the material universe.

"Now, man is not wrong when he regards himself as superior to bodily concerns, and as more than a speck of nature or a nameless constituent of the city of man. For by his interior qualities he outstrips the whole sum of mere things. He plunges into the depths of reality whenever he enters into his own heart; God, Who probes the heart, awaits him there; there he discerns his proper destiny beneath the eyes of God. Thus, when he recognizes in himself a spiritual and immortal soul, he is not being mocked by a fantasy born only of physical or social influences, but is rather laying hold of the proper truth of the matter." (14)

How is it then that man is so beset with profound problems and perplexities? The Council had explained: "Although he was made by God in a state of holiness, from the very onset of his history man abused his liberty, at the urging of the Evil One. Man set himself against God and sought to attain his goal apart from God. Although they knew God, they did not glorify Him as God, but their senseless minds were darkened and they served the creature rather than the Creator. What divine revelation makes known to us agrees with experience." (13)

Then the Council explains how the modern world needs to restore what the "Christian" part of it did not so much lose as throw away: "The intellectual nature of the human person is perfected by wisdom and needs to be, for wisdom gently attracts the mind of man to a quest and a love for what is true and good. Steeped in wisdom. man passes through visible realities to those which are unseen." (15)

Thus, the modern age, though in some respects justifiably proud of its science, has been rendered more unwise than bygone eras, and even compared with parts of the world without the benefit of modern science: "Our era needs such wisdom more than bygone ages if the discoveries made by man are to be further humanized. For the future of the world stands in peril unless wiser men are forthcoming. It should also be pointed out that many nations, poorer in economic goods, are quite rich in wisdom and can offer noteworthy advantages to others." (15)

In the following few paragraphs of Chapter I the Council addresses the human condition according to its practical moral dimension which is operative at the natural/rational level of human nature but made even more visible under the light of Faith. Among the points made: "Hence, the more right conscience holds sway, the more persons and groups turn aside from blind choice and strive to be guided by the objective norms of morality. Conscience frequently errs from invincible ignorance without losing its dignity. The same cannot be said for a man who cares but little for truth and goodness, or for a conscience which by degrees grows practically sightless as a result of habitual sin." (16)

Freedom is intrinsic to the human will. But one needs to carefully distinguish between freedom founded in truth and freedom founded in falsity since will is the appetite for good understood, not just apparent good. This the Council explains in a way that is a presage to the "controversial" declaration on the right of religion freedom: "Only in freedom can man direct himself toward goodness. Our contemporaries make much of this freedom and pursue it eagerly; and rightly to be sure. Often however they foster it perversely as a license for doing whatever pleases them, even if it is evil. For its part, authentic freedom is an exceptional sign of the divine image within man. For God has willed that man remain 'under the control of his own decisions', so that he can seek his Creator spontaneously, and come freely to utter and blissful perfection through loyalty to Him. Hence man's dignity demands that he act according to a knowing and free choice that is personally motivated and prompted from within, not under blind internal impulse nor by mere external pressure". (17)

In paragraph 18 the Council addresses the profound human anxiety about death, which particularly torments the modern mind, for without the natural survival somehow of the spiritual soul nothing to do with human life makes any ultimate sense. The Council puts the Church's position in this regard as follows: "It is in the face of death that the riddle a human existence grows most acute. Not only is man tormented by pain and by the advancing deterioration of his body, but even more so by a dread of perpetual extinction. He rightly follows the intuition of his heart when he abhors and repudiates the utter ruin and total disappearance of his own person. He rebels against death because he bears in himself an eternal seed which cannot be reduced to sheer matter. All the endeavors of technology, though useful in the extreme, cannot calm his anxiety; for prolongation of biological life is unable to satisfy that desire for higher life which is inescapably lodged in his breast."

Finally in this chapter the Council addresses the problem of atheism, which the document has already noted is a strangely unusual feature of the modern age. "Unlike former days, the denial of God or of religion, or the abandonment of them, are no longer unusual and individual occurrences. For today it is not rare for such things to be presented as requirements of scientific progress or of a certain new humanism. In numerous places these views are voiced not only in the teachings of philosophers, but on every side they influence literature, the arts, the interpretation of the humanities and of history and civil laws themselves." (7)

The Council closely examines this profound problem and poses a variety of modes in which it exists today. "The word atheism is applied to phenomena which are quite distinct from one another. For while God is expressly denied by some, others believe that man can assert absolutely nothing about Him. Still others use such a method to scrutinize the question of God as to make it seem devoid of meaning. **Many, unduly transgressing the limits of the positive sciences, contend that everything can be explained by this kind of scientific reasoning alone,** or by contrast, they altogether disallow that there is any absolute truth. Some laud man so extravagantly that their faith in God lapses into a kind of anemia, though they seem more inclined to affirm man than to deny God. Again some form for themselves such a fallacious idea of God that when they repudiate this figment they are by no means rejecting the God of the Gospel. Some never get to the point of raising questions about God, since they seem to experience no religious stirrings nor do they see why they should trouble themselves about religion. Moreover, atheism results not rarely from a violent protest against the evil in this world, or from the absolute character with which certain human values are unduly invested, and which thereby already accords them the stature of God. Modern civilization itself often complicates the approach to God not for any essential reason but because it is so heavily engrossed in earthly affairs." (19) (bold added)

It notes that atheism arises from a variety of causes "including a critical reaction against religious beliefs, and in some places against the Christian religion in particular." We might note that in our view the peculiar vehemence of it in many in modern times evidently stems from the historical rejection of the Catholic Church at the beginning of the modern era. The Council tellingly notes that believing Christians (which must include Catholics) must bear some of the blame for this. Thus, it remarks: "Undeniably, those who wilfully shut out God from their hearts and try to dodge religious questions are not following the dictates of their consciences, and hence are not free of blame; yet believers themselves frequently bear some responsibility for this situation. Hence believers can have more than a little to do with the birth of atheism. To the extent that they neglect their own training in the faith, or teach erroneous doctrine, or are deficient in their religious, moral or social life, they must be said to conceal rather than reveal the authentic face of God and religion." (19)

We may see this as another instance where the rejection of the Church that Christ left as the most precious gift to mankind necessarily brings about evils of an even more powerful kind that in pre-Christian times, as Chesterton noted about the modern sins of cupidity or concupiscence, avarice and lust.

An important and most powerful cause in the modern world known as "Western" is related to its new notion of science that we have dealt with extensively. See what is in bold in the quote from paragraph 19 above. Science in this sense is called "positive" insofar as it does affirm the role of what Aristotle called the particular sciences, natural (but excluding formal and final causes) and mathematical. Its deficiency does not lie in what it posits but in what it mainly negates, which Aristotle and Aquinas call universal science or wisdom, theoretical and practical, Metaphysics and Morals. It is from this fundamental materialist error that atheism follows necessarily.

It is on this purported basis that the conflict between Religion and Science is so strongly argued. Even Catholic modern scientists have difficulty in avoiding the logical conclusion that follows from the very notion of science that is propagated almost universally in the education system of the "West" today. Most religious tend to fall back on the distinction between Faith and Reason, identifying Science, as defined in modern terms, with Reason. This is to fall into another error (Fideism) in order to escape the logical consequence of the first (inevitably leaving oneself open to ridicule by "more rational" scientists). The weakness of the modern educated Catholic in not having the correct notions of philosophy and science as so clearly explained in Aquinas makes for this lamentable failure in rationally defending not just the Faith but also religion itself.

We might note as well that even in ecclesiastical documents there is often not well noted the ambiguity in the use of the word "science" in the modern context. For instance, the word "science" is used extensively in Vatican documents when such use is only valid if we mean it in the traditional sense that does not exclude wisdom, where the modern usage in most cases does, especially when one is speaking of moral science (which as we have seen includes economic and political science).

Why was the name of the "John Paul II Pontifical Institute for Studies on Marriage and the Family" changed to the "John Paul II Theological Institute for Marriage and Family Sciences" without any clarification of how the word "sciences" is being used?

The subject matter is obviously moral if also theological. We might just put it down to ecclesiastical confusion of mind. But there seems some cause for concern that there may be a malign misuse of such ambiguity. Some critics allege that newly appointed officer bearers of the Institute openly express views on contraception and homosexual behaviour that are in flat contradiction of Catholic moral doctrine. St. Thomas classes sins of this kind as unnatural and the most serious of sins against our sexual nature (more directly offending the author of our nature). Such an ambiguous use of the language of science does have practical consequences.

However, we are more directly concerned with the social order that is civil as distinct from domestic. So, we will not go further into the question of marriage and the family, fundamental as it is. Indeed, the Council does not leave out the civil or political order of human association when considering the modern pervasiveness of atheism and its causes. The politico-economic and purely political orders of modern society, to which the social encyclicals, and us, have given such close attention, are most important and powerful factors, not just in regard to the question of social justice (and world peace) but also to the rise of atheism.

Thus, it adds: "Not to be overlooked among the forms of modern atheism is that which anticipates the liberation of man especially through his economic and social emancipation. This form argues that by its nature religion thwarts this liberation by arousing man's hope for a deceptive future life, thereby diverting him from the constructing of the earthly city. Consequently, when the proponents of this doctrine gain governmental power they vigorously fight against religion, and promote atheism by using, especially in the education of youth, those means of pressure which public power has at its disposal." (20)

The focus of our comments in what follows will in fact be on this civil/political aspect of the modern world, though the dimension of the modern world that the Council document sought to reach was at the deepest personal level of the human spirit, faced with ultimate questions of existence itself and the meaning of human life and death. In modern times the philosophical answers to such questions tend to be materialist or time bound, so that even if there is talk of a spiritual side of human nature bodily bodily death is regarded as "final". In the most dominant part of the world this had a particularly atheistic character expressed dramatically in what came to be called "the philosophy of the absurd", a state of mind that was still pervasive at the time of the Council.

There is a difference between the approach of the Catholic Church after and before the Council but it will be seen in what we examine in the second part of the document *Gaudium et spes* that it is not such that it constitutes a discontinuity with social doctrine in the documents of the earlier magisterium – and the Council and subsequent popes repeatedly assert this.

In the last paragraph of Chapter I of Part I the Council discloses what is the only answer to the deep questions and problems faced by Man at all times and therefore "in the world of today". It has said: "The remedy which must be applied to atheism, however, is to be sought in a proper presentation of the Church's teaching as well as in the integral life of the Church and her members." (21)

So, we set out this central paragraph (22) in full both in English and in Latin. Unfortunately, the paragraph has in our view been the occasion for a misunderstanding and widespread misrepresentation of the relation between grace and human nature which we can associate with the *nouvelle theologie* of de Lubac and his many followers, some of whom describe themselves as "postmodern Augustinian Thomists", truer followers of Aquinas than those labelled as "neo-Thomists", such as Garrigou-Lagrange. We have dealt with this most influential misinterpretation in our book "Thomist Tradition: Avoiding Scylla and Charybdis", where we place it in the category of the error of Fideism or Supernaturalism described so clearly by Pope Saint Paul VI in *Lumen ecclesiae.*

As we see it the occasion for the error is in fact the misconception brought into modern thinking from the distorted notion of science which brings about a notion of nature that is decidedly materialistic and this excludes its extension to spiritual nature as was done by Boethius. This exclusion of itself precludes any proper understanding of human nature according to its spiritual soul and hence all metaphysical discussion of immortal life, let alone of the existence of angelic life. The notion of God and eternal life in such a context becomes completely unintelligible.

So it is that we can see that de Lubac, being a Jesuit, with this order's immersion in modern science – admittedly with the best of intentions to show that the modern "conversion" to the quasi-religion of modern science as the sole rule of human reason could be made compatible with the Catholic Faith – acquired a notion of human nature that was focused on the physical and simply could not accommodate the more proper notion that it was in its spiritual "dimension" metaphysical. It is this very narrow physicalist notion of human nature that is naturalistic and secularist, something that de Lubac it seems mistakenly thought the notion of "pure nature" necessarily implied.

There were of course many other features of the notion of nature from Aristotelian philosophy and Aquinas's use of it in the narrow and even strict sense where appropriate. For the notion of nature did first come from what is found (*natus*) in the physical order of reality, our intellectual knowledge being in its beginning dependent on sense knowledge. But Aristotle successfully transcended the sensible order of our knowledge in his *Peri psyche, De anima* in the language of Aquinas, which evidently very few modern Catholic theologians are familiar with, though St Thomas's commentary on it is probably his finest.

On top of that there are difficulties that one encounters in the interpretation of St. Thomas's use of the word "natural" in a supernatural context. The division of potency into natural and obediential is a particular difficulty, which can only be addressed if nature is taken in a spiritual sense. But as we see it the fundamental problem comes from one's thinking, philosophical and theological, being too much infected with how modern science views nature and accordingly human nature.

Here we are only concerned with a correct interpretation of paragraph 22. The English translation overall as usual is not that good. We only refer back to paragraph 2 where *Malignus* is trans-

lated as "personified evil" when it clearly means an actual evil
person, applied customarily to the Devil (note the translation of
the same word in paragraph 13). There is no such thing as personified evil, which makes evil an abstraction that has no "force".
The expression "the truth is that" at the very beginning of paragraph 22 is better translated by "in truth" or "in fact" But we will
let this sort of loose translation pass.

What is important to note about the first sentence is that it is
not talking about the nature or substantial form of man but the
whole mystery of that human nature being taken up into the divine company of the Trinity, so that any natural end or happiness
that necessarily pertains to such natural form becomes graced
with a supernatural end or happiness (beatific vision). As the
document says: "human nature as He assumed it was not annulled, by that very fact it has been raised up to a divine dignity
in our respect too". It also speaks of a union, not a hegelian type
of cancellation of human nature by divine nature or our participation in it by grace. "For by His incarnation the Son of God has
united Himself in some fashion with every man. He worked with
human hands, He thought with a human mind, acted by human
choice and loved with a human heart. Born of the Virgin Mary,
He has truly been made one of us, like us in all things except sin."

The text also says the Christ is "the perfect man". How purely
human can you get? It is Christ as man who died on the cross
and willed by his human freewill to do so. There is of course only
one divine person who is Christ, and his human will is completely in accord with his divine will, but Christ is both man and God.

All this de Lubac manages to blur because of his too gross conception of "pure nature". His followers, particularly in the English-speaking world, are not helped by the standard English translations. *clarescit* is better translated as "has truly become clear". What happened to *vere*? But there is enough in the English translation to show up the error of thinking of de Lubac.

"22. The truth is that only in the mystery of the incarnate Word does the mystery of man take on light. For Adam, the first man, was a figure of Him Who was to come, namely Christ the Lord. Christ, the final Adam, by the revelation of the mystery of the Father and His love, fully reveals man to man himself and makes his supreme calling clear. It is not surprising, then, that in Him all the aforementioned truths find their root and attain their crown.

He Who is 'the image of the invisible God' (Col. 1:15), is Himself the perfect man. To the sons of Adam He restores the divine likeness which had been disfigured from the first sin onward. Since human nature as He assumed it was not annulled, by that very fact it has been raised up to a divine dignity in our respect too. For by His incarnation the Son of God has united Himself in some fashion with every man. He worked with human hands, He thought with a human mind, acted by human choice and loved with a human heart. Born of the Virgin Mary, He has truly been made one of us, like us in all things except sin.

As an innocent lamb He merited for us life by the free shedding of His own blood. In Him God reconciled us to Himself and among ourselves; from bondage to the devil and sin He delivered us, so that each one of us can say with the Apostle: The Son of

God 'loved me and gave Himself up for me' (Gal. 2:20). By suffering for us He not only provided us with an example for our imitation, He blazed a trail, and if we follow it, life and death are made holy and take on a new meaning.

The Christian man, conformed to the likeness of that Son Who is the firstborn of many brothers, received 'the first-fruits of the Spirit' (Rom. 8:23) by which he becomes capable of discharging the new law of love. Through this Spirit, who is 'the pledge of our inheritance' (Eph. 1:14), the whole man is renewed from within, even to the achievement of 'the redemption of the body' (Rom. 8:23): 'If the Spirit of him who raised Jesus from the death dwells in you, then he who raised Jesus Christ from the dead will also bring to life your mortal bodies because of his Spirit who dwells in you' (Rom. 8:11). Pressing upon the Christian to be sure, are the need and the duty to battle against evil through manifold tribulations and even to suffer death. But, linked with the paschal mystery and patterned on the dying Christ, he will hasten forward to resurrection in the strength which comes from hope.

All this holds true not only for Christians, but for all men of good will in whose hearts grace works in an unseen way. For, since Christ died for all men, and since the ultimate vocation of man is in fact one, and divine, we ought to believe that the Holy Spirit in a manner known only to God offers to every man the possibility of being associated with this paschal mystery.

Such is the mystery of man, and it is a great one, as seen by believers in the light of Christian revelation. Through Christ and in Christ, the riddles of sorrow and death grow meaningful. Apart from His Gospel, they overwhelm us. Christ has risen, destroying death by His death; He has lavished life upon us so that, as sons in the Son, we can cry out in the Spirit; Abba, Father".

22.*De Christo Novo Homine.*

Reapse nonnisi in mysterio Verbi incarnati mysterium hominis vere clarescit. Adam enim, primus homo, erat figura futuri, scilicet Christi Domini. Christus, novissimus Adam, in ipsa revelatione mysterii Patris Eiusque amoris, hominem ipsi homini plene manifestat eique altissimam eius vocationem patefacit. Nil igitur mirum in Eo praedictas veritates suum invenire fontem atque attingere fastigium.

Qui est "imago Dei invisibilis" (Col 1,15), Ipse est homo perfectus, qui Adae filiis similitudinem divinam, inde a primo peccato deformatam, restituit. Cum in Eo natura humana assumpta, non perempta sit, eo ipso etiam in nobis ad sublimem dignitatem evecta est. Ipse enim, Filius Dei, incarnatione sua cum omni homine quodammodo Se univit. Humanis manibus opus fecit, humana mente cogitavit, humana voluntate egit (31), humano corde dilexit. Natus de Maria Virgine, vere unus ex nostris factus est, in omnibus nobis similis excepto peccato.

Agnus innocens, sanguine suo libere effuso, vitam nobis meruit, in Ipsoque Deus nos Sibi et inter nos reconciliavit et a servitute diaboli ac peccati eripuit, ita ut unusquisque nostrum cum Apostolo dicere possit: Filius Dei "dilexit me et tradidit semetipsum pro me" (Gal 2,20). Pro nobis patiendo non solummodo exemplum prae-

buit ut sequamur vestigia Eius, sed et viam instauravit, quam dum sequimur, vita et mors sanctificantur novumque sensum accipiunt.

Christianus autem homo, conformis imagini Filii factus qui est Primogenitus in multis fratribus, "primitias Spiritus" (Rom 8,23) accipit, quibus capax fit legem novam amoris adimplendi. Per hunc Spiritum, qui est "pignus hereditatis" (Eph 1,14), totus homo interius restauratur, usque ad "redemptionem corporis" (Rom 8,23): "Si Spiritus Eius, qui suscitavit Iesum a mortuis, habitat in vobis: qui suscitavit Iesum Christum a mortuis, vivificabit et mortalia corpora vestra, propter inhabitantem Spiritum eius in vobis" (Rom 8,11). Christianum certe urgent necessitas et officium contra malum per multas tribulationes certandi necnon mortem patiendi; sed mysterio paschali consociatus, Christi morti configuratus, ad resurrectionem spe roboratus occurret.

Quod non tantum pro christifidelibus valet, sed et pro omnibus hominibus bonae voluntatis in quorum corde gratia invisibili modo operatur. Cum enim pro omnibus mortuus sit Christus cumque vocatio hominis ultima revera una sit, scilicet divina, tenere debemus Spiritum Sanctum cunctis possibilitatem offerre ut, modo Deo cognito, huic paschali mysterio consocientur.

Tale et tantum est hominis mysterium, quod per Revelationem christianam credentibus illucescit. Per Christum et in Christo, igitur, illuminatur aenigma doloris et mortis, quod extra Eius Evangelium nos obruit. Christus resurrexit, morte sua mortem destruens, vitamque nobis largitus est ut, filii in Filio, clamemus in Spiritu: Abba, Pater!

But what we want to take away from this Chapter I of Part I is that the gospel message is not just for Catholics, or those who profess the Christian name (everyone who says Lord, Lord) but for all mankind; grace is meant to be given to human nature as such, "pure nature", as this paragraph ending the Chapter entitled THE DIGNITY OF THE HUMAN PERSON makes clear. "All this holds true not only for Christians, but for all men of good will in whose hearts grace works in an unseen way. For, since Christ died for all men, and since the ultimate vocation of man is in fact one, and divine, we ought to believe that the Holy Spirit in a manner known only to God offers to every man the possibility of being associated with this paschal mystery."

This reaching out to everyman seems to render somewhat "old" the approach that focused on that part of the world that had a close connection with Christian civilisation, in its flowering in medieval times and in its decline in modern. But that impression is a misreading of the history of Catholic Christianity, which becomes clearer when we deal with the process of evangelisation that has taken place since the beginning of the history of the Church as a supernatural association (Body of Christ) whereby the many natural communities are meant to become perfect (as the Father is perfect) and will be made one, as the Father Son and Holy Spirit are one.

Here again we are looking at this mainly from the angle of reason and human association as it is natural and political. So let us move on to examine Chapter II of Part I of *Gaudium et spes.*

Chapter II of Part I: The Community of Mankind

Here we move to the second chapter of Part I of the Council document where it takes into account the fact that, though the human person is necessarily an individual and a being of spiritual soul and thus a creature of such nobility that he (and she) transcends all material nature he is not an isolated individual nor was he created so. St. Thomas puts it that the person is that which is most perfect in all nature but the community condition of human life is clearly brought out. This excellence applies to human nature as such, so that every individual human person is superior to the particular natural social orders of family and civil society. It belongs to their common goods to respect the higher good of individuals as persons. This is also the basis of the principle of subsidiarity whereby the great association exists to supply for what the lesser association cannot do of itself.

The Council document clearly makes this point later when speaking about the politico-economic order: 63. *Etiam in vita oeconomica-sociali personae humanae dignitas eiusque integra vocatio, totiusque societatis bonum, honoranda atque promovenda sunt. Homo enim totius vitae oeconomicae-socialis auctor, centrum et finis est* . "In the economic and social realms, too, the dignity and complete vocation of the human person and the welfare of society as a whole are to be respected and promoted. For man is the source, the center, and the purpose of all economic and social life." Yet an individualistic interpretation of this is to be carefully avoided. It is entrenched in the modern ideology of

Liberalism which, however, modern man blindly reacts to it in taking a collectivist social position.

We might just note that the translation in paragraph 63 is defective, as we will note when we come to the translation of OECONOMICA-SOCIALI in Part II. For the hyphen is ignored and illegitimately substituted by "and". But what is said about the socio-economic order clearly applies to the whole social order.

Here, however, we enter upon a feature of human existence that is mostly overlooked when we concentrate upon man and his social existence exclusive of the rest of nature, or only insofar as he dominates it. The human person, as we have noted, belongs to a universal community that is the whole of creation which includes pure spirits above and purely material things below. Being of spiritual substantial form, however, each person whether angel or man is made in the image of God and is perfectly free under God. God is his (or her) immediate common good.

However, the individual human person belongs in this community and is part of it as an order created by God which so far as the material or physical universe is concerned is made up of individuals having a common nature (species). In the concrete that is what is signified by the word "mankind", Latin *genus humanum*. One needs to be careful here with the use of "humanity" as this signifies the same as humanness, the abstract form of man. It is good in the concrete that is the object of love. As Chesterton has remarked there can be many who say they love humanity but hate their neighbour. He also pointed out the meaning of humanity in modern times is likely to be nothing but the love of oneself universalised. That is the sort of thing that ideologies deal with.

Man is in a peculiar position; for human nature is a complex of spiritual form and material body. Thus, in one respect (as bodily) each man (and woman, which kind of complementarity has its own complication) man (homo) is part of the physical universe, but in the other respect (as spiritual) he is part of the spiritual created order. The whole created order of things has its own unity, goodness and beauty and the human person both individually and community wise is but part of the whole. The matter is difficult to categorise but we might say that by his material or bodily existence man is subordinated to the whole but so far as his spiritual or personal existence is concerned, it is a matter of coordination with the other persons in the whole. This problem is transcended however at the supernatural level so that we need not concern ourselves more with it.

We are concerned here only generally with the significance of man's place (as an individual person) in the whole created order. By virtue of having free will he is not subject to any other creature except as it acts by the authority of the Creator. That is set out in the natural moral order and God has so arranged this that subordination to this order constitutes the perfection of the individual person's freedom in that it is what he naturally/morally (as rational/virtuous) sees as his own good and freely wills. The only true slavery results from sin. St. Augustine remarks that a person has as many slave masters as he has vices.

With that understood, be it inadequately, we can say it is not simply the human person as individual that is what is most perfect in the world of nature but the community of mankind, taken not collectively, but distributively; every man (and woman). Thus, each man has a love of his neighbour that flows out of his love of God. But he also has an affinity with every other thing in creation. And this applies not only at the supernatural level but also at the natural level. There is no opposition between the natural and supernatural; indeed the lower is in some way a reflection of the higher and indeed the highest divine level of being.

What becomes a bit harder to appreciate is that proportionately this applies even to the lowest material order of existence and impinges upon our understanding of the end of the world. Even though the physical universe is not eternal or everlasting but temporal and temporary, as an order of being it ought not to be conceived as being totally annihilated at the end of time. This problem is highlighted in the fate of man, or more properly, his happiness even in natural terms. As Aristotle points out, the concept of happiness requires that there be no possibility of change. But how are we to conceive a state which includes matter, as the human body must, unless it is subject to change?

We know from revelation that the human body, which is naturally subject to constant change will be part of the nature of man even in the most godlike state of supernatural happiness or beatitude. One does not need to speculate about whether natural happiness would necessarily involve a praeter-natural preservation of the body. But the scriptures tell us of a new heaven and a new earth. It seems that this means the preservation of matter at least so far as it would be necessary for human bodily existence.

We know from Scripture that there will be no marriage. Presumably there would be no need for civil rule, though St. Thomas seems to argue there would have existed in the state of original innocence or justice civil society and presumably domestic. However, we do not need to solve these matters.

All that we wish to bring out here is the relation of individual human persons to the rest of creation but especially with regard to the community of mankind. All nature below man is for his use, but not absolutely taken as we have discussed. The natural moral order applies to this use, so that it must be according to reason, both human and divine. Moreover, as all things created have been created out of divine love so too the lowest things ought to be treated with loving care.

This is something that Pope Francis, inspired by Saint Francis of Assisi, has brought out so powerfully in his encyclical *Laudato si*, which he pointedly described as a social encyclical, thus expanding the scope of the subject matter according to the change of focus of Vatican II. Closer to our subject is man's relationship to his fellow human beings which the pope turned to in his second social encyclical *Fratelli tutti*. We will come to these two documents shortly.

Individual human persons have an affinity with other creatures that transcends the limits of the two natural societies of the family and the State. The focus in modern times has been on the last, as if it were the highest, thereby tending to ignore the more fundamental community of the family and the most fundamental natural community of what we might call love of neighbour, without at this stage regarding it as raised to the supernatural level by Christ. This last is first in the order of reality and rationality.

Once again, we must remember that grace does not annul the natural moral order, as the Council document explicitly says. It simply raises human personal life to a higher level of unity and community. We do not wish to enter too much into the theological order. But as we see it, at the divine level for us (by grace) we as individual persons approach as far as possible the divine unity which is as well a community. The Council of course is more focused on this most exalted level of our life and destiny, without neglecting the natural order of creation, to which the participation in divine life has been added in that spiritual part that is obedientially open to it.

With regard to the place of St. Thomas Aquinas in all this it is worth noting that he and St. Francis of Assisi were of one mind and heart when it comes to emphasising the importance of the created material or physical order of things in the praise of God. This was keenly felt by G K Chesterton who wrote marvellously on both saints. Evidently, at first he was more enamoured of Francis than Thomas. But later he came to have an equal devotion to Thomas, and remarked that if we gave to him the customary medieval title the most appropriate would be "St. Thomas of the Creator". Then there is the quote I have used in the front of my book "Economic Science and Saint Thomas Aquinas": "Whilst the two men were a contrast in almost every feature, they were really doing the same thing. One of them was doing it in the world of the mind and the other in the world of the worldly ... it was in every sense a movement of enlargement, always moving towards greater light and even greater liberty".

Hopefully, with this prefatory explanation we can understand how the "new" relationship to the modern world may be understood as different from the "old" and yet following intrinsically from it. The document confirms this in the first paragraph of chapter II: "23. Since the recent documents of the Church's teaching authority have dealt at considerable length with Christian doctrine about human society, this council is merely going to call to mind some of the more basic truths, treating their foundations under the light of revelation. Then it will dwell more at length on certain of their implications having special significance for our day."

These implications are dealt with in Part II where we will concentrate on those that are concerned with the politico-economic, referred to at times as simply "economic", and the political, seeing that is where the primary focus of the earlier social encyclicals, for the reasons given, tended to be.

The consideration of these factors of modern society still contain what is of major concern to all mankind of modern times. But as indicated above the Council broadened the scope and brought into focus the state of the whole world which is in need, not just within that part of the world that had benefited even materially from Christian preaching of the gospel and the charity of the faithful. The power even in material terms of this inheritance was great despite the great abuses that had followed from wholesale rejection of the Faith, most fiercely and destructively in the theory and practice of the ideology of Communism, but also by a more gradual erosion from the theory and practice of Liberalism/Capitalism.

Even when the latter had "progressed", slowly at first but with accelerating speed, to an evident state of social/moral disintegration and political corruption it could still claim superiority over the alternative ideological system. But this became harder and harder to justify as the effects of the sins of injustice in the system were able to be targeted by its opponent ideologues. But we will say more on this below.

For present purposes we stay with the general focus of the document. We will make a few further comments and finish up quoting the final paragraph (32) in which what is contained in this Chapter II of Part I is summed up.

The community of mankind that is in question (from the point of view of reason) is the natural community that transcends the civil order and is governed by what we call personal morality, whose common good is God. The governing body of the civil community has no superiority at this personal level, not even over its own citizens, let alone other persons. The inter-personal relations of men and women therefore are governed by moral obligations. The civil government is not independent of this moral order but must make its laws and policies in accordance with the requirements of the natural moral order, for Christians summed up in the Ten Commandments. It is the Church that has the authority to declare and delimit what is contained in this order of human life and behaviour. The civil government can only add to or further determine what is established under the natural moral law. This is what is called positive law.

The same applies to relations between groups of civil societies, or what today we call international relations. From a natural and human point of view the only viable means of maintaining peace seems to be by agreements or treaties. But if they are broken, up to quite recent times there has been no means of making persons of other nations or nations themselves keep to their agreements than by the exercise of superior force by one nation or group of nations. There seems to be a need for a supra-national association even from a natural/rational point of view. But here, the individualist character of Liberalist ideology seems stronger still. Each nation is unwilling to sacrifice its "national interest" to some perceived "common interest". That would be to surrender its sovereignty.

There are many issues at this level of human association and the Council addresses some of them. But we will not comment on them further, except to say that if all persons, though perfectly free, were perfectly rational and therefore virtuous, there would be no problem at whatever order of association man was engaged in. The world would be peaceful and everyone naturally happy because just. The problem only arises if this natural order is not adhered to, which is clearly the case. The need for a police force as we have seen comes about only because some men are not just. The need is greatly enhanced of course where there is some sort of intrinsic inclination in men (and women) to do evil, especially to others. That is where the supernatural order (because of original sin) comes into play. There is no rational explanation for the fact that men prefer war to peace.

The main thing we wished to bring out in regard to this Chapter of Part I is the bond that exists between all men and women, not just at the particular domestic and civil levels but also universally so that even in the natural order there is a bond of unity whereby we can speak of mankind as one. We tend to speak of that deepest level of unity in terms of family, indeed of all being descended from one father (and mother) which we naturally are. This is raised to an infinitely higher level in the supernatural order with God as Our Father (which is intended to include the notion of Our Mother as well).

We do not see the need to comment on the other two chapters of Part I so we can end by quoting the last paragraph in Chapter II, which brings out the main point we refer to.

"32. As God did not create man for life in isolation, but for the formation of social unity, so also 'it has pleased God to make men holy and save them not merely as individuals, without bond or link between them, but by making them into a single people, a people which acknowledges Him in truth and serves Him in holiness.' (13) So from the beginning of salvation history He has chosen men not just as individuals but as members of a certain community. Revealing His mind to them, God called these chosen ones 'His people' (Ex. 3:7-12), and even made a covenant with them on Sinai. (14)

This communitarian character is developed and consummated in the work of Jesus Christ. For the very Word made flesh willed to share in the human fellowship. He was present at the wedding of Cana, visited the house of Zacchaeus, ate with publicans and sinners. He revealed the love of the Father and the sublime vocation of man in terms of the most common of social realities and by making use of the speech and the imagery of plain everyday life. Willingly obeying the laws of his country He sanctified those human ties, especially family ones, which are the source of social structures. He chose to lead the life proper to an artisan of His time and place.

In His preaching He clearly taught the sons of God to treat one another as brothers. In His prayers He pleaded that all His disciples might be 'one.' Indeed as the redeemer of all, He offered Himself for all even to point of death. 'Greater love than this no one has, that one lay down his life for his friends' (John 15:13). He commanded His Apostles to preach to all peoples the Gospel's message that the human race was to become the Family of God, in which the fullness of the Law would be love.

As the firstborn of many brethren and by the giving of His Spirit, He founded after His death and resurrection a new brotherly community composed of all those who receive Him in faith and in love. This He did through His Body, which is the Church. There everyone, as members one of the other, would render mutual service according to the different gifts bestowed on each.

This solidarity must be constantly increased until that day on which it will be brought to perfection. Then, saved by grace, men will offer flawless glory to God as a family beloved of God and of Christ their Brother."

It is the full development of this communitarian character (or catholic solidarity) that is taken up by the social encyclicals following the Council.

Part II

As indicated, we mean to comment mainly on chapters III and IV of this second part of the Council document as these are most closely connected to the previous social encyclicals. They focus on the politico-economic and purely political aspects of civil society. The three other chapters, I, II and V, are part of the broadening of the scope of the Church's concern. They focus on the other natural social order of the family and on the civil community as a whole, in all its aspects, which we may call cultural in general, and finally on the relation of particular civil communities to mankind as a whole, which as we have seen may be looked upon a the most universal community of creation of which man is the highest part of the physical universe.

We will not spend much time with Chapter I as it takes us into another area of study, domestic ethics, which although civil society is intimately connected with it needs a separate treatment. The central issue of modern times of contraception by way of "the pill" was left by the Council to be resolved by Pope Saint Paul VI which he did in the 1968 encyclical *Humanae vitae*. The Council did but confirm previous teaching on marriage and the family and we simply give two quotations to show this.

"By their very nature, the institution of matrimony itself and conjugal love are ordained for the procreation and education of children, and find in them their ultimate crown. Thus a man and a woman, who by their compact of conjugal love 'are no longer two, but one flesh' (Matt. 19:ff), render mutual help and service to each other through an intimate union of their persons and of their actions. Through this union they experience the meaning of their oneness and attain to it with growing perfection day by day. As a mutual gift of two persons, this intimate union and the good of the children impose total fidelity on the spouses and argue for an unbreakable oneness between them." (48)

"50. Marriage and conjugal love are by their nature ordained toward the begetting and educating of children. Children are really the supreme gift of marriage and contribute very substantially to the welfare of their parents. The God Himself Who said, 'it is not good for man to be alone' (Gen. 2:18) and 'Who made man from the beginning male and female' (Matt. 19:4), wishing to share with man a certain special participation in His own creative work, blessed male and female, saying: 'Increase and multiply' (Gen. 1:28). Hence, while not making the other purposes of matrimony of less account, the true practice of conjugal love, and the whole meaning of the family life which results from it, have this aim: that the couple be ready with stout hearts to cooperate with the love of the Creator and the Savior Who through them will enlarge and enrich His own family day by day.

Parents should regard as their proper mission the task of transmitting human life and educating those to whom it has been transmitted. They should realize that they are thereby cooperators with the love of God the Creator, and are, so to speak, the interpreters of that love."

How any Catholic can reconcile support for "same sex marriage" with the definitive statements of the Council on the matter can only be put down to ignorance, which is all but impossible to regard as invincible. What do they think the word "matrimony" is derived from?The most obvious innovation in the document *Gaudium et spes* was the Chapter on Culture. This was a concept apparently taken from the modern science of Anthropology but given a more philosophical/theological sense so as to apply generally to the understanding of human life as a whole. We may compare this with the way the concept of development was used by Pope Saint Paul VI in the social encyclical *Populorum progressio,* issued almost immediately after the Council in 1967, evidently taking the concept of development from the new science of Economics, but applying it to the development of the whole man at all levels of human social life.

Evidently the usage comes from the felt need to speak to the modern world in language it may understand. There is a risk in adopting this approach but apparently the Council and Pope Saint Paul VI felt it was one worth taking.

In order to understand this, however, let us use an analysis of the levels of human life we have given in regard to the civil community, comparing it to the four aspects of human life in the individual person. As we have noted there are three basic levels, which we may call vegetative, animal and properly human or intellectual/rational, the lower two levels being had in common firstly with plant life and then animal life. It is to be noted carefully though that there is only one actually human life in question (whose one vital principle is the spiritual soul), the two lower levels being only virtually present in the human being, if requiring the co-operation of bodily organs. The highest level, intellectual, depends objectively on the lower but not subjectively; that is, there is no bodily organ for the intellect, but it depends for its operation in this life on being provided with sensible objects from which its objects are drawn (abstracted). This is all masterfully explained by Aquinas in his commentary on Aristotle's *De anima*.

As we have seen, these levels can be subdivided in different ways. For instance, there are two sub-levels of the perfect animal, seen in the functions of the imagination as a higher internal sense and sight as the highest of the external senses. We have noted how the intellect is able to use the imagination in a special way so that in man it is called creative. That is the basis of the arts and it plays an important role in the science of Mathematics. But the most significant subdivision is at the intellectual level, where will comes into the picture and provides the basis of the distinction between understanding theoretical truth (metaphysics mathematics and physics) and practical truth (morals and technics). Logic, as Boethius explains, is not so much a science as the instrument of science.

We have thus used a fourfold division for human life and behaviour, unconscious life (automatic), sense life (spontaneous), intellectual life (theoretical science and natural wisdom) and voluntary life, or practical wisdom and science (free and deliberate). Applying those divisions to the civil order we have used the terms, economic, recreational, cultural and political to refer to these four orders. Cultural is used here specially to refer to the highest intellectual consideration of things in all four aspects. It is used in the Council document to refer to the life and activity of human beings, socially considered, as a general term of the process of development of human life over time, like growth, progression, and development in regard to the individual. As noted, the actual modern use of the word culture seems to have come into modern thought from the special study of the intermediate, ethno-tribal, level of human social life.

It is important to note that the first three aspects are in what we call the natural studies of human life and being. That is to say they are theoretical sciences in Aristotle's classification, which was adopted by Aquinas and forms the background to much of the language of science in magisterial documents. But in regard to the "science" of human nature it is critical that we distinguish the highest spiritual level from the lower material levels. In regard to the highest, "nature" has to accommodate the spiritual order of reality and accordingly the special study of this spiritual order is metaphysical not purely physical, as are the two lower levels. This becomes somewhat difficult to deal with at the higher level of animal life in man because of its immediate subjection to the control of the intellect.

Thus, Aquinas insists along with Aristotle that the study of Mathematics, though an intellectual and rational one has to "terminate" in the imagination. On the other hand, the natural/physical sciences have to terminate in the external senses and sense consciousness. Modern scientists, including Catholics unfamiliar with the works of Aquinas in these areas do not know how to deal with these distinctions, with the distinct risk of falling into a gross sensist interpretation of both natural science and a finer imaginative interpretation of Mathematics when they are studying these sciences in regard to human life. Thus, for instance, modern experimental psychology almost inevitably is underpinned by philosophical materialism. The Council does not go into these thomist details but leaves them understandably to Catholic philosophers and theologians who unfortunately in recent times have almost all fallen down on this job.

But the distinction between the theoretical and practical kinds of sciences, which founds the distinction between metaphysics and morals, and mathematics and physics and technics, is of the utmost importance. For it demands that primary place be given in practical sciences to Ethics, and not to Technical studies. Without understanding this many modern thinkers and scientists readily fall into pairing Science with Technology, simply reinforcing the material(ist) focus. More critical in this context is the fact that strictly speaking Politics (and politico-economics) is a moral science of which the principal practical virtue is political prudence, though materially it needs the expertise of various arts that are technical in a higher sense than we are accustomed to. This we have explained at great length in our previous books. Here again the Council could not have gone into these details though it points generally to the necessary distinctions in various places.

One may appreciate how such a mixed way of using a word like culture can become quite confusing, especially if the translation is not all that carefully done. It is difficult to detach this lower level origin from the purely spiritual nature of the human soul where culture is most properly situated. Anthropology is mainly a study of "primitive" societies that is of the association of peoples that have not reached a properly civilised state as understood by Aristotle, living at the tribal or village stage of social life intermediate between that of the family and the civil community. These intermediate stages can exist separately but continue to exist virtually within the civil community (Aristotle's *polis* or city). They readily remain the focus of the new sciences of culture considered from a material point of view. Within a civil community these new experimental studies have generally been placed with the name of Sociology.

The Council does make note, what some might regard as passing note, of the nuances involved but there is a distinct risk that in naming these new studies as new sciences, they can tend to be regarded as legitimately autonomous sciences, when from an Aristotelian and Thomist point of view they are according to their objects but partial sciences. True enough, as we have discussed earlier, the turn to a proper consideration of the empirical aspect of such studies was a correction of the pre-modern fault of its neglect, which made the previous methods of natural science not just inadequate but, in many cases, false.

But this correction, if taken on its own, did not make them complete natural sciences, and less so properly practical sciences. Sociology as conceived in modern times is an experimental science, like Psychology, which without a proper consideration of natural formal and final causes inevitably leads its proponents to indulge in general theories that are distortions of the nature of human social life and behaviour. Furthermore, without being subordinated to metaphysical and moral principles these modern sciences fall not just into falsity but also into absurdity.

This is a subject that needs much fuller treatment than we can give it here. But the statements in the Council document as to the value of these modern "sciences" have to be read as recognising their material worth, which nonetheless is an important part of the understanding of the human individual and social "psyche" that was lacking before in the too formalistic method of these studies. We should appreciate, however, that it was not a basic fault in Aristotle, though the empirical basis of his science was in many cases limited, but a deficiency in the post Aristotelian study of natural science and also human science (taken even in regard to its moral character). It may be conceded that the "empirical" or factual evidence relied on in Aristotle in some important cases needed to be corrected (as for instance with regard to the development of the human foetus).

The point of the Council's acknowledgement of man's debt to the genuine achievements of modern scientific (empirical) research is well taken. The problem lies in the impression taken by many wishing to defend modern science and its scientific method even in its mistaken philosophical foundations. There is no justification for the proponents of the new sciences rejecting the old fundamental formal and final principles, especially expressed in the old wisdoms. The mathematical science of Geometry for instance depends in its first principles or axioms on metaphysical principles. The whole is greater than its own part is a metaphysical principle common to all reality, but as Aristotle explains, it is used in Geometry as contracted to quantity. To ignore or deny this metaphysical basis of all particular sciences is to descend into a philosophy of pure scepticism, which is common today. So too the desire for material goods in Economics is but a contraction of the desire for good itself. To empty the concept of good or value, or utility, of its objective meaning, as is done in micro economic theory today is to fall into the fallacy and even absurdity of relativism.

What we have said above about the general or formal part of the notion of culture and its more empirical or material sense may be seen put in paragraph 53. We may see how the more concrete realisation of the concept of culture does tend to be expressed in terms of the ethnic and sociological elements in particular societies. Just as Aristotle could discuss the form of civil society as one and universal, so he appreciated that it had to be abstracted from a multitude of particular kinds of civil communities. Unity does not deny diversity; in living things it demands it. Yet this diversity in the concrete does not invalidate the abstract unity of the concept of culture itself, no more than the great diversity of natures in the physical universe prevents us from having a concept of nature as such.

This is how the Council deals with the concept of culture:

"53. Man comes to a true and full humanity only through culture, that is through the cultivation of the goods and values of nature. Wherever human life is involved, therefore, nature and culture are quite intimately connected one with the other.

The word 'culture' in its general sense indicates everything whereby man develops and perfects his many bodily and spiritual qualities; he strives by his knowledge and his labor, to bring the world itself under his control. He renders social life more human both in the family and the civic community, through improvement of customs and institutions. Throughout the course of time he expresses, communicates and conserves in his works, great spiritual experiences and desires, that they might be of advantage to the progress of many, even of the whole human family."

Aristotle is said to have studied 150 kinds of political constitutions (including the Constitution of Athens) and no doubt his science of Politics would have been improved if he had studied more. That is the advantage modern research has over ancient. Its disadvantage in too many cases is that it cannot define what it is studying, or perhaps it is better to say it does not admit the need to. So, this state of foolishness leaves many a researcher subject to the sophistry of ideologues.

Paragraph 53 continues: "Thence it follows that human culture has necessarily a historical and social aspect and the word 'culture' also often assumes a sociological and ethnological sense. According to this sense we speak of a plurality of cultures. Different styles of life and multiple scales of values arise from the diverse manner of using things, of laboring, of expressing oneself, of practicing religion, of forming customs, of establishing laws and juridic institutions, of cultivating the sciences, the arts and beauty. Thus the customs handed down to it form the patrimony proper to each human community. It is also in this way that there is formed the definite, historical milieu which enfolds the man of every nation and age and from which he draws the values which permit him to promote civilization."

In paragraph 54 the Council document brings out the immense scope of the diversity of cultures over time and space so that the study of culture and society has reached a new level unimagined to previous generations. Nonetheless the goodness of each particular culture can be judged by the extent to which it measures up to the intelligible "form" of the meaning of culture we have. The new age of human history is not to be taken as if it has resulted in a new notion of humanity, as is the fashion today in talk about transhumanism.

"54. The circumstances of the life of modern man have been so profoundly changed in their social and cultural aspects, that we can speak of a new age of human history. New ways are open, therefore, for the perfection and the further extension of culture. These ways have been prepared by the enormous growth of natural, human and social sciences, by technical progress, and advances in developing and organizing means whereby men can communicate with one another. Hence the culture of today possesses particular characteristics: sciences which are called exact greatly develop critical judgment; the more recent psychological studies more profoundly explain human activity; historical studies make it much easier to see things in their mutable and evolutionary aspects, customs and usages are becoming more and more uniform; industrialization, urbanization, and other causes which promote community living create a mass-culture from which are born new ways of thinking, acting and making use of leisure. The increase of commerce between the various nations and human groups opens more widely to all the treasures of different civilizations and thus little by little, there develops a more universal form of human culture, which better promotes and expresses the unity of the human race to the degree that it preserves the particular aspects of the different civilizations."

Though the Council does laud the contribution of these new "sciences" it does point to what is a danger in their promotion.

"Indeed, today's progress in science and technology can foster a certain exclusive emphasis on observable data, and an agnosticism about everything else. For the methods of investigation which these sciences use can be wrongly considered as the supreme rule of seeking the whole truth. By virtue of their methods these sciences cannot penetrate to the intimate notion of things. Indeed, the danger is present that man, confiding too much in the discoveries of today, may think that he is sufficient unto himself and no longer seek the higher things." (57)

In my view, this potential is in fact so widely realised that it may be fairly characterised as the state of mind of the majority of modern scientists. However, the Council insists on our not forgetting the positive side of things modern. We should also remember that mankind is progressing to its end regardless of particular setbacks and the apparent triumph of sin and error.

"Those unfortunate results, however, do not necessarily follow from the culture of today, nor should they lead us into the temptation of not acknowledging its positive values. Among these values are included: scientific study and fidelity toward truth in scientific inquiries, the necessity of working together with others in technical groups, a sense of international solidarity, a clearer awareness of the responsibility of experts to aid and even to protect men, the desire to make the conditions of life more favorable for all, especially for those who are poor in culture or who are deprived of the opportunity to exercise responsibility. All of these provide some preparation for the acceptance of the message of the Gospel a preparation which can be animated by divine charity through Him Who has come to save the world." (57)

There are those, we believe, who mistakenly criticise the document for taking such a positive view of modern culture. We have discussed their position at length in our book "Thomist Tradition: Avoiding Scylla and Charybdis". It is difficult to strike the right balance and subsequent history of modern culture may seem to prove that the arguments of such critics had some force. However, the more important consideration is to bring out the true attitude the Church should have towards modern culture. And it will be found that the Council gave the appropriate warnings and was not so concerned about condemnations. An important statement is a confirmation of the teaching of Vatican I regarding the relation between Faith and Reason. One just needs to be careful to interpret the word "sciences" so as to accord with reason.

"This Sacred Synod, therefore, recalling the teaching of the first Vatican Council, declares that there are 'two orders of knowledge' which are distinct, namely faith and reason; and that the Church does not forbid that 'the human arts and disciplines use their own principles and their proper method, each in its own domain'; therefore 'acknowledging this just liberty,' this Sacred Synod affirms the legitimate autonomy of human culture and especially of the sciences." (59) Notice the careful use of the word "legitimate".

A final warning at the end of paragraph 59 is most telling given the nature of State sponsored education in a modern educational system that is (free – paid for by the State) compulsory and now become aggressively secularist. "As for public authority, it is not its function to determine the character of the civilization, but rather to establish the conditions and to use the means which are capable of fostering the life of culture among all even within the minorities of a nation. It is necessary to do everything possible to prevent culture from being turned away from its proper end and made to serve as an instrument of political or economic power."

If one looks closely enough there is sufficient in the document to satisfy the severest critic of modern culture and the ideologies by which it is driven. As for the references to the benefits of the new modern sciences, one will notice that they are mainly to do with their "findings". Not that this excludes a student's consideration of theories, even when false. Aristotle had already said we should be grateful for those who have fallen into error in a genuine search for the truth. This requires of course the exercise of prudence, and competence where appropriate.

At the end of this Chapter on Culture the Council indicates what it wishes from the teaching of theology in seminaries and universities. "Let those who teach theology in seminaries and universities strive to collaborate with men versed in the other sciences through a sharing of their resources and points of view. Theological inquiry should pursue a profound understanding of revealed truth; at the same time it should not neglect close contact with its own time that it may be able to help these men skilled in various disciplines to attain to a better understanding of the faith. This common effort will greatly aid the formation of priests, who will be able to present to our contemporaries the doctrine of the Church concerning God, man and the world, in a manner more adapted to them so that they may receive it more willingly." (62)

Here, to avoid being possibly misled by the English translation we put the Latin. *Qui theologicis disciplinis in Seminariis et Studiorum Universitatibus incumbunt, cum hominibus qui in aliis scientiis excellunt, collatis viribus atque consiliis, cooperari studeant. Theologica inquisitio insimul profundam veritatis revelatae cognitionem prosequatur et coniunctionem cum proprio tempore ne negligat, ut homines variis disciplinis excultos ad pleniorem fidei scientiam iuvare possit. Haec socia opera plurimum proderit institutioni sacrorum ministrorum qui Ecclesiae doctrinam de Deo, de homine et de mundo aptius coaevis nostris explanare poterunt, ita ut verbum illud etiam libentius ab eis suscipiatur.*

That will have to be enough in our comments on Chapter II of Part II. We move on to consider Chapter V which involves a broadening of the focus of the social doctrine of the Church. It is concerned with that social order of mankind that transcends and ought to be the final unifying principle of the civil or political orders that Aristotle and the Greeks tended to see as the perfection of human association.

Chapter V THE FOSTERING OF PEACE AND THE PROMOTION OF A COMMUNITY OF NATIONS

There are three other chapters in Part II. They are chapters III, IV and V. We have elected to deal with chapter V following I and II as it is part of the broadening of the scope in the treatment of the social doctrine of the Church that we have noted. It concerns the most universal association of mankind and coincides with that universal community that we have seen to come under Personal Ethics and the Natural Moral Law. This order of relationship extends to all creation and so includes man's relation to all things above and below his nature, though our knowledge and interests are to a large extent immersed in the material order or physical universe.

More directly however our concerns are with the relations within mankind itself. That is where the problems and conflicts are focused by reason of original sin. But, as we now are so painfully aware, these have repercussions on the whole of nature below us, upon the goodness of which we necessarily depend. In this final chapter then the Council addresses the problem of world peace and justice at their most profound levels. As it notes these problems cannot be resolved at the level of natural morality and will only be resolved at the supernatural level at the end of time. Nonetheless, in the meantime mankind must work as best it can to foster peace and promote the organisation of individuals, groups and nations (civil communities) to ensure justice on a world scale.

We should remember however that the modern condition and history of things social and civil do not readily fall into the categories of Aristotle and Aquinas. The picture of the state of nations and their attempts to dominate others seems more to resemble the state of "kingdoms" described by St. Augustine: **"Justice being taken away, then, what are kingdoms but great robberies? For what are robberies themselves, but little kingdoms? The band itself is made up of men; it is ruled by the authority of a prince, it is knit together by the pact of the confederacy; the booty is divided by the law agreed on. If, by the admittance**

of abandoned men, this evil increases to such a degree that it holds places, fixes abodes, takes possession of cities, and subdues peoples, it assumes the more plainly the name of a kingdom, because the reality is now manifestly conferred on it, not by the removal of covetousness, but by the addition of impunity. Indeed, that was an apt and true reply which was given to Alexander the Great by a pirate who had been seized. For when that king had asked the man what he meant by keeping hostile possession of the sea, he answered with bold pride, "What thou meanest by seizing the whole earth; but because I do it with a petty ship, I am called a robber, whilst thou who dost it with a great fleet art styled emperor." St. Augustine (354-430), in Book IV of *The City of God*.

As we have noted, the desire for "political" power, like that for money, tends to be thought of in terms of quantity, as the modern mind has been accommodated to thinking of science exclusively in mathematico-empirical concepts. To Aristotle and Aquinas the lack of a natural limit (which comes from natural forms and ends) that that mode of thinking promotes, is, like the condition of a cancerous growth, a sure sign of something unnatural. This lack of finiteness or definition spills over into many "scientific" concepts, such as evolution, development and progress. They have their place and importance, within limits. There is a risk though in adopting these words indiscriminately, as many Catholics wanting to dialogue with their modern philosophic and scientific colleagues do. The Council does endorse the role of dialogue in regard to the danger of war, but adds "with prudence".

Though this sinful condition has been redeemed by Christ and the world has the great blessing of the Church that he has bestowed on mankind, with which he is always, each human person remains free and capable of rejecting the grace needed to obtain salvation during this life. Such rejection which evidently can be on a large scale means that the spectre of war and its violence hangs over humanity. In the 1960's the evil aspect of such a human condition could be seen to cover the whole earth and more and more led many to fear the total destruction of mankind and indeed of the whole natural world.

Chapter V of Part II is divided into two sections, the first entitled "On the Avoidance of War", meaning between nations or groups of nations, and the second "The Setting Up of a World Community". In regard to the second we need to be careful with the use of terms such as "community", "nation" in regard to which we also have the use in Latin of *gens, civitas* and so on. It takes some effort in fitting them into the Greek Aristotle's and the Latin Aquinas's terminology. We will address this problem in the second section.

As to the first, about participation in wars, the Council says this: "As long as the danger of war remains and there is no competent and sufficiently powerful authority at the international level, governments cannot be denied the right to legitimate defense once every means of peaceful settlement has been exhausted. State authorities and others who share public responsibility have the duty to conduct such grave matters soberly and to protect the welfare of the people entrusted to their care. But it is one thing to undertake military action for the just defense of the people, and something else again to seek the subjugation of other nations." (79)

Before we get too excited about outlawing all violent action we should note what the Council also says here: "Those too who devote themselves to the military service of their country should regard themselves as the agents of security and freedom of peoples. As long as they fulfill this role properly, they are making a genuine contribution to the establishment of peace." Aristotle will say that the end of the warrior is victory. But more fundamentally it is peace and so long as that is his end his measured use of violence can be justified. It is based on the moral principle justifying necessary self-defence.

The world conditions in this regard have as all are aware changed dramatically since the Council. Within thirty years one of the two great modern "nations" (USA and USSR) that, even if granted, on both sides (subjectively) good intentions, sought "the subjugation of other nations", had as a bloc (modern word for empire) disintegrated. We are just finishing a further period of thirty years where wars have multiplied at the behest of the remaining powerful nation, purporting to act to free other nations and install its own style of democracy (the only good form of government). How genuine this "good" intention has been is more and more being brought into question.

The Council goes on to say: "82. Today it certainly demands that they [world leaders] extend their thoughts and their spirit beyond the confines of their own nation, that they put aside national selfishness and ambition to dominate other nations, and that they nourish a profound reverence for the whole of humanity, which is already making its way so laboriously toward greater unity ... It does them no good to work for peace as long as feelings of hostility, contempt and distrust, as well as racial hatred and unbending ideologies, continue to divide men and place them in opposing camps."

We will not go into the merits of present conflicts about which the whole world is in turmoil. We simply say that all should carefully consider on which side, or sides, is there a stirring up of "feelings of hostility, contempt and distrust, as well as racial hatred and unbending ideologies", which inhibits any prospects for peace?

The realism about human nature and confidence in the divine comes out at the end of the section. "But we should not let false hope deceive us. For unless enmities and hatred are put away and firm, honest agreements concerning world peace are reached in the future, humanity, which already is in the middle of a grave crisis, even though it is endowed with remarkable knowledge, will perhaps be brought to that dismal hour in which it will experience no peace other than the dreadful peace of death. But, while we say this, the Church of Christ, present in the midst of the anxiety of this age, does not cease to hope most firmly. She intends to propose to our age over and over again, in season and out of season, this apostolic message: 'Behold, now is the acceptable time for a change of heart; behold! now is the day of salvation'."

THE COMMUNITY OF NATIONS

In the second section of Chapter V the Council addresses the problem of how a "competent and sufficiently powerful authority at the international level" might be set up. The need for this was seen already at the secular level at the end of World War II in order to avoid a third world war after the harrowing experience of two. So it was that the two emerging superpowers, one Capitalist and the other Communist, were prepared to "co-operate" in the formation of an international organisation by a number of nations entering into agreement styled the "United Nations' Charter".

Necessarily it reflected the condition of the world at the time. The Charter was in fact flawed verbally and conceptually but all signed up so as to allow the parties to at least have the semblance of concordance. Verbally a charter signified an agreement but in the context of a concession or privilege conceded by a superior to inferiors, as in the historic case of *Magna Carta*. But in this case, there was no real superior in a legal sense, or of political right, but there was in a modern sense of "political", of military power.

At the time there were or were thought to be not one but five such powers, USA, USSR (later the Russian Federation), UK, France and the Republic of China (later the People's Republic of China), though the first two were or were close to becoming the major players. UK and France qualified as being on the winning side. Germany, Italy and Japan were noticeably excluded initially. China in a way represented the Asian (non-Christian) part of the world that had not been involved in the wars. It would become more significant after 1949 when it had "converted" to Communism.

The document was in reality a compromise in that the five "permanent" members reserved to themselves the power of veto. The other members were prepared to go along with this arrangement and over time nearly all other countries (many previous colonies) signed up so that the organisation grew not only in size but also in moral status. The virtual ineffectiveness of the UN as a political or legal body did enable important declarations to be promulgated. So it was that the moral authority of the Church was able to be an important influence. This "moral" influence could of course be abused and perverse ideological positions of member states came over time to be more vigorously promoted through the very organisation that was meant to promote peace.

However, we do not wish to dwell on this topic here. What is of more interest is how the status of international organisations might be seen in the light of Aristotle's and hence Aquinas's ethical and political philosophy. We have set out the basis on which these organisations may be judged in our books, "Ethics Today and Saint Thomas Aquinas". "Political Science and Saint Thomas Aquinas" and "Economic Science and Saint Thomas Aquinas". We need therefore make only a few observations.

As noted, for Aristotle the *polis* (city) which we may more generally call the civil community is the perfect human society in natural terms. For Aristotle saw it as able to provide its members with all that they required or rationally desired not just at the lowest level of the exchange of external/material goods and services but also going up to the highest level of the communication of spiritual goods, such as wisdom, science and arts. It should be noted that this extends to practical wisdom and sciences which rule human behaviour through the cardinal virtues of prudence, justice, fortitude and temperance. It is important to notice that religion is a virtue in the order of justice.

The higher levels have been called cultural in our scheme of the levels of human life set out earlier, but we also use the word culture in the widest sense to include all levels, even modes of production and exchange of goods or trade. For culture in its best sense means all that is good for human nature on its way to perfection. It is in modern times that these divisions get muddled and in translation into English it becomes near impossible to untangle. But we keep trying.

Aquinas has said that the city so conceived is the greatest thing that man can know and constitute. It is the best thing that man can "make" even though it is based on human nature and therefore in some sense natural. (Aristotle, "man is by nature political"). Because of original sin however such a natural society is rarely if ever to be found. Indeed, it is quite evident that lacking justice, which is the very essence of such a system of human communication in goods, man tends to constitute "civil communities" that are more like what St. Augustine describes as robber kingdoms.

We should refer back here to the grouping of human beings that is imperfect and to which in Latin the name *natio* was given. It is significant that though in the perfect state of human communications the city would be of a limited population sufficient to work to satisfy all the needs and wants of its members (and any surplus membership would have to take steps to found another city – it being a matter of thinking in terms of human quality of life and allowing for passage of time, not in gross abstract numerical terms as is the modern mentality). The concept of a civil association has been changed in modern times so that a nation is made up of many cities. This brings in another feature of the modern notion of civilisation – that there is no limit to the size of a nation and indeed the tendency is for political power to grow to the proportions of an empire, itself ever expandable.

It was possible to conceive of a city as a perfect civil community in the era of ancient Greece and Christendom but it is unintelligible in the modern era. The modern notion of a world order of civilisation therefore is not to be identified with the Aristotelian. What it is, is anyone's guess; it is hardly definable. That is one hidden difficulty that the Church's communicators with the modern world have to contend with. Vatican documents are often using terms taken from Aristotelian and Thomist philosophy (and science) that are at odds with the meanings in modern "scientific" language. This is particularly noticeable in their English translations from the original Latin.

A world "civil" order conceived in modern terms has to be put in terms of agreements, treaties and charters between civil communities. It may perhaps be put in terms of "nations" that have a capital city which is the core political centre of rule, that corresponds somewhat today to the idea of a State. But beyond that we resort to the notion of a federation or confederacy of states. In the "Middle Ages", cities and towns did combine and coordinate in that way forming such combinations as the Hanseatic League.

The word "federal" has the same origin in the notion of an agreement between states. The word "feudal" does not come from the same root but from one attached to the possession of land, whereby tribal type associations pledged their loyalty to one chief lord or landlord. The political and legal terms such as federation, union and commonwealth take some sorting out.

Modern international empires or grouping of nations are better thought of as positively based associations rather than natural ones. In many cases they may indeed be viewed as unnatural, according to St. Augustine's picture of kingdoms/ empires even in ancient times. In modern times, as we have noted, the loss of the connection of the very concept of political (and the various levels within such civil life, such as economic) with natural morality, together with the focus of science (in this case practical science) upon quantity rather than (moral) quality, has meant that the population of the civil community is thought of in terms of numbers without any natural limit. So it is that there is a strong tendency in modern superpowers, ideologically driven, to want to dominate the whole world. One does not have to look very far to verify this.

After the First World War, looking back to European unions of States, by now called Nations, there was formed The League of Nations, based on the Treaty of Versailles. After World War II, perhaps unconsciously thinking of more modern kinds of formation of federations, such as the United States of America (a somewhat presumptuous title when you come to think of it), the body replacing the League was called the United Nations. With the notion of sovereignty retained, this union was in essence a marriage of convenience (military or economic), but over time took on a quasi-sacral nature. Ironically, this quasi-religious worship of collective human authority was used early to try to exclude the Vatican State from membership. Though the Vatican could argue that it does have the necessary human and political status this exclusion from full membership still obtains, but apparently by the Church's choice.

However, what we want to bring out is the change in intelligibility of the terms used for political reality. First there was the substitution of a civil association founded "by free agreement", absolutely considered, a Lockean notion, instead of "by nature". The Aristotelian notion of natural has to be understood in moral terms, so that a political entity is still a work of man, based on human free will (like marriage), but morally bound. Being "under God" its' positive law and political prudence (policy) has to conform with the natural moral law.

With the new positivist political philosophy, the "force" of the promises based on agreement of free wills was much weakened. Personal interest and national interest tended to trump such a single act of will. The history of modern ethics and politics provides ample evidence of the subordination of treaties to "the national interest", considered absolutely.

But we should note here another feature of modern political discourse. In ancient political philosophy such as conceived by Aristotle and Aquinas, external goods, the communication in which was called commerce or trade, the "soul" of the economic level of civil life, like all other communications, was conceived to be sufficient to provision the natural needs and rational wants of

citizens within the city or civil community – that was its very notion. Remember that the city was not as conceived today as the
central "business" district but the territory under one ruler extending to the fields of agriculture with the towns or villages of
manufacturing industrial areas place outside the city centre, so
the importation of "foreign" goods was thought unnecessary and
possibly disruptive of social order. This applied at all levels including the lowest, trade in external goods. In the concrete
though, there were social advantages to be had by such trade
where the city could not provide itself with all its reasonable
wants. So, the thinkers of practical wisdom like Aristotle warned
against it but the politicians were not so worried.

This applied to trade in ordinary terms, which we have symbolised as CMC, so that in theory at least there should not arise a
situation where a city depended on another for its agricultural or
manufacturing products or one kind of them. But there would
soon enter into this kind of trade (it was a feature of trade within
the one city) the second mode of exchange MCM discussed by
Aristotle, where someone acting as other than the "householder"
who produced and sold what he did not require for his household in order to use the money gained to buy what he needed
otherwise, produced nothing essentially but simply bought in
order to sell "at a profit" (in money).

We have to be careful here get the essential sense of Aristotle's
language. We have used the example of a bootmaker (not a
bookmaker). The second mode of exchange pertains to what is
called a merchant who first bought goods (MC) and sold them
where one could expect a good profit (CM). Foreign trade tends

to be dominated by this second mode which Aristotle criticised and it no doubt influenced him in his aversion to a city coming to rely on foreign trade – notice the almost opposite trade situation of the modern city or nation.

We have discussed this distinction between natural and non-natural (tending to unnatural) exchange of material goods at great length, for we see it as the key to understanding both modern Capitalism and its opposing politico-economic ideology Communism – refer particularly to my two books "Economic Science and Saint Thomas Aquinas" and "Political Science and Saint Thomas Aquinas". But here we wish to bring out the huge difference between basic concepts in pre-modern and modern times. This comes out most dramatically in practical terms in the political and economic orders pertaining to the civil life now "enjoyed" by all mankind.

In the era of Christendom under the Church's watchful eye the economic/ commercial disorders (to which the injustice of finance/usury was closely connected) were with more or less success kept in check. The changed feature of modern times in this regard is that, with the diminution of the influence of the Church as the guardian of morals, and especially social morals, the temptation to gain by moneymaking and money lending became too great and there was a "commercial and financial" revolution, an important prelude to the religious and political revolutions that followed.

What we particularly wish to focus on is the loss, or rejection, of any notion of limit, natural and moral, to the fulfilment of human desires in social/civil intercourse. This lack of reason and limit is everywhere; in modern science's love of Mathematics and quantity as the only form to be applied to empirical observations; in Evolution as the guiding principle and ultimate explanation in modern science.

In the order of politico-economics this irrationality is expressed in the love of money for its own sake and the profitmaking possible in the use (or rather abuse) of money, whether in "commerce" by unnatural exchange, or in "finance" by charging interest where not justified or excessive interest where it is (usury). We can apply this infinitization of our notions to politics taken in the sense of power politics where it manifests itself in the love of political dominance to monstrous proportions. It is more than enough (and we have not mentioned the disorder the domestic/sexual relations) to reduce the conscientious rational animal to anger and despair. But wisely the Council counsels against that temptation for the reasons it and previous popes have given.

That should be enough to indicate how huge was the adjustment needed to enter into a conversation or dialogue with the modern world. But there is one other matter that we want to bring out. It is in our view the second key to the understanding of what is meant by modern life but it does involve on our part a preliminary excursus into fundamentals, "philosophy". We ask for a little forbearance in this regard.

Just as the lowest level of human life is commonly called simply "life" and is so basic that occupation with the other higher levels has to suspended if this lowest level is disordered or "diseased"; so the lowest level of civil or political life, the economic, occupies such a basic place in the social life of a civil community that any disorder or disturbance at this level (which can be equated with injustice) will draw attention of all, especially those in positions of authority, away from interest and intercourse at the higher levels (except perhaps sport). All is interconnected of course but even the highest levels such as of wisdom and science will be brought to focus on the problems at the most vital level of activity.

In the civil order of human life the activity that is most relevant is that of communication, or commerce in economic terms, and the disorder most critical is in the sphere of exchange or the market. To make a comparison, it is like having a problem with the circulation of the blood in its doing its job of making sure that all parts of the body are supplied with the requisite life-giving elements required for their health and the health of the whole body. This dis-ease (peace being ease spiritually taken) can arise from and cause all sorts of other problems relating to the material cells or organs. So, we are not to suppose that the market is the only thing that is important for the health of the political economy. The productive contribution of the economic parts, capital and labour, whether individual or organised, also need to be sound and able to function well.

Thus, we may see the whole economic life of the civil community as one of production and exchange. But, considered in Aristotelian terms, it is the exchange process that is the formal or unifying part of the economy and the productive that is the material part or aspect. Less properly, we can divide products into the formal consideration as artificial or technical works of man (with the aid of tools) and natural resources as the materials needed.

To anticipate, what we are getting to is that modern social life is so materially focused that nearly all of people's attention is dominated by health and sickness in the case of individuals and the "economy" and economic ills in the case of social life. This plays into not just interpersonal relations within on political unit but right to the widest international relations. Wars between nations and empires have been for the most part "trade wars". For reasons we now go into the domination has been expressed for material advantage, with the economic order being much focus on the ability to produce military weapons. The reader can imagine how little room is left for cultivation of the higher spiritual goods of human life.

Relative to our present subject, that is the state of the modern mind with which the Church meant to engage in dialogue with. The issues with which the Church wished to engage the world were generally seen from this point of view rather remote and non-urgent. But we wish to develop this focus on the material more fully in order to bring out not the impossibility of the problem (for we are all human and rational in nature) but of its enormity.

Now we have a problem in using the distinction between the formal and the material in the context of the life of a civil community. What we want to say is that the difference between the vision of Aquinas and the modern is that the modern scientific focuses almost purely on the material aspects (gross and subtle) and it is fair to say that the whole modern educational approach at least as far as scientific method is concerned is materialistic. But we have to be clear in what sense we use that term.

What can be said at this point is that this approach fits into the feature we adverted to above of the infinitization of modern thought. For as Aristotle notes, quantity is the property of a body that flows from its matter. Primary matter, considered in itself, has what is called potential infinity – it does not have a form but is able to have any bodily form. So too we can understand that quantity considered in itself is without any limit, it is potentially infinite. That is not to be confused with actual infinity.

Now one who thinks materialistically will lose the notion of a natural limit and will tend to see, and desire goods, in terms of quantities rather than qualities. We have adverted to that phenomenon in modern thinking. That is already an indication of materialism in one's view of the world.

Now coming to the problem at hand: how to view the modern world with which we want to dialogue? We cannot converse or dialogue without both parties using language with words that are mutually agreed to have the same meaning. This is not such an easy task even in small groups. When we are dealing with communication between people who are "worlds apart" which in a real way describes the religious world of the Catholic as related to that of the non-Catholic we may appreciate how daunting it is. Do not expect it can be done without much misunderstanding and at least a lot of talking at cross purposes.

Let us just introduce here an example of the problem as it relates to translating the Latin language of the Council into the English language commonly used in regard to discussing the state of things socio-economic which, as may be appreciated, is a core subject matter in the dialogue.

In paragraph 85 we have this sentence in English: "The development of a nation depends on human and financial aids." The Latin is: *Incrementum alicuius nationis ex adiumentis humanis et pecuniariis pendet.* There is no great problem with reference to human aids. For these evidently refer to the internal goods of human sciences and arts. In traditional Catholic discourse the Council Fathers, being educated in Sacred Theology, would have included wisdom and prudence. The only problem here is that the modern meanings would exclude the metaphysical and moral senses. That is significant but not so much to the point as the use of financial for *pecuniariis*.

The basic point is that civil development requires the aid of both internal and external aids. The internal from the modern point of view are science and technology. What are the external goods that should be provided to assist underdeveloped nations? The first thing that comes to the modern "educated" mind is of course money. That is a translation of the Latin *pecunia*. But more fundamentally it is not money as it is "lent" but money that is the common medium of exchange and accordingly the common measure of value of the natural or real goods in exchange. Thus, it has come from a word for sheep, as capital comes from cattle, stock, natural wealth in Aquinas's terms, not artificial wealth (a measure of debt). So, we have a subtle shift from something positive as an aid, not money but what money can buy, to something privative. The heart of the problem of usury lies here but we refer to our book "Economic Science and Saint Thomas Aquinas" for a proper discussion of this.

It is so easy for the borrower to shift money received as "aid" to purposes not really intended by the lender, whose focus is anyhow on the "interest" able to be charged. The foreign aid may very well end up aiding the official(s) who received the money or his favorites rather than the country he serves. The modern financial system is in many ways designed to cover up what happens to the loans, which might have to become gifts when the poor country finds it still has not enough money, and pleads for more "aid".

That is just one way, perhaps the most fundamental, in which an education in modern "Economics" and "Monetary Theory" influences and in effect deceives even the experts in the sciences and arts involved. What chance has the English reader of the Council document (rich or poor, cleric or layperson) in this regard? He or she just feels the need to work harder to persuade the government and rich corporations to lend more money. Why with so little real effect?

So, the first thing to do is spend money on education, no need to ask what education? Thus, it is that the best intentions of the Council expressed in the clearest language from Christian tradition can be and no doubt have been derailed. We are, remember, up against "principalities and powers". We will not go into the many other deceptive ploys used, such as talking of "financial systems". The real creditors, the few people of money, do not mind passing off the responsibility for the burden of debt taken on by those who cannot meet their current needs (including governments that put themselves into "bondage" to meet urgent needs) as owing to unfeeling systems (as was the fashion with the first exponents of the modern science of Political Economy – the mathematization of the science only makes the human persons responsible more invisible).

But let us finish up by looking a little more closely at what is said in the last paragraphs of the section of Part II of *Gaudium et spes*. Though it is as it were breaking new ground it is critical that we keep in mind what the Council has said about its dependence of previous social encyclicals. It is a mistake to try to make sense of what is stated here as if it can be understood independently of previous social doctrine. That only exacerbates the difficulties we have referred to.

As we have noted the lowest level of political/civil life is what we call the economic. This has to do with the communication of goods, but these goods are in the main and for the majority, workers and debtors, products pertaining to bodily welfare, food, clothing, shelter, transport and services related thereto.

These all have to be conducted in a moral manner, justly, rendering to each his due for labour and materials contributed but there are a multitude of technical sciences and arts involving scientists and technical workers having to be paid. Their due recompense is not arbitrarily estimated by their employers but according to a common estimation that is objectively based. In a just society or market one individual or group does not determine or make the exchange value or price but takes its measure from the community evaluation that is commonly known without any difficulty within a range of fairness if not exactly. That is what is meant by the just price for goods or wages for services. Particular injustices do occur even in a generally just society.

But where the order of justice is so deeply structurally distorted, as is obvious in the system of Capitalism, where the materials of production (natural resources) and the instruments of labor, collectively called "capital", have been so maldistributed and misappropriated, "legally", at the behest of a powerful tyrant or oligarchical few, the majority of the population is reduced to poverty readily recognised as propertyless named even by popes a proletariat. They are left to rely for a living upon the owners or controllers of virtually all "capital" needed in order to labor to produce the goods and services for themselves their families and the community as a whole (including the capitalists who do not have to work because they can live on the income from the capital which is seen to include the "labor" they have purchased/employed from/by those who have nothing else to "sell" in the labor market.

It is this actual situation of the modern employed laborers that Pope Leo XIII openly described and obviously condemned as under "a yoke little better than slavery". That desperate condition of impoverishment and virtual servitude of the "workers" has been ameliorated by various reforms mainly legal, if much of this improvement has produced a dependency on the Welfare State. Overall, though, it does not substantially alter the economic condition of virtual servitude. It only means that those now dependent in one way or another are relatively better off in their quasi-servile condition. This obtains even though the same employed workers are legally considered politically free in having some say collectively in electing the government they are under. Who guards the guardians is another matter. Generally speaking, the party system gives one a choice between two politico-economic ideological "systems", whilst the power of money acts quietly in the background.

In an exchange system, which automatically arises in a civilised community, it is not difficult to see how such "capital" comes to be associated with the possession and control of money, which is the common measure of wealth in exchange. This enables the capitalists to be dissociated with any particular kind of possession of wealth, such as land and buildings, and to be simply regarded as people of money, which is as it were the debt that the community as a whole owes to individuals or associations that are parts of it. Such enormous credit had by a few enables even governments to borrow seemingly without limit on behalf of the "taxpayers".

The problems of monetary inflation and depression, booms and busts, are closely linked to this. Trying to plot the course of the "pathology" of these "economic" matters is practically impossible. As a doctor friend of mine replied, when asked by his patient what could happen if he tried to run with his broken leg, "anything". The modern political governments are full of experts willing to predict what might happen. Their predictions generally prove to be all wrong, but, if they have not foresight, they have great hindsight.

The Council was well aware of the existence of this unjust state of affairs but does not go into any detail. Here they are content to trace things back to the deeper causes where the remedy consists in repentance. "83. In order to build up peace above all the causes of discord among men, especially injustice, which foment wars must be rooted out. Not a few of these causes come from excessive economic inequalities and from putting off the steps needed to remedy them. Other causes of discord, however, have their source in the desire to dominate and in a contempt for persons. And, if we look for deeper causes, we find them in human envy, distrust, pride, and other egotistical passions."

Nonetheless the Council does address what should be done in terms of international cooperation" "85. The present solidarity of mankind also calls for a revival of greater international cooperation in the economic field. Although nearly all peoples have become autonomous, they are far from being free of every form of undue dependence, and far from escaping all danger of serious internal difficulties."

It even enters into particular counsels, but from what we have already pointed out, we need to keep in mind the difficulties attending their implementation:

"The development of a nation depends on human and financial aids. The citizens of each country must be prepared by education and professional training to discharge the various tasks of economic and social life. But this in turn requires the aid of foreign specialists who, when they give aid, will not act as overlords, but as helpers and fellow-workers. Developing nations will not be able to procure material assistance unless radical changes are made in the established procedures of modern world commerce. Other aid should be provided as well by advanced nations in the form of gifts, loans or financial investments. Such help should be accorded with generosity and without greed on the one side, and received with complete honesty on the other side."

In view of the course of events following the Council, though initially giving some cause for hope of improvement its final plea appears somewhat forlorn.

"If an authentic economic order is to be established on a world-wide basis, an end will have to be put to profiteering, to national ambitions, to the appetite for political supremacy, to militaristic calculations, and to machinations for the sake of spreading and imposing ideologies."

Nonetheless, we should not forget the great good effect that has followed from the efforts of individuals and organisations referred to in paragraph 84. "In view of the increasingly close ties of mutual dependence today between all the inhabitants and peoples of the earth, the apt pursuit and efficacious attainment of the universal common good now require of the community of nations that it organize itself in a manner suited to its present responsibilities, especially toward the many parts of the world which are still suffering from unbearable want.

To reach this goal, organizations of the international community, for their part, must make provision for men's different needs, both in the fields of social life - such as food supplies, health, education, labor and also in certain special circumstances which can crop up here and there, e.g., the need to promote the general improvement of developing countries, or to alleviate the distressing conditions in which refugees dispersed throughout the world find themselves, or also to assist migrants and their families."

It is only the pleas and warnings addressed to governments and large corporations that seem to have gone unheeded. But we will see more of this when we come to the papal encyclicals that followed the Council. These we may conveniently divide into those that seem to constitute a second series of social encyclicals from *Populorum progressio* to *Sollicitudo rei socialis* and *Caritas in veritatem,* and the two social encyclicals of the present pope *Laudato si* and *Fratelli tutti.*

Before this we need to complete our comments on *Gaudium et spes* by going back to chapters III and IV of Part II. We will however do this in reverse order.

Chapter IV THE LIFE OF THE POLITICAL COMMUNITY

This chapter is the shortest in Part II and indeed in the whole document. One would have thought that being concerned with the whole of civil life it would have attracted more attention than Chapter III which is concerned with only one aspect of modern civil or political life, that is the economic. However, that difference perhaps has its own significance. For as we have seen and as is evident in the focus of the Church's social doctrine in modern times it is the economic life of people that dominates the political scene.

It is not only of course in that part of the world that has developed a civilization that we may call of Christian heritage where political or other rule is perverted to serve the economic interests of a few rather than turned as it should to serve the common good of all. In the general history of mankind, whether civilized or not, the basic wants of life have to be first satisfied and those in power tend to make sure that theirs are met to their satisfaction (or avarice and cupidity) by the labour of the people they rule.

But here we are not talking about a stage of mankind where the civilization is pagan or the people live any more in a primitive pre-civilized state. If not directly through the good rule of Christian nations but rather through their misrule the peoples of the world have reached a stage in which virtually all have come into contact with Christian civilization.

Prior to the modern era which we may date roughly from the Protestant Reformation, the influence of Christianity was transmitted by heretical movements that opposed the Church then called Catholic, among which we may include Islam, derived from Nestorianism, which became so politically and militarily powerful as to threaten the very existence of Christendom.

But we are talking about the modern world that has mainly developed out of Christendom and from which it drew and retained, if with diminishing force, much of value at all the levels of civil society we have discussed. If, as we have argued, the Christian civilization that has roots going back to Athens and Rome to Jerusalem and other oriental nations and beyond those still, has spread in modern times to the whole world, its influence has not always been in its pure or Catholic form obviously, but the name of Christ and the gospel he preached has become known in some way or other even by those who regard it as an object of disdain and distrust.

It is true as the Council says at the beginning of *Gaudium et spes* that we have reached a new era of history; indeed, some might fear it is the end of human history. But what we wish to focus on, as does the Council, is that there has been progress in human consciousness of the good kind so far as the rights and responsibilities pertaining to civil or political life for man is concerned. This we may credit mankind as a whole with, as it is a progress in moral consciousness, but its ultimate source must be put with divine grace and therefore with the Catholic Church as the body of Christ, as the channel of grace in this world. That from a philosophical point of view is the formal and final cause

The material and proximate efficient cause of this may be said to be the spread of the knowledge of the gospel with the "progress" of the domination of the rest of the world, by military means, by ideologically driven superpowers, just as early Christianity providentially spread within and with the extension of the Roman Empire. We do not wish to enter into details of this sort which have to be theological, but simply to provide some basis for reconciling what may appear to be a worldly concession to human nature as a cause of moral goodness independently of the source of grace.

The Council has put the position as follows: "73. In our day, profound changes are apparent also in the structure and institutions of peoples. These result from their cultural, economic and social evolution. Such changes have a great influence on the life of the political community, especially regarding the rights and duties of all in the exercise of civil freedom and in the attainment of the common good, and in organizing the relations of citizens among themselves and with respect to public authority." *Nostris temporibus profundae advertuntur transformationes etiam in compage et institutionibus populorum, quae ipsorum evolutionem culturalem, oeconomicam ac socialem consequuntur; quae transformationes magnum influxum in communitatis politicae vitam exercent, praesertim quod attinet ad omnium iura et officia in libertatis civilis exercitio ac in bono communi attingendo et ad civium relationes inter se et cum publica auctoritate ordinandas.*

It mentions other positive aspects such as freedom of association and other rights "against" the ruling power. This extends to the rights of labourers to have trades' unions, something that was fiercely fought against by the "liberal" capitalists of the nineteen century and we must say it was only through Pope Leo XIII that such a right was accepted. So it was that other rights for all to participate in political rule (even argued for by Aristotle) came again to be accepted, through the better awareness of natural morality only preserved intact by faith in the Catholic Church, as not confined to persons of property.

However, the Council did not fail to point out the negative side to modern political life. Thus, it said: "However, those political systems, prevailing in some parts of the world are to be reproved which hamper civic or religious freedom, victimize large numbers through avarice and political crimes, and divert the exercise of authority from the service of the common good to the interests of one or another faction or of the rulers themselves." *Reprobantur autem quaecumque formae politicae, in aliquibus regionibus vigentes, quae libertatem civilem vel religiosam prae-*

pediunt, victimas cupiditatum et criminum politicorum multipli-
cant ac exercitium auctoritatis a bono communi ad commodum
cuiusdam factionis vel ipsorum moderatorum detorquent.

Considering the state of the world at the time some might think it could have put things a bit stronger. But no one would be unaware of which nations or political "blocs" were being referred to.

That is basically what is said in the first numbered paragraph (73) of four. The next (74) simply sets out the traditional Aristotelian and Thomist position on the formation of civil or political communities as natural. Thus, it says: "It is clear, therefore, that the political community and public authority are founded on human nature and hence belong to the order designed by God, even though the choice of a political regime and the appointment of rulers are left to the free will of citizens." *Patet ergo communi-*
tatem politicam et auctoritatem publicam in natura humana
fundari ideoque ad ordinem a Deo praefinitum pertinere; etsi
regiminis determinatio et moderatorum designatio liberae civium
voluntati relinquantur.

Read without reference to the rest of the chapter, and in the context of most, even Catholics, being educated in modern political philosophy or science, it is quite possible, even likely, that this paragraph be given a liberalist interpretation. The translation may help in this regard by translating *moderatorum* as "rulers" leaving out any indication of the rulers having to be moral in their ruling, let alone all voters in their choices. All politicians in a liberal democracy are honourable, are they not?

Here again the Council points to a real possibility of political abuse of authority to the point of oppression. Thus, it adds: "where citizens are oppressed by a public authority overstepping its competence ... it is legitimate for them to defend their own rights and the rights of their fellow citizens against the abuse of this authority, while keeping within those limits drawn by the natural law and the Gospels." No mention of any political rule in particular, but no problem in concluding where it does exist to one not blinded by ideology.

In paragraph 75 the Council simply expands upon the rights and responsibilities of citizens in a civil community as well as the obligations of rulers or politicians, in the legislative judicial and executive spheres, in this regard. We do not find any particular need to add further comment.

In the last paragraph (76) of Chapter IV the document treats of the relation between Church and State. This is a most important subject in the modern age in that since the Protestant Reformation there has been a determined effort to diminish the influence of the Church (which obviously means the Catholic Church) not just in political affairs, meaning pertaining to those in government, but also in all public affairs, that everything connected with civil society and civilization. What the reformers did not count on was that this has led inevitably not only to the exclusion of morality and religion from law and lawmaking (which law is seen as purely positive) but also from any kind of public discussion.

Keep your faith and morals to yourself is the theory behind having your religion as private and your politics as public. It has come to the situation where even to express and try to rationally defend moral convictions (held from time immemorial) is irrationally ridiculed as seeking to "impose" one's private beliefs on others. The contradiction of this with the liberalist fundamental principle of freedom of speech is simply too great for the modern mind to cope with, so it loudly trumpets the one and supinely suppresses the other.

But what we want to bring out here is how the distinction between the objects of concern and authority of Church and State have sophistically been taken as meaning the separation of the two. Separation of Church and State has gained the secular status of a proverb: Church is Church and State is State and never the twain shall meet. But ignorantly the new "educated" recall only the first line of Kipling's verse.

"East is East and West is West and never the twain shall meet,

Till Earth and sky stand presently at God's great judgement Seat.

But there is neither East nor West, Border, nor Breed nor Birth,

When two strong men stand face to face though they come from the ends of the earth!"

Rudyard Kipling, who some might regard as an Imperialist (or White Supremacist), was no racist. "You're a better man than I am Gunga Din!" The same cannot be said of those who would divide Mankind into those who are God-fearing and those who are not.

Vatican II's "Constitution" gives only one paragraph to this most burning question of the modern age. Here then it is most important to relate what it says to the doctrine enunciated by previous popes, where it is to be found in none more clearly and powerfully than Pope Leo XIII. It would seem, however, at least in the English-speaking world, that those who most assiduously study the Vatican document (in a defective translation), not having the moral strength of Kipling's real men, believe they can start and finish with the generality of its "pastoral sentiments" and dispense with the "doctrinal dogma" which it itself declares it is based upon.

Part II: Chapter III ECONOMIC AND SOCIAL LIFE

Finally, however, we turn to Chapter III of Part II where the Council puts in general terms the truth, which is the Church's doctrinal strength, about the lowest level of modern socio-political life, the socio-economic, or what I prefer to call the politico-economic, the light of which truth had been shone so brilliantly in modern times by Pope Leo. By his time the condition of this level of civil life had reached such a critical point that the very life of what remained of the civilized part of the modern world owing its origin in some way to Christendom was threatened with extinction.

That was the focus of the social doctrine of the Church in Leo's time, and we may say things hung in the balance through a World War, the First, a politico-economic Great Depression and another World War, the Second, bringing us to only a little more than a decade before the opening of the Council.

Unfortunately, but typically, the English translator makes a mistranslation in the very heading of this chapter. It may not seem significant. But, besides being a blatant failure to adhere to the simple grammatical structure of a word combination or phrase, it shows up such a profound ignorance of the precise subject matter being dealt with that it is seriously misleading.

We have earlier noted that the translation in paragraph 63 is defective. The Latin is OECONOMICA-SOCIALI. Quite blithely the translator has turned the hyphenated word into a phrase ECONOMIC AND SOCIAL, as if this was of no consequence. It cannot be excused as an accidental error, for he has used the correct hyphenated word later in the text. The mistranslation is in the heading, for goodness sake! One has to conclude that he does not think it makes any difference. The heading is meant to focus on the subject matter as an aspect of the social order, as we might have referred to the chapter on culture as CULTURAL-SOCIAL life or to the chapter on politics as POLITICO-SOCIAL life.

This elementary error discloses a serious looseness not just in the use of language but also in the use of the mind of the translator. He has no clear idea of what he is dealing with and so his translation should not be trusted at all in this part of the document and indeed makes one suspicious of his translation ability in regard to the whole document. But as may be clear by now all English translations of Vatican documents from the Latin on our subject have to be suspect. It is a "cultural" problem with all academics "educated" in the modern sciences of socio-ethical subjects dealt with by the Church. That is not necessarily from a lack of expertise in the skill of translating, but more likely comes from a mentality trapped in a set way of thinking (a more polite way of saying ideological indoctrination) – no doubt quite subliminal by this stage. But checking the English against the Latin as we go, we press on.

This is not the only mistranslation but we will go through the chapter and note the others as we go. Let us first note that there is an introductory paragraph 63 and the rest of the chapter is divided into two sections, the first from paragraph numbered 64 to 66 and the second from 67 to 72, making 10 paragraphs in all. This is more than for Chapter IV. But considering the part played by politico-economic life in modern social life it still gives room for hardly anything but a brief mention of the topics needed to be covered. This is where the Council's indication of its dependence on previous social encyclicals that are "rather recent" should be kept in mind.

"Since rather recent documents of the Church's teaching authority have dealt at considerable length with Christian doctrine about human society, this council is merely going to call to mind some of the more basic truths, treating their foundations under the light of revelation. Then it will dwell more at length on certain of their implications having special significance for our day." (23)

It is in the area of political and politico-economic matters that we might say the treatment of the Council is rather thin and this applies particularly to chapters III and IV of Part II. Even though it is said that "it will dwell more at length on certain of their implications" of "some of the more basic truths" in Part I in these two chapters of Part II, the extent of the treatments of chapters III and IV of Part II, if read alone, would leave a lot to be desired.

We have already noted the sparsity of matter covered in chapter IV. To repeat, there is more in Chapter III but it is still very general and obviously depends greatly on the documents of the Church's teaching authority that have gone before.

We may interpose at this point the question: what is the difference in the world condition that the Council saw had arisen seemingly after the modern world had survived the Second World War? Pope Saint Paul VI put it in terms of a shift of focus, present already in Pope Saint John XXIII, from a crisis within limited, or what might be termed national, boundaries to unlimited, or truly global, proportions. More precisely, we might put it as a shift from a focus on Christian/Western "civilized" nations, or rather groups of nations, to a whole world focus.

This is clearly the case but it is not as great a shift as some might think, because as pointed out above, virtually the whole world was becoming dominated by the two great power blocs, espousing one or other of the two opposed politico-economic ideologies of Capitalism and Communism, which, we have already noted, are Christian/Western in the perverse sense of heresies and false socio-political philosophies (appropriating to themselves the name of sciences). It is this clash between the ideologies of Capitalism and Communism that Leo was faced with. The capitalist process of domination had begun to expand under the British Empire, with other less powerful nation-based (European) empires providing some competition. This had resulted in a period of colonialism not so much by forming colonies as did the

Greeks but after the fashion of subjugating weaker communities (militarily) as did the Romans.

But Communism had not risen to openly challenge Capitalism in "power politics" as it was to do after the Russian Revolution at the end of the First World War. Up till then it was a kind of underground movement, a new politico-economic ideology of revolution against the dominance of Capitalism, or more concretely of that part of the world that was capitalist in its political implementation of that ideology. Communism had its roots in a political philosophical error, Socialism, which thought the problem of mass poverty lay in the institution of property and therefore the solution lay in abolition of the institution. That was a far greater error, comparable to an attempt to cure a severe migrane by cutting off one's head.

However, we may see that in practical/historical terms this irrational rejection was not too far off the mark. That is why it has proved to be so intellectually influential. The migrane was so severe that one might be said to have a splitting headache. Capitalism was an ideology which in principle justified the majority of the population being deliberately and legally excluded from "owning" originally anything but their bodies. The regime that subscribed to this view of political rule argued for the disproportion in their favour in the distribution of external goods, wealth/capital, so that a few virtually commandeered all "capital" in the civil community so that the rest could only live off being employed by the capitalists. (Recall Chesterton's definition of Capitalism).

In Aristotelian terminology it fell on the perverse side of political constitutions, oligarchical, but of such a concentration of property into the hands of a few that its unnatural character would have astounded even Aristotle. For, theoretically, the difference between all and nothing of property is infinite. Of course, its theory being so extremely wicked it could never be put fully into practice. But at its acme (nadir) in the nineteenth century, with the aid of its modern scientific support, the "fortunate few" did their best to "implement" it by law, so that many laborers perished (unfortunately).

That perverse theory was something only a mind educated in modern science, applied to an economic science based on the desire for wealth as money, could conceive. Habit or custom is, however, a powerful social force and the "system" had become so longstanding and deep rooted that it was only a few, like Marx, who could conceive of any alternative kind of regime. Yet, even Marx could not escape thinking of it as somehow "natural". Indeed, with the help of the logic (dialectic) of Hegel, he thought of his own Communist theory as the natural/ historical successor to Adam Smith's Political Economy, which itself was making use of Newton's modern scientific method in what is strictly a moral subject matter.

By a stroke of (devilish) genius Adam Smith, we may assume innocently, had invented a physical science "An Enquiry into the Nature and Causes of the Wealth of Nations". This he gave to the modern world, or rather to its wealthy part, as a substitute physicalist/naturalist science for the old natural/moral science of Politics, taken however at its lowest "economic" level of life. Marx outdid Smith (or thought he did) and converted to his theory of revolution that part of the world that was not committed to Capitalism.

Marx's social philosophy had many and complex influences. Deep down he shared the materialism and atheism that the intellectuals of the modern age, the Enlightened, had descended into. There was, however, a religious influence. He was deeply affected by his Jewish/religious background (his family like other German Jewish families had converted to Protestantism) and thus had an almost visceral aversion to social injustice. He lived in the midst of the rise of Socialism in Europe and particularly in France. Hence, he was influenced by the socialists like Proudhon, who stated boldly: "Property is robbery". Taking Proudhon literally one could not be but consumed by anger at a society that would tolerate such a depth of injustice that threatened a multitude of one's compatriots' very survival, and then tried publicly to justify it in its official academies.

However, we have dealt with the analysis and critique of Capitalism and Communism in our previous books, and the more particular picture may be gathered from the appendices to my book "Political Science and Saint Thomas Aquinas". What we are concerned with here is simply the historical point of the shift of focus on the part of the Church in its dealing with the question of structural injustice and conflict in the modern world. The problem of poverty or an impoverished population in a rich nation or world, though not unconnected with the conflict between the Capitalist and Communist controlled parts of the world, has its own dimension on a world scale so that the division between rich and poor was not confined within nations or even empires but had a fully international spread.

We need to be careful in talking about rich or developed nations and poor or undeveloped or developing nations as opposed to the simple platonic division between rich people and poor people. For one thing as is clear there was and is within the one nation or empire a great gap between the pecunious few and the impecunious many (much affected and even reduced by the dominance of rich nations and empires, the British later called "commonwealth", over poor nations).

We should not forget Pope Pius XII's penetrating point that a so-called rich nation in which there is this gross imbalance in the sharing of wealth (and consequent control of the means of exchange) is in truth not rich in the good sense but decidedly poor and not just in terms of spiritual goods, in a situation of real servitude to sin, but also in the enjoyment of its material possessions.

The Council points to this in an indirect way after noting that in the modern age there is more capacity to produce and exchange goods and hence to meet the needs of "the human family".

"Reasons for anxiety, however, are not lacking. Many people, especially in economically advanced areas, seem, as it were, to be ruled by economics, so that almost their entire personal and social life is penetrated with a certain economic way of thinking. Such is true both of nations that favor a collective economy and of others. At the very time when the development of economic life could mitigate social inequalities (provided that it be guided and coordinated in a reasonable and human way), it is often made to embitter them; or, in some places, it even results in a decline of the social status of the underprivileged and in contempt for the poor. While an immense number of people still lack the absolute necessities of life, some, even in less advanced areas, live in luxury or squander wealth. Extravagance and wretchedness exist side by side. While a few enjoy very great power of choice, the majority are deprived of almost all possibility of acting on their own initiative and responsibility, and often subsist in living and working conditions unworthy of the human person."

The anxiety expressed about the attention of many being too much focused on economics, though a fault, seems to us not such an extensive one as may be suggested. Taken in the context of the extremity of the modern divide between the rich and the poor that is within modern capitalist society as described by Leo XIII (even when the position of the working majority has improved in "economically advanced areas" since World War II, for various reasons not excluding the exploitation by the rich areas of the labourers in the not so advanced areas, the focus is understandable and in a way to be expected.

At least one should not be too hard on the working majority within the so-called rich countries. It is the excessively rich as such that are "too much focused on economics". Even with the subsidiary functions of association private and public performing better the workers are still basically bereft of their due share of property according to distributive justice. True enough, at the time of the Council in the economically advanced areas they could afford a house to live in (and did well for a few years after the end of the second world war) but they were in a social condition like that of a healthy person worried about what might happen to him and his family if he should become ill or disabled. Would you criticise him for thinking too much about his future economic health? His economic situation is still pretty precarious. Of course, the super-rich are happy for the obligation arising from distributive injustice to be spread to all "taxpayers" in the "rich" nations, called so mainly because of the excessive riches of the few. Somehow or other the occupation of tax lawyer, expert in the art of avoiding, not evading, tax is a thriving business. It is rather expensive trade however and only the very rich can afford taking advantage of it.

In calling for the "more advanced areas" or "developed nations" to provide more "finance" to the less advanced areas or developing nations we need to be careful that a reading of the document here does not play into the hands of the super-rich and end up causing the poor peoples to be more impoverished and even heavily burdened with debt. Strange how that has happened. What is the solution? The economic experts' advice is: extend the time for repayment of loans and lower the rate of interest so that the nation does not collapse immediately into bankruptcy. What is the sense in killing the golden goose?

We should not be too surprised then if pleas to rectify the gross inequality in the distribution of the world's wealth (natural and artificial) generally fall on deaf ears, or requires much negotiation of terms satisfactory to the givers of aid mostly in the form loan of money. For, the "fortunate" few's desire for wealth and money is "measured" by avarice; there is never enough cash to spare. Secondly, the "unfortunate" many are on the whole weighed down with the struggle to provide for the present let alone for the future.

The points the Council makes are true enough. Where the plight of the world's poorest is desperate, dying by starvation, there is an urgent obligation in justice, not charity alone, on everyone who can to go to their aid, not just out of their "surplus" wealth but also out of what might eat into their substance in the short term; to provide food and drink necessary for survival. All in the developed world who ignore the plight of anyone they know is in such a parlous situation are to some extent guilty.

Of course, one has to be prudent to ensure the aid reaches those who need it. There are people (mostly rich) so wicked who would intercept it. For the ordinary citizen it is a dilemma - who to trust? Less urgently, there is the obligation to ensure all fellow human beings have the necessary clothing and shelter and medical needs for a healthy life. Here even the rich nations fall down in regard to their own fellow citizens.

What is the general attitude of those educated in modern economics? Sorry, but things seem scarce from whichever way you look at them. The best we can do is follow the advice of the experts in international finance and offer some "financial" relief to poor nations drowning in debt.

This seems to be a rescue package agreeable to the lenders. Better to keep the slave alive than to have him die from being overburdened. No thought of looking at the root of the problem in the abuse of the institution of property caused by legally sanctioned gross distributive injustice. That would undermine the

hallowed principles of Liberal(ist) Capitalism. That would be
Communism. That would be to attack the institution of property
itself, which is absolutely sacrosanct and subject to no higher so-
called principle in justice of the universal destination of goods.
Just trust the rich man *Dives* to throw a few crumbs to poor Lazarus. In modern economics there is no place for such moral values
as justice. What is justice, anyway? Science, even something like
Economics which concerns human social/moral behaviour, is
about facts not value-judgments. What's the latest score in the
cricket, the game by gentlemen?

However, let us proceed with comments upon the paragraphs
in section I of Chapter III. The opening paragraph (64) simply
states what is obvious to any rational person, namely, that all elements making for economic development at the economic level
of socio-political life must be promoted" (a better translation for
the last word is "supported"). What the modern mind might fail
to grasp (for reasons we have discussed) is the meaning of the
following sentence (a point made strongly by Pope Pius XII) :
"The fundamental finality of this production is not the mere increase of products nor profit or control but rather the service of
man, and indeed of the whole man with regard for the full range
of his material needs and the demands of his intellectual, moral,
spiritual, and religious life; this applies to every man whatsoever
and to every group of men, of every race and of every part of the
world."

Indeed, the modern economist will find the reference to morality in the sentence of the paragraph following this one quite
unintelligible. "Consequently, economic activity is to be carried

on according to its own methods and laws within the limits of the moral order, so that God's plan for mankind may be realized." Does that mean the desire for wealth without limit or for money for its own sake is immoral? Is not Economics but a science of choice of scarce means in the effort to satisfy unlimited wants?

However, we have given sufficient space to showing the irrationality of the first principle of modern economic science. Let us move on to paragraph 65. "Economic development must remain under man's determination and must not be left to the judgment of a few men or groups possessing too much economic power or of the political community alone or of certain more powerful nations."

Nor is it the capitalist protests. We are not dealing with human wills but with natural laws. You may wish to criticise the "system" as the Council document does here: "Growth is not to be left solely to a kind of mechanical course of the economic activity of individuals ..." but it might as well protest against the laws of geometry. Adam Smith proved that the economic law of free enterprise or individual self-interest was a natural law and in fact is ultimately the best way to a thriving economy.

We notice how the document ends this sentence: "... nor to the authority of government." We (the modern economists) can agree on that. Why then does the document go on to condemn both us and the socialists? "For this reason, doctrines which obstruct the necessary reforms under the guise of a false liberty, and those which subordinate the basic rights of individual persons and groups to the collective organization of production must be shown to be erroneous." Do not Catholics understand that if you are against the capitalist individualist economic system you must be for a collectivist socialist one?

In the last paragraph (66) of this first section of the chapter the Council calls for heightened efforts to eliminate the "immense inequalities" that exist and "in many cases are growing": "To satisfy the demands of justice and equity, strenuous efforts must be made, without disregarding the rights of persons or the natural qualities of each country, to remove as quickly as possible the immense economic inequalities, which now exist and in many cases are growing and which are connected with individual and social discrimination."

Put in such general terms and in view of subsequent history the call has had its effect not we cannot say it has been greatly heeded. In the next section II, the Council gives more specific directives, that we might have expected to have a more telling effect.

This section is divided into two parts, the first dealing with labor, and the second with property, the two most relevant elements of the subject matter with which we are concerned, human civil life at the lowest economic level, though they pre-exist the civil or political order according as understood by Aristotle and Aquinas. It is within civil or civilized society as perfected within Christian times but disrupted subsequently that the division has been reflected in modern Capitalism, as that between Capital and Labor.

Though not limited to the contest between Capitalism and the opposition it has generated, Communism in the eyes of Marx, the world problem of the relation between the rich and the poor that the Church has turned its attention to, which extends beyond the conflict between the two ideologies, is very much a product of that context. Accordingly, it is necessary to have the right understanding of property and labour, in its global context.

So it is that the Council has addressed these two elements, going beyond their notions as understood in Capitalism and Communism (basically not all that different). It is just necessary to be careful to purify the notions of their modern connotations. Labour is more or less identified in modern times with hired or employed labour, with wages paid in money (from capital) whereas the notion of work (opus) has no such association: the independent shoemaker is paid in shoes that in a civilized community he sells for money. He works for a living and he will need materials and tools to do this. He is both, a capitalist and a worker, a tradesman and a trader.

We have seen how the ambiguity in these two words have entered deeply into the English language even to the serious confusion of translators of theological documents. Unfortunately, it may be expected also to have entered into the thinking of theologians advising the magisterium. Its damaging effect is avoided in keeping to the Latin language (having mercifully died before the modern era). But it is a real problem especially in English translation.

Let us see what the document says: "67. Human labor which is expended in the production and exchange of goods or in the performance of economic services is superior to the other elements of economic life, for the latter have only the nature of tools." This is obvious to common sense but sadly that is not a valued commodity in modern thought. Things are a bit more complicated if you understand labor as employed by capital. The laborer cannot begin to work without materials or tools. Where does he get this capital from? Do to the modern economist (even if Catholic) it must appear that the statement has got things back the front.

The document continues: "This labor, whether it is engaged in independently or hired by someone else, comes immediately from the person, who as it were stamps the things of nature with his seal and subdues them to his will." The attempt by the document to explain itself seems rather unrealistic. How many workers are there in the workforce who are "independent"? They are not even called workers but "independent contractors". How many independent shoemakers are there today? Are the tennis players paid huge sums to advertise the excellence of their wares? This is only further proof that the Church is not living in the real world.

Not much point, the economist thinks, to reading the rest of the paragraph. It is all just airy-fairy stuff, sounds good but someone espousing it would not get past Economics 101. Let us move on to paragraph 68.

"68. In economic enterprises it is persons who are joined together, that is, free and independent human beings created lo the image of God" This tries to justify workers having the right to form associations or trades unions." There it is in black and white: "Among the basic rights of the human person is to be numbered the right of freely founding unions for working people."

Notice the modern elision of the final 's' on trades to convert it to trade unions – gives it a commercial look does it not; might cause problems in the labour market; interference with freedom of trade (of capitalists/employers)! Moreover, what is this talk about labor being persons who are joined together? What for, to go on strike, causing great harm and inconvenience to the community (not to speak of business and profits). Capitalists/employers have no interest in combining to keep prices of their products higher than they otherwise would be. It seems that the Church does not know much about modern industrial relations.

There are many other issues on this subject of labour and wages that are not much referred to, like treating a human being's labour as if it were a commodity in the exchange market. This is however dealt with in previous social encyclicals so we cannot complain about that. Even the social encyclicals do not go into the causes of how this could happen in the treatment of commutative justice. Apart from my books there is no place where the theologians might have studied what Aquinas says about exchange in II-II q. 77 of the second part of the *Summa Theologiae* and been able to relate the modern problem of labour to a particular use of money in the exchange market. This neglect would seem to come about because they are bewitched by modern economics and feared to look foolish in their failure to understand modern economic science. There is little prospect of course that they will give serious consideration to what I say.

Let us move on however to the other contentious issue of the institution of property which in our view is where they are completely at sea, despite the repeated statements of the Magisterium about the Natural Moral Law in this regard. This is an issue that involves knowledge of that kind of particular justice called distributive, which is even more unknown in modern studies of Catholic Theology. This is the opening statement of the Council on this matter: "69. God intended the earth with everything contained in it for the use of all human beings and peoples. Thus, under the leadership of justice and in the company of charity, created goods should be in abundance for all in like manner."

For a modern economist, even one who is most committed to his Faith, that is the most counter-intuitive thing you could say about the economic situation of the world today. Let us leave aside the reference to justice, and the scriptural "Seek ye first the Kingdom of God and his Justice", as a moralistic platitude that has no place in modern economic science. What is this talk about created goods, natural material wealth having to be made available for all to enjoy in abundance? What hallucinogenic drugs were the Fathers of the Council on? The whole science of Economics is based on the notion of scarcity. If everyone could have enough there would be no exchange. Human wants are ever pursuing scarce resources.

The facts are there is an abundance of poverty and only a few able to enjoy wealth or resources that are limited compared to wants. Are you proposing that the limited wealth of the fortunate few be spread around to all? It might make a few crumbs difference; that is all. Forget about distributive justice; it is a religious delusion.

The Council goes on with this economics of unreality profess-
ing such sharing of material goods as a right with which went a
most serious obligation. "... the right of having a share of earthly
goods sufficient for oneself and one's family belongs to everyone.
The Fathers and Doctors of the Church held this opinion, teaching that men are obliged to come to the relief of the poor and to
do so not merely out of their superfluous goods." The seriousness
of the obligation is highlighted by a quote from the early Fathers
of the Church: "... remember the aphorism of the Fathers, 'Feed
the man dying of hunger, because if you have not fed him, you
have killed him' ..."

Yet not even that seems to give pause to the modern mind
over which the veil of economic science has been drawn. Perhaps
we need to read again the story of *Dives* and Lazarus (*Lk. 16: 31*).
"... neither will they be convinced if someone should rise from
the dead." The Council is deadly serious.

In paragraph 70 the document says in English translation:
"Investments, for their part, must be directed toward procuring
employment and sufficient income for the people both now and
in the future.

In monetary matters they should beware of hurting the welfare of their own country or of other countries. Care should also
be taken lest the economically weak countries unjustly suffer any
loss from a change in the value of money."

The Latin is: *Bonorum collocationes, ex sua parte, tendere debent ad occasiones laboris redditusque sufficientes tam populo
hodierno quam futuro procurandos.* The only problem with this is
the Latin obviously refers to physical goods, capital as materials

or instruments, whereas in English it tends to be taken in terms of money and loans, finance. We have had occasion to discuss the ambiguities this causes and even the deceit perpetrated in speaking of "foreign aid" to a country by giving it a debt instead of wealth. (Refer to discussion of paragraph 85 earlier.)

In paragraph 71 deals directly with the right of property both from the personal and civil point of view. Thus it says: "Since property and other forms of private ownership of external goods contribute to the expression of the personality, and since, moreover, they furnish one an occasion to exercise his function in society and in the economy, it is very important that the access of both individuals and communities to some ownership of external goods be fostered.

Private property or some ownership of external goods confers on everyone a sphere wholly necessary for the autonomy of the person and the family, and it should be regarded as an extension of human freedom. Lastly, since it adds incentives for carrying on one's function and charge, it constitutes one of the conditions for civil liberties."

What is perhaps of more importance to be brought out in a context of liberalist capitalism which regards it as an absolute right, is its subjection to the more basic right of every person to access to material goods in the case of necessity. "By its very nature private property has a social quality which is based on the law of the common destination of earthly goods." Possession of goods, as St Thomas says, has to be proper but their use has to be common. There also has to be distributive justice in the possession given to individuals (and associations, subject to the principle of subsidiarity) of natural or community goods. It is this level of social justice that Capitalism has perpetrated the most fundamental structural injustice of the modern era. As Pope Leo XIII put it by it the majority of people (now extended to peoples) have been subjected to a "yoke little better than slavery". What needs to be done about it we have seen explained by the social encyclicals. It is not a recipe for pacifism.

So finally paragraph 72 puts it this way: "Christians who take an active part in present-day socio-economic development and fight for justice and charity should be convinced that they can make a great contribution to the prosperity of mankind and to the peace of the world. In these activities let them, either as individuals or as members of groups, give a shining example. Having acquired the absolutely necessary skill and experience, they should observe the right order in their earthly activities in faithfulness to Christ and His Gospel. Thus their whole life, both individual and social, will be permeated with the spirit of the beatitudes, notably with a spirit of poverty."

Chapter Seven

Part I

Pope Saint Paul VI's *Populorum progressio* (1967)

In this chapter we mean to deal with the social encyclicals following *Gaudium et spes* but only *Populorum progressio* (1967) and *Solicitudo rei socialis* (1987). In Chapter Eight we will deal with *Caritas veritatem* (2009), and the two of Pope Francis. It is acknowledged by all that the first encyclical listed here marked a changed approach in regard to the social doctrine of the Church, something which we have already discussed.

This change needs some further discussion since it has not been represented accurately, especially in English translations, and may even to some extent be misrepresented to suit the modern way of looking at things economic, or politico-economic as we prefer to describe them. What the problem is can be best seen as put by Pope Saint John Paul II in his SRS.

The nature of the shift from the Church's point of view is rather subtle, and should not be seen quasi-mechanically as some sort of shift from a narrow vision to a broader one. For reasons already dealt with, that is a distinct tendency for modern minds inured in mathematico-empirical type of scientific thinking.

Adverting to earlier signs of this shift the Polish pope puts it this way: "However, the social teaching of the Church had not yet reached the point of affirming with such clarity that the social

343

question has acquired a worldwide dimension, nor had this affirmation and the accompanying analysis yet been made into a 'directive for action,' as Paul VI did in his Encyclical."

He even warns of a possible misunderstanding: "In the first place a possible misunderstanding has to be eliminated. Recognition that the 'social question' has assumed a worldwide dimension does not at all mean that it has lost its incisiveness or its national and local importance. On the contrary, it means that the problems in industrial enterprises or in the workers' and union movements of a particular country or region are not to be considered as isolated cases with no connection. On the contrary they depend more and more on the influence of factors beyond regional boundaries and national frontiers." (9)

In Latin: *Quae oriri forsan potuerit, in primis necesse est auferre ambiguitatem. Quod "quaestio socialis" extensionem sibi accepisse dicitur illam "universalem", non inde sequitur ut deminutum ipsius sit pondus neque ut momentum suum singulis pro nationibus locisque amiserit. Officinas ex contrario significat atque fabricas vel opificum motum ipsorum eorumque collegia certa aliqua in civitate aut regione non esse dispersas tamquam insulas habendas sine ullis alibi coniunctionibus, verum magis pendere magisque illas ex impulsione rationum iam exstantium extra cuiusque provinciae nationisve fines.*

A further statement in this regard brings out both the worldwide character of the situation of injustice but also its connection with the spread of the two "economic" ideologies that had arisen within the field of European nations.

"In fact, if the social question has acquired a worldwide dimension, this is because the demand for justice can only be satisfied on that level. To ignore this demand could encourage the temptation among the victims of injustice to respond with violence, as happens at the origin of many wars. Peoples excluded from the fair distribution of the goods originally destined for all could ask themselves: why not respond with violence to those who first treat us with violence? And if the situation is examined in the light of the division of the world into ideological blocs a division already existing in 1967 - and in the light of the subsequent economic and political repercussions and dependencies, the danger is seen to be much greater." (10)

There are other nuances missed by modern minds in this regard but we will leave comment on them till we come to SRS. What is of particular relevance here is the way the division between rich and poor can be shifted from that between rich "people" (capitalists) and laboring poor (workers) within a nation to that between rich nations ("peoples") and poor nations to give the impression that there are only rich people (capitalists) and no poor people (with little or no property) in the "developed" world (say the USA) and that is how it has always been in the modern era, even in the British Empire in the nineteenth century. Thereby, a huge hunk of modern history is conveniently glossed over so that the population, the majority of whom living by their labour, who went to the wars, could be led to believe that the wars had been fought, not to preserve the dominant position of the rich or the system of modern Capitalism, but for the glory of Empire (defending or building), in the case say of the British

Empire, or, in the case say of the American hegemony (to adopt a current term), "to make the world safe for (or by imposition of) 'Democracy'".

Insofar as this misunderstanding Pope Saint John Paul II refers to might be taken in, it then becomes the responsibility of the rich nations to give foreign aid to poor nations, but not of rich people personally or as a group within a nation or more commonly these days living internationally, for them to have any direct responsibility for the plight of the poor, whether internally or externally. It is up to individual nations to raise taxes (that as we have noted may come mainly from "workers") and give aid not directly to the poor in other nations, but to their governments (often corrupted by connection with their own nation's excessively rich).

Moreover, the question becomes seen as one of charity, justice having dropped out of the picture for the experts in economics and international finance. The Church may be listened to sympathetically on the picture of worldwide distress, but its views on justice are dismissed as its business is charity. Even the unjust applaud the work of all in this regard. If people wish to donate some of their wealth to help others who is to object? But, religious people should not meddle in matters of economics and finance.

How this impression can be touched up in translation we may illustrate from comparison of the English with the Latin of the primary encyclical of *Populorum progressio*. Even the two words, "peoples" and "progress" are fertile sources for deception, mostly too devious to be detected by the best educated of modern Catholic readers.

Let us just take paragraph 3, first in Latin and then in English (from the Vatican website). We have highlighted the words in question.

3. *Illud hodie maxime interest omnes pro certo habere ac veluti sentire, socialem quaestionem nunc ad universam coniunctionem inter homines hominum magnopere pertinere. Quod Decessor Noster fel. rec. Ioannis XXIII ositis ambagibus asseveravit (6), et Concilium Vaticanum II edita Constitutione pastorali de Ecclesia in mundo huius temporis comprobavit. Quarum praeceptionum cum gravissimum sit pondus et momentum, iis propterea mature parere necesse prorsus est.* __Fame laborantes populi__ *hodie divitiis praepollentes populos miserabili quadam voce compellant. Quapropter Ecclesia, anxiis huiusmodi clamoribus quodammodo cohorrescens, singulos omnes vocat, ut amore impulsi quasi fratribus opem implorantibus tandem suas dedant aures.*

"3. Today it is most important for people to understand and appreciate that the social question ties all men together, in every part of the world. John XXIII stated this clearly, and Vatican II confirmed it in its Pastoral Constitution on The Church in the World of Today. The seriousness and urgency of these teachings must be recognized without delay.

The **hungry nations** of the world cry out to the peoples blessed with abundance. And the Church, cut to the quick by this cry, asks each and every man to hear his brother's plea and answer it lovingly."

Anyone see "nations" in the Latin? No, because the Latin can simply be translated by: "peoples suffering from hunger". The comparison between rich and poor can be made on the basis of nations but it is not primary. For the point is clearly made in the magisterial documents that in poor nations there is a scandalous disparity between few who are rich (generally connected with the ruling class) and the many who are poor. It is not all in poor nations who are poor.

It is just that in modern times for various reasons, some connected with exploitation of the poor of poor nations by the rich of rich nations, that paradoxically it is those of Christian (European) heritage, "reformed" religiously (ending up atheistic today), and perverted politically, that have achieved superiority in empirio-mathematical science and technology, fundamentally inherited, but attributed all to themselves, so that the world has become divided into the "advanced" and "advancing" peoples. The majority in the "developing" nations are now those most cruelly subject to a "yoke little better than slavery", as were the majority in the advanced nations in the nineteenth century, when the Church "intervened" to forestall revolution.

Since then, despite two world wars and a great economic depression the "advanced" nations have recovered somewhat with the rich capitalists turning their attention away from their own fellow citizens to the richer pickings to be had abroad. The working poor in the advanced nations no longer are left to perish and if necessary are looked after by their governments, which governments of late having to borrow heavily - from whom? But, "unfortunately" this rescue operation is not working that well worldwide.

This a very rough, and if you like simplistic, description of the modern situation. There are all sorts of complexities to be taken into account, going back to the basic distinction between the two kinds of capital and the two kinds of particular justice. The two kinds of capital are materials necessary in any productive process, and tools necessary for the laborer the lower levels of whom, as we shall see, can to a certain extent be dispensed with in recent times.

Natural resources are of course the basic material, but they come in different forms; a worker needs land if only to stand on and if this is the property of the capitalist the worker can be charged for the space he needs. In an "advanced" economy this can have a high "land value", charged by the square foot. Henry George saw how this "site value" increased the nearer you got to the centres of exchange, for it is to a large extent a community generated value.

The materials needed to work on then can enter into the value of products not just statically as the elements of a building on it but also dynamically, like burning coal. But the most lucrative "land value" in a civil community (city) is its "commercial" value. Such capital therefore has its exchange value which will be reflected in a market. This sort of value, even if "unearned" is natural and the proprietor is entitled to the exchange value expressed in a commonly estimated money price. But this is only valid in a civil community in which the materials or natural resources, such as land and the natural minerals, vegetation (forests) and untamed animals, are distributed by the government according to distributive justice. We do not exclude other rights to first possession at a pre-civil level.

In the modern Capitalist system, with connivance of (oligarchical) government this distribution has been either violated by "legal" expropriation, facilitated by generation of hatred of the Catholic Church, as happened in England and Europe at the beginning of the modern age, or by "legal" maldistribution in the settlement of new lands (*res nullius*), no man's land, in the modern colonial period. We are not talking only about injustice to aboriginal inhabitants but even to the "white" workers, "convicts" and "free settlers". The inevitable effect of such modern Capitalism was the reduction of those without property to a form of servitude and consequent impoverishment. It is this latter kind of distributive injustice that practically all in the part of the modern world that is capitalist (if now greatly mixed with socialism) are blind to. It is almost as if the focus on the injustice to the indigenous part of new nations like Australia is something that is able to be used as a distraction from the injustice to the poor "white" working majority.

But we should interpose the other lack of distinction that complicates the understanding of the modern politico-economic situation that goes by the name Capitalism. As Aristotle and Aquinas make clear there are two kinds of particular injustice, distributive and commutative. They are mixed up in the modern notion of social justice. Capitalism is built upon the most extreme case of misappropriation of external goods or wealth within a community so that, in principle at least a privileged few claim all right to property or capital in both forms of natural materials (land) and instruments of production as explained, whilst the many have only their labour whereby to claim a share in the goods produced and exchanged in a civil community. Thus arises the notion that it is capital and not labour that has priority in the production of "the wealth of nations". In a capitalist economic system no amount of insistence by the Church that labour must be held to have priority over capital can shift this "scientific truth" of modern Economics.

The situation is further complicated by the way it involves commutative justice, or the justice of exchange. By this notional priority of capital (in the form of money) the capitalist system can operate non-naturally (MCM), where the labour of the labourer, since it is hired labour for which there is a price (wage), can be treated as a commodity (C) in a Labour Market. In fact, there are those who work outside this system as "independent contractors" if they have some capital of their own (or borrowed), but in the capitalist system the expropriation by the capitalists is so complete that the majority of workers are "employed", either directly or indirectly, by the men of property or money.

So entrenched is this system of "Employment" that it is considered as a natural part of the modern economy, with its own specific social problems. Why these philosophical distinctions and their application to the modern economy, drawn from Aquinas's *Summa* (see my book "Ethics Today and Saint Thomas Aquinas"), are not picked up by modern Catholic theologians, nor even used explicitly in the Church's documents, is something we will address at the end of this book.

Now it has been noticed that the Church is most concerned with the misery of the poor's impoverishment, especially if extreme, as it became even in "advanced" nations in the nineteenth century, and as it has become even with the real benefits from "Christian"/ Western civilisation in many new nations in post-colonial times. Radical change in well entrenched economic/political systems can only be effected by revolutions which on the whole result only in changing one bad form of regime for a worse. That has certainly been proved in modern times with the change from Capitalism to Communism.

One other thing to notice is that the Church does not counsel revolution and this is repeated in the encyclical of 1967. In paragraph 30 Pope Paul certainly paints a grim picture that must prompt many to succumb to the temptation to stir up revolt. "The injustice of certain situations cries out for God's attention. Lacking the bare necessities of life, whole nations are under the thumb of others; they cannot act on their own initiative; they cannot exercise personal responsibility; they cannot work toward a higher degree of cultural refinement or a greater participation in social and public life. They are sorely tempted to redress these insults to their human nature by violent means."

Yet, he warns against succumbing to the temptation which in the modern situation plainly leads to a worse situation: "31. Everyone knows, however, that revolutionary uprisings - except where there is manifest, longstanding tyranny which would do great damage to fundamental personal rights and dangerous harm to the common good of the country - engender new injustices, introduce new inequities and bring new disasters. The evil situation that exists, and it surely is evil, may not be dealt with in such a way that an even worse situation results."

Ironically, it is the "Catholic" colonies in South America that fell first for Communism and into political chaos, whilst the "Protestant" colonies avoided this fate and the majority retained the still quasi-servile but nonetheless less socially critical condition in Capitalism, especially as it was in attenuated form owing to the influence, waning it is true, of Christianity. This seems however to be a passing phase as the USA and allied capitalist nations are rapidly succumbing to communist influence, and the capitalists seem unable to do anything about it, precisely because of their commitment to a politically superficial "democracy".

Putting things in as near as we can to modern terminology the close alliance between the rich and "conservative" capitalists, who wield power in one way or another, is changing to that between the rich and "neo-conservative" liberalists, who imitate what Lenin envisaged as the vanguard needed to produce the new world order. Thus, we seem headed for a totalitarianism not necessarily wedded to the cause of Communism, nor to the good of anyone but that of the few "idealists" (still in the grip of the people of money). However, this excursus into contemporary history is by the way and we need to return to our immediate concern which is that of the Church.

We need first to complete what we have been saying about the complexity of the modern politico-economic situation. The other kind of capital is of tools needed for production, with which has to be joined the science and art of the production and use of such tools, which is called technology. Capital as materials is of course more basic and is needed to make tools, so they are products. But they are intermediate products. Initially they can be very primitive, such as an axe or spear but with civilization they reach a power and perfection that seems to be beyond imagination. It is in this regard that materially at least, and in military terms, the capitalist nations, come to be empires, have achieved a level of dominance that is quasi-infinite – able to annihilate any opposition that has not achieved the same power.

Ironically, this technological supremacy cannot be withheld from the nations or empires that ideologically oppose Capitalism, such as Communism. For they are derived from the same source of Christendom, from which the powers of modern empirio-mathematical science and technology are derived, if in a form without wisdom and therefore oriented more to destruction than to construction. As well, the two opposed ideological politico-economic systems are intimately related, as Pope Saint John Paul II noted, as did Chesterton, so that Socialism is but State Capitalism. Political liberalism has within it its opposite, totalitarianism, as we can see before our eyes today.

This brings in a third complicating feature of the modern political situation, which has come out most forcefully with the invention of the computer. Such is the mesmerising effect of this technical product upon a population without wisdom or common sense that we are led to imagine that we have produced something that has an intelligence of its own, artificial intelligence. The believers in scientific evolution pose the possibility that man himself has thus "evolved" into what is "transhuman", something superior to human reason. That kind of discussion is taken seriously, proof only of to what level of idiocy science without wisdom can lead man to descend.

However, what we are meaning to bring out here is the extent to which humans can so fall in love with and into admiration for their own creations, i. e. Technology, as to think in terms of "systems", apparently able to act automatically, like a robot, that they treat them as able to operate independent of human intelligence. In the politico-economic order this comes out in speaking of the "mechanisms" of the market, of commercial and financial "systems", as if they were objects to be admired or feared, of praise or blame. Indeed, that is how the opposed ideologies regard them.

However, to return to the division of people and peoples into the rich (few) and the poor (majority) that is the social product of modern Capitalism, we need to remember that the simple division between rich and poor is not a social condition that is peculiar to modern Capitalism, which is actually only a very refined ("civilised") perversion of Christian civilization. The non-Christian forms of the division are more brutal, even when expressed in law, as in ancient times was chattel slavery. Christianity introduces a beneficent influence where it meets this relationship but its concrete form must await political maturity for it to be eliminated or outlawed. Capitalism, however, is a post-Christian political phenomenon which, as Chesterton has noted, has the potential for being even more vicious and cruel than pagan forms of viciousness and cruelty. At least other forms of economic subjugation retained some sort of personal connection between the master and the servant. The "commercial" nature of Capitalism's "economic laws" is absolutely impersonal.

As history shows it is only Christian moral and theological virtue that has kept the modern yoke, that is only a little better than (chattel) slavery, in the words of Pope Leo XIII, from triggering the catastrophe modern "Western" civilisation was heading for in the nineteenth century. Just how successful this rescue mission will be on the world stage remains to be seen.

It may be acknowledged that some Christian sentiment lasted for a while after the revolt against the Catholic Church (it was even present in the treatment of black slaves in the American South – the slaveowners were not all monsters). But that moral sentiment has been gradually eroded and is now all but gone so that the ugly nature of the ideology is returning to its raw "natural" state. It operates at the politico-economic level of modern civilised life, but in close association with the purely political, which as we have noted exists at a superficial level in modern Capitalism.

We are of course speaking from the point of view of nature and reason. From this level of assessment, the future looks ominous and causes many to give up hope. The viewpoint of the Church is at a much higher level. There will always be hope. Chesterton described the theological virtue of hope as "of the hopeless", just as he described Christian love as "for the unloveable". And that is the message of the social doctrine of the Church that we will come to.

So, we do not wish to go against the Council's and popes' seemingly unrealistic optimism in view of the turn of events since. It is just that it is proper to express (righteous) anger at an injustice, and greater anger the greater the injustice. But to return to the point we were making about the misleading character of the English translation let us look at paragraph 4. That is the tendency in English translation to talk as if the modern problem were solely a matter of comparing and contrasting rich nations and poor nations.

Let us begin with a quote from paragraph 4 of *Populorum progressio*.

Accedit etiam quod, fere in Concilii Vaticani II exitu, rerum adiuncta disponente Deo, licuit Nobis sedem omnium Consociatarum Nationum petere, ibique, veluti in honestissimo Areopago, **populorum pauperiorum** *causam publice suscipere.*

"Before the close of the Second Vatican Council, providential circumstances allowed Vs to address the United Nations and to plead the case of the **impoverished nations** before that distinguished assembly." (4)

Here again "nations" is put for peoples. As we shall see, it may be appropriate to talk about nations and the responsibility of their governments in this subject matter. But it is not precisely the point the pope is making here right at the beginning of his encyclical.

The word "nations" does appear in the next paragraph 5. But it comes in as something supplementary to the fundamental problem of poverty and indeed as a question of justice between nations and therefore their governments. The fundamental responsibility rests primarily on those who are rich, to come to the aid of those who are poor (especially if desperately so where it is a matter of justice), but with a greater focus on aid at the national and governmental level where presumably there is greater facility in providing aid (sad experience does not always verify this).

We should take a more careful look at paragraph 5.

Extremum, ut simul optata Concilii efficeremus, simul os-tenderemus quantopere Apostolica Sedes iustae atque magnae causae faveret **populorum ad progressionem nitentium,** *recens Nostrarum esse partium censuimus, ad cetera Romanae Curiae primaria officia Pontificiam Commissionem adicere, quae sibi proponit populum Dei universum excitare ad plenam adipis-cendam conscientiam muneris sibi hisce temporibus demandati; ita quidem, ut hinc* **pauperiorum populorum progressus** *promoveatur,* **ac socialis iustitia inter nationes** *foveatur, illinc vero subsidia* **nationibus minus progressis** *praebeantur, quorum ope eaedem incrementis suis per se ipsae consulere possint (8). Quae Commissio a Iustitia et Pace iam appellationem, iam agendarum rerum indicem consecuta est. Ad huiusmodi autem cogitatas res efficiendas non dubitamus, quin cum filiis Nostris catholicis cumque fratribus christianis homines quiviscumque bonite voluntatis suos conatus, suos labores consociare velint. Quamobrem graviter omnes universos hodie hortamur, ut, collatis consiliis, compositis operibus, eo contendant, ut sive singulus quisque homo plene excolatur,* **sive hominum coniunctio com-muniter progrediatur.**

"5. Even more recently, We sought to fulfill the wishes of the Council and to demonstrate the Holy See's concern for the **developing nations**. To do this, We felt it was necessary to add another pontifical commission to the Church's central administration. The purpose of this commission is 'to awaken in the People of God full awareness of their mission today. In this way they can further the **progress of poorer nations** and **international social justice,** as well as **help less developed nations** to contribute to their own development.' (8)

The name of this commission, Justice and Peace, aptly describes its program and its goal. We are sure that all men of good will want to join Our fellow Catholics and fellow Christians in carrying out this program. So today We earnestly urge all men to pool their ideas and their activities for man's complete development **and the development of all mankind.**"

We need only note how the word "nation" does appear but is used indiscriminately in the English translation to suggest it is all about the rich nations helping the poor nations. Coming to paragraph 6 the focus is on human beings, men generally, so poor that they struggle even to feed themselves and their families. The notion of nations does come in but only to indicate the difficulties the people in such new nations have of obtaining the basic economic and political structures and processes of a civil community to help their own peoples.

*Nostris hisce diebus dum **homines** id appetere videmus, ut exploratius inveniant quo alantur, quo aegroti curentur, quo firmiter occupati teneantur; ut ab omni vexatione tuti, ab omnique liberi deformitate, hominis dignitatem labefactante, maiora in dies de se praestare possint; ut se doctrina magis expoliant: hoc est, ut magis operentur, discant, possideant, ut ideo pluris valeant; interea*

magnam eorum partem *videmus in eiusmodi vitae condicionibus versari, quae iustas eorum appetitiones* **frustrentur.** **Ceterum populi,** *qui recens suis legibus suisque iudiciis uti coeperunt, quasi necessitate cupiunt ad civilem adeptam libertatem sociales et* **processus** *oeconomicos* <u>addi</u>, *homine dignos suisque viribus sibi partos, ut primum cives iusta incrementa, uti homines, capiant, ut deinde ipsi in* **nationum consortione** *debitum sibi locum consequantur.*

"6. Today we see **men** trying to secure a sure food supply, cures for diseases, and steady employment. We see them trying to eliminate every ill, to remove every obstacle which offends man's dignity. They are continually striving to exercise greater personal responsibility; to do more, learn more, and have more so that they might increase their personal worth. And yet, at the same time, **a large number of them** live amid conditions which frustrate these legitimate desires.

Moreover, those **nations** which have recently gained independence find that political freedom is not enough. They must also acquire the social and economic structures and processes that accord with man's nature and activity, if their citizens are to achieve personal growth and if their country is to take its rightful place in the international community."

So, we may go on. There are numerous places throughout the translation where what Pope Saint John Paul II called a possible misunderstanding of the intent of Pope Saint Paul VI's encyclical is actually reinforced; we do not say intentionally but strange to say it works in a way that suits the Capitalist "narrative" (a new euphemism for political spin or propaganda).

We have dealt here only with one kind of mistranslation but there are others showing the same kind of alien "doctrinal" influence on the Catholic mind trying to come to terms with the modern politico-economic situation in that part of the world that is, or has been up to date, pretty well dominated by the ideology of Capitalism at war with Communism.

All we wish to bring out at this point is that the division between rich and poor that is characterised by Capitalism (or as Chesterton would prefer to call it "Proletarianism") that belongs to the post-Christendom era has not gone away. It has taken on a modified form since the end of the Second World War, in good ways and bad. The rise of its politico-economic competitor, Communism, has changed the relation between its rich and poor elements, not only externally but also internally, and quite profoundly, even by 1967. The pace of change has been dizzying, and growing apace since.

Into all this has come the great political "revolutions" at the end of the previous colonial period, which though freed from the old colonial powers became enmeshed in the new power blocs. The circumstances of the rise of these modern infant nations compared to the existing "adults" (this comparison come to be spoken in terms of "developing" and "developed") were almost impossibly diverse. Shortly after the formation of the United Nations a new vision came about of a world in which everyone had to be considered as a citizen. Without bringing in the theological meaning of St. Augustine let us call it "The City of Man". This is what the Council and Pope Paul were faced with, wanting to focus on its naturally good aspects and tell to all "the good news".

We do not mean therefore to deny that a great gap between the rich and the poor on a national basis has become most evident with the rise of many new nations after World War II and the end of the previous period of colonialism. The peoples that had become colonies under British and other European rule which had, as Pope Paul notices, not only been exploited by the colonising powers but also had benefited from the good elements in them, not just Christian at the moral level but also secular at the material level. The relationship was somewhat complicated. But, overall, the newly formed nations were placed at a disadvantage to their more "mature" brothers (not all that brotherly, bits of bullies actually).

This is something the encyclical comes to focus on directly in its second part, beginning at paragraph 43, the pope referring to his trips overseas and speech to the UN. Let us look at what is said here. Notice that there is a heading placed in the English translation.

43. *Omnimoda singuli hominis progressio coniungi debet cum progressione generis humani, mutuo peragenda conatu. In urbe Bombaya haec sumus elocuti: Oportet homo homini occurrat, nationes inter se, ut fratres et sorores, ut filii Dei, occurrant. Hac mutua cum benevolentia et amicitia, hac sacra cum animorum concordia nos pariter aggredi debemus opus, communem prosperitatem futuram humani generis apparandi. Suasimus etiam ut subsidia certa et efficacia exquirerentur, quibus recte disposita instituta conderentur et incepta sociarentur ad opes, quae praesto es-*

sent, cum aliis communicandas, atque adeo vera inter nationes constabiliretur necessitudo.

II. THE COMMON DEVELOPMENT OF MANKIND

"43. Development of the individual necessarily entails a joint effort for the development of the human race as a whole. At Bombay We said: 'Man must meet man, nation must meet nation, as brothers and sisters, as children of God. In this mutual understanding and friendship, in this sacred communion, we must also begin to work together to build the common future of the human race.' We also urge men to explore concrete and practicable ways of organizing and coordinating their efforts, so that available resources might be shared with others; in this way genuine bonds between nations might be forged."

The pope is focusing on the obligations of nations, i. e. of governments. It is in so far as some nations have more wealth that they have obligations to those which have less. The pope however lists a threefold duty. First there is that of the basic bond that should be between nations, the second a due correction of trade relations and third of simple charity by which a more human association should be promoted by all.

44. **Locupletiores primum hisce devinciuntur officiis,** *quorum partes fraternitate humana et supernaturali continentur, triplicem exhibente rationem:* **prius est officium mutuae necessitudinis,** *auxilium nempe a divitioribus nationibus afferendi iis, quae ad progressionem adhuc nituntur;* **deinde occurrit officium iustitiae**

socialis, *quae in eo est posita, ut rationes mercatoriae, populis for-*
tunatioribus cum infirmioribus intercedentes, in melius restitu-
antur; **denique officium caritatis universalis,** *qua pro omnibus*
consortio humanior promovetur, in qua cuncti dare debeant et
accipere, neque aliorum processus progressionem praepediat ali-
orum. Gravis sane est haec causa, cum ex ea cunctorum hominum
cultus civilis, qui futuris erit temporibus, pendeat.

"44. **This duty concerns first and foremost the wealthier na-**
tions. Their obligations stem from the human and supernatural
brotherhood of man, and present a three-fold obligation: 1) **mu-**
tual solidarity - the aid that the richer nations must give to developing nations; 2) **social justice** - the rectification of trade relations between strong and weak nations; 3) **universal charity** - the
effort to build a more humane world community, where all can
give and receive, and where the progress of some is not bought at
the expense of others. The matter is urgent, for on it depends the
future of world civilization."

Thus, it is a call to all as brothers, at the level of government as
well, to act "so that a more human way of living is opened to all".
(n. 82) The appeal is made to the rulers of nations, but it is obviously directed to them in so far as they have or have control over
surplus wealth within their population. It would hardly be satisfied by imposing a tax on the income of their working poor,
without "independent means", weighed down by debt. So here
again it comes back to those who are in fact people of property
and money. But in the English translation this will not be so
clear.

Pope Paul makes the fundamental point with a quote from St. James: 45. *Si autem frater et soror - ut ait S. Iacobus - nudi sint et indigeant victu quotidiano, divat autem aliquis ex vobis: Ite in pace, calefacimini et saturamini, non dederitis autem eis quae necessaria sunt corpori, quid proderit? Hisce temporibus nemo iam potest ignorare, in nonnullis continentibus terris innumerabiles viros et feminas fame vexari; innumerabiles pueros puellasque inedia languere, ita ut non pauci eorum in ipso flore aetatis morte absumantur; apud multos alios corporis incrementum et mentis profectum ea de causa impediri, ideoque totarum regionum incolas, in maerore iacentes, deficere animis.*

"45. If a brother or a sister be naked and in want of daily food," says St. James, and one of you say to them, 'Go in peace, be warm and filled,' yet you do not give them what is necessary for the body, what does it profit?" Today no one can be unaware of the fact that on some continents countless men and women are ravished by hunger and countless children are undernourished. Many children die at an early age; many more of them find their physical and mental growth retarded. Thus, whole populations are immersed in pitiable circumstances and lose heart".

This will be most obvious to the rulers of the nations (or empires) that have control over vast amounts of capital (materials and technical means), able to expend billions on weapons, and able to provide their own majority working poor with ample "bread and circuses", and so should be able to provide foreign aid readily to the starving populations of poor nations. Even the propertyless in such "advanced" nations should feel under some obligation to provide food and warmth to those brothers (and sisters, young and old) who they are quite aware by modern means of communication are perishing as they watch and listen. But they do to a large extent trust their governments to meet their obligations at a national level.

Pope Paul has acknowledged that the appeals of the Church have met with some positive action.

46. *Anxie edita voce iam sunt postulata auxilia. Rogatus Decessoris Nostri fel. rec. Ioannis XXIII cum alacritate est auditus; Nos ipsi cum iteravimus nuntio ob sollemnia Nativitatis Domini anno MDCCCCLXIII prolato, ac denuo anno MDCCCCLXVI Indiam iuvaturi. Incepto omnium nationum Consilii victui et agriculturae accurandae, compendiariis litteris FAO appellati - cui proposito Apostolica Sedes studiose favit - liberaliter est obsecundatum. Institutum Nostrum, cui nomen Caritas internationalis, ubique terrarum suscipit labores, ac multi catholici, a Fratribus Nostris in Episcopatu adacti, nihil sibi parcentes conituntur, ut egentibus opitulentur, ac paulatim eorum amplificent numerum, quos ut proximos foveant.*

"46. Anxious appeals for help have already been voiced. That of Our predecessor John XXIII was warmly received. We reiterated his sentiments in Our Christmas message of 1963, and again in 1966 on behalf of India. The work of the Food and Agriculture Organization of the United Nations (FAO) has been encouraged by the Holy See and has found generous support. Our own organization, *Caritas Internationalis*, is at work all over the world. Many Catholics, at the urging of Our brother bishops, have contributed unstintingly to the assistance of the needy and have gradually widened the circle of those they call neighbors."

However, the moral problem has proved to be intractable and the world situation as it was expressed more than 20 years later by Pope Saint John Paul II in an address to FAO would seem to be not much improved.

"Absolute poverty is a condition in which life is so limited by lack of food, malnutrition, illiteracy, high infant mortality and low life expectancy as to be beneath any rational definition of human decency. The persistence of such degrading poverty, and especially the lack of the absolutely basic minimum of food, is a **scandal of the modern world**, in which one finds enormous contrasts of income and standards of living between rich countries and countries that are materially poor." *ADDRESS OF JOHN PAUL II TO THE PARTICIPANTS IN THE 21st SESSION OF THE FAO CONFERENCE Friday, 13 November 1981* (bold added).

The scandal comes out today most glaringly at the international level but it ought not be forgotten that it is the rich few whether in rich or poor countries (capitalists, communists or not) who are the principal scandalmongers. Putting it in terms of distributive justice Pope Saint John Paul II expressed it this way: "The primary destination of the resources of the earth to the common good demands that the necessities of life be provided for all human beings before individuals or groups appropriate for themselves the riches of nature or the products of human skill." (ibid)

Pope Saint Paul VI puts in his encyclical the root of the problem simply: *Cum enim nationes tum homines, qui avaritiae labe inficiantur, mores minus progressos quam manifestissime ostendunt.* "Avarice, in individuals and in nations, is the most obvious form of stultified moral development." (n. 19) The translation is a paraphrase rather than literal. For one thing, *mores* does not necessarily mean "moral". It can signify a broader concept of development. Morality is the key to full human growth but lack of it can stunt human development in many aspects. Scripture says: "Seek ye first the Kingdom of God and his justice and all these things will be added unto you". The obverse of this is "and other good things will be subtracted from you". So it is that as the pope says in the preceding sentence: "… the exclusive pursuit of material possessions prevents man's growth as a human being and stands in opposition to his true grandeur." Both individual persons and nations suffer in this regard.

Pope Paul goes on in his encyclical: "23. He who has the goods of this world and sees his brother in need and closes his heart to him, how does the love of God abide in him?" Everyone knows that the Fathers of the Church laid down the duty of the rich toward the poor in no uncertain terms. As St. Ambrose put it: "You are not making a gift of what is yours to the poor man, but you are giving him back what is his. You have been appropriating things that are meant to be for the common use of everyone. The earth belongs to everyone, not to the rich." These words indicate that the right to private property is not absolute and unconditional.

No one may appropriate surplus goods solely for his own private use when others lack the bare necessities of life. In short, "as the Fathers of the Church and other eminent theologians tell us, the right of private property may never be exercised to the detriment of the common good." When "private gain and basic community needs conflict with one another," it is for the public authorities "to seek a solution to these questions, with the active involvement of individual citizens and social groups."

The scriptural parable that all popes quote in this connection is that of the rich man *Dives* and the poor man Lazarus. It is here that the warning to the heartless rich is put most starkly, not only in terms of their end without repentance, but also in terms of the hardness of heart they risk, so as not to take seriously their perilous position - "neither will they be convinced if someone should rise from the dead". (*Lk 16: 31*)

From a natural point of view, one will be rather sanguine about the possibility of moving the hearts of the fortunate few even with the prompting of those exercising political power. Indeed, we will see in dealing with Pope Saint John Paul II's 1987 encyclical after 20 years the problem of world poverty if anything got worse. But the Church is not operating only at the natural moral level. If we might paraphrase a question put by one of the apostles in this regard: how can anyone (rich) be saved; we have the Lord's answer: "nothing is impossible to God".

Pope Paul treats of many matters in this encyclical reinforcing much of what has been said in the social encyclicals of his predecessors. Thus, he puts in his own terms the nature of Capitalism. "21. What are less than human conditions? The material poverty of those who lack the bare necessities of life, and the moral poverty of those who are crushed under the weight of their own self-love; oppressive political structures resulting from the abuse of ownership or the improper exercise of power, from the exploitation of the worker or unjust transactions."

Then again, he strongly confirms the principle of the universal destination of goods and points to its blatant ignoring by the champions of the absolute notions of property and free trade of liberalist economists in modern times: "every man has the right to glean what he needs from the earth. The recent Council reiterated this truth: 'God intended the earth and everything in it for the use of all human beings and peoples. Thus, under the leadership of justice and in the company of charity, created goods should flow fairly to all.' All other rights, whatever they may be, including the rights of property and free trade, are to be subordinated to this principle. They should in no way hinder it; in fact, they should actively facilitate its implementation. Redirecting these rights back to their original purpose must be regarded as an important and urgent social duty." (n. 22)

Other basic principles of modern economic science are also strongly condemned: " ... the exclusive pursuit of personal gain is prohibited." (n. 24)

In the context of discussion of these prominent features of modern liberalist Capitalism, Pope Paul condemns explicitly Liberalism as an ideology that makes human freedom into an absolute and pointedly notes Pope Pius XI's insight at the time of the Great Depression that these ideas had produced a system of politico-economic tyranny that preceded it (a feature of Capitalism that has reasserted itself after the end of the Second World War). "26. However, certain concepts have somehow arisen out of these new conditions and insinuated themselves into the fabric of human society. These concepts present profit as the chief spur to economic progress, free competition as the guiding norm of economics, and private ownership of the means of production as an absolute right, having no limits nor concomitant social obligations. This unbridled liberalism paves the way for a particular type of tyranny, rightly condemned by Our predecessor Pius XI, for it results in the international imperialism of money. Such improper manipulations of economic forces can never be condemned enough ...".

Yet the English translator fails to understand the intent of what he is translating and, in the process (no doubt subconsciously), gives words a translation that accommodates a favourable or neutral taking of Capitalism. First of all, take the phrase in the part of the paragraph already quoted, "the international imperialism of money." The Latin is: *rei nummariae internationalismus seu imperialismus internation-alis.* The correct translation is: "the internationalism of money or international imperialism."

Leaving out the *seu* (or) may only indicate mental laziness, or it may indicate something missing in the translator's understanding of what the pope is trying to get across, a politico-economic domination that is tied to power politics of those ambitious of empire. As translated, one gets the impression that money is somehow an evil "mechanism". There are no real evildoers; they are indeed hidden, but the translation, conveniently for those who somehow profit from the international financial "system", has made them invisible.

But let us look at the end part of the paragraph. The Latin is: *At si fatendum est, e quadam* **capitalismi, uti aiunt,** *forma ortum duxisse tot aerumnas, tot patratas iniquitates fraternasque dimicationes, quarum effectus etiam nunc experimur, falso tamen quis tribuat* **artium et artificiorum incremento** *mala illa, quae verius calamitosis de re oeconomica opinionibus vitio vertenda sunt, quae cum eodem incremento coniungebantur. Immo vero iustitia postulat, ut suscipiamus, non modo* **laboris temperationem,** *sed etiam* **artium et artificiorum profectum ad** *progressionem provehendam necessarium adiumentum conferre.*

The English is: "But if it is true that a type of capitalism, as it is commonly called, has given rise to hardships, unjust practices, and fratricidal conflicts that persist to this day, it would be a mistake to attribute these evils to the rise of **industrialization** itself, for they really derive from the pernicious economic concepts that grew up along with it. We must in all fairness acknowledge the vital role played by **labor systemization and industrial organization** in the task of development."

We will pass over "a type of capitalism as it is commonly called" for "a certain capitalism as it is called" which suggests the pope is talking about only one kind of capitalism when the existing economic system of the West is actually before our eyes. It is to this that the pope attributes the evils he lists. Let us, however take a closer look at the highlighted words "industry" and "labour". As we have dealt with at length, the labour understood in modern times, in the very science of Economics, is one "under the thumb" of capital, as also described at length, So, too, the great advances in industry (lauded in modern history as "The Industrial Revolution") is seen only as owing to the new mode of production in which Labour is exploited by Capital. This mode of production can be very powerful in material terms, building pyramids and railways, or modern football stadiums and weapons of war.

The point the pope wants to make is that it is not labour relations or industrial organisation as such that is the evil but the abuse of them that produces the evils he describes so graphically. The translator does a good job (unwittingly no doubt since he has had a good modern education) of shifting attention from the evil side to the good side in the use of the words. Notice the Latin words used in relation to industry, **artium et artificiorum**, "of arts and artifacts". Try to apply that to the labour of a factory worker in an "assembly line" today, or in a textile factory in Manchester England in the nineteenth century.

The Scottish poet Robert Burns (a diamond cutter by trade) caught the spirit of the Industrial Revolution, so lauded by modern economists and all admirers of Capitalism, in verses he scratched on a window of the Inn at Carron (North England) in 1787 when visiting the Carron Iron Works (famously considered to be at the forefront of the Industrial Revolution). As you can see, his poetic mind saw the virtues of modern industry differently, almost a difference between heaven and hell.

We cam na here to view your warks

In hopes to be mair wise

But only lest we gang to hell

It mae be nae surprise

There is no word more abused in modern "economic" language than "industry". It simply refers to an intensification of activity or work. Work is then emptied of any qualitative differences so we end up with the wonderful modern notion of "sex workers". The word "profession" has fared no better by its connection only with making money in some way or other. In the new scale of ("Western") values it is probable that the profession of prostitute has gained on that of the university academic. I do not want to be flippant. But that is the level of idiocy to which a scientific education without wisdom must descend. The modern English translator of social encyclicals that use words according to their natural meanings has not a hope where words of politico-economic significance are concerned.

In the following paragraphs the pope refers to the significance of the word "labour". He says that although sometimes a certain mystical teaching about labour is unduly glorified, nonetheless it does not lessen the fact that God has commanded and approved it. 27. *Item, quamvis quandoque plus aequo extollatur mystica quaedam de labore doctrina, tamen non minus constat Deum laborem iussisse atque bene ei dixisse.*

The English is: "The concept of work can turn into an exaggerated mystique. Yet, for all that, it is something willed and approved by God." Not that the looseness of the translation in this case is of great import but we leave the reader to ponder how accurately it renders the Latin.

After addressing the basic issues of property and labour Pope Saint Paul VI moves to highlight the worldwide extent of the critical situation, its depth and urgency and the need for all to apply themselves to fight against and conquer the injury being done. The language of the pope is put in terms of a battle as it were to the death. By contrast the English translation is tame. We just draw attention to two weakening of the force of words by placing them in bold.

32. *Volumus ut sententia Nostra plane intellegatur: huic, qui nunc obtinet, rerum statui, animo forti occurri debet et, quas secum fert, iniuriae* **impugnari** *debent atque evinci. Progressio mutationes postulat audacter aggrediendas, quibus rerum forma penitus renovetur. Sine ulla mora annitendum est, ut eaedem res, quae tantopere urgent, in melius corrigantur.* **Unusquisque animo magno et alacri in eo habeat partem,** *ii praesertim qui pro ingenii cultu, munere, potestate plurimum possint.*

"32. We want to be clearly understood on this point: The present state of affairs must be confronted boldly, and its concomitant injustices must be **challenged** and overcome. Continuing development calls for bold innovations that will work profound changes. The critical state of affairs must be corrected for the better without delay. **Everyone must lend a ready hand to this task**, particularly those who can do most by reason of their education, their office, or their authority."

Just how serious the pope is may be seen from the sentence he adds: "They should set a good example by contributing part of their own goods, as several of Our brother bishops have done."

Most of the rest of the encyclical develops this need to address and redress the critical situation the whole world finds itself in. Older dictums of reason and Faith, justice and charity, need to be brought to bear not just in respect of those who are near to us but also to those who before were far away but now are as close as the television. Thus, the pope says: "The rule, by virtue of which in times past those nearest us were to be helped in time of need, applies today to all the needy throughout the world." (49) The urgency and the emergency that Pope Leo faced at the end of the nineteenth century has now spread worldwide.

In a way the Christian notions of neighbour and charity have acquired their full existential significance. But at the same time so too has the opportunity for evangelisation. For, now the Church can reach most readily into the minds and hearts of all mankind. This is what the popes after Paul VI have taken up as we shall see, but still drawing on the social doctrine of the Church best expressed for modern times by Pope Leo XIII. Much of this, though seen with the help of the light of Faith, is within the order of natural morality and justice applied to the politico-economic level of modern civilized life, the principles of which are masterfully expounded upon by Saint Thomas Aquinas, the Common Doctor of the Church who Pope Leo so admired and recommended.

So, we will just treat of a few more paragraphs by way of completion of our comments on this encyclical of the great Pope Saint Paul VI. There are two words that recur in paragraph 56 that we have already commented upon, but further illustrate the problem of English translation that is so basic and distorting for readers of the social encyclicals in the "leading" countries of the "developed" world, that we ought to say something more about.

Highlighting the relevant passages that contain the words they are:

Omnes autem conatus, sane non mediocres, qui ad iuvandas **civitates gradatim progredientes sive pecuniariis sive technicis auxiliis** *capiuntur, fallaces inanesque plane evadant, si ab his comparata remedia magna ex parte irrita fiant ob mutabiles nego-tiationum rationes, quae inter ditiores et tenuiores populos inter-cedant. Etenim alteri omni exspectatione et fiducia destituantur, ubi manant, ne alteri id ab ipsis repetant, quod iam dederint.*

"Efforts are being made to help the **developing nations financially and technologically.** Some of these efforts are considerable. Yet all these efforts will prove to be vain and useless, if their results are nullified to a large extent by the unstable trade relations between rich and poor nations. The latter will have no grounds for hope or trust if they fear that what is being given them with one hand is being taken away with the other."

The use of the word "nations" for *civitates* is not so significant except that it shows the difficulty of getting straight for the modern reader the Aristotelian notion of civil community. But it is the use of the word "financial" for *pecuniariis* that immerses one deep into the distorting effect of modern economic thought and science. We have already noted that the modern word is tied to moneylending, and therefore to the moral issue of usury, which we will not go into here (refer to book "Economic Science and Saint Thomas Aquinas).

The root of the Latin is the word for sheep. It came to refer to money, as the measure of "economic" wealth or goods, just as capital comes from cattle (counted according to head *caput*). But money is a derived meaning. Aquinas commonly used *pecuniae* to signify wealth in the context of exchange, yet signifying natural wealth as opposed to artificial wealth. So, the likely intent of the pope's combination of *pecuniariis* and *technicis* is to aid by giving (even if in the form of a loan, like lending a tractor) capital in the form of natural materials and tools as explained above. That is to give real help, whether by way or donation or loan, not "loans" of money to which most of the *mutabiles negotiationum rationes* ("unstable trade relations") attach in all the machinations of modern finance systems.

Just imagine even those clerics (in this area mostly English speaking I would guess) working in the Vatican trying to sort these meanings out. For it is not a simple matter of translating but a complication and confusion coming from a neglect of the study of Aristotle and Aquinas and immersion in modern education in matters of Economics and high finance.

The critical situation has different causal levels but the pope indicated in paragraph 66 the true root cause, lack of justice and charity, which is the Church's primary concern and the only way finally to resolution of the crisis and world peace. "Human society is sorely ill. The cause is not so much the depletion of natural resources, nor their monopolistic control by a privileged few; it is rather the weakening of brotherly ties between individuals and nations."

Yet we must not ignore the subsidiary causes and fail to take steps to remedy them. The encyclical sums up the situation in paragraph 80. "We must travel this road together, united in minds and hearts. Hence, We feel it necessary to remind every-one of the seriousness of this issue in all its dimensions, and to impress upon them the need for action. The moment for action has reached a critical juncture. Can countless innocent children be saved? Can countless destitute families obtain more human living conditions? Can world peace and human civilization be preserved intact? Every individual and every nation must face up to this issue, for it is their problem."

The pope has not ignored the difficulty of the task from ideo-logical causes much of the effects of which have subsequently come to pass in our own times He says in paragraph 11. "In such troubled times some people are strongly tempted by the alluring but deceitful promises of would-be saviors. Who does not see the concomitant dangers: public upheavals, civil insurrection, the drift toward totalitarian ideologies?"

After addressing particular ways in which various sections of people may be able to contribute, Pope Paul ends by making a final appeal to all. What is of particular interest to us as laypeople is the role that the laity may have: "81. We appeal, first of all, to Our sons. In the developing nations and in other countries lay people must consider it their task to improve the temporal order. While the hierarchy has the role of teaching and authoritatively interpreting the moral laws and precepts that apply in this mat-ter, the laity have the duty of using their own initiative and taking action in this area - without waiting passively for directives and precepts from others. They must try to infuse a Christian spirit into people's mental outlook and daily behavior, into the laws and structures of the civil community. Changes must be made; present conditions must be improved. And the transformations must be permeated with the spirit of the Gospel.

We especially urge Catholic men living in developed nations to offer their skills and earnest assistance to public and private organizations, both civil and religious, working to solve the problems of developing nations. They will surely want to be in the first ranks of those who spare no effort to have just and fair laws, based on moral precepts, established among all nations."

The situation of the world in this regard as already noted is constantly changing. Two encyclicals follow commemorating *Populorum progessio*. The first on the twentieth anniversary is that of Pope Saint John Paul II in 1987 *Solicitudo rei socialis*, to which we now turn.

Part II

Saint Pope John Paul II's *Solicitudio rei socialis* (1987)

With this encyclical the problem with the English translation raises its ugly head again and in fact it seems more annoyingly than ever. We will stop to note only the more egregious as frankly it has become exceedingly tiresome to have to correct the translator. I suspect that the fault is mainly in the English translation though I have occasionally checked other ones, such as the French, Italian and Spanish and notice them falling into the same holes. I would put this down to them coming increasing under the spell of modern Economic "Science" and American educational influence.

Just to provide some idea of the sloppiness of translation indicative of laziness (or slanting) of thinking, particularly evident in the subject matter the social encyclicals have to be primarily concerned with, the problem of poverty in countries under the dominance of Capitalist ideology, we will just compare the very first paragraph of the encyclical of 1987, setting out the two versions one in English and the other in Latin. The terms and phrases most relevant have been highlighted.

"1. The social concern of the Church, directed towards an **authentic** development of man and **society** which would **respect** and promote all the **dimensions** of the human person, has always expressed itself in the most varied ways. In recent years, **one of**

the special means of intervention has been the Magisterium of the Roman Pontiffs which, beginning with the Encyclical *Rerum Novarum* of Leo XIII **as a point of reference**, has frequently dealt with **the question** and has sometimes made the dates of publication of the various social documents coincide with the anniversaries of that first document.

The Popes **have not failed to throw fresh light** by means of those **messages** upon new aspects of the social doctrine of the Church. As a result, this doctrine, beginning with the **outstanding contribution** of Leo XIII and enriched by the successive contributions of the Magisterium, has now become an updated doctrinal "corpus." It builds up gradually, as the Church, in the fullness of the word revealed by Christ Jesus and with the assistance of the Holy Spirit (cf. Jn 14:16, 26; 16:13-15), reads events as they unfold in the course of history. She thus **seeks** to lead people to respond, with the support also of rational reflection and of the human **sciences,** to their vocation as **responsible** builders of earthly society.

*1. Sollicitudo rei socialis Ecclesiae **veram** hominis et **communitatis** respiciens progressionem, quae pariter ips ius hominis omnes servet facultates ac provehat, multimodis est patefacta. Praecipuum quidem **eiusdem doetrinae tradendae instrumentum** novissimis temporibus in Romanorum Pontificum **potissimum** invenitur Magisterio, quod quidem a Leonis XIII Litteris Encyclicis sumens exordia, quarum verba initialia sunt Rerum Novarum, quasi **a capite ad quod reliqua referuntur,** identidem **hac de re** pertractavit, dum varia documenta socialia foras edenda interdum cura-*

bat ipsis anniversariis temporibus, quibus illa occurrebat memoria.

*Nec vero Summi Pontifices suis ipsorum **dissertationibus** doctrinae socialis Ecclesiae **collustrare** etiam **novas rationes neglexerunt**. Ipso igitur initio repetito a Leonis XIII **luculentis monitis**, subsequentibus <u>additamentis</u> locupletato Magisterii, pervenitur ad "corpus" quoddam doctrinae, quod gradatim contexitur, cum scilicet Ecclesia, Verbi a Christo Iesu revelati spectans plenitudinem, Spirituque Sancto affiante (cfr. Io 14, 16. 26; 16, 13-15), vitae hominum scrutatur eventus, dum per historiae cursum evolvuntur. Ratione **humanisque cognitionibus** adhibitis, ipsa profecto perdu cere homines **nititur** ad vocationi parendum, quae est **prud entium** societatis terrestris conditorum.*

Let us list first some basic terms:

veram This is translated as "authentic". Now there is an exact word in English to translate this that is "true" and there is another word in Latin for "authentic" *authenticam*. They do not mean quite the same but "authentic" is oh so modern, because it has a tinge of subjectivism. I can be authentically myself even if I am Lucifer, but I am not true to my real self, for "I did it my way". True development is simply development that is true to reality, not necessarily to the American way of life (Capitalism).

communitatis This is translated as "of society". Now you would not think there is much difference in the meanings but here again there is an exact word in English "community". Why the switch? Oh well, it may be explained in scientific Sociology (which the translator may have studied), where there is an important "technical" distinction made (by Tonnies) between "community" and "society". The German words that Tonnies used are *Gemeinshaft and Gesellschaft,* the former supposedly characterized by a strong sense of common identity, shared norms (the nearest the modern mind can get to acknowledging moral law), and close personal relationships, the latter by "a rationally developed mechanistic type of social relationship characterized by impersonally contracted associations between persons" (Merriam-Webster's dictionary).

The technical sociological notion of "society" seems to fit better the kind of social life one lives in a capitalist system, all about money? The Church does of course admit it has no reason to enter into the "technical" details of the modern studies of Economics and Sociology, so it leaves them alone. Things get complicated, however, when these "sciences" claim to be "value-free" and want to talk about "norms" as distinct from morals. Different human communities have different "norms" (customs and systems of positive laws) as everyone (modern) knows, so talk about a natural moral law common to all mankind is so much religious nonsense. I am not so sure even the clerical "elect" are all that clear about how to apply the distinction. But we will say something more about this shortly.

servet The better translation is "preserve", or save the integrity of. "Respect" today is a word that hardly means anything, like respecting another's false opinions, when what one can mean is respecting another as a person despite the falsity of his opinions. But "everyone is entitled to their opinion".

Facultates An aunt of mine used to talk of someone who had lost the use of his "facilities". That is closer to the meaning than the use here of "dimensions". Like charity "dimensions" covers a multitude of linguistic sins. It will generally serve when we do not know the right and proper word to use. Faculty stands for an ability and in this context mainly for rational and related ability. It is not difficult to detect where the translator got this fall-back word from, for modern thought is riddled with mathematics and terms of quantity. The modern value/quality free "sciences" of Economics and Sociology speak hardly any other kind of language.

Hac de re Question is supposed to translate *hac de re*. *Res* is a thing or matter not a question. But the translator cannot see the difference (see next).

Dissertationibus Messages translates *dissertationes* which means reasoned discussions, but it is quite likely that the translator has not encountered any such in modern university studies – they are all about questions that have no final answer in truth.

nititur The meaning of the Latin is closer to strives of even struggles. The translation thus weakens the force of "to lead" as if the leader has as much clue of where to go as those following. There is this aversion to speaking about the Church in "triumphalist" terms; very anti-democratic. Better to avoid speaking of Christ as King or the Triumph of the Cross?

Cognitionibus Here we have the word "science" used that we have discussed extensively and pointed to its deceptive connotations in the context of modern thought. The word translated is not even *scientia* in the Latin but *cognitio*, a general word for knowledge which need not be intellectual. It seems that the translator cannot get out of his mind that all human knowledge has to be scientific in the modern sense.

Prudentium Finally, the translator eschews using the English equivalent word "prudent" and substitutes "responsible". He apparently does not consider that the pontiff may have used the word advisedly because of its moral significance, which "responsible" does not necessarily have.

Not all of these loose translations have the same import. But they all point to a poor understanding of the subject matter being treated. We have dealt only with the very first paragraph and then only with terms. We could also find fault with a number of phrases.

eiusdem doetrinae tradendae instrumentum ... potissimum For this we have "one of the special means of intervention". A most powerful means of handing down the same doctrine becomes a "special intervention". Beside inserting a phrase of its own of which no element is in the Latin the translation weakens the forcefulness of the expression, from which Pope Saint John Paul II will go on to refer to the primary encyclical *Rerum novarum* and the fact that subsequent encyclicals will regard it as a head from which others take their lead. Subsequent popes have described it as the *Magna Carta* of social encyclicals.

quasi a capite ad quod reliqua referuntur This in turn is translated lamely as "a point of reference".

collustrare *etiam* **novas rationes neglexerunt** The translation of this part of the sentence is "they have not failed to throw fresh light … upon new aspects". *Rationes* are more than aspects but reasons or explanations. It would be better to say "to show up new reasons concerning the social doctrine of the Church".

luculentis monitis Leo's brilliant criticisms/warnings become "the outstanding contribution of Leo XIII".

That is one obstacle we need to overcome in attempting to comment on the encyclicals that follow the Council. It is by no means a minor one and seems to be one that becomes more and more of a problem. But there is what appears to be a more worrying problem that we need to address and here is a convenient point to begin to do so, though we will come back to it in our Afterword.

The problem we are referring to is in the order of thinking rather than of language. It may be already appreciated that it underlies the problem of translation we have encountered. For the main cause of mistranslation seems to be in the difference of the modern mind set from that to which the Church had been accustomed in pre-modern times for 1500 years. The difference between the very understanding of the notion of science we have said a lot about.

If we were to give a more general description of the difference, we could put it as the change of focus of the modern mind onto accidentals rather than essentials. In other terms modern knowledge is focused on appearances (Gk. Phenomena) rather than essences (ousia), the primary meaning for which in Aristotle is substance. It is no coincidence that the word "to understand" is but another way of saying knowing sub-stance. So, in strict philosophical terms all modern thinking is without substance – but no matter, let's carry on without understanding, seems to work in getting us to the moon (the home of happy lunatics).

The change of focus to empirical knowledge in the study of physical nature, which as we have admitted was to some extent justified, unfortunately locked the human mind into the sense level of human knowledge. Philosophically, this was "solidified" by the English empiricists beginning with John Locke. As Hume argued quite logically, this actually destroyed the basis for intellectual knowledge, or science of any kind, for it led to a radical scepticism.

But Kant came to the rescue with his reinterpretation of the notion of phenomenon giving the sense impressions a mathematical form, as Newton had done with his phenomenally successful modern version of physics, where he applied a mathematical form to empirical material. This union was somewhat like Aristotle's concept of a special kind of mixed science, examples of which were astronomy and optics. Aquinas called them medial sciences, but the special mixed method that was peculiar to this kind of science was so universalized as to constitute the modern notion of "the scientific method". The mathematical form too, however, was locked at sense level, internal not external, of the imagination. So, what there was of truth in the Newtonian physics gave way eventually to science fiction, big bangs and all. This was given the name "New Physics", with Einstein and Planck perhaps the most creatively imaginative of modern "applied" mathematicians until Gell-Mann came along.

We need not be surprised if the mathematical theories produce some results, for quantity is after all based in physical reality. Neither do the human senses lie, though appearances or impressions can cause us to jump to false conclusions. But without the penetration of intellectual understanding the kaleidoscope of phenomena does not make much "sense" of the substance of physical things, let alone things spiritual like the human soul or psyche. Read again Aristotle's *Peri psyche*, but you will understand it better if you have on hand Aquinas's masterful commentary on it *In de anima*. I know, even the modern Catholic theologians do not have time for this – too busy keeping up with the ever-changing theories of mathematico-empirical (experimental) psychology (Freud, Jung and Co. are already long out of date, not to speak of Rogers and Maslow).

However, we cannot spend any great time or space here on the problem at this fundamental level. We have other works (yet to be published) where we have dealt with the problems of modern thinking from the theoretical side of things. Here we wish only to draw attention to the difficulty that comes into this practical matter of morality (if in a theological context) in the social doctrine of the Church. The problem lies in the equivocation in the meaning of science that underlies much not only of the mistranslations but even of the Council's and pope's ability to address the relation between the Church and the modern world.

The line between the moral and "technical" in the discussion is not all that easy to draw when we are dealing with metaphysical and moral matters in sciences that are distorted by ideologies. In Economics, for instance, what is ideological is put up as if it belonged to the "technical" vocabulary of the modern science. That makes many a Catholic theologian shy away from entering into any debate upon Capitalism, for, if he does, he will be ridiculed, even by Catholic economic experts with not having any competency in microeconomic theory, let alone the Global Financial Crisis.

To elaborate a little on this practical aspect of modern thinking since it is so central to all modern social life, I will just mention some other features if I may. The GFC brings to mind the complications of macroeconomic theory introduced by J. M. Keynes in order to rescue (neo) "classical" Economics upon the "scientifically" inexplicable happening of the Great Depression. The neoclassical Economics was highly mathematized (and subjectivist) as opposed to the ("objectivist") natural science of the old classical Political Economy of Adam Smith, Ricardo and Malthus. There was already a crude mathematical element in the old political economy with Malthus's principle of population - poverty of the masses was inevitable because of the law that food production increased arithmetically whilst human reproduction increased geometrically. The idea of margin came in with Ricardo and his Law of Rent. Even the law of comparative advantage in foreign trade was incipient in Adam Smith's idea that exchange profits came from specialization; in the production of pins one set of workers concentrates of pin heads whilst another on pin points, all very mechanically efficient.

It is no accident that Keynes was a mathematician (in the new Mathematics pioneered by those constructing a new Logic as well as a new Mathematics, such as Stanley Jevons – a prelude to computer logic, even aside from Boole) with such a creative imagination that someone is supposed to have said he could have invented a new economic system every few days. Whether that is true or not his "General Theory" so mesmerized a whole generation of young economic "scientists" (with eyes on government jobs) that the science became permanently divided into two sections "microeconomics" and "macroeconomics", the pure individualist/ psychological part of "marginal utility" and the collectivist/socialist part of monetary and fiscal political management.

So, one may imagine the difficulty for the student of moral theology in having to sort out what is moral and what is "technical" in the examination of modern politico-economic life under Capitalism. Having eschewed any "technical" expertise, but asserting an "expertise in humanity", even the popes seem to struggle when calling for instance for a reform of the international trade system. We mention at this point only one place where this appears to be the case (in paragraph 43).

We quote both English and Latin extracts for not only is the problem evident in the Latin but the English translation as usual is misleading. We have highlighted the relevant words.

*Singillatim, ad haec quod spectat, memorare volumus reformationem internationalis systematis commercii, quod quidam nimio favore et synallagmaticis commutationibus sibimet vindicant; reformationem praeterea **nummariam et fiscalem** per orbem terrarum, quod hodie insufficiens esse agnoscitur; quaestionem permutationum technologicarum earumque aptus usus; necessitatem recognoscendi structuram institutorum internationalium,* *quae nunc sunt, intra ambitum ordinis iuridici internationalis...* **Systemati nummario et fiscali** *per orbem terrarum vigenti id est proprium et peculiare ut methodi permutationis et quaestus faciendi varientur, quo fit ut generalis ratio creditorum ac debitorum ac status aeris alieni, quibus regiones pauperes conflictantur, inde capiat detrimentum.*

"In this respect I wish to mention specifically: the reform of the international trade system, which is mortgaged to protectionism and increasing bilateralism; the reform of the world **monetary and financial system**, today recognized as inadequate; the question of technological exchanges and their proper use; the need for a review of the structure of the existing international organizations, in the framework of an international juridical order... The world **monetary and financial** system is marked by an excessive fluctuation of exchange rates and interest rates, to the detriment of the balance of payments and the debt situation of the poorer countries."

But before commenting on the text we should refer the readers to the celebrated two tools of modern politico-economic "management", monetary policy and fiscal policy. The pope or his household theologian (a Dominican) is evidently familiar with the distinction (the translator is not). For in the quote in the Latin we have the distinction between the monetary and the fiscal systems clearly made. Now even the man in the street has come to know that the first is to do with the lending and borrowing of money (mainly through banks) and the second with taxation rates (levied by government). The political order can try to "manage" the economic life of its citizens by manipulating changes in both respects. But as may be seen in the last sentence in Latin quoted from the paragraph it seems that the fiscal tool has dropped out of the picture. This may be seen better in the English translation though the translator had already mistranslated fiscal as the more general notion of "financial" (which usually gets associated with the lending and borrowing of money).

So, the translator is all at sea, not even having the knowledge of such matters of an ordinary citizen. But the pope does not seem to have the matter in question all that clear. For the encyclical goes on to speak of what belongs to monetary policy only, exchange rates and interest rates and debt. Ecclesiastics, as such, should not be expected to have any expertise in such "technical" economic matters. They are to do with tools of government, if the tools are those of a socialist type of government. A moral judgement needs to be made but at a deeper ideological level. That in fact is where the encyclical insists there is need for reform. One can see that though it is quite evident to the Magisterium that there is something seriously wrong with the existing politico-economic order it is a matter of great difficulty to judge it in the concrete.

This is where I believe that Pope Leo's call for all to assist in the solution, and especially the laity with some experience in worldly politico-economic affairs, comes into play. The concerns of the Church are with "profane" or secular affairs in so far as they impinge upon Faith and Morals but, as Pope Benedict XVI pointed out at Regensburg, these sorts of matters, even that of social justice as it pertains to the natural moral order, are the proper concern of man as rational and political. This is where I fear modern Catholic men (and women) have fallen down badly. The remedy for this failure I have tried to show in my books can be found in that part of the work of St. Thomas moral theology to which for some reason, which may not be strange, the theologians of modern times have paid little or no attention.

The Catholic moral theologians and moral philosophers may be regarded as hardly to blame given that the modern system of education under liberalism and capitalism is probably the most powerful of the works of the master deceiver in his war with Catholicism. Early in the piece we might even suspect that an alliance was forged between Protestantism (in its most powerful theology, Calvinism) and Capitalism as indeed Max Weber argued.

The battle simply cannot be fought even at the level of reason without the assistance of the master theologians that the Church has given to us and St. Thomas is the acknowledged supreme master in this regard. So, the failure to pay special attention to Saint Thomas Aquinas post Vatican II has a particular importance. This it is to be noted is despite the constant insistence of the popes, even the very latest, for all Catholics involved in education to pay special attention to the works of St. Thomas. (cf. *Veritatis Gaudium, 2017*) However, in their general education in "advanced" countries the faithful have been well indoctrinated to focus on accidentals rather than essentials. with which goes a worship of the new (*rerum novarum*).

We might mention some indices that lead people to think that Aquinas is now regarded as passe, with particular reference to the more recent documents to do with the social doctrine of the

Church. Prior to the Council the encyclicals were replete with references and footnotes to Aquinas; the theological reputation of St. Thomas could not have been held higher, and it was as it were, shouted from the roof tops. After the Council these references and footnotes have virtually vanished, and one might be tempted to think so has the exalted status of Aquinas. Now this can be explained by the fact that the Council explicitly stated it was assuming all that was taught by the Magisterium prior to the Council and by the additional fact that there was a change in focus. That explanation some might feel is not enough.

There is one other noticeable change that has occurred that may have some influence upon the way things are perceived by Catholic academics. That is the change as it were in the background experience of the popes who have followed Pope Saint Paul VI. Superficially, it may be seen as a new line of non-Italian popes. Some may see it however a change from a narrow Italian way of thinking to a broader one, necessarily bringing with it a reaction against too much attention given to Aquinas.

It is true indeed that prior to their pontificates Pope Saint John Paul II was particularly taken with Phenomenology and the writings of Max Scheler and Pope Benedict XVI seemed to show a preference for Augustine and even Bonaventure over Aquinas. Certainly, Pope Francis might be interpreted as holding St. Francis of Assisi in higher regard than St. Thomas Aquinas. Yet their pronouncements as pope do not show any desire to oppose the assessments of their predecessors (*Lumen ecclesiae* of Pope Saint Paul VI, for instance, is cited prominently in *Veritatis Gaudium*). It may be noticed that in his most controversial statements Pope

Francis has pointed to Aquinas for support in regard to the position he has taken.

What can be forgotten is that it is one thing to commend great saints and their works, and different ones at different times, but this should not be taken as displacing the position of Aquinas in the Church. St. Thomas is not the only great theologian or Doctor of the Church but he is called the Common Doctor for a reason, which a pope is said to have expressed in this way, that every work of other theologians, including doctors as great as St. Augustine, is recommended and regarded as safe only insofar as it is in harmony with that of St. Thomas.

One does not know how this can be but it is possibly providential, for there is no field in which unity is more essential to Catholic thinking than in the work of theologians. If one wants to understand why the pope's household theologian has always been a Dominican one may read Pope Benedict's XV's encyclical on the seven hundredth anniversary of the death of St. Dominic, *Fausto appetente die* (1921), just on 100 years ago.

The turning of attention away from the masterful insights of Aristotle and Aquinas that can be readily applied to the modern economy (because they are applicable to every and any) has a lot to do with the difficulty of the theologians. We have brought out how in our books so far. But there are difficulties to do with the nature of the subject matter in the modern context that we need to bring out more. We have already referred to the problem of discerning what is a moral aspect of the subject matter and what is technical and how the ideological character of modern science is ever present, especially as applied to what is the strictly speaking practical moral science of Politics (refer to my "Political Science and Saint Thomas Aquinas) within which is to be included what is referred to today simply as "Economics" (refer to my "Economic Science and Saint Thomas Aquinas").

Now modern day thinking on these two areas of human civil life today are dominated greatly by the politico-economic ideologies of Capitalism and Communism. The roots of both are in the revolutions the occurred at or shortly before the beginning of the modern age, at the centre of which was the Protestant Reformation. But a concurrent revolution that was occurring was the commercial and financial one that we have described. This involved a matter of (social) justice and one important aspect of it was that it took the form of a new kind of servitude or rule of the many by the few. Not that the many were excluded from nominal citizenship bur were effectively subjugated economically through the operation (a diabolically devised misuse of the institution) of property rights, as we have explained. It was something altogether new in the history of mankind, where slavery was logically inconsistent with being regarded as a free citizen. Pope Leo XIII therefore described the position of the majority proletariat (propertyless) as in a condition "little better than slavery".

This is not to deny that beforehand there has been subjugation of poor citizens by a few rich, for that is what Aristotle categorized as oligarchy but this post Christendom perversion of civil rule was a political disorder that reached a level of evil exercised on one's own fellow citizens beyond "civilized" pagan barbarity. For in order to reduce fellow human beings to the level of degradation that occurred in the nineteenth century one normally would have to regard them as in some way sub-human. Within a Christian context one has to think of it as so treating a member of one's own family. The class divide was not made in terms of human nature or political status but in terms of property. This is what makes the modern social situation so peculiar and perplexing. All are equal before the law, but this was to be considered after "the law" had determined that all possession of wealth that was in any way common belonged to a "fortunate" few who then became distinguished as people of property, upon whom the "unfortunate" many depended for their livelihood by way of "employment".

When considering the course of Capitalism since the end of the nineteenth century, and effectively since the end of the Second World War, it is to be kept in mind that though the condition of impoverishment under the system of Capitalism has improved for various reasons, political and "humanitarian", greatly influenced by the Catholic and Christian "interventions", the politico-economic system (of Capitalism) that justifies the practico-political divide between the modern rich and the modern poor, called capitalists and workers, has not been changed in principle. The economic science has indeed undergone "adjustments" even to the extent of compromise with its opposite ideology (Socialism), so as to be seen to be about a "mixed" economy. But the new mode of servility that originated in Capitalism remains. It exists today however not without having to struggle with Communism, which previously could be thought of as an external threat but is now, as it ever was, an internal one, now much more powerful.

When we speak of a battle between Capitalism and Communism we should not be thinking in terms of a struggle between a few rich and the many poor. We should rather be thinking in terms of two sets of groups or cohorts of relatively few exercising political power either by virtue of their economic power (as is characteristic of Capitalism as such) or by virtue of political power gained by this or other means, including threats of violence, deceit and some kind of corrupt conduct. With Communism that is where the Party came in, justified by Lenin as a sort of vanguard. But the party system is but a public way of exercising power unjustly seized. There are other more clandestine modes of operating, common today to political systems espousing Capitalism or Communism. Significantly, both Pope Saint John Paul II and Chesterton, identified a radical socialist system with State Capitalism. The *modus operandi* of either is in the end not all that different.

There is one moral feature of the modern situation within the Capitalist world that needs to be brought out into the light. It is so subtle and effectively hidden that one might think it was being referred to in Scripture as such as "to deceive even the elect". For though its truth can be found in the magisterial documents if one looks closely enough it is hardly highlighted in the commentaries on the social encyclicals. It is important to highlight it because it is with the system of Capitalism in the concrete that we are principally concerned and it is there that its moral or rather immoral character has to be fully and frankly confronted.

What we have to deal with is the use of the language of good and evil in the modern discussion within the liberalist Capitalist

West. It is generally discussed in terms of the opposition between Capitalism and Communism. What we want to draw notice to is the distinct tendency to put the opposition in terms of good and evil with Communism being presented as obviously evil and Capitalism as its opposite obviously a good politico-economic system. Indeed, seeing the systems as mutually exclusive it is thought to follow logically that Capitalism is necessarily the only good economic system.

There is some historical background to this. For the modern political era was founded upon a belief in Liberalism, which is a belief in the rejection of any authority over the individual and as we have seen arises out of a rebellion against the authority of the Catholic Church (whose root is religious and can be traced back to Lucifer's declaration, *non serviam*). Having rejected religious authority it naturally extended to any human authority, and especially political authority. Both Capitalism and Communism subscribe to political liberalism.

But what we need to bring out here is that the opposition is not between one thing good and another evil but between two evil things. Indeed, as may be seen, they both are deficient from the same root evil which could hardly be more grave considered at every level from personal to political. Superficially, Liberal Capitalism can seem to be less wicked than Communism but that is from external and accidental factors that are brought into its assessment, such as its apparent defence of the natural institution of private property and its defence of the individual against the State. But such "virtues" are founded in the same notion of absolute liberty resting in the individual person that extends to rejection of divine authority (hence atheism is ultimately common to both). As may be seen from within one's own lifetime experience the evils in either of the ideologies soon come to the surface and the only power on earth that can check them is that which is divine in the Catholic Church.

What is noteworthy in those living in a capitalist economic system is the tenacity with which they cling to the belief that the battle is between good and evil and not between two forms of evil. Such however must be attributed to the power of propaganda and compulsory public education. It is particularly noticeable in the USA, the champion of modern Capitalism.

But we need to move on to our commentary upon the social encyclical *Solicitudo rei socialis*. We have put these remarks here as they bear upon all of the social encyclicals that follow the Council.

There is nothing in the first few paragraphs of the encyclical that needs commenting on which has not been commented upon before. Paragraph 3 shows the same laxness as usual in the English translation. We will not delay to comment on this but will come to paragraph 7 just to highlight two particular matters that the pope wishes to take up again out of the tradition of the social doctrine of the Church (dealt with also in *Gaudium et spes*) namely, a reference to "the notorious inequalities in the situations of those same people" and the "confirmation of the Council's teaching, a faithful echo of the centuries - old tradition of the Church regarding the 'universal purpose of goods'". These two issues tend to get lost in the discussion in Capitalist countries. No need to ask why.

The English translation of what is quoted may be allowed to pass, though "centuries old" is not quite the same as "the oldest". The Protestant Reformation is centuries old. *animadversio, ex qua permagnae dissimilitudines perquirendae sunt, ipsarum personarum statum afficiunt quasque Constitutio pariter ipsa ostendit;doctrinae conciliaris confirmatio, fidelis vetustissimae velut vox traditionis, quae "bonorum universalem destinationem" commemorat;*

But more serious is the mistranslation of what is stated before: *Sensus et argumenta, quae Litterae Encyclicae recolunt, sunt rursus confirmanda:* The English is: "With regard to the content and themes once again set forth by the Encyclical, the following should be emphasized". There is an important difference between content and themes that should be merely emphasised and meanings and arguments that are to be again confirmed. This is but another instance of the poverty of the translator's understanding of what he is supposed to be translating. It is also a sad reflection on the personnel in the Vatican. Does no one of the requisite intelligence check what is being done? Does anyone in the Vatican care about the integrity of translations of magisterial documents?

In the next three paragraphs, 8, 9 & 10, the encyclical deals with three points wherein the pope believes the originality of *Populorum progressio* may be shown. The first lies in the fact that the Church has turned its attention to the subject matter, which is not limited to any aspect of the human condition, but is applied to all, from the lowest level of human life, which we have described as vegetative (biological), through the animal, to the properly human (rational), but rather considered in its social life, the lowest being economic, the highest we have called cultural, with what we have called recreational in between.

But though the distinctions can be clearly made philosophically (if one knows anything of Aristotle – they are there in the *Peri psyche*), the nomenclature, in any language, is quite confused to say the least. Culture for instance is a word like growth, or development, that can be applied to any level of social life, though in things human it is usually applied to the highest level. But even here the distinction between the highest animal level of human life and the purely spiritual is difficult to discern and more often than not involves the imagination, a higher internal sense.

The intent of the paragraph of the encyclical is able to be seen but the confusion introduced by using such a flexible term as development, without supposing a solid background in Aristotelian or Thomist philosophy (which Pope Saint Paul VI did nave), have to give rise to problems of communicating that intent which may have been underestimated. Then there remains the great problems to do with getting involved with the "technical" language of modern Economics (centred on money) we have already discussed.

In paragraph 8 itself the pope uses the phrase **disciplinarum socialium ac nummariarum**. This is too much for the translator, who makes it **"of the social and economic sciences."** Apart from substituting "sciences" for "disciplines" he has ignored the fact that *nummeriarun* means "of monies" and put in its stead the most general concept economic to cover his ignorance. But it appears that the pope himself has some trouble finding the right words for the subject matter he wants to cover. What hope have the theologians who have little or no acquaintance with the relevant distinctions in Aristotle and Aquinas to understand the issues, let alone sort out the problems involved?

We have already used a quote from paragraph 9 where the pope points to a possible misunderstanding that needs to be "eliminated" if we are to properly read the change to a worldwide focus. This means importantly that the deep divide within modern politico-economic life that still persists when we look at the modern world as a whole has not magically gone away but in fact has spread like a contagion that weakens, particularly in terms of morality and justice, all modern nations. This includes of course those countries which were previously dominated by Communism (a failed experiment in the former USSR) but also those which are currently "under the thumb" of one ideology or the other. The old "cold war" that was confined before to USA and USSR has now spread worldwide particularly with China's "conversion" to Communism, with Russia though no longer officially atheistic being pushed by "the West" (led by the USA) to ally with the Chinese Communist Party. That is looking at things from the point of view of external relations but the ideology of Communism is probably a bigger threat to Capitalism in the West internally. As Pope Francis has said ours is not so much an era of change as a change of era. How it will turn out from a natural point of view is unpredictable.

The politico-economic picture as put by the pope in 1987 remains basically the same: "We are therefore faced with a serious problem of unequal distribution of the means of subsistence originally meant for everybody, and thus also an unequal distribution of the benefits deriving from them. And this happens not through the fault of the needy people, and even less through a sort of inevitability dependent on natural conditions or circumstances as a whole." Where is the fault then?

The responsibility for providing some relief to the needy people (regardless of the cause of their need especially if desperate) is also basically the same as that on Dives for the plight of his neighbour Lazarus, where the notion of "neighbour" and even "brother" has taken on its full Christian intensity and extension.

Pope John Paul II put it: "In this framework, the originality of the Encyclical consists not so much in the affirmation, historical in character, of the universality of the social question, but rather in the moral evaluation of this reality. Therefore, political leaders, and citizens of rich countries **considered as individuals,** especially if they are Christians, have the moral obligation, according to the degree of each one's responsibility, to take into consideration, in personal decisions and decisions of government, this relationship of universality, this interdependence which exists between their conduct and the poverty and underdevelopment of so many millions of people. Pope Paul's Encyclical translates more succinctly the moral obligation as the 'duty of solidarity'; and this affirmation, even though many situations have changed in the world, has the same force and validity today as when it was written." (highlight added)

The concept of "Development" is taken out of the confines of the lowest level of socio-economic life to extend to all levels of human life, even the highest, as ordered (like to maturity in physical growth) to what is due to every human being, as a matter of justice and right. The priority to be given to the lowest economic level is in the order of necessity, not to be thought of as sufficient once this level has been satisfied.

Man is a noble creature, made in the image of his Creator even from a natural point of view, so the nobility of this nature in each individual human person has to be given its due. For the Christian, which means de facto everyone, the obligation is not only in terms of justice but also in charity. That is what the new word "solidarity" is meant to convey. Paragraph 10 focuses on the notion of development as intended to be taken, but this intent is sufficiently indicated already.

In paragraphs 11 to 26 the pope provides a survey of the world as it existed at the time of his encyclical, 20 years after that of Pope Paul VI. He concedes that the world situation has not improved in many respects even at the lowest economic level of human social life for the majority of the world's population and of its nations. Thus, he says: "it is sufficient to face squarely the reality of an innumerable multitude of people - children, adults and the elderly - in other words, real and unique human persons, who are suffering under the intolerable burden of poverty. There are many millions who are deprived of hope due to the fact that, in many parts of the world, their situation has noticeably worsened. Before these tragedies of total indigence and need, in which so many of our brothers and sisters are living, it is the Lord Jesus himself who comes to question us (cf. Mt 25:31-46)." (n. 13)

From a higher perspective, however, there are positive signs and the Christian never loses Faith, or Hope, in the true progress of mankind. Thus, all is not negative in the contemporary world, nor could it be. "Thus, all is not negative in the contemporary world, nor could it be, for the Heavenly Father's providence lovingly watches over even our daily cares (cf. Mt 6:25-32; 10:23-31; Lk 12:6-7, 22- 30)." (n. 26)

We will not comment on this section of the encyclical as it needs none and may be simply read as a view of history. Besides, the world situation has again changed dramatically since. The next section of the encyclical from paragraphs 27 to 34 also needs little comment by us. It has a heading in English, "Authentic Human Development", that is not had in the Latin. We would simply refer the reader to our remarks on the word "authentic" at the beginning of our comments on the encyclical.

The problems of translation continue, such as **oeconomica-sociali** being translated as **economic and social.** We will not go to the trouble of correcting such mistakes as in the main what the pope says in this section simply confirms points we have already made, if focusing more on the supernatural. For instance. in paragraph 28 he says: "This then is the picture: there are some people - the few who possess much - who do not really succeed in 'being' because, through a reversal of the hierarchy of values, they are hindered by the cult of 'having'; and there are others - the many who have little or nothing - who do not succeed in realizing their basic human vocation because they are deprived of essential goods."

In the next section, however, from paragraphs 35 to 40, just six numbered paragraphs, we do have something that we wish to comment upon. For in it the pope comes to the heart of the subject matter, in its substance and significance, if he introduces a new kind of terminology. It is not expressed in typically Aristotelian or Thomist language, but can be readily "translated" into such. It is presented in a strictly theological context but then again being concerned with what belongs also to the moral/political side of human life can be examined under the light of reason, that is to say philosophically as well as theologically.

The pope wishes to bring out the moral character of the modern situation and so uses the language of sin. This in itself is not an innovation for an ecclesiastical document but then he talks about "structures of sin". This probably came as a bit of a shock to Catholic academics in the fields of economics and politics, and even in the field of Ethics.

There are a couple of things to be said about this. But first let us try to express what he says in the language of traditional personal and political moral philosophy. (This may be had by a read of my books Ethics Today, Economic Science and Political Science) Sins, naturally considered, are simply immoral acts, but we must remember that there are three orders of moral sciences or Ethics, personal, domestic and political. We are excluding domestic ethics in this discussion, for a reason that has been given, but we are including Economic Science as within Political Science, as has also been explained.

Now primarily sin is personal, as the pope himself explains in the encyclical. But there is a way it becomes "structural" in a *polis* or civil community, if in modern times we prefer to use the terms "nation", "state" or the like.

In order to understand this in Aristotelian terms (based on common sense) we need to distinguish between human acts and habits. In personal terms a bad act is a sin but a bad habit is called a vice. Vices are acquired through the deliberate repetition of bad acts, where there is an added "natural" disposition to commit the same sin. A civil community (city, state, nation, empire) can be conceived of as acting badly, through the political will of all or most, which is principally in the government, and correspondingly can acquire a bad habit in this regard, habit (*ethos*) here being called a custom (*mores*).

This we believe is what the pope is referring to when he speaks of "structural sin". Personal responsibility for a political vice may be avoided by resisting a social sin that has become customary (or, if necessary, publicly disavowing any approval of it - to take a religious example we can cite the cases of Saints John Fisher and Thomas More). Examples of structural sins today are the customary practice of murder (abortion), assisted suicide, same sex marriage and a host of other vicious habits socially approved (legal toleration is a separate issue).

But the pope is evidently referring particularly in this context to "social" injustice embedded within a civil community. These we can identify as sins against distributive and commutative justice elaborated upon in our books and which can be related to the politico-economic ideologies of Capitalism and Communism.

The pope has evidently expressed himself in this modern kind of language ("structure" is a quantitative notion usually applied to something like a building) and avoided traditional "scholastic" language. But we can get the "picture". Nonetheless, it is a difficult exercise as may be noted by the copious reliance upon putting words and phrases within quotation marks. This confuses the English translator somewhat as he only selectively follows the Latin in this respect, thus missing the import of many a word and phrase.

But let us put down paragraph 35. It is convenient to quote the paragraph in full, in both English and Latin. "Precisely because of the essentially moral character of development, it is clear that the obstacles to development likewise have a moral character. If in the years since the publication of Pope Paul's Encyclical there has been no development - or very little, irregular, or even contradictory development - the reasons are not only economic. As has already been said, **political motives also enter in**. For the decisions which either accelerate or slow down the development of peoples are **really political in character**. In order to overcome the misguided mechanisms mentioned earlier and to replace them with new ones which will be more just and in conformity with the common good of humanity, an effective political will is needed. Unfortunately, after analyzing the situation we have to conclude that this political will has been insufficient.

In a document of a pastoral nature such as this, an analysis limited exclusively to the economic and political causes of under development (and, *mutatis mutandis*, of so-called super development) would be incomplete. It is therefore necessary to single out the moral causes which, with respect to the behaviour of individuals considered as responsible persons, interfere in such a way as to slow down the course of development and hinder its full achievement.

Similarly, when the scientific and technical resources are available which, with the necessary concrete political decisions, ought to help lead peoples to true development, the main obstacles to development will be overcome only by means of essentially moral decisions. For believers, and especially for Christians, these decisions will take their inspiration from the principles of faith, with the help of divine grace."

35 *Quoniam progressus est magna parte indolis moralis, patet idem affirmandum esse de impedimentis, quae ei obstant. Si annis actis post vulgatas Litteras Encyclicas, quae inscribuntur Populorum Progressio, progressus defuit - aut parvus fuit, inconstans, si non omnino contradictorius causae non possunt ex sola origine oeconomica oriri. ut iam antea memoravimus, hac in re **causae etiam "politicae" se interponunt.** Rationes enim, quae "populorum progressionem" provehunt aut infrenant, **nonnisi indolis "politicae" sunt.** Ut perversae machinationes superentur, de quibus diximus, et iis novae subiciantur rectiores et bono communitatis communi congruentiores, necessaria est efficax **voluntas "politica".** Re indagata, est concludendum hanc non sufficientem fuisse.*

In documento pastorali, ut hoc est, indagatio, quae causas oeconomicas et politicas solum expendat minoris prosperitatis et incrementi (et, portione necessaria servata, etiam maioris prosperitatis et auctus), est imperfecta. Sunt inde causae indolis moralis inveniendae, quae industriae hominum, utpote personarum moraliter officiis astrictarum, intersunt ut progressionis cursum frenent et plenam eiusdem impediant adeptionem.

Pariter, cum praesto sunt opes scientiae et technicae, quae necessariis consiliis politicis intervenientibus, possunt et debent ad populos incitandos tandem in verum progressum prodesse, sola consilia natura sua moralia, quae credentes, praesertim christiani ponunt in fidei principiis, omnia removebunt, quae obstant et impediunt, gratia divina auxiliante.

We will only note, following upon what we have just said, that the word for political in Latin is given within quotation marks which the English translator ignores (three times). The pope is evidently wanting us not to take the word "political" according to its proper meaning (as political prudence) but in a sense, common today, of an art that serves sectional interests. Failing to apply the quotation marks destroys any attempt to make that distinction between good politics and bad "politics". But then it is not likely that any reader of the English translation (well educated in "politics") will know the difference.

This has important repercussions in our confused age when we come to the question of keeping religion out of politics, as, say, even some bishop might insist the priests under him do. If one candidate, following his party line, approves of murder of the unborn and the other disapproves, the priest, a bishop may argue, should refrain from advocating election of the latter rather than the former for the question is obviously a "political" issue. [No allusion to any particular case is intended here]

It is, however, fundamentally a moral issue, a matter of personal conscience, even if one has to go against a preferred political party's line. Whether it should affect one's choice between two evils in the form of candidates' overall defective positions is a relevant consideration. Another possible consideration is whether not to permit an evil would result in worse evils. But this is presumptively a case of murder which is the worst crime possible against a fellow human being. When one wills to kill one human person in a way one wills to kill one's own human nature.

When we come to paragraph 36 it is clear that the pope is alive to the place of ideologies in the social situation; this is where he introduces the notion of "structural" sin. This involves questions of justice which may even as the Church Fathers asserted amount to murder, by a sin of omission, failing to feed a human person so that he dies from lack of food you could have supplied him with. We are not concerned with "academic" questions here.

"36. It is important to note therefore that a world which is divided into blocs, sustained by rigid ideologies, and in which instead of interdependence and solidarity different forms of imperialism hold sway, can only be a world subject to structures of sin. The sum total of the negative factors working against a true awareness of the universal common good, and the need to further it, gives the impression of creating, in persons and institutions, an obstacle which is difficult to overcome.

If the present situation can be attributed to difficulties of various kinds, it is not out of place to speak of 'structures of sin,' which, as I stated in my Apostolic Exhortation *Reconciliatio et Paenitentia*, are rooted in personal sin, and thus always linked to the concrete acts of individuals who introduce these structures, consolidate them and make them difficult to remove. And thus they grow stronger, spread, and become the source of other sins, and so influence people's behaviour.

'Sin' and 'structures of sin' are categories which are seldom applied to the situation of the contemporary world. However, one cannot easily gain a profound understanding of the reality that confronts us unless we give a name to the root of the evils which afflict us.

One can certainly speak of 'selfishness' and of 'short sighted-ness,' of 'mistaken political calculations' and 'imprudent eco-nomic decisions.' And in each of these evaluations one hears an echo of an ethical and moral nature. Man's condition is such that a more profound analysis of individuals' actions and omissions cannot be achieved without implying, in one way or another, judgments or references of an ethical nature.

In this consists the difference between sociopolitical analysis and formal reference to 'sin' and the 'structures of sin.' Accord-ing to this latter viewpoint, there enter in the will of the Triune God, his plan for humanity, his justice and his mercy. The God who is rich in mercy, the Redeemer of man, the Lord and giver of life, requires from people clear cut attitudes which express them-selves also in actions or omissions toward one's neighbor. We have here a reference to the 'second tablet' of the Ten Com-mandments (cf. Ex 20:12-17; Dt 5:16-21). Not to observe these is to offend God and hurt one's neighbor, and to introduce into the world influences and obstacles which go far beyond the actions and brief life span of an individual. This also involves interfer-ence in the process of the development of peoples, the delay or slowness of which must be judged also in this light."

36. Est inde animadvertendum mundum, in adversarum na-tionum compages divisum, rigidis fultum doctrinis, in quo, potius quam copulatio inter se, ut talis agnita et consensione roborata, imperii libidinis diversae dominantur formae, esse non posse nisi mundum "structuris peccati" obnoxium.

Iniquarum causarum summa, quae agunt contra veram conscientiam boni communis universalis et necessitatis ei favendi, videtur condicionibus astringere personas et institutiones, victu difficilibus (64).

Si praesens status tribuendus est condicionibus diversae indolis, alienum non est de "structuris peccati" loqui, quae, ut diximus in Adhortatione Apostolica Reconciliatio et Paenitentia, peccato personali inhaerent et ideo actibus personarum definitis annectuntur, quae eas inducunt, confirm ant efficiuntque ut difficile diruantur (65). Hinc corroborantur, diffunduntur atque aliorum peccatorum fons fiunt hominum mores condicionibus astringendo.

"Peccatum" et "structurae peccati" genera sunt, quae non saepe usurpantur in statum mundi huius temporis. Sed res, quas ante oculos habemus, non acriter intelleguntur, nisi malorum origini, quae patimur, nomen imponimus.

Verba fieri possunt de "nimio sui amore" deque "brevi visione"; potest mentio fieri de "consiliis poli ticis mendosis", de "imprudentibus oeconomicis consultis". Et quaevis harum nominationum vocem resonat ethicam moralem. Hominis condicio talis est, ut difficilem reddat actionum et omissionum personarum acriorem inquisitionem, quae aliquo modo iudicia vel designationes naturae ethicae non comprehendat.

Haec consideratio utilitatem habet, praesertim .si usque ad extrema consequens fit et in fide Dei et in eius lege fundatur, quae bonum iubet et malum prohibet.

In hoc differunt quidam typus inquisitionis socialis-politicae et respectus formalis ad "peccatum" et ad "structuras peccati". Pro hac visione agunt Dei voluntas ter Sancti, eius de hominibus consilium, eius iustitia eiusque misericordia. Deus dives in misericordia, redemptor kominis, Dominus et auctor vitae, ab hominibus agendi modo; exigit accuratos etiam in actionibus et praetermissionibus erga proximum. Hic "secundue tabulae" decem mandatorum memoria renovatur (cfr. Ex 20, 12-17; Dt 5, 16-21); horum violatione Deus offenditur et proximus laeditur, cum in mundum condiciones introducantur et impedimenta, quae multum actus et brevem hominis vitam transcendunt. Intervenitur etiam cursui progressionis populorum, cuius mora vel tarditas hac luce collustrante iudicandae sunt.

We quote the paragraph in full but really want only to note the pope's elaboration on the notion of "structural sin" and how its moral character may be linked to the politico-economic ideologies of Capitalism and Communism, to the evils of which the first social encyclical of Leo XIII was primarily addressed.

The Council has simply brought out the fuller and deeper implications for and causes of this radical attack on the "vitals" of human life as it affects the whole world today. Indeed, it seems not coincidental that in a way it is a time when the evangelizing mission of the Church is able to be more fully realised. The world can then find the true way of development to lasting peace. We do not enter into the mystery of divine providence in order to understand the enormity of the evils in the world at present apart from quoting St. Augustine: *For the Omnipotent God, whom even the heathen acknowledge as the Supreme Power over all, would not allow any evil in his works, unless in his omnipotence and goodness, as the Supreme Good, he is able to bring forth good out of evil.*

In paragraph 37 the pope relates the "structures of sin" which he has in mind to the modern ideologies that dominate the politico-economic and political life and most particularly the *mores* that come from the "Spirit of Capitalism".

"This general analysis, which is religious in nature, can be supplemented by a number of particular considerations to demonstrate that among the actions and attitudes opposed to the will of God, the good of neighbor and the 'structures' created by them, two are very typical: on the one hand, the all-consuming desire for profit, and on the other, the thirst for power, with the intention of imposing one's will upon others. In order to characterize better each of these attitudes, one can add the expression: 'at any price.' In other words, we are faced with the absolutizing of human attitudes with all its possible consequences.

Since these attitudes can exist independently of each other, they can be separated; however, in today's world both are indissolubly united, with one or the other predominating.

Obviously, not only individuals fall victim to this double attitude of sin; nations and blocs can do so too. And this favors even more the introduction of the 'structures of sin' of which I have spoken. If certain forms of modern 'imperialism' were considered in the light of these moral criteria, we would see that hidden behind certain decisions, apparently inspired only by economics or politics, are real forms of idolatry: of money, ideology, class, technology.

I have wished to introduce this type of analysis above all in order to point out the true nature of the evil which faces us with respect to the development of peoples: it is a question of a moral evil, the fruit of many sins which lead to 'structures of sin.' To diagnose the evil in this way is to identify precisely, on the level of human conduct, the path to be followed in order to overcome it."

In paragraph 38 the pope points up the complexity of the problem and the need for all to participate in its resolution. This needs no further comment from us. "This path is long and complex, and what is more it is constantly threatened because of the intrinsic frailty of human resolutions and achievements, and because of the mutability of very unpredictable and external circumstances. Nevertheless, one must have the courage to set out on this path, and, where some steps have been taken or a part of the journey made, the courage to go on to the end.

In the context of these reflections, the decision to set out or to continue the journey involves, above all, a moral value which men and women of faith recognize as a demand of God's will, the only true foundation of an absolutely binding ethic.

One would hope that also men and women without an explicit faith would be convinced that the obstacles to integral development are not only economic but rest on more profound attitudes which human beings can make into absolute values. Thus one would hope that all those who, to some degree or other, are responsible for ensuring a 'more human life' for their fellow human beings, whether or not they are inspired by a religious faith, will become fully aware of the urgent need to change the spiritual attitudes which define each individual's relationship with self, with neighbor, with even the remotest human communities, and with nature itself; and all of this in view of higher values such as the common good or, to quote the felicitous expression of the Encyclical *Populorum Progressio*, the full development 'of the whole individual and of all people.'

For Christians, as for all who recognize the precise theological meaning of the word 'sin,' a change of behavior or mentality or mode of existence is called 'conversion,' to use the language of the Bible (cf. Mk 13:3, 5, Is 30:15). This conversion specifically entails a relationship to God, to the sin committed, to its consequences and hence to one's neighbor, either an individual or a community. It is God, in 'whose hands are the hearts of the powerful' and the hearts of all, who according his own promise and by the power of his Spirit can transform 'hearts of stone' into 'hearts of flesh' (cf. Ezek 36:26).

On the path toward the desired conversion, toward the overcoming of the moral obstacles to development, it is already possible to point to the positive and moral value of the growing awareness of interdependence among individuals and nations. The fact that men and women in various parts of the world feel personally affected by the injustices and violations of human rights committed in distant countries, countries which perhaps they will never visit, is a further sign of a reality transformed into awareness, thus acquiring a moral connotation.

It is above all a question of interdependence, sensed as a system determining relationships in the contemporary world, in its economic, cultural, political and religious elements, and accepted as a moral category. When interdependence becomes recognized in this way, the correlative response as a moral and social attitude, as a 'virtue,' is solidarity. This then is not a feeling of vague compassion or shallow distress at the misfortunes of so many people, both near and far. On the contrary, it is a firm and persevering determination to commit oneself to the common good; that is to say to the good of all and of each individual, because we are all really responsible for all. This determination is based on the solid conviction that what is hindering full development is that desire for profit and that thirst for power already mentioned. These attitudes and 'structures of sin' are only conquered - presupposing the help of divine grace - by a diametrically opposed attitude: a commitment to the good of one's neighbor with the readiness, in the gospel sense, to 'lose oneself' for the sake of the other instead of exploiting him, and to 'serve him' instead of oppressing him for one's own advantage (cf. Mt 10:40-42; 20:25; Mk 10:42-45; Lk 22:25-27)."

In paragraphs 39 and 40 the pope elaborates on the concept of solidarity which has arisen in the context of the modern social situation and he relates to Pope Pius XI's expression "social charity". Though it does not therefore mean anything more than charity that enfolds love of God with love of neighbour it is a notion that has an appeal to all even if not religious.

One cannot help notice, however, its affinity with modern science's focus on empirio-mathematics, "solid" being mathematical form applied to empirical "mass". It thus can describe the bond between the poor considered as the "masses". One thinks too of the Polish use of the term in the uprising against the Communist oppression of the USSR.

With its proper Christian intent it has been taken up as a theological "term", just as Pope Leo XIII "baptized" the word "democracy" when given a Christian (supernatural) "form". The disciples of St. Thomas will just have to get used to this new terminology even though the purist might prefer to use the traditional terms, like constitutional rule which in Aristotelian political philosophy already meant "by the many for the common good" and Christian brotherhood, which necessarily co-signified the Fatherhood of God. Whether this new modern sounding language will make the necessary connection with the modern world remains to be seen. We will not make any further comment on this section of the encyclical.

From paragraphs 41 to 45 the encyclical offers some particular guidelines. We will make some comments though much of what we say has been touched on already. Paragraph 41 begins with this statement: "The Church does not have technical revolutions to offer for the problem of underdevelopment as such, as Pope Paul VI already affirmed in his Encyclical. For the Church does not propose economic and political systems or programs, nor does she show preference for one or the other, provided that human dignity is properly respected and promoted, and provided she herself is allowed the room she needs to exercise her ministry in the world."

Ecclesiae praesto non sunt solutiones technicae quaestionis incrementi deficientis ut talis. Quod quidem iam Paulus PP. VI in Encyclicis Litteris, quas commemoramus, affirmavit. Ecclesia enim non systemata vel rationes ordine compositas rerum oeconomicarum et politicarum proponit neque horum alia aliis anteponit, dummodo dignitas hominis recte servetur et promoveatur ac necessarium detur spatium proprio ministerio gerendo in mundo.

We have already commented upon how we have to be careful how "technical" is taken. There is a technical side to Politics which needs various arts of management just as the prudence of the general needs troops with various arts of war. But the "technical" language of modern ideology under the disguise of "science and technology" gets mixed up with this here. It is probable that what we have said has not had much effect on even Catholic moral theologians or philosophers, let alone the army of "fat cats", professional experts in Economics and Sociology working in the public service, or in the private service of multinational corporations.

The other part of the quote is no doubt taken by most as the Church staying out of politics altogether, ignoring the fact that the proviso only makes in other words Aristotle's distinction between good and bad political constitutions on the score of acting for or not for the common good. The Church necessarily shows preference for good political constitutions and not just "democratic" ones. But at this stage getting any such intelligibility through is perhaps a forlorn hope.

The last part of the paragraph makes the famous statement that the Church's social doctrine is not a third way between liberal Capitalism and Marxist collectivism. It may have helped if it was also said that Aristotle's moral/political doctrine is not a third way, no more than a virtue is not a third way between two opposed vices.

In paragraph 42 the pope brings home the worldwide situation of poverty to each one of us: "Today, furthermore, given the worldwide dimension which the social question has assumed, this love of preference for the poor, and the decisions which it inspires in us, cannot but embrace the immense multitudes of the hungry, the needy, the homeless, those without medical care and, above all, those without hope of a better future. It is impossible not to take account of the existence of these realities. To ignore them would mean becoming like the 'rich man' who pretended not to know the beggar Lazarus lying at his gate (cf. Lk 16:19-31)."

Yet in the very same paragraph he does not forget to state again the fundamental principle not just of Christian social doctrine but also of distributive justice whose deliberate rejection (in the liberalist ideology of Capitalism) lies at the root of what has come to be called the problem of social justice in modern times. "It is necessary to state once more the characteristic principle of Christian social doctrine: the goods of this world are originally meant for all. The right to private property is valid and necessary, but it does not nullify the value of this principle. Private property, in fact, is under a 'social mortgage,' which means that it has an intrinsically social function, based upon and justified precisely by the principle of the universal destination of goods."

In paragraph 43 he turns his attention to the world trade organizations and the obvious need for the reform of the international monetary "system". This is something that is hugely immersed in the "technical" order of things economic and political, which we have already commented upon. The "sciences" and "arts" employed at this international level are affected by the same lack of theoretical and practical wisdom that bedevils them at the national level. The prospects for reform then are rather remote. But that is considering things from the point of view of nature and reason. Man has to play his part at this level.

In paragraph 44 the pope makes the point that the responsibility of each nation to develop its potential rest primarily on its own efforts, it must carry out the necessary reforms to its own constitution, just as each individual person must first of all be true to himself, before calling upon the help of others, even if this is necessary. Thus, he says: "Other nations need to reform certain unjust structures, and in particular their political institutions, in order to replace corrupt, dictatorial and authoritarian forms of government by democratic and participatory ones. This is a process which we hope will spread and grow stronger. For the 'health' of a political community - as expressed in the free and responsible participation of all citizens in public affairs, in the rule of law and in respect for the promotion of human rights - is the necessary condition and sure guarantee of the development of 'the whole individual and of all people'."

What he makes is a general point applying to all civil communities, including good ones. Unfortunately, the way it is put can give the impression that he is referring to less "advanced" nations and to the political corruption commonly to be found in them. They should reform themselves by imitating the "advanced" nations which have no "plank" in their own eyes.

It is clear that this impression is counter to the whole tenor of the Church's social doctrine and even to the intent of the text when seen in Latin *Aliae nationes quasdam structuras suas iniustas reforment oportet praesertim instituta sua politica, eo consilio ut pro regimine corrupto, dictatorio vel imperioso formam democraticam etparticipalem substituant.* Why is a corrupt empire called simply "authoritarian? "A democratic form" evidently refers to the participatory character that ought to belong to every good political constitution, even regal. But, almost inevitably, it will be equated with the modern form of democracy that a capitalist system boasts of its workers enjoying.

It just shows how risky it is to adopt modern terms in politics and how careful one has especially to be in adopting words such as "democratic". However, we must end our commentary on *Solicitudo rei socialis* here. The remaining paragraphs (ending on para. 49) do not require any particular further comment. We move on then to consider Pope Benedict XVI's *Caritas in veritate* (2009).

Chapter Eight

For reasons indicated, our criticisms of aspects of the encyclicals of popes Benedict XVI and Francis should be taken as provisional and needing a closer and fuller treatment. This we will endeavour to make in our two remaining books in this series.

Part I

Pope Benedict XVI's *Caritas in veritate* (2009)

Pope Benedict XVI issued only one social encyclical. It was intended to be issued on the 40th anniversary of *Populorum progressio* but was delayed to 2009 by the happening of the Global Financial Crisis (GFC). It has 79 numbered paragraphs and is divided into 6 parts, called chapters. It has159 footnotes only one of which refers to the work of St. Thomas. But then again there is only one footnote referring to St. Augustine. Most of the references are to works of the popes since Vatican II including Benedict.

Though the pope is very strong on stating that the Council and popes since are fully in accord and continuity with the tradition of the social doctrine of the Church one might gain the impression from the treatment of questions that *Rerum novarum* had faded into the background and a fresh approach was called for. Indeed, in the encyclical itself the pope puts it that *Populorum progressio* had replaced *Rerum Novarum* as the primary document for our time. It is clear that Pope Benedict himself did not want his statements to be taken as diminishing the fundamental importance of the previous encyclicals. But other factors, some within the wording of the encyclical itself, even in the Latin, appear to work to bolster the impression that the social situation has changed and a more spiritual, or directly scriptural, approach was needed. We have noted the almost total absence of any explicit reference to the work of Aquinas, not just in regard to the philosophical principles of the natural moral law but also to the treatment of justice in the *Summa Theologiae*. The principles are referred to but without referencing Aquinas.

There is the usual problem with the English translation which we will illustrate by quoting the first paragraph in English and Latin. Astoundingly, although "true" is in the title and central to the whole document, the word used to translate it is almost invariably "authentic". We simply refer the reader to our previous comments in this regard.

But the difficulty with the text goes deeper than this. As previously noted, Cardinal Ratzinger's adherence to the thought of Aquinas was not as wholehearted as that of previous members of the hierarchy. We do not say that being a German rather than an Italian was a factor, but no doubt differences of temperament condition one's thinking on practical matters.

Though rather of remote relevance it is to be remembered that Luther was an Augustinian and hated Aquinas's reliance on Aristotle and human reason in his theology. The mood after the Council was not as crude as this but many had tired of the sameness and even certainty in stating Catholic social doctrine that seemed to leave no room for its development. It is of course an exaggeration and caricature of the mood, but Carl Jung for instance considered that there was good reason to believe there were four persons in God. Why are we not free, some may say, to consider this as a theological possibility? The new approach, is it not, an openness to dialogue with all and sundry?

There was some basis to the complaints as to the way the teaching of theology was being presented, as Pope Saint Paul VI himself acknowledged, but one can detect the old itch for new things (*Rerum novarum*) that Pope Leo XIII noted was a feature of modernity; and it is evidently a continuing one.

How this might be seen as relevant to a shift post Vatican II from following Aquinas so strictly to taking in more broadly the work of other theologians, such as Augustine and the earlier Fathers (with the Council's call for an approach that was closer to Scripture), may be gathered from a quote from Chesterton comparing the way Aquinas and Augustine expressed their thought:

"There is no thinker who is so unmistakably thinking about things and not being misled by the indirect influence of words, as St. Thomas Aquinas. It is true in that sense that he has not the advantage of words, any more than the disadvantage of words. Here he differs sharply, for instance, from St. Augustine who was, among other things a wit. He was also a sort of prose poet, with a power over words in their atmospheric and emotional aspect; so that his books abound with beautiful passages that rise in the memory like strains of music; the *illi in vos saeviant*; or the unforgettable cry, 'Late I have loved thee, O Ancient Beauty!' It is true that there is little or nothing of this kind in St. Thomas; but if he was without the higher uses of the mere magic of words, he was also free from that abuse of it, by mere sentimentalists or self-centred artists, which can become merely morbid and a very black magic indeed."[1]

St. Thomas, in his theological method, as Saint Paul VI noted, was akin to the scientist. This does not mean that he did not have a poetic soul. There is no greater poetry than his hymns on the Blessed Sacrament. In his theology, however, he was totally impersonal in order to express and defend the objective truth of the Catholic Faith. Chesterton notes this deeper and almost unique quality of his mind. "And yet I confess that, in reading his philosophy, I have a very peculiar and powerful impression analogous to poetry ... I mean the elemental and primitive poetry that shines through all his thoughts; and especially through the thought with which all his thinking begins. It is the intense rightness of his sense of the relation between the mind and the real thing outside the mind."[2] Those who prefer St. Augustine to St. Thomas, which often is a mere matter of intellectual temperament, can miss this deeper beauty of the latter's mind.

Chesterton's point is not to oppose the poetic to the analytic. He himself was rather a poet than anything else. Nor is he denigrating Augustine's theological/linguistic method. Applying this characteristic to the interpretation of Scripture we may note that St. Thomas did not regard his literal interpretation of Scripture as

---

[1] G. K. Chesterton, "The Dumb Ox", Ch. VIII, "The Sequel to St. Thomas".
[2] "The Dumb Ox", ibid.

superior to the spiritual modes (allegorical, moral and anagogical). Rather he saw that the Fathers and other doctors had done this kind of commentary as well as anyone. What he saw needed to be done was to provide the literal "body" with which such spiritual soul must co-exist, or the rational basis with which it must co-operate. We should note here that "literal' means something other for St. Thomas than ordinarily taken today – it meant what the author intended to express even if metaphorically. The scriptural sense was simply of a higher order.

What he did say was that the truths expressed in the other modes needed to be grounded on the literal meaning and one could only argue definitively from the literal meaning. This has important implications for the interpretation of Scripture and the subjectivity that can enter into interpretations. The history of Protestantism attests to this loss of objectivity with the inevitable result in an abundance of contradictory private interpretations.

With theology St. Thomas saw the need for this "science" to reflect the relation in human nature of the body to the soul. Our mental life even in terms of Faith and Reason had to reflect that. Just as the soul lives naturally in a body, grace must exist and operate in our human nature. Faith transcends Reason, but it cannot contradict it. Indeed, as grace perfects our nature, so does Faith perfect our Reason.

But what we wish to take from Chesterton's observation is the last part of it where he warns of the possibility, and even tendency for some (lesser minds than Augustine and Bonaventure), become "mere sentimentalists or self-centred artists," to abuse their mastery of language. Which can become "merely morbid and a very black magic indeed."[3]

I am afraid that many modern theologians, in wishing to return to the Augustinian approach in theology, have become very "wordy" indeed, and in some cases their wordiness is reminiscent of that famous Augustinian, "brooding, sincere, decidedly morbid", as described by Chesterton, "and his name was Martin Luther".

In preferring St. Augustine to St. Thomas, but without the genius of St. Augustine (or St. Bonaventure), modern theologians risk falling into the trap of being mere abusers of words or language. What Pope Saint Paul VI said in *Lumen ecclesiae*, bears repeating here, with particular attention needed to be paid to the danger of supernaturalism or fideism: "In this matter there is evident danger of falling into either of two opposite errors: a *naturalism* which completely eliminates God from the world and especially from Man's life, and a false *supernaturalism*, or *fideism*, which seeks to avoid any doctrinal or spiritual decline by using the principle of authority to suppress the legitimate demands of reason and the development of the natural order. In fideism, however, the principle of authority is extended beyond its proper sphere, namely, the truths of faith revealed by Christ which are the seeds in us of the life to come and which completely transcend the limits of the human intellect.

---

[3] G. K. Chesterton, "The Dumb Ox", Ch. VIII, "The Sequel to St. Thomas".

These two dangers have often arisen throughout the centuries, both before and after St Thomas's time. In our own day they wait, like Scylla and Charybdis, for those who incautiously involve themselves in the many problems raised by the relations between faith and reason. In thus involving themselves, men may be showing the kind of innovative daring St Thomas showed in his day, but they often lack the clear vision and balance which the great doctor possessed in a supreme degree." (Refer to my book "Thomist Tradition: Avoiding Scylla and Charybdis.")

There is, then, this general and legitimate difference of approach in Theology between the Augustinians and the Thomists (which, of course, did not prevent St. Thomas from paying great deference to Augustine's thought). But if one does not give special attention to the approach of St. Thomas, and follow it faithfully, there is a distinct risk of losing one's balance not only in Theology but also in Philosophy (in my book referred to above I argue that the former applies in the case of de Lubac and the latter in the case of MacIntyre, two of the most innovative Catholic academics of our day).

Now it is well known that early in his academic career, well prior to his pontificate, Josef Ratzinger was sympathetic to the excitingly new developments in the study and teaching of Catholic Theology that proposed a return to the sources (*Ressourcement*) and later acquired the title *Nouvelle Theologie*. Nonetheless, there were strong Thomist counter influences if somewhat outside the mainstream in Josef Pieper, perhaps the most significant German lay Catholic theologian/ philosopher of his time, together with the Catholic priest Romano Guardini who, though

Italian by birth, grew up in Germany and evidently was a great influence on the thinking of Cardinal Ratzinger. Though not necessarily identified as a Thomist Guardini was solidly founded in the common sense philosophy of Aristotle with which went a profound insight into the modern situation. It is interesting to note that Pope Francis seems to be much influenced by him. These two modern Catholic philosophers /theologians were thinkers who possessed the vision and balance of Saint Thomas that Pope Saint Paul VI believed the modern world sorely needed.

In the case of Pope Benedict XVI, it is evident that his early enthusiasm for the novelties arising in modern Catholic theology gradually subsided during the pontificate of Pope John Paul II and was all but absent on his election as pope. This can be seen quite clearly in his social encyclical. Though, like the new enthusiasts, he highlighted divine Charity as the fundamental "force" that drives (impels) us in the necessary development of our human life, including social life, to the final state of justice and peace according to God's eternal will, he was careful not to disconnect it from divine Truth, which sets us free. He gives a marvelous analysis of the interdependence of charity and truth.

It is a mistake to give one aspect of the divine nature priority over the other. One might as well set up what is appropriated to one person of the Trinity against another, in this case the third against the second. God is Love, but so is God Truth. True it is that Pope Benedict uses language that makes it look as if Love has a certain priority over everything else. He applies physical terms like "force" (*vis*) that tends to create this impression. The English translation only reinforces this impression, even adding (without warrant) "driving" to the word to bring out its elemental mechanical sense. This only shows how much the modern "educated" mind is set in a physicalist mould. The pope has to be using the term analogically or even metaphorically, which can be done in Theology

We set out below paragraph 1 in Latin and English with the relevant words highlighted in support of what we have said.

*Caritas in veritate, quam sua terrestri vita ac potissimum suam per mortem et resurrectionem testificatus est Iesus Christus, praecipua est **vis**, quae **verum** in omnibus humanis personis universaque humanitate producit progressum. Amor – "caritas" – **magna** est **vis** quae personas **impellit** ut animose studioseque in iustitiae ac pacis provincia agant. Est **quidem vis**, quae a Deo principium sumit, Amore sane aeterno absolutaque Veritate. Unusquisque suum bonum reperit, Dei de se accipiens consilium, ut in plenitudine perficiatur: hoc in consilio suam veritatem is invenit atque huic veritati adhaerens fit liber (cfr Io 8, 32). Cum quis veritatem tuetur eandemque humiliter certeque in vita testatur, caritatis **rationes impellentes** praebet, quae substitui non possunt. Ipsa "congaudet autem veritati" (1 Cor 13, 6). Homines universi ad **vere amandum ex animo impelluntur**: amor perinde ac veritas eos numquam plane deserunt, quandoquidem vocationem prae se ferunt, quam Deus in cuiusque hominis corde menteque **posuit**. Mundat Iesus Christus et a nostris paupertatibus humanis amorem et veritatem conquirendam abducit atque in plenitudine amoris voluntatem vitaeque verae **propositum** ostendit, quod pro* *nobis comparavit Deus. In Christo caritas in veritate Vultus fit eius Personae, vocatio fit nobis ad nostros fratres in veritate eius propositi diligendos. Etenim Ipse Veritas est (cfr Io 14, 6).*

"Charity in truth, to which Jesus Christ bore witness by his earthly life and especially by his death and resurrection, is the principal **driving force** behind the **authentic** development of every person and of all humanity. Love – *caritas* – is an extraordinary **force** which leads people to opt for courageous and generous engagement in the field of justice and peace. It is a **force** that has its origin in God, Eternal Love and Absolute Truth. Each person finds his good by adherence to God's plan for him, in order to realize it fully: in this plan, he finds his truth, and through adherence to this truth he becomes free (cf. Jn 8:32). To defend the truth, to articulate it with humility and conviction, and to bear witness to it in life are therefore **exacting and indispensable forms** of charity. Charity, in fact, "rejoices in the truth" (1 Cor 13:6). All people feel the interior **impulse** to love **authentically**: love and truth never abandon them completely, because these are the vocation **planted** by God in the heart and mind of every human person. The search for love and truth is purified and liberated by Jesus Christ from the impoverishment that our humanity brings to it, and he reveals to us in all its fullness the **initiative** of love and the **plan** for true life that God has prepared for us. In Christ, *charity in truth* becomes the Face of his Person, a vocation for us to love our brothers and sisters in the truth of his plan. indeed, he himself is the Truth (cf. Jn 14:6)."

This tying of charity or love to truth (or wisdom) is an important and necessary correction to the popular mood that was expressed in the Beatles' song (1967): "all you need is love". This mood or emotion has however become entrenched in modern sexual immorality, which has now "progressed" to the deepest level of depravity. Pope Benedict points out how the words can be misused and to such an extent as to signify their very opposite. But so deep seated had become this exaltation of "free love" in modern culture not just generally but also in Catholic life, even of the clergy, that it must have put enormous strain on the pope himself. One can well understand that its difficulty may have played some part in the pope's resignation. He was already an old man at the time of his election, and apparently pleaded want of strength to bear the burdens of office as a reason for giving it up.

We will make some initial comment on the Introduction in which Pope Benedict makes this fundamental point of the relation between Charity or divine love and Truth or divine wisdom. This can readily be given a supernatural interpretation in terms of the relation between the persons of the Trinity. However, this inter-relationship is detectible in the created order, but only if one founds it in the metaphysical order of being as true and good. The correction made by the pope was a necessary one in the concrete context of the social situation in the modern world, as explained above. However, it is pitched at a rather general and even abstract level so that one may think it does not really come to grips with the burning issues of the day. This may even be seen when the pope applies his mind to two particular aspects that are central to the traditional social doctrine of the Church, namely, the notions of justice and the common good.

The discussions of justice and the common good are all very necessary and important but they need to be taken well beyond the most general level. They are also applicable at the level of nature and reason, where St. Thomas gives them a most detailed treatment even in his *Summa Theologiae* (Refer to my book "Ethics Today and Saint Thomas Aquinas"). Pope Leo XIII and subsequent popes did apply them most strongly to the situation of the times Ih they were in. This continued through to Pope Saint John Paul II. But one cannot help noticing a weakening of concrete focus in the encyclical of Pope Benedict.

The points he makes are all very true and well made but somehow fall short in their application, for instance, to the deteriorating condition of the world's poor and their increasingly brutal exploitation at the hands of those already excessively rich, whether considered individually or nationally, and this continuing unabated even after the fall of the USSR in 1989. This is not necessarily seen as a fault in the pope but rather an early sign of his failing strength. The problems on all sides even in his times were indeed overwhelming. They have not of course gotten any less so after his resignation.

We will examine more particularly the rest of the encyclical, which is divided into six chapters. However, chapter one (paragraphs 10 to 20) needs little comment since it does not add anything to what is already in *Populorum progessio* and other documents of Pope Saint Paul VI. We will refer to only one point made.

In paragraph 10 the pope refers to the unity of the tradition with regard to the social doctrine of the Church as applying to

Populorum progressio as to all other social encyclicals: "The correct viewpoint, then, is that of the *Tradition of the apostolic faith,* a patrimony both ancient and new, outside of which *Populorum progressio* would be a document without roots – and issues concerning development would be reduced to merely sociological data." In Latin: *Recta quidem animadversio est fidei apostolicae Traditionis, patrimonii antiqui novique, extra quod Litterae encyclicae Populorum progrogressio si versarentur, documentum essent sine radicibus progressionisque quaestiones in sociologica tantum elementa reciderent.* (10)

It is noteworthy how Pope Benedict describes what the encyclical would amount to without its traditional roots. We have to appreciate that this tradition refers not only to the light of Faith but also to that of Reason (as the pope insists on in good Thomist fashion time and time again). In his testament revealed after his death it is clear that the pope well understood that much of what was called science in modern times was but false philosophy.

"What I said before to my countrymen, I now say to all those in the Church who have been entrusted to my service: Stand firm in the faith! Do not let yourselves be confused! It often seems that science – the natural sciences on the one hand and historical research (especially exegesis of Sacred Scripture) on the other – are able to offer irrefutable results at odds with the Catholic faith. I have experienced the transformations of the natural sciences since long ago and have been able to see how, on the contrary, apparent certainties against the faith have vanished, proving to be not science, but philosophical interpretations only apparently pertaining to science …".

The Faith is not opposed to science which is true to reason even it is the imperfect science of material causes or empirical investigations. It is not opposed to the mixed science that derives from subjecting such "matter" to mathematical forms or formulas. But it is opposed to philosophical falsity masquerading as science which is the notion of science for many if not most scientific experts occupying "professorships" in modern universities, who unfortunately indoctrinate their students so that they become atheists. That debased idea of science is what is put up as opposed not only to supernatural faith but also to natural religion.

Pope Benedict was alive to this deception if he relied more on his experience than on the completeness of his grasp of Aquinas. It is this quasi-Aristotelian insight based in common sense that stood him in good stead in his pontificate. In our opinion, admittedly unable to be verified, the tension coming from pressures both internal and external that we have alluded to was a large factor in his resignation.

Be that as it may, we need to examine and comment upon the encyclical as it is. We move on to a consideration of Chapter Two.

However, before doing this let us briefly advert to a most peculiar problem of translation within this encyclical. It occurs in paragraph 55 the first sentence of which we first quote in Latin highlighting the word concerned. 55. *Revelatio christiana de unitate generis humani interpretationem quondam prae se fert metaphysicam humani in quo **rationalitas** elementum est essential.*

Then we put the English: The Christian revelation of the unity of the human race presupposes a *metaphysical interpretation of the "humanum" in which **relationality** is an essential element.*

Notice the mistranslation? Relationality is not rationality. This seems to be a blatant error on the part of the English translator. But, extraordinarily, the same error of translation appears in other languages. I have checked the Spanish, French and Italian and they all make the same mistake! Moreover, the context of the paragraph seems to support such a reading. Is the mistake in the Latin version published? If the mistake is in the Latin is there any way of correcting such a blatant error? The Latin is supposed to be the official text and the author has now died. Why has not the problem been realised before?

It may not be of much doctrinal significance since though the pope seems to be making a point that philosophically (metaphysically) relation or relationality (not just to God but as such) belongs to the essence/substance of human nature (when more properly it is rationality that does) he is evidently speaking about unity and community in the order of grace. Relation does come into the essence of the "definition" of person in the Trinity but there was an effort to transport such a definition into the concept of person taken generally and substitute it for Boethius's "individual substance of rational nature". We have discussed this issue in regard to an article by the pope as cardinal on the concept of person (put in an appendix).

In the first paragraph (21) of Chapter Two the pope goes over the various aspects of the social situation at his time which we must remember was in the midst of the Global Financial Crisis of

2008. On reading what he says one would not gain any idea that it was a crisis of Capitalism. Thus, he ends up saying: "The current crisis obliges us to re-plan our journey, to set ourselves new rules and to discover new forms of commitment, to build on positive experiences and to reject negative ones. The crisis thus becomes *an opportunity for discernment, in which to shape a new vision for the future.* In this spirit, with confidence rather than resignation, it is appropriate to address the difficulties of the present time." What are these new rules, new forms of commitment? This is what we meant by saying there seems to have been a loss of critical awareness of what was wrong with "the system".

In paragraph 22 the pope does point to "glaring inequalities" and the injustice of the divide between the rich and the poor, and the use by the rich of their advantage gained by exclusive possession or control of property, backed up by law. Thus, he observes: "On the part of rich countries there is excessive zeal for protecting knowledge through an unduly rigid assertion of the right to intellectual property, especially in the field of health care". What is "an unduly rigid assertion of the right of property"? Even so it is put mainly at the level of rich nations and poor nations.

In paragraph 23 the pope refers to the changes that have occurred since 1987 and especially the dissolution of the USSR. He initially makes the point that human social development means more than political economic and technological. We believe such a point can be made too much of in the discussion, as if it were not obvious. However, the word development being taken from this limited context perhaps it is necessary to remind modern moral philosophers and Catholic theologians that Pope Paul VI was using it in its most extensive sense. It is the rest of the paragraph that needs some comment, so we put in English and Latin:

"After the collapse of the economic and political systems of the Communist countries of Eastern Europe and the end of the **so-called *opposing blocs,*** a complete re-examination of development was needed. Pope John Paul II called for it, when in 1987 he pointed to the existence of these blocs as one of the principal causes of underdevelopment, inasmuch as politics withdrew resources from the economy and from the culture, and **ideology** inhibited freedom. Moreover, in 1991, after the events of 1989, he asked that, in view of **the ending of the blocs,** there should be a comprehensive new plan for development, not only in those countries, but also in the West and in those parts of the world that were in the process of evolving. This has been achieved only in part, and it is still a real duty that needs to be discharged, perhaps by means of the choices that are necessary to overcome current economic problems."

Post ruinam oeconomicorum et politicorum ordinum apud Nationes communistas Europae Orientalis, et post conclusionem **"consociationum inter se oppositarum",** *necessarium fuisset progressionem summatim retractare. Quod quidem postulaverat Ioannes Paulus II, qui anno MCMLXXXVII docuerat exsistentiam harum* **"consociationum"** *esse unam ex praecipuis causis huius exiguae progressionis [57], quatenus res politica opes ex oeconomia et cultura subtrahebat, et* **ideologia** *coërcebat libertatem. Anno MCMXCI, post eventus anni MCMLXXXIX, ipse quoque flagitavit ut, superatis* "oppositionibus", *sequeretur novum globale progres-*

sus propositum, non tantum in iis Nationibus, sed etiam in Occidente et in iis mundi regionibus quae paulatim progrediebantur [58]. Quod tamen partim tantum contigit et pergit esse vera obligatio, cui satisfacere necesse est, ceterum illas adhibendo optiones quae hodiernas quaestiones oeconomicas superare valeant.

The Latin has difficulty in expressing the modern notion of "bloc" but it is no different from the notion of empire which might be applied to the rule of Alexander the Great or Napoleon Buonaparte. It would fit also the modern examples of empire such as the Spanish and the British. But most relevantly it is applied to the contemporary examples of the USA and USSR. The English translation typically gives it a slant whereby one would think that with the fall of the USSR the American Super Power (more euphemistically called "hegemony) had ceased to be a bloc.

The popes are referring to the "Cold War" between the two opposing blocs, the USSR through its engagement in two world wars having benefited from the technological heritage of the "West" to an extent where it was able to challenge the existing powers, the British and other European empires having declined and their superiority overtaken by the USA (with its allies being the remnant of the British and European empires (NATO) and their former colonies).

But what is the picture that tends to emerge, not from the original Latin but from the English translation? All of a sudden, the world has become free of oppression of the many working poor by the rich few in the system of Capitalism and, more in the picture, from the exercise of overpowering military might by the remaining "bloc" now able to rule the world virtually unopposed.

Jeffrey Sachs, an adviser to key governments since the fall of the USSR and appointed by Pope Francis to the Pontifical Academy of Social Sciences (despite his apparently anti-Catholic position on abortion and other moral issues) says that in his opinion the USA has been engaged in wars of world significance virtually continuously ever since the disappearance of its opposing bloc. So much for the era of peace that was hoped for with the end of the opposition between the two blocs in 1989. We do not go into the present war in Ukraine and the threat of war over Taiwan. Look up Jeffrey Sachs and see what he says on these matters.

In paragraph 24 this focus on the difference between rich nations and poor nations, as developed and developing, continues. What happened to Pope Pius XII's observation that so called rich nations manifestly based on unjust political systems (glaring inequalities) should be regarded as impoverished? It seems to be simply assumed that the poorer nations need to catch up with the "advanced" ones. The encyclical cannot mean that. But the treatment is pitched at such a general level that a reader could gain such an impression.

Then in paragraph 25 the social encyclical seems to take the existing politico-economic order (disorder) for granted, without any radical criticism not just of the situation of injustice between nations but also within (rich) nations, the State finding it more difficult to supply for the needs of the (working) poor and to moderate the global depredations of the capitalist "employers" (thought of now as rich nations). "From the social point of view, systems of protection and welfare, already present in many countries in Paul VI's day, are finding it hard and could find it even harder in the future to pursue their goals of true social justice in today's profoundly changed environment. The global market has stimulated first and foremost, on the part of rich countries, a search for areas in which to outsource production at low cost with a view to reducing the prices of many goods, increasing purchasing power and thus accelerating the rate of development in terms of greater availability of consumer goods for the domestic market. Consequently, the market has prompted new forms of competition between States as they seek to attract foreign businesses to set up production centres, by means of a variety of instruments, including favourable fiscal regimes and deregulation of the labour market."

The right note, however, is struck in paragraph 27: "Life in many poor countries is still extremely insecure as a consequence of food shortages, and the situation could become worse: *hunger* still reaps enormous numbers of victims among those who, like Lazarus, are not permitted to take their place at the rich man's table, contrary to the hopes expressed by Paul."

However, the division of the rich and poor is still put in terms of rich and poor nations, and injustice is put in the most extreme terms so that the impression may be given that there is no problem of poverty or injustice in the distribution of wealth within "rich" or capitalist nations. That impression however is becoming harder to maintain in recent times. Poverty is manifest in many ways, not just in lack of food or water which indeed can be so extreme that the injustice perpetrated may amount to the crime of murder, as the Fathers of the Church made clear.

Our main worry with the direction the discussion has taken since the Council is that attention is taken off the real villains in the piece who are behind the "excessive inequalities" between the modern rich and poor, which system of injustice is deep rooted and so long standing as able to be traced back to the beginning of modern times as we have described over and over again. This systematic disorder of social injustice which we can call Capitalism (or Proletarianism) was in place well before Communism appeared on the scene and would presumably remain in place if there were no opposition to it. But like every false ideology the roots of its decay and dissolution are within it.

As we have seen, and as Pope Leo XIII discerned in its heyday, it is a rule by or for the benefit of a few, and what is peculiar to it is that it can operate under the cover of a political rule that we now call "democracy" – since the majority "under its thumb" are politically free to elect their government (one party or another) – so that is not legal slavery but rather "a yoke little better than slavery".

What is a puzzle to many is that the Church does condemn features of Capitalism but does not condemn it outright as it has now condemned all other forms of slavery. Yet it may be noticed that such condemnation was not evident during the periods when these forms of slavery were a quasi-natural condition of the social order. Our view is that the explanation may be put briefly as twofold.

We have the example of Christ who was portrayed by his own people, the Jews, as the Messiah who would set his people free, yet he meekly submitted to the authorities of the day even though their decrees were unjust. So too the apostles lived in a time of chattel slavery and in the case of St. Paul sent one legally a slave back to his master. The primary reason then has to be supernatural, "My Kingdom is not of this world". There is the Christian point of view that suffering serves a higher purpose. Joined with Christ's sacrifice it is the very means of salvation of all.

The secondary reason we would suggest is natural, a matter of natural (and supernatural) prudence. The Church counsels against revolution, which generally results in a worse situation, as is obvious in the case of Communism. Thus, the Magisterium did not approve of the theology of liberation. Moreover, justice and the promotion of the natural common good is the proper concern of the human community and principally of its government. The Church is the conscience of the State and does condemn social injustice but must act with prudence. This does not affect the judgment that any social system is evil. But it does affect how one should deal with an evildoer especially if he is a tyrant.

However, we do not want to discuss at length here these profound issues. The remaining paragraphs of this chapter (28 to 33) treat of other moral issues such as the right to life, which abortion as widely practised and even supported by governments violates. These bring into focus questions of injustice of a much graver kind than robbery no matter on how great a scale, except where it amounts to murder. We need only remember St. Paul's dictum "the love of money is the root of all evil" to see how all other evils may arise within a social system driven by greed.

We will draw attention to a couple of passages that highlight what we have observed about the modern social situation, in respect of both practical political science and morals (justice). The first brings out the rejection of metaphysics in modern thinking and the second the relevance of "economic choices".

"Paul VI had seen clearly that among the causes of underdevelopment there is a lack of wisdom and reflection, a lack of thinking capable of formulating a guiding synthesis, for which 'a clear vision of all economic, social, cultural and spiritual aspects is required'. The excessive segmentation of knowledge, the rejection of metaphysics by the human sciences, the difficulties encountered by dialogue between science and theology are damaging not only to the development of knowledge, but also to the development of peoples, because these things make it harder to see the integral good of man in its various dimensions. The 'broadening [of] our concept of reason and its application' is indispensable if we are to succeed in adequately weighing all the elements involved in the question of development and in the solution of socio-economic problems". (n. 31)

Yet earlier in the paragraph the document speaks of the need for "faith, theology, metaphysics and science to come together in a collaborative effort in the service of humanity". What concept of science is being used there – one that counts as science the "human sciences" of Economics and Sociology which reject metaphysics? There does not appear to be a clear notion of science as propounded in modern thought. It is difficult to see how the encyclical can address the concrete situation affecting modern society dominated by a notion of science without wisdom.

Then we have the further quote in the next paragraph: "The dignity of the individual and the demands of justice require, particularly today, that economic choices do not cause disparities in wealth to increase in an excessive and morally unacceptable manner, and that we continue to *prioritize the goal of access to steady employment* for everyone." (32) What about the economic choices of the historic past whose effect persists into the structural injustice of the present? There seems to be no awareness as in past encyclicals of the existence of the politico-economic system of Capitalism, which Pope Leo XIII condemned so severely, nor any reference to the ideology of Liberalism that underpins it.

And what about perpetuating a system of employment, for people of little or no means of living apart from their labour, that Leo described as "a yoke little better than slavery". The extremity of the workers of the nineteenth century, who were not even guaranteed survival as were the slaves of the pagan era, was changed so that they are now not left to perish. But what has changed in their dependence upon the people of property (or the State) for "steady employment"? No mention is made of the increasing indebtedness with which the working majority is burdened. How close to a servile condition can one get for most but those who are astute enough to work the system to their advantage one way or another?

Pope Saint John Paul II stated that the change of focus introduced by the Council did not mean that the social doctrine of the Church had lost the incisiveness and particular focus of previous encyclicals, such as those of popes Leo XIII and Pius XI. But one cannot but think that this has happened to a certain extent in the more recent Catholic works on the modern social condition.

We can seek to discover what may be the causes of this but one would have to be a failure to pay special attention to St. Thomas in his works where he discusses, with great precision, the most fundamental questions of distributive and commutative justice. This he does not just in general terms but also in such a way that the principles exposed can be directly applied to the solution of the politico-economic problems even of our own day.

When we come to the four last parts of *Caritas in veritate* we cannot help noticing how the particular politico-economic focus in which Liberalist Capitalism is the social system that is responsible for the condition of the modern working poor majority becomes somewhat of a shadowy presence and attention is turned to more general matters of social concern such as fraternity, culture and injustice as sin in general. These are all matters of great concern to the Church and apply to all human development. It is not that the division of people into rich and poor is lost sight of but the sins of the rich, and particularly as found in modern society of European/Christian heritage (called 'the West") tend to be attributed to humanity as a whole. So much is this so in more recent times that one might think that the modern equivalents of the poor man Lazarus are responsible for the parlous state of the world since his kind form the great majority of mankind. Man is to be held responsible for the deterioration of the environment, not the greedy rich few who have turned to exploit natural resources as well as their fellow man. There are still working poor

In "advanced" or "developed" nations. Are they to be morally required to go to the aid of poor nations?

What compounds this it seems is the weakness of the knowledge of the world of modern theologians closeted away in their universities, afraid to venture into the complex fields of modern economic and political science, lamenting from afar the exclusion of morality (and justice) from such "secular" disciplines, using the excuse that the moral theologian has no competence in the "technical" side of such studies.

One can perhaps see a sign of this even in the headings of the encyclical. Chapter Three is headed: "Fraternity, Economic Development and Civil Society". The central focus of this chapter is on Economic Development. To envelop this aspect of the social condition with more general considerations of social life within a civil community let alone considerations of universal fraternity introduces a multitude of difficulties in sticking to one subject. We have seen how the civil community needs to be divided into various levels of life, of which we have enumerated four, economic, recreational, cultural and political, all with special meanings in Aristotelian and Thomist terms. This makes the treatment of the politico-economic aspect hard enough. But then when we use the word "political" in its debased modern sense it becomes all but impossible to follow any discussion let alone argument even in the original Latin. Then when we try to follow things in English translation the potential for confusion is potentially infinite.

Let us try to indicate this problem by taking one numbered paragraph (35) and examine it in Latin and English. Various parts will be put in bold.

35. *Mercatus, si adsit mutua et pervulgata fiducia, est instiio oeconomica quae conventui favet hominum, quatenus sunt operatores oeconomici qui utuntur contractu uti suarum necessitudinum norma et qui permutant bona et servitia **inter se fungibilia** ad proprias necessitates et desideria exsequenda. Mercatus obnoxius est principiis **sic dictae iustitiae commutativae**, quae temperat necessitudines dandi et recipiendi* **inter homines pari numero constitutos.** *Sed doctrina socialis Ecclesiae numquam destitit in lucem proferre momentum iustitiae distributivae et iustitiae socialis pro ipsa oeconomia mercatus, non solum quia immittitur in reticula amplioris contextus socialis et politici, sed etiam ob complexionem relationum in quibus peragitur.* **Etenim mercatus, relictus soli principio peraequationis valoris bonorum permutatorum, haud idoneus est ad creandam illam socialem cohaesionem, quae requiritur ad recte operandum. Absque internis formis solidarietatis et mutuae fiduciae, mercatus proprium munus oeconomicum plene exsequi nequit. Et hodie ipsa haec fiducia deest in ambitu internationali, et amissio fiduciae gravis est amissio.**

Quapropter Paulus VI in Litteris encyclicis "Populorum progressio" luculenter affirmabat nempe quod eadem methodus oeconomica commodum caperet ex diffusis iustitiae actionibus, quatenus primi beneficiis gaudentes ex progressu populorum pauperum essent populi locupletes [90]. Iuxta mentem Pontificis, non agebatur tantummodo de emendandis erroneis functionibus per assistentiam. **Pauperes enim minime reputandi sunt uti "sarcinae" [91], sed uti subsidium quoque sub aspectu stricte oeco-**

nomico. Attamen, erratum iudicandum est iudicium eorum qui censent oeconomiam mercatus quadam indigere portione paupertatis et exiguae progressionis quo melius effici possit. Ad mercatum interest ut emancipationem promoveat, ad cuius finem vere exsequendum soli sibi confidere nequit, quoniam nequit ex se gignere ea quae superant eius capacitatem. Ipse vires morales haurire debet ex aliis subiectis, quae eas generare valeant.

"35. In a climate of mutual trust, the *market* is the economic institution that permits encounter between persons, inasmuch as they are economic subjects who make use of contracts to regulate their relations as they exchange goods and services **of equivalent value between them,** in order to satisfy their needs and desires. The market is subject to the principles of **so-called** *commutative justice*, which regulates the relations of giving and receiving **between parties to a transaction.** But the social doctrine of the Church has unceasingly highlighted the importance of *distributive justice* and *social justice* for the market economy, not only because it belongs within a broader social and political context, but also because of the wider network of relations within which it operates. **In fact, if the market is governed solely by the principle of the equivalence in value of exchanged goods, it cannot produce the social cohesion that it requires in order to function well.** *Without internal forms of solidarity and mutual trust, the market cannot completely fulfil its proper economic function.* **And today it is this trust which has ceased to exist, and the loss of trust is a grave loss.**

It was timely when Paul VI in *Populorum progressio* insisted that the economic system itself would benefit from the wide-ranging practice of justice, inasmuch as the first to gain from the development of poor countries would be rich ones [90]. According to the Pope, it was not just a matter of correcting dysfunctions through assistance. **The poor are not to be considered a "burden" [91], but a resource, even from the purely economic point of view. It is nevertheless erroneous to hold that the market economy has an inbuilt need for a quota of poverty and underdevelopment in order to function at its best. It is in the interests of the market to promote emancipation, but in order to do so effectively, it cannot rely only on itself, because it is not able to produce by itself something that lies outside its competence. It must draw its moral energies from other subjects that are capable of generating them.**

Why say that the economic level of consideration is not enough? The point is, is the economy doing what it is supposed to be doing if it is justly managed. Does the focus of the medico on life at the lowest level not to be considered properly focused if the highest cultural/moral level of life of the patient and doctor is not taken into account. That has its point in the appropriate context. But bringing in these higher considerations can distract one from the study of what one is focusing on.

Let us deal with the Latin first. *Fungibilia* does not seem to be the appropriate word in the context. Their "exchange" is usually described as a loan, like when someone gives another a dozen eggs on the understanding that he will get back their "equivalent" at a later time. The word signifies that what is given back is not the same eggs but things of the same kind, that "do" the same job (function). For the use of them involves them being "consumed".

As St. Thomas notes there is no real distinction between the thing and its use so one cannot charge "interest" on their use since it does not have any distinct existence. Such a charge is for nothing that is now in the possession of the "borrower", as is the case with money borrowed whose only purpose in receiving it is to get rid of it in exchange for what one needs. The concept is applicable mainly in the discussion of usury in the "borrowing" and "lending" of money. The common use of money is as a medium of exchange so that in using it one loses it.

If one borrows money one cannot return the same notes, coins or whatever material things are used to stand for it (even electronic) but one must return what serves the same function. Without understanding this one has no hope of discussing usury. The charging for the use of money is therefore an intrinsically immoral and unjust just as much as if one demanded 15 eggs back from one's neighbour who had been "lent" 12, the extra charge being for his use and enjoyment in consuming the eggs. There are extrinsic titles that may justify a charge of interest and this is the case especially in modern times as I explain in my book "Economic Science and Saint Thomas Aquinas". But hardly anyone pays special attention to St. Thomas's clear demonstration of the serious sin of injustice of usury, and this applies especially to Catholic moral theologians today, for they are bewitched with the "Economics" they are taught in school and university.

Pope Benedict was clear in his condemnation of usury (as was Pope Leo) but it is doubtful from how the word *fungibilia* is used in this document that he was all that familiar with St. Thomas's treatment of it in the Summa (*II-II q 78*). For as used here it is clear that this special kind of exchange/loan is not distinguished from ordinary exchange of goods, where in the case of durables, such as motor cars and clothing, one can distinguish between the thing and its use so that it is legitimate to charge for the use (hire or loan) separately from sale of the thing. These non-consumables (non-fungible goods) are exchanged at an equal exchange value and the parties go away with different things of the same value.

It is this sense of exchange of goods that the translator has picked up and ignorant of the meaning of *fungibilia* has given the translation "of equivalent value" (we pass over the clumsiness of saying equivalent value instead of equal value). But if one considered as the leading theologian of our time is not clear about the difference what hope have lesser theologians? So far as the document is concerned however this misuse of the term does not affect the sense intended to be conveyed, as is picked up by the translator.

The expression used "so called commutative justice" is a bit of a worry. Though not all that significant it does give the impression that the scholastic language traditional to the thought of Aristotle and Aquinas in the discussion of politico-economic issues in such an important area as justice may be a bit "archaic" and unfamiliar to the modern mind in matters economic.

I cannot make much literal sense of the phrase *inter homines pari numero constitutos*. Neither it seems can the translator. So, he gives a rough translation without using any of the English equivalents of the Latin terms.

The passage put in bold at the end of the first part of the quote makes the point that we cannot properly discuss one aspect of justice in society without having a grasp of the whole. That is true in this case but it is a point applicable to every discussion. Here it seems only to serve to distract what should be an examination of a distinct part of justice by the introduction of extrinsic factors – it seems to be a common fault with a theological discussion of matters of reason that one tends to "over-spiritualize" it. All that is said is true; one can hear the applause of the Augustinians. But it can distract from a properly rational treatment of a particular topic. Why say we should not focus too exclusively on the market in goods being ruled by equality of exchange value when that is its very "form"?

Certainly, there are other matters to be considered and they need to be in order as well. But as St. Thomas says a socio-political issue can be flawed by reason of four causes of which the formal cause is central. Thus, even a law made for the common good but involving inequality in form is a bad law. Here the modern Catholic theologian throws all the emphasis on the final cause, common good, and tends to forget the necessity of justice in the very form of exchange, just price. Why is that? We suspect it is because in their secularist education they are told that the notion of just price is a scholastic nonsense. The only price is the market price determined by "supply and demand". Justice or morality has no place in real economic science. Most fall for this as it seems so close to "reality". So, we have the moral theologians mouthing the need for order to the common good without any real notion of what it is and its relation to commutative justice.

The encyclical is aware of the perverse language of modern economic science which can be seen in the last part of the paragraph put in bold. But the market "must draw its moral energies from other subjects". So it must; but not to the neglect of the moral aspect of commutative justice, which is also called justice in exchange. It may be appreciated then how difficult it is to apply proper moral thinking (both philosophical and theological) to the subject matter the social encyclical is trying to deal with.

It is evident that the pope is not comfortable in discussing the matter in its most proper terms and limits himself to higher more "spiritual" considerations. But these tend to be of a general kind that do not come to grips with the issues, as would be done if one paid special attention to the relevant parts of St. Thomas's treatment of the subject. That is a pity, even if the elevation of mind that the encyclical does bring about is necessary and otherwise justified.

We will not comment on the other paragraphs of this chapter, simply asking the reader to note how they are all pitched at the same level. The relation of "business" to morality as attempted to be applied in modern times is affected by the lack of a fundamental understanding of the principles of justice. Ethical considerations tend to be "plastered" on business practices as they exist with all their modern capitalist "institutions", such as money driven investment by large "corporations". Shareholders are discouraged from putting their money with "unethical" projects, which are tainted by slave labour, or some other immoral or unjust oppression of workers. Or the immorality may be seen in the very nature of the projects, such as profiting from commerce ("trafficking" is the word used) in organs taken from human corpses even persons killed for the purpose of "harvesting" their organs. (Where money is to be made it is rather tempting to see other human beings, of no wealth or property, as disposable and dispensible; money tends also to distance the one profiting, the "investor" or "shareholder" in the investment, "stakeholder", from the nasty nature of the "transactions"). All sorts of heinous and horrendous crimes are covered up in a society dominated by a capitalist mentality focused on "profit" as the driver of the modern economy, which makes, as we are taught in school and university, countries like USA, UK, Australia and Canada such marvellous examples of the success of the liberlaist/capitalist way of life.

This ethical "tinkering" does salve the conscience and of course is not to be denied its moral value. But in one way it too does distract from addressing the deeper causes of moral disorder and injustice present in the existing economic "system" There is a tendency as well for such championing of virtue to be applied beyond human nature to nature generally so that the environment takes centre stage and one's grandmother will be denounced for having possessed a fur coat.

The treatment of the relation between the Economy (as Market) and the State falls short in our view of coming to grips with the actual social situation of the modern division between the rich few (capitalist) and the majority poor (workers). The State (politics) is seen as having to adjust the system somehow to make it more "human" (and Christian) but here again this is done mainly by working at the edges of the existing system. No mention is made of the state of quasi-servility of those dependent solely or even mainly on their own hands and brains, nor on the seemingly inevitable forcing down of their wages and increasing resort to debt to meet basic living needs, like houses, transport and at times even non-junk food for the family.

The obligation in the State to redistribute some of the natural resources and other wealth of society to those without is referred to but somehow without highlighting the fact that the existing distribution is grossly unjust and that the "redistribution" is but an implementation of distributive justice. This is such a radical idea that it may stir up thoughts of revolution and threaten our democracy. So perhaps it is wiser and more prudent to play it low key. It is not suggested that there is any fault in the encyclical in this respect. Even Pope Leo did not demand that the system be reformed as a whole (perhaps for the same reason that the early Christians were instructed to live with ancient chattel slavery).

To be oppressed and persecuted in this world is not the worst thing that can happen to a Christian, nor to any man. It can even be a blessing in disguise – consider the fates of the rich man *Dives* and the poor man Lazarus! As St. Rose of Lima remarked: "Without the burden of afflictions it is impossible to reach the height of Grace. ... The gift of Grace increases as the struggle increases. ... No one would complain about his cross or about troubles that may happen to him, if he would come to know the scales on which they are weighed when they are distributed to men." It is not a shock for a true Catholic to learn of how the saints rejoiced as they were burnt at the stake, like Joan of Arc after having to suffer the ignominy of being judged by a Catholic bishop with being an evil witch.

The remaining three chapters of the encyclical show much the same trend to shift focus on to the higher spiritual aspects of the social development needed to bring all to not just a fully natural level of human life but to that highest level of supernatural life won by Christ the good news of which he commissioned his Church to proclaim to all nations. Amid all the vicissitudes of history since, including the seemingly fatal disasters of the Protestant Reformation and the consequent disintegration of Christian civilizations, the Christian knows that all works to the good and the end intended by God from the beginning, indeed from eternity. Even the enormity of evils that visit humanity and seems in the latest times to justify for many the taking of a position of atheism and its twin complete despair does not displace the truth of St. Augustine's defence of the absolute goodness of God.

But we must address the social condition of our times as God has given us not only the gift of Faith but also of Reason. Human society has been affected at all levels of life not only supernatural but also natural. We have been primarily concerned with that level where God expects us to help ourselves so far as we can, namely, with our reason. Faith comes to our aid here, but this does not dispense us with using our reason which in this subject matter involves that of practical science and practical wisdom.

Unfortunately, since the beginning of the modern era the rejection of Catholic Faith has inevitably involved the rejection of natural wisdom (Metaphysics) together with practical wisdom (Ethics). The loss of Metaphysics cripples the particular sciences (Physics, Mathematics and Physico-mathematics) but the loss of Ethics, if allowing some space to Technics, which at its highest includes Medicine and Psychiatry, is fatal to all practical sciences such as Politics, within which must be included what is today called Economics. This is because "practical science" here means practical wisdom which needs to be completed in the virtue of prudence.

For a detailed explanation of how this is so one may refer to my previously published books. Anyone who is familiar with the work of Aquinas would know the nature and division of the sciences set out in my books. But who makes a special study of the works of Aquinas these days?

Now we have remarked on a falling off in the study of Aquinas particularly as it affects our subject matter, which is much the same as that of the social doctrine of the Church, but we should note that its primary focus is on the politico-economic part of Political Science (Wisdom). We have repeated these matters here so that the reader may appreciate the point we are making about the encyclical in so far as it is affected by the "new theology" and the tendency to lose focus on the specific topic that the social encyclicals were focused on, namely, that particularly modern phenomenon of social injustice to the working poor that is concreted in the system of Capitalism. There have arisen of course a host of evil "side" effects that overwhelm modern society and inhibit the proper development of human beings and to which the Church has to give attention. We can include in this the attack on the institutions of marriage and the family and the coincident descent into sexual depravity. So too may we include a deterioration of the very order of civil society and the corruption of political government. But we ought not forget the original injustice rooted in the sin of cupidity or greed. This disorder in our view is what has tended to be overlooked even in more recent magisterial documents, paying more attention (not for that unnecessary) to all sorts of works of the social evils.

With this in mind we should not need to make much comment on the last three chapters of *Caritas in veritate* but will make some short comments. But we first use a quote in Latin and English of the first sentence of Chapter Five to back up what we are saying above: Paragraph 53. *Una ex gravissimis paupertatis formis quas homo experiri potest est solitudo.* "One of the deepest forms of poverty a person can experience is isolation."

If "poverty" is taken metaphorically or in a wider sense than normal, the sentence makes a point. But the meaning of poverty up to this point has been the normal one of a lack of the external material goods one needs to sustain one's bodily life or physical existence. In the wider sense, ill-health may be a kind of poverty, so too may be ignorance or lack of a knowledge of elementary maths. But the meaning of poverty the encyclicals have been concerned with is the ordinary one, meaning lack of sufficient food, water and those material goods that if one does not have leads to starvation and death. So it was that the Church Fathers said that if you do not feed the hungry and they die because of your wilful neglect you are guilty of murder. No one is going to die simply because of lack of company. In famines whole families die, whole villages perish from lack of food. So we may appreciate that though there is a point to what is said in the encyclical it is somewhat off focus. It takes attention away from the poverty that comes from the injustice in the distribution and exchange of external goods in the modern system of Capitalism, which was the occasion for Pope Leo's original intervention. As well as this the encyclical inserts at this point a theological discussion of the place of relation in human nature, paralleling its place in the divine nature. That may be an important question in theology, but it is rather remote from the precise question in issue.

That is an example of the tendency to shift focus of the discussion of social justice from the condition of the poor (modern "workers") to wider and wider concerns that are undoubtedly important and of great importance in current times. But we may safely assume from a human point of view that most derive from the effects of unjustly imposed poverty most properly taken. Why do children of today isolate their parents from their families in institutions called "homes"? All sorts of evils have entered into the condition of humanity as a result of a long-standing structural injustice that is for the most part ignored. The real beneficiaries of the "system" (the fortunate few rich) are of course quite happy for the blame to be set upon humanity as a whole.

To return to Chapter Four. We note its heading, first in English: "The Development of People, Rights and Duties the Environment. In Latin *Populorum progressio: Iura et Obligationes, Rerum natura.*

A more correct translation is "The Development of Peoples Rights and Obligations, The Nature of Things". We may pass over the mistranslation of what is the title to Pope Saint Paul VI's encyclical and the use of duties for obligations. But why has the translator not used "The Nature of Things" and simply assumed the pope is referring to what we call today the environment. It may be so assumed were it not for this phrase in paragraph 48 of the encyclical: "When nature, including the human being ...". It is clear that the encyclical is seeing nature in a more traditional and even Aristotelian sense than as the ambience of natural material things in which we live. The phrase "Our nature, constituted by matter but also by spirit ..." also occurs in the same paragraph. But we have become so accustomed to opposing ourselves (the human being) to nature that any reference to nature is simply assumed to mean "the environment". The translator is simply following this fashionable use of language and thus totally confused about the meaning of this section of the encyclical.

As already noted, bringing into the discussion rights and duties is introducing general considerations that though relevant to the parlous moral condition of modern society does also draw attention away from the main moral issue (of justice) in question. The pope does try to address in this context "the relationship between business and ethics". But it is here that the weakness in the ecclesiastical understanding of precisely what modern business practices involve shows up. We will not go into details.

Let us move on to the next Chapter Five. The heading is "The Cooperation of the Human Family" In Latin: *Humanae Familiae Consociata Opera*. It is rather an awkward heading. One might ask "with whom?" But the intent I suppose is that the works (opera) are self-referential, for family means an association that, though not self-sufficient in natural terms, when transferred to the supernatural order signifies what is complete and a perfect unity or community. So here we see again a shift to theological heights of what we want to deal with in philosophical terms if with the aid of the light of Faith.

We have already commented upon the strange situation in the mistranslation of the first sentence. This curious situation occurs again within the same paragraph 53 where the Latin *Creatura humana, quatenus est spiritalis naturae, in necessitudinibus inter personas adimpletur;* is rendered "As a spiritual being, the human creature is defined through interpersonal relations." Where is "is defined" in the Latin? *Adimpletur* means 'is filled up'. Human nature is filled up with many accidents (qualities/powers) like intellect and will and many relations like being social, belonging to a family and as Aristotle said "by nature" a political animal.

By definition though a human being is by nature a rational animal and as an individual a human person. So where do you think the translator got the idea that even at the natural level being rational came after being social? Perhaps he knew the mind of Cardinal Ratzinger and his early piece where he (along with von Balthazar) argued for redefining human person in the same way as a divine person. Higher considerations do indeed come into the "definition" of a person when we move to the supernatural divine level where as St. Thomas points out a divine person is constituted "essentially" by relation.

Well, what do you know the new theologians argued that since we have been divinized by grace our personhood has taken on this divine character, and since de Lubac had shown that nature was rubbed out by grace, we ought now to "define" the human person in terms of relationality rather than rationality (leaving out that old Aristotelian notion of individual substance). Sublime stuff for the Christian no doubt but a horrible confusion of the orders of nature and grace. That however would explain how the translators have confused the words "rationality" and "relationality" even when the actual word used in the encyclical is "rationality" and relationality is referred to not as defining human being but as something that fills it up.

This is not to deny that community is what the unity of the individual human being is meant to end up in even at the natural level. But such intimacy with others is not to be equated at the natural level with the divine intimacy between the divine community. God has brought us as close as possible to it but even in the order of grace there still remains an infinite distance between the mode of our being one with each other and that of the divine persons.

However, this is but another instance where the later discussion of the social condition of man is shifted as it were into another key, appropriate for a Christian but hardly intelligible to non-Christians. Should we not try to address the conditions of injustice that can be argued from the level of reason that may serve to break down the prejudices against the social doctrine of the Church? This point is even made in this chapter of the encyclical: "57. Fruitful dialogue between faith and reason cannot but render the work of charity more effective within society, and it constitutes the most appropriate framework for promoting *fraternal collaboration between believers and non-believers* in their shared commitment to working for justice and the peace of the human family."

Most of what remains of Chapter Five has been covered by points already made. We will however finish with a quote of paragraph 65 in Latin and English as it demonstrates the difficulties inherent in the encyclical's attempt to pronounce upon modern "economic" ideas and propositions and the horrible mess the translators make of it. The more important relevant parts are put in bold.

65. *Oportet proinde ut* **res nummaria ipsa**, *necessario renovatis structuris operandique rationibus, malum post usum qui realem oeconomiam pessumdedit, munus recuperet meliorem copiarum progressionisque proventum obtinendi. Oeconomia cuncta resque nummaria, non modo quaedam earum partes, ut instrumenta, ethice adhibeantur oportet, ut condiciones hominis populorumque profectus congruae exsistant. Commodum quidem est, et nonnumquam necessarium,* **nummaria incepta** *suscipere, in quibus humana ratio antistet. Hac nimirum re non est obliviscendum* **totam nummariam rationem** *ad veram sustinendam progressionem esse convertendam. Necesse est potissimum ut boni faciendi consilium certae facultati bonorum gignendorum non opponatur.* **Rerum nummariarum operatores** *ipsum ethicum fundamentum recipere debent suarum industriarum, ne instrumentis his subtilissimis abutantur, quae parcis hominibus decipiendis inservire possint. Aequum propositum, honestas bonique effectus persequendi admitti possunt atque numquam seiungantur oportet. Si amor prudens est, rationes quoque ad providam iustamque con-*

venientiam operandi reperire valet, **quemadmodum insigniter complures cooperationis crediti experientiae ostendunt.**

Cum huius **provinciae moderatio,** *quae debiliores homines servet ipsaque turpia quaestus studia prohibeat, tum* **rei nummariae nova genera** *adhibita, quae ad progressus incepta iuvanda destinantur, solidae sunt experientiae, roborandae et confirmandae, ipsa parci hominis responsalitate concitata.* **Tenuis rei nummariae** *quoque experientia, quae in cogitationes atque humanistarum civilium opera radices agit – de Montibus Pietatis constitutis cogitamus – est roboranda atque definienda, his potissimum temporibus, quibus* **rerum nummariarum quaestiones** *dificillimae fieri possunt, quod ad debiliores plebis partes attinet,* **ab usurae aut desperationis discrimine eripiendas.** *Debiliores homines* **de usura arcenda** *sunt docendi, ac simul* **inopes populi** *sunt instituendi, quomodo* **tenui credito** *iuventur, ita ut duabus his in provinciis quarundam abusionum genera infringantur. Quandoquidem divitibus in Nationibus nova exstant paupertatis genera,* **tenuis res nummaria** *certa adiumenta suppeditare potest, ut in debiliorum societatis ordinum beneficium incepta novaeque condiciones admittantur, etiam cum ipsa societas in paupertate forte versetur.*

"65. **Finance**, therefore – through the renewed structures and operating methods that have to be designed after its misuse, which wreaked such havoc on the real economy – now needs to go back to being an *instrument directed towards improved wealth creation and development*. Insofar as they are instruments, the entire economy and finance, not just certain sectors, must be used in an ethical way so as to create suitable conditions for human development and for the development of peoples. It is certainly useful, and in some circumstances imperative, to **launch financial initiatives** in which the humanitarian dimension predominates. However, this must not obscure the fact that the **entire financial system** has to be aimed at sustaining true development. Above all, the intention to do good must not be considered incompatible with the effective capacity to produce goods. **Financiers** must rediscover the genuinely ethical foundation of their activity, so as not to abuse the sophisticated instruments which can serve to betray the interests of savers. Right intention, transparency, and the search for positive results are mutually compatible and must never be detached from one another. If love is wise, it can find ways of working in accordance with provident and just expediency, as is illustrated in a significant way by much of the experience of credit unions."

Both the regulation of the financial sector, so as to safeguard weaker parties and discourage scandalous speculation, and experimentation with **new forms of finance**, designed to support development projects, are positive experiences that should be further explored and encouraged, highlighting *the responsibility of the investor*. Furthermore, the *experience of **micro-finance***, which has its roots in the thinking and activity of the civil humanists – I am thinking especially of the birth of **pawnbroking** – should be strengthened and fine-tuned. This is all the more necessary in these days when **financial difficulties** can become severe for many of the more vulnerable sectors of the population, who should be protected from the **risk of usury** and from despair. The weakest members of society should be helped to defend themselves against **usury**, just as poor peoples should be helped to derive real benefit from **micro-credit,** in order to discourage the exploitation that is possible in these two areas. Since rich countries are also experiencing new forms of poverty, **micro-finance** can give practical assistance by launching new initiatives and opening up new sectors for the benefit of the weaker elements in society, even at a time of general economic downturn."

We will not devote time or space here to sorting out the muddle that permeates this paragraph. We suggest the reader consult the chapter Usury and Debt in my book "Economic Science and Saint Thomas Aquinas". All that the translator knows is that finance has something to do with money and its use. The pope evidently knows what he wants to say but transposing modern terms into Latin creates enormous difficulties. He is talking about money (*nummaria*) and its "investment" in lending. He is aware of the sinfulness of usury and its existence in modern times.

Where are the Catholic moral philosophers and theologians, not to mention those Catholics who claim to be experts in Economics, who write books showing the Church has long since abandoned this "mediaeval" moral doctrine, shouting down Pope Benedict XVI for even suggesting it still exists as a rational thought, let alone as a sin of injustice? Most likely they have swallowed the modern line that belief in usury went out with that in fairies and the spirit world. Nonetheless, it must be a bit embarrassing for them to have such a "progressive" pope holding so strongly to such a moral position. Best I suppose to pretend he did not say it and praise the more "spiritual" parts of the document they approve of.

The last chapter (6) is headed *Populorum Progressio Et Technica Ars*. In English, "The Development Of Peoples And Technology". At least "peoples" is got right this time.

We will not devote much comment to this chapter though the amazing advances in technology have given it a kind of mystique and even induced in many an awe of its magical power. This has a lot to do with how modern physico-mathematics has developed.

But as for political and politico-economic domination, who do you think have most profited from this, especially as applied to weapons of war? The working poor, of course, those without any property in capital as instruments of producing wealth. Who gets the blame for its misuse and leading the world to the edge of the abyss? The propertyless poor, of course, since they are the vast majority of humanity. How could a fortunate few have managed to monopolise virtually all property in modern society, both in natural resources, lately discovered to contain enormous energy, especially destructive, and in "technology"? This knowledge side of technology, coming into modern life from the heritage of reason in Christendom, but "taken over" by what St. Augustine referred to as "robber kingdoms", has mushroomed into the modern "mass weapons of destruction".

There is of course a positive side, in the miracles of modern medical technology, and even in the development of nuclear energy for peaceful purposes. But given the continuing effects of original sin, we may expect that the negative side will predominate and modern technology will be used to serve the interests of the fortunate few who have ownership in its products. Governments try to get into the act with less and less effect it seems.

"Humanity", however, is up against the "forces" of evil in a moral sense. The devils, and their human co-operators, do not mind if we think the danger of misuse is inherent in the material and mechanical forces themselves. So, we school the children and well indoctrinated into believing in the artificial intelligence of robots, and, not believing in evil spirits, being as fearful of robots and even technology itself as primitive man was of ghosts.

Part II

Pope Francis' *Laudato si* (2015) and *Fratelli tutti* (2020)

We put these two social encyclicals together for various reasons. Firstly, because we do not intend to deal with each in detail because for some strange reason the Latin version is not on the Vatican website for the latter and only appeared quite recently for the former, even though the encyclical came out in 2015. There does not seem much point in dealing with only one and not the other in the way we have proceeded comparing the English translation to the original and official Latin version.

A second reason is that Pope Francis is still issuing magisterial documents and may write another social encyclical. We would prefer to have his complete teaching in order to give an adequate commentary on his contribution to the social doctrine of the Church.

A third reason is that his writings on the subject matter are of much greater length and complexity than previous ones and have their own peculiar difficulty because of his background, such that to do justice to them would require in my view a book of its own.

We will indicate something of the nature of this difficulty and complexity shortly. It is not suggested that they indicate any fault on the part of the pontiff, but we might say that modern Jesuit thinking is perhaps the furthest removed from that of Aquinas (despite St. Ignatius's injunction that his order should adhere

most strictly to the study of St. Thomas). One has only to think of
Marechal, de Lubac, Rahner and the like. Generally, it has a lot to
do with a keen desire to be in tune with the modern mind. This
creates problems more in the field of modern philosophy, in the
reliance on Kant and Heidegger, than modern science when its
notion is properly limited.

In the case of Pope Francis there are counter-influences, as we
have noted with Pope Benedict. We might just cite Romano
Guardini and even Hugh Benson. In regard to modern science, in
line with an Aristotelian assessment of it as we have outlined, the
pope is aware of its limited scope.

Thus, in *Laudato si* n. 199 he says: "It cannot be maintained
that empirical science provides a complete explanation of life, the
interplay of all creatures and the whole of reality. This would be
to breach the limits imposed by its own methodology." The Latin
is: *Censeri non potest empiricas scientias vitam, intimam essentiam omnium creaturarum ac totam realitatem omnibus ex partibus explanare. Si ita esset, angusti eorum fines methodologici haud
iure superarentur.* We will only note that the English translator
"improves" on the Latin by putting the singular "empirical science" for the plural.

Despite this papal caution what we do notice is that the notion
of science is taken at times as if its modern usage is unaffected by
the longstanding rejection of the metaphysical principles to
which it is necessarily subject and even by the disdain for formal
and final causality within natural science. Not only is natural science limited to empirical/ material causality and formal causality
is as had in mathematics but also the notion of "the scientific

method" does not go beyond the mixed method appropriate to physico-mathematical sciences.

Then much more seriously little notice is taken of the distortion of the understanding of science as applied to the practical sciences of Ethics and Politics as understood by Aristotle and Aquinas, the latter science being reduced to the distorted versions of science in modern politics and economics. Modern science has its usefulness, but it is much more limited than most of its Catholic supporters think. The Jesuits have been able to do good work in such mixed sciences as Astronomy for there the deficiencies of the modern method are least in evidence.

But in the area of "social justice", in which today Jesuits are deeply involved, there is a great risk of them falling for ideological errors such as Communism. Allied to this in recent times are all the sub-ideologies of Feminism and a host of others often to do with sexual perversion. Though not perhaps a Jesuit there are reports of a bishop promoting the moral legitimacy of homosexual behaviour in the name of modern science!

All are aware of the association of the modern experimental/ empirical science of Psychology with depraved philosophical theories of human sexuality. There are clear connections with modern psychology's use in commercial "advertising" and political propaganda, after the theory and practice found its home in Capitalist USA.

It is a worry when the pope himself seems to use the notion of science without taking into account these serious distortions attaching to the modern usage of the word. At times one wonders if he has the requisite clarity of mind on the nature of science to make the proper distinctions. The testament of the late Pope Benedict XVI should be given more public attention in this regard.

Initially, however, we will draw attention to some problems with the English translation of the first encyclical where the Latin version has now been made available. The document is too long to go through it all in such an exercise. There are parts where the mistranslation is serious, but we give here a sample only and leave the rest for another book. We will take examples only from paragraphs 189 to 199.

The focus of these paragraphs is on "politics" and "the economy". It evident that the pope has a sense of the problem which ought to be called politico-economic, but such is the poverty of knowledge of Aristotle's treatment and St. Thomas's masterly commentary in which the basic distinction is made between natural and non-natural (or artificial) exchange, the latter readily falling into an unnatural state, that the language used to express the problem now become a "crisis" is hopelessly confused, even in the Latin. The popes know it is something to do with the use of money but the distinction between the two kinds of its use CMC and MCM is not clearly made. The distinction between commerce and finance cannot be made in such a mind-set.

What is worse, the unnatural is seen in much the same way as in modern economics, that is, as what the market is "normally" engaged in. The notion of profit suffers from the same confusion, no one able to distinguish between the ordinary good notion and *lucrum*. At times, when this "investment" is too deranged it is called "speculation". But what we get in the Latin is the word *res nummeria,* which simply means the thing that is money, having to carry all the distortions in the meaning of "financial dealings". The other word for money is *argentaria,* which serves to refer to the operation of the modern banking system. In such a state of confusion there is no way that the sin of usury can be clearly understood, so its mention is avoided.

Apart from the other mess in trying to deal with sexual morality in the face of the "authority" of the modern science of Psychology, it appears that this politico-economic mess (concreted in the system of Capitalism) proved to be too much for Pope Benedict XVI, even though he was no doubt wise to what is going on. Pope Francis, I believe, has the necessary insight, but it is rather what is crudely referred to as "gut". The reliance of certainty derived from strong feeling, even if it be grounded in goodness, however, does cause difficulties in interpretation of what he says and writes. He has been known to apologize for statements made "off the cuff".

The complexities of the problem cannot be properly exposed without the distinctions we have drawn out from Aristotle and Aquinas. Sadly, it seems, the more modern Catholic theologians including those in the Vatican have not paid special attention to the work of St. Thomas precisely in this area of moral philosophy and theology. This is even more the case evidently with the English-speaking translators so that it is all but impossible to sort out the confusion.

We will not attempt to do this but starting with paragraph 189 simply highlight the words most concerned in both the Latin and English versions.

"IV. POLITICS AND ECONOMY IN DIALOGUE FOR HUMAN FULFILMENT"

189. **Res politica** *oeconomiae non est subdenda, quae technocratiae imperanti et specimina efficientiae demonstranti se tradere non debet. Hodie, de bono communi cogitantes, procul dubio necesse habemus ut* **res politica** *et oeconomia colloquentes vitae sine cunctatione inserviant, praesertim vitae humanae. Quod* **argentariae** *quacumque ratione servantur, quodque pretium populis est solvendum, absque firma deliberatione recognoscendi atque totum propositum reformandi, absolutus* **rei nummariae** *dominatus confimatur, quae nihil in posterum consequetur quaeque, post diuturnam, sumptuosam vanamque curationem, novas tantum difficultates afferre potest.* **Rei nummariae** *discrimen annis MMVII-MMVIII occasionem praebuit ut nova oeconomia susciperetur, quae studiosior esset moralium principiorum, atque* **mercatorium rei nummariae opus** *nec non virtuales divitiae denuo componerentur. Sed nihil contra factum est, ut rationes obsoletae, mundum adhuc moderantes, iterum ponderarentur. Quae efficiuntur non semper sunt rationalia, quae saepe oeconomicis variationibus sociantur, quibus fructus aliter aestimantur atque re valent. Ex eo evenit ut saepenumero quaedam merces plus aequo gignantur, ambitali impactione haud necessaria addita, quae eadem opera multis regionum oeconomiis detrimentum affert. [133] Subitaneus* **rei nummariae auctus** *plerumque est quoque subitaneus proventus auctus. Itaque quod firma voluntate non agitur est* **oeconomiae realis** *argumentum, quae efficit ut varien-*

tur atque bona effecta meliora reddantur, societates bonis gignendis congruenter operentur, parvae mediaeque societates augeantur atque opus praebeant.

"189. **Politics** must not be subject to the economy, nor should the economy be subject to the dictates of an efficiency-driven paradigm of technocracy. Today, in view of the common good, there is urgent need for politics and economics to enter into a frank dialogue in the service of life, especially human life. Saving banks at any cost, making the public pay the price, foregoing a firm commitment to reviewing and reforming the entire system, only reaffirms the absolute power of a financial system, a power which has no future and will only give rise to new crises after a slow, costly and only apparent recovery. The **financial crisis** of 2007-08 provided an opportunity to develop a new economy, more attentive to ethical principles, and new ways of regulating **speculative financial practices** and virtual wealth. But the response to the crisis did not include rethinking the outdated criteria which continue to rule the world. Production is not always rational, and is usually tied to economic variables which assign to products a value that does not necessarily correspond to their real worth. This frequently leads to an overproduction of some commodities, with unnecessary impact on the environment and with negative results on regional economies. [133] The **financial bubble** also tends to be a productive bubble. The problem of the real economy is not confronted with vigour, yet it is the **real economy** which makes diversification and improvement in production possible, helps companies to function well, and enables small and medium businesses to develop and **create employment**."

Just a couple of further comments are in order. *Res politica* simply means the thing that is the object of political science. This science for Aristotle and Aquinas is a practical moral science completed by political prudence – for the modern mind it is a technical science completed by political art. We assume that the pope generally means the good meaning but he is not clear and the English translator takes it in the modern sense where, being divorced from the moral order, it is readily equated with the emphasis on "animal" in the phrase "political animal". In fact, the political thing in the modern context is not the art to do with a good art but a devious astuteness serving partisan ends. What is intended is "party politics" where opposing ideologies, principally Liberalist Capitalism and Socialist Communism, war for dominance through the "democratic" election system (largely manipulated by "money interests").

In paragraph 190 we will not try to sort out the confusion caused by trying to express in English what the pope has tried to express in Latin. We have dealt with the use of "financial" for "money" but point out how reasons (*rationes*) become forces according to the mechanical mode of modern thinking.

190. *Hac in re oportet memoria semper teneatur "ambitalem tutelam **per rationem tantum nummariam** impendiorum ac beneficiorum praestari non posse. Ambitus ad bona illa pertinet quae **mercatus rationes** tueri aut congruenter promovere non valent".* [134] *Iterum vitetur oportet magica mercatus opinio, quae putat*

*quaestiones per auctum societatum aut singulorum **lucrum** expediri. Num re cogitari potest illum, qui flagranter maximis lucris studeat, ambitalibus effectibus detineri, quos ad proximas generationes transferat? **Intra quaestus ordinem** nullus datur locus naturae ordinibus, temporibus ipsius degradationis ac regenerationis, implicatis oecosystematibus, quae graviter hominibus operantibus vitiari possunt. Praeterea cum de biodiversitate fit mentio, summum respicitur uti copia oeconomicarum opum, quae adhiberi potest, at serio animo **verum rerum pondus**, earum momentum apud personas et culturas, commoditates necessitatesque pauperum non considerantur.*

"190. Here too, it should always be kept in mind that "environmental protection cannot be assured solely on the basis of **financial calculations** of costs and benefits. The environment is one of those goods that cannot be adequately safeguarded or promoted by **market forces**". [134] Once more, we need to reject a magical conception of the market, which would suggest that problems can be solved simply by an increase in the **profits** of companies or individuals. Is it realistic to hope that those who are obsessed with maximizing profits will stop to reflect on the environmental damage which they will leave behind for future generations? Where **profits alone** count, there can be no thinking about the rhythms of nature, its phases of decay and regeneration, or the complexity of ecosystems which may be gravely upset by human intervention. Moreover, biodiversity is considered at most a deposit of economic resources available for exploitation, with no serious thought for the **real value** of things, their significance for persons and cultures, or the concerns and needs of the poor."

There is not much in paragraph 191 in which the pope merely chides the modern economists for accusing those who criticise them with opposing the march of rational economic thought. The intellectual hubris of the modern economist is so ingrained as to be almost incorrigible.

191. *Cum tales quaestiones agitantur, nonnulli ceteros insimulare perinde nituntur, quasi irrationaliter progressum et humanum provectum cohibere studeant. At nobis est persuadendum: cum praestitutus productionis consumptionisque ordo tardatur, alius progrediendi ac provehendi modus praeberi potest. Conatus ad tolerabilem naturalium opum usum non sunt inutile impendium, sed bonorum collocatio, quae alia oeconomica beneficia brevi offerre potest. Si haud anguste conspicimus detegere possumus magis innovatae productionis variationem, minore impactione ambitali cum efficiatur, emolumenti multum afferre posse. Aditus ad varias opportunitates non est intercludendus, quae non postulant ut humanum ingenium cohibeatur eiusque progressus studium, sed potius ut talis vis nova ratione dirigatur.*

"191. Whenever these questions are raised, some react by accusing others of irrationally attempting to stand in the way of progress and human development. But we need to grow in the conviction that a decrease in the pace of production and consumption can at times give rise to another form of progress and development. Efforts to promote a sustainable use of natural resources are not a waste of money, but rather an investment capable of providing other economic benefits in the medium term. If we look at the larger picture, we can see that more diversified and innovative forms of production which impact less on the environment can prove very profitable. It is a matter of openness to different possibilities which do not involve stifling human creativity and its ideals of progress, but rather directing that energy along new channels."

In paragraph 192 the pope elaborates on what he has said. We include it mainly to highlight the different Latin terms besides *lucrum* that are translated simply as "profit". The pope is evidently trying to make the distinction between the notion of profit that is good or indifferent but the English translator only knows one kind, which modern economics takes in the perverse sense.

192. *Exempli gratia, productionis progressus cursus magis **ingeniosus** meliusque ordinatus disparitatem emendare potest inter immodicam rerum consumendarum technologicam **tractationem** atque **modicum** ad prementes quaestiones **hominum** expediendas usum; quaedam genera res sapienter **quaestuoseque** iterum adhibendi, recuperationis functionalis atque multiplicati usus gignere potest; efficacem virium usum in urbibus amplificare potest. Productionis diversitas ad creandum ac novandum complures humano intellectui praebet facultates, dum ambitum tuetur atque operandi plus dat opportunitatis. Fecunda esset ista operositas hominis nobilitatem rursus concitatura, quia dignius est intellectu uti, simul cum audacia ac responsalitate, ut provectus tolerabilis aequique genera reperiantur, ampliore habita notione vitae qualitatis. At contra minus est dignum et ingeniosum leviusque instare*

ut vastationis naturae inveniantur formae, oblaturae tantum con-
*sumendi ac **subitaneum profectum** habendi facultates.*

"192. For example, a path of productive development, which is more **creative** and better directed, could correct the present disparity between excessive technological **investment** in consumption and **insufficient** investment in resolving urgent problems facing the **human family**. It could generate intelligent and **profitable** ways of reusing, revamping and recycling, and it could also improve the energy efficiency of cities. Productive diversification offers the fullest possibilities to human ingenuity to create and innovate, while at the same time protecting the environment and creating more sources of employment. Such creativity would be a worthy expression of our most noble human qualities, for we would be striving intelligently, boldly and responsibly to promote a sustainable and equitable development within the context of a broader concept of quality of life. On the other hand, to find ever new ways of despoiling nature, purely for the sake of new consumer items and **quick profit**, would be, in human terms, less worthy and creative, and more superficial."

In paragraph 193 the pope tries to deal with the notion of "economic growth" which in modern economic "science" is tied to money profit but which naturally has the same function as bodily growth. It is good up to a point (ad-ult). But what is enough in politico-economic terms is something entirely foreign to the modern mind. Do you mean one can have enough money or purchasing power? Ask a billionaire. One cannot have sufficient shoes for every occasion. The modern notion of Economic Growth is like the "scientific" concept of Evolution – it has no end, it is an end in itself. The economic notion of development gets caught up with the scientific notion of evolution and we invent the buzz word "sustainable development". But no one has any idea what it is supposed to mean – sounds good and rational though.

Consult Jeffrey Sachs who has been made chief of the UN department that is commissioned to deliver it in global terms. I do not know but I suspect the pope consults him on matters political and economic. He is, in what little I know about him, despite his unfortunate educational exposure to modern Economics, which is probably where he lost his way in the understanding of population control, a sincere and courageous person with a deep knowledge of the "deep state" of politics in the USA and internationally since the fall of the USSR.

193. *Quidquid est, si hinc **tolerabilis progressus** novas crescendi rationes secum feret, illinc, coram avido inconsideratoque incremento, quod multa per decennia est productum, est cogitandum de remorando gradu, quibusdam **rationabilibus finibus** ponendis, vel retrocedendo, antequam nimis sero sit. Scimus intolerandum esse morem illorum qui consumunt ac magis magisque vastitatem faciunt, dum alii adhuc propriae humanae dignitati vitam accommodare non valent. Quam ob rem tempus est decrementum quoddam in aliquibus orbis partibus opibus susceptis tolerare, ut aliis in partibus **sanum incrementum** obtineatur. Ait Benedictus XVI: "Necesse est ut societates technologice cultae consuetudinibus temperatis favere velint, propriam energiae consumptionem imminuentes eiusque usus meliores facientes condiciones". [135].*

"193. In any event, if in some cases **sustainable development** were to involve new forms of growth, then in other cases, given the insatiable and irresponsible growth produced over many decades, we need also to think of containing growth by setting some **reasonable limits** and even retracing our steps before it is too late. We know how unsustainable is the behaviour of those who constantly consume and destroy, while others are not yet able to live in a way worthy of their human dignity. That is why the time has come to accept decreased growth in some parts of the world, in order to provide resources for other places to experience **healthy growth**. Benedict XVI has said that "technologically advanced societies must be prepared to encourage more sober lifestyles, while reducing their energy consumption and improving its efficiency". [135]

In paragraph 194 the pope actually questions the use of the phrase "sustainable growth" obviously where it is used as a way for covering up the furthering of other ends. The familiar translation of money as to do with finance continues.

194. *Ut novae progressus rationes exstent, necesse habemus ut "ex toto progressus ratio immutetur", [136] quod secum fert officii conscientia cogitare "de re oeconomica eiusque finibus, ad ipsius infirmitates ac depravationes emendandas". [137] Per mediam viam naturae curam **nummariis copiis**, vel ambitum servandum progressui conciliare non sufficit. Hoc de argumento mediae viae parum tantum ruinam remorantur. Agitur modo de progressu iterum finiendo. Technologicus oeconomicusque progressus qui meliorem mundum et vitae qualitatem integre superiorem non relin-*

quit, progressus haberi non potest. Ceterum personarum realis vi-
tae qualitas pluries extenuatur – propter ambitum in deterius mu-
tantem, humilem alimentorum qualitatem vel exhaustas quasdam
opes – intra rei oeconomicae augmentum. **Hac in provincia toler-**
abilis incrementi sermo saepenumero mentem avertit datque
excusationem, *qui bona exhaurit sermonis oecologici intra* **rei**
nummariae *ac technocratiae fines, atque inceptorum socialis am-*
bitalisque responsalitas in quandam seriem rationis mercatoriae et
simulacrorum plerumque contrahitur.

"194. For new models of progress to arise, there is a need to change "models of global development"; [136] this will entail a responsible reflection on "the meaning of the economy and its goals with an eye to correcting its malfunctions and misapplications". [137] It is not enough to balance, in the medium term, the protection of nature with **financial gain,** or the preservation of the environment with progress. Halfway measures simply delay the inevitable disaster. Put simply, it is a matter of redefining our notion of progress. A technological and economic development which does not leave in its wake a better world and an integrally higher quality of life cannot be considered progress. Frequently, in fact, people's quality of life actually diminishes – by the deterioration of the environment, the low quality of food or the depletion of resources – in the midst of economic growth. **In this context, talk of sustainable growth usually becomes a way of distracting attention and offering excuses.** It absorbs the language and values of ecology into the categories of **finance** and technocracy, and the social and environmental responsibility of businesses often gets reduced to a series of marketing and image-enhancing measures."

In paragraph 195 the pope addresses the famous economic principle of the maximization of profit. Interestingly he uses a good word for profit, *profectus,* when the principle is taken from the bad, *lucrum.* But the criticism can be applied to either insofar as even a desire for natural wealth (e.g. shoes) can be taken to excess. This confusion of ideas is unfortunate as it further obscures the nature of exchange and "investment". It seems that the pope also does not have the distinction all that clear though the points he is making are valid. What he says though will hardly make any sense to a modern economist.

195. **Principium maximi obtinendi profectus,** *quod a qualibet alia consideratione abduci vult, quaedam est depravata rei oeconomicae opinio: si productio augetur, parum interest an detrimento futurarum opum vel ambitus salutis id accidat; si silva quadam excisa productio augetur, nemo hac in computatione damnum metitur, quod territorium in solitudinem redigit, biodiversitatem vastat aut contaminationem auget. Hoc nimirum vult societates profectus obtinere computantes ac solventes minimam expensarum partem. Unus ethicus putari mos potest, cum fit "ut impendia oeconomica et socialia, ex communium opum naturae usu exorta, translucida agnoscantur ratione ac plene sustineantur ab omnibus qui iisdem perfruuntur, non autem ab aliis populis vel a venturis generationibus". [138] Instrumentalis rationalitas, quae immotam solummodo secum fert realitatis analysim, illius momenti consid-*

erata necessitate, adest tum cum ipse mercatus opes impertitur, tum cum id efficit ordinans Status.

"195. **The principle of the maximization of profits**, frequently isolated from other considerations, reflects a misunderstanding of the very concept of the economy. As long as production is increased, little concern is given to whether it is at the cost of future resources or the health of the environment; as long as the clearing of a forest increases production, no one calculates the losses entailed in the desertification of the land, the harm done to biodiversity or the increased pollution. In a word, businesses profit by calculating and paying only a fraction of the costs involved. Yet only when "the economic and social costs of using up shared environmental resources are recognized with transparency and fully borne by those who incur them, not by other peoples or future generations", [138] can those actions be considered ethical. An instrumental way of reasoning, which provides a purely static analysis of realities in the service of present needs, is at work whether resources are allocated by the market or by state central planning."

In paragraph 196 the pope alludes to the social phenomenon of multi-national corporations. That phenomenon only brings out the fact that the power of (mis)appropriation of natural wealth and the allied control of money (used well or ill) and the market that underlies the system of Capitalism transcends ordinary national boundaries. For to an extent it took over from the unifying civilizing reach of the Catholic Church. In a real sense it is a new kind of religion, the worship of money. Whereas the Catholic religion being supernatural is the foundation of all good in the world this new religion is the root of all evil. It works for mastery of mankind and is basically the work of the devil Lucifer. But although allowed by God to purify man it cannot prevail over the Church.

Nonetheless, in the eyes of the unwise it can seem to do so. The truth is that one cannot serve two masters; one must choose God or Mammon. The natural authority of the various civil communities over their members, however, is able to be overpowered by Mammon. The counter power at this global level can only be the Catholic Church, not to be taken merely at its clerical level but as the people of God. That is called the Church Militant. Everyone is "called up".

We simply set out this paragraph and highlight certain phrases but our comments already made should cover what is needed to be remarked upon.

196. ***Qui rei politicae est locus?*** *Memoria subsidiarietatis principium repetimus, quod libertatem tribuit ad praesentes facultates omnibus in ordinibus explicandas, sed eodem tempore a potentioribus erga bonum commune responsalitatis plus postulat. Verum est hodie nonnullos **oeconomicos ordines** plus pollere quam **ipsos Status**. At **res oeconomica sine re politica** probari non potest, quae aliam logicam conciliare non valeat, varias species moderaturam hodierni discriminis. Logica, in qua nullus est locus sincerae ambitus sollicitudinis, eadem est in qua nulla est sollicitudo de debilioribus involvendis, quia "in vigenti specimine **"felicis exitus"** ac **"privatae rationis"** pecuniam collocare insanum videtur, ut ii*

qui tardantur, debiles vel minus habentes vitae decursu prosperare possint". [139]

"196. **What happens with politics?** Let us keep in mind the principle of subsidiarity, which grants freedom to develop the capabilities present at every level of society, while also demanding a greater sense of responsibility for the common good from those who wield greater power. Today, it is the case that some **economic sectors** exercise more power than **states themselves**. But economics without politics cannot be justified, since this would make it impossible to favour other ways of handling the various aspects of the present crisis. The mindset which leaves no room for sincere concern for the environment is the same mindset which lacks concern for the inclusion of the most vulnerable members of society. For "the current model, with its emphasis on success and self-reliance, does not appear to favour an **investment** in efforts to help the slow, the weak or the less talented to find opportunities in life". [139]

Much the same can be said about paragraph 197 where "politics" is awkwardly put in the Latin as a thing and then translated into English confusedly as the "crazy" world of modern political government. Genuine good government, on which Aristotelian political science (Politics) is primarily focused, cannot be responsible for the actual corruption that attends most modern forms of political rule. So the confusion is further compounded.

197. ***Re politica opus est*** *nobis quae lato prospectu cogitet, atque omnibus ex partibus rem aggrediatur, per dialogum variarum disciplinarum diversas complectens discriminis facies.* ***Ipsa***

res politica pluries suae infamiae responsalis est, propter corruptelam atque defectum bonarum politicarum actionum publicarum. Si Status suum officium quadam in regione non exsequitur, quidam oeconomici coetus benefactores videri possunt ac re habere potestatem, cum sibi dari a quibusdam legibus vacationem sentiant, ut perveniant ad varias scelerum instructorum species, personarum commercium, stupefactivorum medicamentorum commercium et violentiam, quae difficulter eraduntur. Si res politica perversam logicam frangere non valet, ac praeterea vanis sermonibus implicatur, magnas hominum quaestiones neglegere pergemus. Realis immutationis ordo requirit ut omnes processus denuo considerentur, quoniam non sufficit oecologicas leves considerationes inserere, dum logica non excutitur, hodiernae culturae subdita. Sana res politica sibi hoc certamen instituere debet.

"197. **What is needed is a politics** which is far-sighted and capable of a new, integral and interdisciplinary approach to handling the different aspects of the crisis. **Often, politics itself is responsible** for the disrepute in which it is held, on account of corruption and the failure to enact sound public policies. If in a given region the state does not carry out its responsibilities, some business groups can come forward in the guise of benefactors, wield real power, and consider themselves exempt from certain rules, to the point of tolerating different forms of organized crime, human trafficking, the drug trade and violence, all of which become very difficult to eradicate. If politics shows itself incapable of breaking such a perverse logic, and remains caught up in inconsequential discussions, we will continue to avoid facing the major problems of humanity. A strategy for real change calls for rethinking processes in their entirety, for it is not enough to include a few superficial ecological considerations while failing to question the logic which underlies present-day culture. A healthy politics needs to be able to take up this challenge."

The same crossover from understanding "politics" as a proper practical ethical study in Aristotle and Aquinas shows up here in paragraph 198. The true practical science and prudence of Politics as understood by them does not need to acknowledge their mistakes. Here it seems the pope himself slips into using the word "politics" in the debased sense that it commonly has.

198. ***Res politica et oeconomica alia in aliam refert culpam,*** *quod ad paupertatem et ambitalem degradationem attinet.* ***Sed illud postulat ut proprios errores agnoscant*** *nec non mutuae actionis reperiant genera ad bonum commune obtinendum. Cum alteri oeconomicae utilitati solum studeant, alteri dominatui servando augendoque flagranter operam dent, supersunt contentiones vel dubiae pactiones, ubi minus interest utriusque partis ambitum servare ac debiliores curare. Etiam hic principium valet "unitatem concertationem superare." [140]*

"198. **Politics and the economy tend to blame each other** when it comes to poverty and environmental degradation. **It is to be hoped that they can acknowledge their own mistakes** and find forms of interaction directed to the common good. While some are concerned only with **financial gain**, and others with holding on to or increasing their **power**, what we are left with are conflicts or spurious agreements where the last thing either party is concerned about is caring for the environment and protecting those who are most vulnerable. Here too, we see how true it is that "unity is greater than conflict". [140]"

We have already commented upon the first sentence of paragraph 199. The only further comment is that the pope seems to think that the deficiency in the modern empirical scientific method is by reason of leaving out final cause as well as poetic and other non-analytical modes of reason but the most important deficiency is perhaps the leaving out of the natural formal cause (for which a mathematical form or formula is substituted in the modern scientific method). This is a sign that the pope himself has not studied as completely as he should St. Thomas's treatment of the nature and division of the sciences. However, his point is well made anyway.

199. *Censeri non potest empiricas scientias vitam, intimam essentiam omnium creaturarum ac totam realitatem omnibus ex partibus explanare. Si ita esset, angusti eorum fines methodologici haud iure superarentur. Si hoc exiguo prospectu cogitatur, aestheticus sensus, poesis vel et rationis facultas significationem finemque rerum complectendi dissolvuntur. [141] Memorare cupimus "religiosa scripta potiora quandam significationem omnibus aetatibus praebere posse, suadentem habent vim ad novum usque prospectum patefaciendum .... Estne rationis intellectusque ea in obscuritatem detrudere eo quod in quodam religiosae opinionis contextu tantum sunt orta?". [142] Leve est reapse cogitare ethica principia meris verbis demonstrari posse, ab omni contextu seposita, atque quod per religiosum sermonem manifestantur, in*

publicis disputationibus vi ac pondere non exuuntur. Ethica principia quae ratio percipere potest per diversas species semper redire et per varios sermones, religiosos quoque, exprimi possunt.

"199. It cannot be maintained that empirical science provides a complete explanation of life, the interplay of all creatures and the whole of reality. This would be to breach the limits imposed by its own methodology. If we reason only within the confines of the latter, little room would be left for aesthetic sensibility, poetry, or even reason's ability to grasp the ultimate meaning and purpose of things. [141] I would add that "religious classics can prove meaningful in every age; they have an enduring power to open new horizons... Is it reasonable and enlightened to dismiss certain writings simply because they arose in the context of religious belief?" [142] It would be quite simplistic to think that ethical principles present themselves purely in the abstract, detached from any context. Nor does the fact that they may be couched in religious language detract from their value in public debate. The ethical principles capable of being apprehended by reason can always reappear in different guise and find expression in a variety of languages, including religious language."

We will now leave making comments on particular paragraphs of the present pope's social encyclicals, for the reasons given. This means that our comments to follow are necessarily general and dependent upon a prima facie understanding of what is said. On a general impression of the documents we must say that the documents are rather disappointing from several aspects. Without saying that they wander too much off the subject they do tend to discuss all sorts of issues related but often only remotely so to the burning issues of the times.

As noted with the social encyclical of Pope Benedict one gets a notion that there is such a politico-economic system as one ruled either by an identifiable few or for the benefit of the few, but not clearly equated with Capitalism as it has operated and is operating in the modern world. Nor is this now world-pervasive politico-economic system of Capitalism clearly named as the system of gross inequalities that is in fact the prime cause of the "challenges" listed by the pope in his Apostolic Exhortation *Evangelii gaudium.*

As he put it there, "we have to remember that the majority of our contemporaries are barely living from day to day, with dire consequences. A number of diseases are spreading. The hearts of many people are gripped by fear and desperation, even in the so-called rich countries. The joy of living frequently fades, lack of respect for others and violence are on the rise, and inequality is increasingly evident. It is a struggle to live and, often, to live with precious little dignity. ... We are in an age of knowledge and information, which has led to new and often anonymous kinds of power. (52) How is this any different essentially from the "condition of the worker" described by Pope Leo XIII in 1891?

Pope Francis then elaborated on the politico-economic condition of our times.

an economy of exclusion

"53. Just as the commandment 'Thou shalt not kill' sets a clear limit in order to safeguard the value of human life, today we also have to say 'thou shalt not' to an economy of exclusion and inequality. Such an economy kills. How can it be that it is not a news item when an elderly homeless person dies of exposure, but it is news when the stock market loses two points? This is a case of exclusion. Can we continue to stand by when food is thrown away while people are starving? This is a case of inequality. Today everything comes under the laws of competition and the survival of the fittest, where the powerful feed upon the powerless. As a consequence, masses of people find themselves excluded and marginalized: without work, without possibilities, without any means of escape."

"54. In this context, some people continue to defend trickle-down theories which assume that economic growth, encouraged by a free market, will inevitably succeed in bringing about greater justice and inclusiveness in the world. This opinion, which has never been confirmed by the facts, expresses a crude and naïve trust in the goodness of those wielding economic power and in the sacralized workings of the prevailing economic system. Meanwhile, the excluded are still waiting. To sustain a lifestyle which excludes others, or to sustain enthusiasm for that selfish ideal, a globalization of indifference has developed. Almost without being aware of it, we end up being incapable of feeling compassion at the outcry of the poor, weeping for other people's pain, and feeling a need to help them, as though all this were someone else's responsibility and not our own. The culture of prosperity deadens us; we are thrilled if the market offers us something new to purchase. In the meantime all those lives stunted for lack of opportunity seem a mere spectacle; they fail to move us."

the new idolatry of money

"55. One cause of this situation is found in our relationship with money, since we calmly accept its dominion over ourselves and our societies. The current financial crisis can make us overlook the fact that it originated in a profound human crisis: the denial of the primacy of the human person! We have created new idols. The worship of the ancient golden calf (cf. Ex 32:1-35) has returned in a new and ruthless guise in the idolatry of money and the dictatorship of an impersonal economy lacking a truly human purpose. The worldwide crisis affecting finance and the economy lays bare their imbalances and, above all, their lack of real concern for human beings; man is reduced to one of his needs alone: consumption."

"56. While the earnings of a minority are growing exponentially, so too is the gap separating the majority from the prosperity enjoyed by those happy few. This imbalance is the result of ideologies which defend the absolute autonomy of the marketplace and financial speculation. Consequently, they reject the right of states, charged with vigilance for the common good, to exercise any form of control. A new tyranny is thus born, invisible and often virtual, which unilaterally and relentlessly imposes its own laws and rules. Debt and the accumulation of interest also make it difficult for countries to realize the potential of their own economies and keep citizens from enjoying their real purchasing power. To all this we can add widespread corruption and self-serving tax evasion, which have taken on worldwide dimensions. The thirst for power and possessions knows no limits. In this system, which tends to devour everything which stands in the way of increased profits, whatever is fragile, like the environment, is defenseless before the interests of a deified market, which become the only rule."

a financial system which rules rather than serves

"57. Behind this attitude lurks a rejection of ethics and a rejection of God. Ethics has come to be viewed with a certain scornful derision. It is seen as counterproductive, too human, because it makes money and power relative. It is felt to be a threat, since it condemns the manipulation and debasement of the person. In effect, ethics leads to a God who calls for a committed response which is outside the categories of the marketplace. When these latter are absolutized, God can only be seen as uncontrollable, unmanageable, even dangerous, since he calls human beings to their full realization and to freedom from all forms of enslavement. Ethics – a non-ideological ethics – would make it possible to bring about balance and a more humane social order. With this in mind, I encourage financial experts and political leaders to ponder the words of one of the sages of antiquity: "Not to share one's wealth with the poor is to steal from them and to take away their livelihood. It is not our own goods which we hold, but theirs". [55]"

"58. A financial reform open to such ethical considerations would require a vigorous change of approach on the part of political leaders. I urge them to face this challenge with determination and an eye to the future, while not ignoring, of course, the specifics of each case. Money must serve, not rule! The Pope loves everyone, rich and poor alike, but he is obliged in the name of Christ to remind all that the rich must help, respect and promote the poor. I exhort you to generous solidarity and to the return of economics and finance to an ethical approach which favours human beings."

the inequality which spawns violence

"59. Today in many places we hear a call for greater security. But until exclusion and inequality in society and between peoples are reversed, it will be impossible to eliminate violence. The poor and the poorer peoples are accused of violence, yet without equal opportunities the different forms of aggression and conflict will find a fertile terrain for growth and eventually explode. When a society – whether local, national or global – is willing to leave a part of itself on the fringes, no political programmes or resources spent on law enforcement or surveillance systems can indefinitely guarantee tranquillity. This is not the case simply because inequality provokes a violent reaction from those excluded from the system, but because the socioeconomic system is unjust at its root. Just as goodness tends to spread, the toleration of evil, which is injustice, tends to expand its baneful influence and quietly to undermine any political and social system, no matter how solid it may appear. If every action has its consequences, an evil embedded in the structures of a society has a constant potential for disintegration and death. It is evil crystallized in unjust social structures, which cannot be the basis of hope for a better future. We are far from the so-called "end of history", since the conditions for a sustainable and peaceful development have not yet been adequately articulated and realized."

Is it too much to relate this state of the world, which is lamented by the pope, to the dominance exercised by the politico-economic system we know as modern Capitalism? Such a politico-economic system will be strenuously defended in name by those committed to its liberalist ideology, which commitment we must concede is in many cases genuine, whether from personal conviction or successful indoctrination. We might add though that, having the money, the capitalists can call upon for its defence the best advocates that money can buy in the various professions.

It is true that it may be claimed for Capitalism that it should be credited with the tremendous material benefits that have come through the peoples who adopted it, as for instance the Protestant countries of England and Europe, and their colonies (especially the one which first divorced itself from English rule). This seems to have confirmation from the spectacular advances in science and technology that followed almost immediately after the rejection of the authority of the Catholic Church.

It is curious however how this burst of industrial production came through a system in which the majority of workers were treated little better than slaves. Though a crude analogy it is a bit like the Egyptian civilization proudly claiming its superiority from the marvels of the pyramids. Who benefited from this industrial revolution? Was it not principally the rich few, those who had commandeered the material and intellectual wealth and technical knowledge that had been developed by a Christian civilization to a point where it might blossom so that it could be used to conquer the world, but such a religiously minded society was not interested in doing so except spiritually?

It was only this advantage of wealth (capital), material and technical, made possible from their privileged inheritance from a previous civilization that the ruling minority could, rather miserly, dole out to their own(ed) majority poor a seemingly comfortable living so as to present themselves as rulers of a great country. On the whole, however, the poor majority were used as hired workers in time of peace and as cannon fodder in time of war. For the military superiority of the post Christian nations came from their (inherited) technological advantage in the production of weaponry.

Modern wars are not won by brave soldiers defeating equally brave soldiers on the other side but by wholesale slaughter by the possession of "weapons of mass destruction". That is what makes war in modern times so senseless. But how else can one powerful nation defend itself if threatened by another preparing to overthrow it with such means?

In his social encyclicals Pope Francis has discussed the evils that mankind is made to suffer, but he has not discussed the obvious modern root cause except in general terms. Admittedly, one cannot name the culprits (except historically) for they manage to keep anonymous. The accidental billionaires of the day, like George Soros and Bill Gates are in the scheme of things rather minor players compared to those to whom, by reason of their vast control of capital and money, all, including governments, are in debt.

This leads on to a couple of curious features of the recent social encyclicals. Firstly, there is this absence of any specific reference to the system of Capitalism (the last reference seems to have been in *Centesimus annus* (in which, even there, it was given a possible benevolent alternative interpretation). Secondly, there is this apparent shift to blaming all "humanity" for the "challenges" posed by the depredation of the environment and the oppression of our fellow man.

To me that is to fall into the trap of deflecting attention away from the real cause, namely, the injustices in the order of distributive and commutative justice perpetrated by "the fortunate" (or privileged) few in the historical manner that we have outlined in our books and which can be clearly identified as behind the modern politico-economic system of Capitalism. But in polite company no one wants to call it by its name except those who laud it.

However, there may be good reason for this ecclesiastical strategy. An explanation for the reluctance may be hidden in Scripture where the rich man (*Dives* in Latin) is nameless and only the poor man Lazarus is named. Considering the fate of

Dives it is perhaps a charity not to identify anyone of the relevant rich, even according to his adherence to a particular ideology.

However, what we seem to have in the two social encyclicals of the present pope (we must remember that we are going only on English language translations) is the constant reference to "we" as all human beings, having to fix the problem. Now it is true that all have some responsibility, even for the sins of others, since we are one people, but plainly it is not Lazarus who was primarily responsible for his condition of poverty and temporal misery, nor is it the masses ("the majority of our contemporaries") that are in any position to do much about the degradation of the environment or their own hunger, many to the point of starvation before our "virtual" eyes.

It is obvious that Pope Francis's lament is directed to the fortunate, mainly the beneficiaries of the politico-economic system in the "West", since that is his main audience. But the language is such as to suggest at least that it is humanity as such that is to blame. The Latin in this regard in not easy to interpret, because there are so many nuances with the word "human", or man (*homo*). It has reached a stage of insanity in regard to the difference between man (*vir*) and woman (*femina*).

But even in every context there is nothing but complete confusion. First, there is the elementary logical distinction between the abstract and the concrete, as when we can say that Socrates is man (*homo*) but not that he is humanity –no individual man is, not even all men. The English, the least logical of all peoples, constantly use the abstract form for the concrete.

Then we have mixed up the interchange between the two forms of man in universal but concrete (*genus humanum*), mankind and human race. Socrates is an individual member of the human race but he is not mankind. The English translator is all over the place in this regard. It is not even worth the effort to sort it all out here. (One may refer to a forthcoming book of mine on Logic, Science and Saint Thomas Aquinas).

When we come to trying to understand the mind of the popular movements desiring to remedy the parlous condition of the human race (is that racist?) it is like trying to eat a bowl of spaghetti one spaghetto at a time. As for the activists, are they as concerned about the fate of the poor as they are about their own perceived impending discomfort? Is the Vatican aware of the possibility of the unclear language of its documents giving the impression that it is on the side of the popular push? We think the Church leaders should be careful whose lead they themselves may be following. As already noted, the unjustly rich, now obscenely so, do not mind if everybody, that is "humanity", gets the blame.

However, we do not wish to prolong our commentary on the social encyclicals of the present pope. We will briefly say something regarding the other encyclical *Fratelli tutti*, but our comments so far apply generally also to it.

One annoying thing we notice in the English translation of *Fratelli tutti* (not having the benefit of the Latin, if any) is how St. Francis of Assisi is portrayed as if he was not interested in Catholic doctrine. Let us quote part of paragraph 4. "Francis did not wage a war of words aimed at imposing doctrines; he simply spread the love of God. He understood that "God is love and those who abide in love abide in God" (1 Jn 4:16). In this way, he became a father to all and inspired the vision of a fraternal society. Indeed, "only the man who approaches others, not to draw them into his own life, but to help them become ever more fully themselves, can truly be called a father".[4] *Exil et tendresse*, Éd. Franciscaines, Paris, 1962, 205.

Now, the two statements at the beginning and the end of this passage taken separately (as we are sure the persons concerned intended them) can stand a good interpretation. Firstly, that one should not preach to others as if one were in a debate in which winning was the end (and being given the accolade of winning the debate). Or preaching with an aim other than telling the good news to others to be freely received, without promises, threats, or inducements of any kind except the inducement that lies in coming to know the very truth and goodness of the message.

The word "proselytize" means to attempt to convert another. It did not have any pejorative meaning originally (the Greek "proselyte" being simply a convert) but having become associated with religion it has acquired such. Presumably, this pejorative connotation came into the English language to denigrate the conversion of Protestants to Catholicism, there having to have been some devious means employed, knowing how evil the Catholic Church was. "Law Reform" by a parallel process has come to mean to totally deform and destroy the effect of a law, for example, the law against abortion or suicide.

Words such as a woman's right to choose (to kill) and euthanasia (good death) are good examples of what Chesterton called evil euphemisms. The father of lies has been hard at work in modern times. It is remarkable how many "good" Catholics have fallen for the deceit; it says a lot for their "good" modern Jesuit (?) education.

Ironically, it is Protestantism that has undergone since "The Reformation" the historical process of deformation and self-destruction. But the pejorative meaning has survived applying now to religion itself. The conversion method of Islam is taken to be the norm. No doubt, the pope is aware that what he is referring to is proselytism.

The second statement (by a Franciscan ELOI LECLERC, O.F.M.) can be allowed if "to his own life" is not opposed to the life of Christ and "become ever more themselves" is not taken to exclude to become ever more Christ-like. But it does sound like helping one "to do it my way". It is not to be taken in this sense, but we may be sure that many of the readers will want it to be taken in this sense. A little more clarity is hopefully in the Latin when it comes out. Leaving the English as it is, however, in our view does run the risk of the text being twisted to suit the modern self-centred meaning.

The danger here is what Pope Benedict was warning of in his encyclical, of opposing love or charity to wisdom or truth. Pope Francis does later make the same point. "227. Truth, in fact, is an inseparable companion of justice and mercy." It is not just something that applies in the supernatural order. Aristotle himself says that it belongs to the wise to teach, and what do they teach but doctrine (natural wisdom).

It is easy to lose one's balance in this regard. That is why the theologians need to pay special attention to the work of St. Thomas Aquinas. We will however, leave our commentary on Pope Francis's social encyclicals for the reasons already given and end our book with an Afterword that follows.

Afterword

We have completed as best we can our commentary on the Social Encyclicals as they relate to the subject matter we have been focused on, namely, the politico-economic aspect of civil society (*polis*) as understood by Aristotle and Aquinas. It was not meant to treat of every aspect brought out by the social encyclicals since Pope Leo XIII's *Rerum novarum,* but only that precise aspect upon which that pope focused originally, which was the burning question of the condition of the worker within the economic system that had come to dominate modern socio-political life.

It is quite clear what the historical name of that system is, Capitalism. One can pretty well name also the countries of the "West" which closely identify their politico-economic systems with it, and have been proud to have it as their "Economy". They are rather touchy however about the injustice of its familiar features with regard to the possession of property or capital being concentrated in the hands of a minority and the quasi-servile condition of those (the majority) who as a consequence possess little or no capital, whether by way of natural resources or the instruments/technology needed by labour to engage in the production of wealth.

The only access to such consumption/wealth by the "workers", even such as is necessary for survival, is by the receipt of wages the exchange value or "price" of which is determined through a market system wherein the owners of the capital (let us call them as is customary Capitalists, not necessarily the direct employers but generally operating through their well rewarded stewards – we do not go into the modern legal subterfuge of the "corporate veil"), offer "employment" to a "pool" of those desperate for work at a "price" (set by the "market" it is alleged), on a "take it or leave" it basis.

In its "unbridled" heyday towards the end of the nineteenth century the only alternative to "agreeing" to this wage price, which generally (for reasons that should be obvious to all not blinded by greed or modern economic "science") was for the worker, not to go "on the dole" as the "safety net" provided by a now improvident State, but to perish by starvation along with his family and dependents – unless some good Samaritan came to the rescue.

Compassion was alien to the system, for its mantra was "economic" means efficient in a world of "scarcity" and the mechanism of the market would break down if clogged with the milk of human kindness. "It's the Economy, stupid", is the modern expression, a true enough statement if the adjective is put in the right place.

However, despite valiant efforts, after its collapse between two world wars, to reform this politico-economic system, without any change in understanding the basic cause of its malfunctioning, it has lasted into recent times, but evidently now is "on its last legs", not so much because of external opposition (from Socialism and Communism) but because of its internal rottenness that has brought its deep rooted immoral condition (beginning with injustice) to its (un)natural end.

That potted version of the history of Capitalism in modern times has been filled out somewhat in the books we have previously devoted to the subject matter. But we are not so much concerned to trace the complex history of the system, with all its attendant evils, both political and moral, as it has "progressed", but to examine the causes and this mainly from a philosophical point of view, even though the present book has necessarily to take into account related theological issues.

The understanding of the subject matter has to begin, as it does with most philosophical subjects, including moral, with the remarkable Aristotle. A fundamental problem with the understanding of the questions of justice that are central to the issues involved has to come from the well known fact that the modern mind right at the beginning of the modern era rejected his contribution, not just to the study of the ethical issues involved here, where his contribution had been classical for more than a thousand years, and whose genius is even grudgingly admitted by the best of scholarship today, but virtually to throwing away every one of his writings, including those of anyone connected with him, the most illustrious being St. Thomas Aquinas.

We will come shortly to explaining how such an act of unbelievable cultural vandalism could have come about, though we have already given some indication of it. It has a great deal to do with the religion to which Aquinas belonged and it can be argued that the works of Aristotle were spat out in disgust because they had become too closely aligned with the theology of the Catholic Church best expounded by Aquinas.

Arguments were found to justify the rejection of Aristotle and to give its rejection a veneer of plausibility. As we have explained the objections did not apply to Aristotle's own method of science, that of his natural science being insufficiently empirical, but to those so overawed by his genius as to use his authority (which he regarded as the weakest of arguments) to close down further discussion and even investigation of an assumed scientific "fact". So natural science in particular languished until starting to recover about the time of Saint Albert the Great, the teacher of Aquinas. The moderns would not of course admit any debt to the despised "scholastics".

Any argument against Aristotle's scientific work, however, would have been gladly received. For the rejection of the divine authority of the Catholic Church, that we know as the Protestant Reformation, struck deep and wide. At the time it seemed to carry all before it. The most saintly, wise and rational of those who resisted it promptly lost their heads.

It is even reported that of the Catholic bishops of England at the time (presumably well educated clerics/clerks) all but one went over to Henry's new Church of England protesting against "Rome". This would have to be attributed not only to fear of losing their heads, but also to the great degree of the dissatisfaction with the Catholic Church authorities of the age.

Such was the vehemence in the way the protest was expressed, with which political and national enmities were mixed, that the Church that had been recognised for 1500 years as founded by Christ, the Son of God, was painted as a work of the devil. Any work of harm and destruction against it, unjust according to normal criteria of justice, could be seen as justified, even demanded by God.

It is hard to imagine the depth of feeling that occurred once the "Reformation" was embarked upon. The protestors were out for blood and robbery was seen as a virtue so far as Catholic religious property was concerned. Over a relatively short time of domination and demolition of things Catholic the social and political situation "cooled" down and those enriched by the legally sanctioned rapine settled down to enjoy their lives of luxury and being regarded as respectable lords of the realm. The *hoi polloi* (the majority working poor – the Greek simply means the ordinary citizens) were schooled to accept the justice of the protest and to look up to their lords with gratitude for their newfound freedom from the religious persecution by the papist secret service police recruited from overseas (mostly the new guard Jesuits, of which St. Edmund Campion was of course the chief persecutor).

The nature of the new divide between the rich and the poor was reflected in that of "The Church of England" into High Church and Broad Church, the former clinging to their belief that it could be regarded as but a branch of the Catholic Church (hence the name Anglo-Catholic) in the same way the Orthodox argued. The latter followed the more radical idea of a clear break with the old superstitions about a ministerial priesthood and the *hocus pocus* (*Hoc est Corpus Meum ?*) of a sacrament of the Eucharist. The notion of thanksgiving (eucharist) to God was kept but in the USA it became a national holiday period and is celebrated with turkey.

However, we do not want to dwell on these now historical enmities (just think of what the protestors did with the day before All Saints' Day, the eve of All Hallows, Halloween). A large part of the reason for the loss of their sharpness comes from the social decline of attachment to any religion, and the fall by the modern "educated" into a sophisticated atheism. What we want to bring out is the fact that in the background there remains the deep divide of the population into a rich few and a majority working poor that constitutes the essence of modern Capitalism, even when claimed to be "bridled". Many a political leader of socialist leanings has felt that he can bridle the beast but is soon thrown off. But we have discussed enough the power conferred by control of the capital and money of a politico-economic system of a civil community.

We have also discussed attendant problems in the apparent position of the Church, even in its official stance, towards a manifest state of structural injustice, of cultivating a *modus vivendi* for the sake of social stability ("law and order") and a degree of peace that may be accorded to the members of the Church in the practice of their Faith.

The administration of Church finances involves difficult prudential decisions made even more difficult by not having any understanding of the moral dilemmas through not having paid special attention to the relevant parts of the work of Saint Thomas Aquinas (particularly II-II, qq. 77 & 78). The bishops seeing these matters of finance as requiring technical expertise happily hire (at considerable expense) CFOs to assist the CEOs running the diocesan church bureaus. The deacons would not be up to the job.

We do not wish to belittle the work of such ecclesiastical administrations but the modern ecclesiastical *modus operandi* brings out how much the Church hierarchy has become entangled with the financial and multiple other woes of the modern "capitalist" way of life. They have become dependent upon "management" modelled on large corporations, not only in regard to their "finances" but also their "labour force".

That is complicated in more modern times by the "intervention" of the State (following through the Keynesian "revolution" in Economic Science - more government jobs for graduate macro-economists). The Catholic education system, even the education of priests, not just as for funds but also as to curriculum, has become greatly dependent upon the public education system, which sets "standards of excellence" (mostly ending in failure) and involves all students in a paralysing octopus of bureaucracy. Being expensive the students now have to bear a portion of the cost of their education, the payment for their "contribution" to their "higher" education/ indoctrination helped by a wonderful system of indebtedness that adds another expensive arm of government bureaucracy to the system.

We do not enter into the numerous problems arising from such involvement of the Church not just with a secularist/atheist State but also in a politico-economic system that is liberalist/capitalist, where society is divided into a two sections, one of which is of a few people of "property", or capital, and the other is of a great majority of little or no property, mostly dependent solely upon their labour for a livelihood.

Things are of course complicated by numerous auxiliary factors, such as the employment of many by the moneyed section to manage their property, commercial and financial interests, such as collecting rents from tenants of the estates, lands and farms, managing factories and businesses and looking after investments (interest on loans etc.)

Then when the State comes into the picture there is the need for accountants and lawyers one of whose services is to ensure as much tax as possible is legally avoided (and not illegally evaded). In the provision of all these kinds of "services" the servants are well rewarded and can be counted as part of a "middle class" escaping somewhat from the struggle for existence of those of the "lower" classes. We do not include here those (by no means a small number) who simply curry favour with the rich, or obtain their patronage, and thus are generously provided for. Amongst the middle class we should include the more skilled of labourers, plumbers etc., who can operate as independent contractors and earn enough to be able to set aside some "savings".

But we are more interested here in a particular feature of the capitalist system that is open to all, rich and poor alike, though the rich have obviously a great advantage. It consists in astuteness in the commercial "art" of buying and selling at a profit that we have described and some indeed can make a great profit thereby even with borrowed money. Some, like real estate agents, thrive on this kind of "business'.

It is in fact the feature that distinguishes modern capitalism the most, and really defines it in being applied to the "labour market", as we have explained. Generally applied, however, it is a feature that has important implications, of a grave moral kind, for the engagement of ecclesiastical and religious institutions in the operations of the modern market. How did the Vatican do in its purchase of a luxury property in Chelsea the fashionable part of London? This is obviously important when we are considering it in the context of the social doctrine of the Church.

Simply put, the feature consists in engagement in the market according to the second mode of exchange distinguished and described as long ago as Aristotle and which we have clearly set out with St. Thomas's assistance in our book "Economic Science and Saint Thomas Aquinas". It is the mode of non-natural exchange that we have symbolised as MCM, as opposed to the natural mode CMC.

We need to understand the causes for the total neglect of this distinction in modern thought (even extending into Catholic theology). An obvious one is the rejection of anything to do with Aristotle's legacy. But there had to be more than that. In our view it came about from a convergence of many causes that were coming to a head towards the end of the era of Christendom.

The best way to put it is that the modern age was ushered in, not by one revolution or kind of social turmoil, but by many, both Christian/supernatural and civil/natural. By the latter we mean to include many facets of social life, political, economic and cultural, but also so as to include changes in scientific knowledge of the world that was acquired from investigation of the physical world, not just by the newly invented instruments for investigating the stars above (telescope) and the elements below (microscope), but also all regions of material reality, giving rise to the new experimental and physico-mathematical sciences of astronomy (replacing astrology), chemistry (replacing alchemy), multiplying as the investigations reached into more and more corners of the physical world, as in geology, mineralogy and so forth.

The possibilities of investigation and invention awakened by the new empirical spirit seemed endless. All this was further stimulated by the voyages of discovery which opened up vast regions beyond the then known world. Those living in those times must have felt like a child in a world of adventure and excitement. Add to this the stimulation of the human creative imagination and the fact that, when the imagination takes over, science takes on an infinite character and it becomes at times difficult to distinguish modern science from science fiction.

However, as may be appreciated, we are more concerned with the area of the new social sciences and in particular that part of political science originally named Political Economy, but now called Economics, that has declared its independence from Politics as understood by Aristotle. It is in this area that the revolution we are concerned with is, what we may call commercial and financial, in which the moral questions dealt with by St. Thomas in II-II, qq. 77 & 78, that are most relevant to the rise of Capitalism, can best be understood.

Though it was intertwined with the religious life of late Christendom, the one redounding on the other, it is not religion as is supernatural that is concerned, but rather as it is part of natural morality, as shown by St. Thomas in his discussion of Justice in the second part of the second part of the *Summa* (refer to my "Ethics Today and Saint Thomas Aquinas"). The moral issue is in commutative justice, to do with "voluntary commutations" covering the two areas of exchange, natural and non-natural, the latter being symbolised by MCM (with money as an end in itself) and usury, which is a kind of exchange of monies for the sake of "making" a money profit.

What appears to have been occurring was that the opening of trade routes to foreign lands had opened up as well the opportunities for merchants to make fortunes from the mode of exchange that distinguishes their mercantile activity (MCM). This created a great desire to have money with which to undertake (Fr. entreprise) such a mode of exchange, and borrowing from those who had money was just as good a means as having one's own stock of money.

The existing laws against usury constituted a hindrance to "capitalizing" on such a profitable mode of exchange and thus on the ballooning business of the merchants. They were not the least concerned with having to pay some "interest" on the borrowed money, for it was generally a minor cost in the making of profits from the merchants' "trade" in the new world of opportunity for making fortunes. A ban on the lender receiving interest seemed so much nonsense.

As seen in our book, the discussion of the moral issues involved in the new circumstances of the time, even considered from a moral point of view, had certain complications. We have seen, for instance, that St. Thomas himself ruled out one of the extrinsic titles that were later found to be valid. (We discuss the reason for this in the book). Some Catholic moral theologians shifted ground, and when the Reformers came into power the more powerful of these, e.g. John Calvin, did so quite definitively. We need not go into the railings of such as Thomas Hobbes. However, we refer to our book for a discussion of how the question ought to be viewed according to the principles enunciated by Aquinas. The Church has not changed its position in this regard though many Catholic moralists have worked strenuously to "bring it around" to conform to modern thought.

In any case at the time of the ending of Christendom there was great pressure put on the religious authorities to ease the restrictions on "freedom of trade". This was an important part in the push for "laissez faire laissez passer" that formed the first principle of the new economic science. We have noted its roots in the first principle of all modern thought and practice: "I am servant of no man or god".

In the more civilized "West", therefore, Church authorities, apart from the popes, seem generally to have felt it inevitable to have to bow to the "best practice" of the worldly, and concede there is nothing sinful in charging for the use of money provided it is not excessive or harmful to the poor. Otherwise, as the economists tell us, the whole economic system would collapse. The lending of money, or financing, after all, is a large part of the driving force of all socio-economic activity.

In the event, a fundamental pillar of Capitalism was enshrined in modern society. Usury was "legitimized" and freedom of trade won the day. What we have wanted to notice is the important part this played in the series of revolutions that rocked Christendom and facilitated the consignment to the past of its notions of a natural moral law, at the same time that the principles of Capitalism were adopted in their stead.

But let us look a little more closely at the implications this has for the involvement of the Church in modern commercial and financial practices. We do not want to go over all what we have already said in previous books. What we want to focus on is something St. Thomas says about the involvement of clergy and religious in "investments" in the market in the mode of the second kind of exchange (MCM). It is not easy to identify the exact point in view of the general ignorance regarding the twofold modes of exchange. So what we propose to do is quote the relevant article (II-II, q. 77, art. 4) in Latin and English and then extract the point we wish to bring out. This will involve first going over some mistranslation of the English, the awfulness of which we have seen accounts for English speakers, even moral theologians, relying on the translation, having no hope of understanding the issues involved.

We set out below the two versions, the Latin first:

ARTICULUS 4

[42253] IIª-IIae q. 77 a. 4 arg. 1 Ad quartum sic proceditur. Videtur quod non liceat, **negotiando**, aliquid carius vendere quam emere. Dicit enim Chrysostomus, super Matth. XXI, *quicumque rem comparat ut, integram et immutatam vendendo, lucretur, ille est mercator qui de templo Dei eiicitur.* Et idem dicit Cassiodorus, super illud Psalm., *quoniam non cognovi littera-*

turam, vel negotiationem secundum aliam litteram, *quid, inquit, est aliud negotiatio nisi vilius comparare et carius velle distrahere?* Et subdit, *negotiatores tales dominus eiecit de templo.* Sed nullus eiicitur de templo nisi propter aliquod peccatum. Ergo talis negotiatio est peccatum.

[42254] IIᵃ-IIae q. 77 a. 4 arg. 2 Praeterea, contra iustitiam est quod aliquis rem carius vendat quam valeat, vel vilius emat, ut ex dictis apparet. Sed ille qui, negotiando, rem carius vendit quam emerit, necesse est quod vel vilius emerit quam valeat, vel carius vendat. Ergo hoc sine peccato fieri non potest.

[42255] IIᵃ-IIae q. 77 a. 4 arg. 3 Praeterea, Hieronymus dicit, *negotiatorem clericum, ex inope divitem, ex ignobili gloriosum, quasi quandam pestem fuge.* Non autem negotiatio clericis interdicenda esse videtur nisi propter peccatum. Ergo negotiando aliquid vilius emere et carius vendere est peccatum.

[42256] IIᵃ-IIae q. 77 a. 4 s. c. Sed contra est quod Augustinus dicit, super illud Psalm., *quoniam non cognovi litteraturam, negotiator avidus acquirendi pro damno blasphemat, pro pretiis rerum mentitur et peierat. Sed haec vitia hominis sunt, non artis, quae sine his vitiis agi potest.* **Ergo negotiari secundum se non est illicitum.**

[42257] IIᵃ-IIae q. 77 a. 4 co. Respondeo dicendum quod **ad negotiatores pertinet commutationibus rerum insistere.** Ut autem philosophus dicit, in I Polit., duplex est rerum commutatio. Una quidem quasi naturalis et necessaria, per quam scilicet fit commutatio rei ad rem, vel rerum et denariorum, propter necessitatem vitae. **Et talis commutatio non proprie pertinet ad negotiatores,** sed magis ad oeconomicos vel politicos, qui habent

providere vel domui vel civitati de rebus necessariis ad vitam. Alia vero commutationis species est vel denariorum ad denarios, vel quarumcumque rerum ad denarios, non propter res necessarias vitae, sed propter lucrum quaerendum. **Et haec quidem negotiatio proprie videtur ad negotiatores pertinere.** Secundum philosophum autem, prima commutatio laudabilis est, quia deservit naturali necessitati. Secunda autem iuste vituperatur, quia, quantum est de se, deservit cupiditati lucri, quae terminum nescit sed in infinitum tendit. Et ideo negotiatio, secundum se considerata, quandam turpitudinem habet, inquantum non importat de sui ratione finem honestum vel necessarium. Lucrum tamen, quod est negotiationis finis, etsi in sui ratione non importet aliquid honestum vel necessarium, nihil tamen importat in sui ratione vitiosum vel virtuti contrarium. Unde nihil prohibet lucrum ordinari ad aliquem finem necessarium, vel etiam honestum. Et sic negotiatio licita reddetur. Sicut cum aliquis lucrum moderatum, quod negotiando quaerit, ordinat ad domus suae sustentationem, vel etiam ad subveniendum indigentibus, vel etiam cum aliquis negotiationi intendit propter publicam utilitatem, ne scilicet res necessariae ad vitam patriae desint, et lucrum expetit non quasi finem, sed quasi stipendium laboris.

[42258] IIa-IIae q. 77 a. 4 ad 1. Ad primum ergo dicendum quod verbum Chrysostomi est intelligendum de negotiatione secundum quod ultimum finem in lucro constituit, quod praecipue videtur quando aliquis rem non immutatam carius vendit. Si enim rem immutatam carius vendat, videtur praemium sui laboris accipere. Quamvis et ipsum lucrum possit licite intendi,

non sicut ultimus finis, sed propter alium finem necessarium vel honestum, ut dictum est.

[42259] IIᵃ-IIae q. 77 a. 4 ad 2. Ad secundum dicendum quod non quicumque carius vendit aliquid quam emerit, negotiatur, sed solum qui ad hoc emit ut carius vendat. Si autem emit rem non ut vendat, sed ut teneat, et postmodum propter aliquam causam eam vendere velit, non est negotiatio, quamvis carius vendat. Potest enim hoc licite facere, vel quia in aliquo rem melioravit; vel quia pretium rei est mutatum, secundum diversitatem loci vel temporis; vel propter periculum cui se exponit transferendo rem de loco ad locum, vel eam ferri faciendo. Et secundum hoc, nec emptio nec venditio est iniusta.

[42260] IIᵃ-IIae q. 77 a. 4 ad 3. Ad tertium dicendum **quod clerici non solum debent abstinere ab his quae sunt secundum se mala, sed etiam ab his quae habent speciem mali.** Quod quidem in negotiatione contingit, tum propter hoc quod est ordinata ad lucrum terrenum, cuius clerici debent esse contemptores; tum etiam propter frequentia negotiatorum vitia, quia *difficiliter exuitur negotiator a peccatis labiorum*, ut dicitur Eccli. XXVI. Est et alia causa, quia negotiatio nimis implicat animum saecularibus curis, et per consequens a spiritualibus retrahit, unde apostolus dicit, II ad Tim. II, *nemo militans Deo implicat se negotiis saecularibus*. **Licet tamen clericis uti prima commutationis specie, quae ordinatur ad necessitatem vitae, emendo vel vendendo.**

And then the English:

Article 4. Whether, in **trading,** it is lawful to sell a thing at a higher price than what was paid for it?

Obj 1. It would seem that it is not lawful, in trading, to sell a thing for a higher price than we paid for it. For Chrysostom [Hom. xxxviii in the Opus Imperfectum, falsely ascribed to St. John Chrysostom] says on Matthew 21:12: "He that buys a thing in order that he may sell it, entire and unchanged, at a profit, is the trader who is cast out of God's temple." Cassiodorus speaks in the same sense in his commentary onPsalm 70:15, "Because I have not known learning, or trading" according to another version [the Septuagint]: "What is trade," says he, "but buying at a cheap price with the purpose of retailing at a higher price?" and he adds: "Such were the tradesmen whom Our Lord cast out of the temple." Now no man is cast out of the temple except for a sin. Therefore such like trading is sinful.

Obj 2. Further, it is contrary to justice to sell goods at a higher price than their worth, or to buy them for less than their value, as shown above (Article 1). Now if you sell a thing for a higher price than you paid for it, you must either have bought it for less than its value, or sell it for more than its value. Therefore this cannot be done without sin.

Obj 3. Further, Jerome says (Ep. ad Nepot. lii): "Shun, as you would the plague, a cleric who from being poor has become wealthy, or who, from being a nobody has become a celebrity." Now trading would not seem to be forbidden to clerics except on account of its sinfulness. Therefore it is a sin in trading, to buy at a low price and to sell at a higher price.

On the contrary, Augustine commenting on Psalm 70:15, "Because I have not known learning," [Cf. Objection 1 says: "The greedy tradesman blasphemes over his losses; he lies and perjures himself over the price of his wares. But these are vices of the man, not of the craft, which can be exercised without these vices." Therefore trading is not **in itself** unlawful.

I answer that, **A tradesman is one whose business consists in the exchange of things.** According to the Philosopher (Polit. i, 3), exchange of things is twofold; one, natural as it were, and necessary, whereby one commodity is exchanged for another, or money taken in exchange for a commodity, in order to satisfy the needs of life. **Such like trading, properly speaking, does not belong to tradesmen,** but rather to housekeepers or civil servants who have to provide the household or the state with the necessaries of life. The other kind of exchange is either that of money for money, or of any commodity for money, not on account of the necessities of life, but for profit, and this kind of exchange, properly speaking, regards tradesmen, according to the Philosopher (Polit. i, 3). The former kind of exchange is commendable because it supplies a natural need: but the latter is justly deserving of blame, because, considered in itself, it satisfies the greed for gain, which knows no limit and tends to infinity. Hence trading, considered in itself, has a certain debasement attaching thereto, in so far as, by its very nature, it does not imply a virtuous or necessary end. Nevertheless gain which is the end of trading, though not implying, by its nature, anything virtuous or necessary, does not, in itself, connote anything sinful or contrary to virtue: wherefore nothing prevents gain from being directed to some necessary or even virtuous end, and thus trading becomes lawful. Thus, for instance, a man may intend the moderate gain which he seeks to acquire by trading for the upkeep of his household, or for the assistance of the needy: or again, a man may take to trade for some public advantage, for instance, lest his country lack the necessaries of life, and seek gain, not as an end, but as payment for his labor.

Reply to Objection 1. The saying of Chrysostom refers to the trading which seeks gain as a last end. This is especially the case where a man sells something at a higher price without its undergoing any change. For if he sells at a higher price something that has changed for the better, he would seem to receive the reward of his labor. Nevertheless the gain itself may be lawfully intended, not as a last end, but for the sake of some other end which is necessary or virtuous, as stated above.

Reply to Objection 2. Not everyone that sells at a higher price than he bought is a tradesman, but only he who buys that he may sell at a profit. If, on the contrary, he buys not for sale but for possession, and afterwards, for some reason wishes to sell, it is not a trade transaction even if he sell at a profit. For he may lawfully do this, either because he has bettered the thing, or because the value of the thing has changed with the change of place or time, or on account of the danger he incurs in transferring the thing from one place to another, or again in having it carried by another. On this sense neither buying nor selling is unjust.

Reply to Objection 3. **Clerics should abstain not only from things that are evil in themselves, but even from those that have an appearance of evil.** This happens in trading, both because it is directed to worldly gain, which clerics should despise, and because trading is open to so many vices, since "a merchant is hardly free from sins of the lips" ['A merchant is hardly free from negligence, and a huckster shall not be justified from the sins of the lips'] (Sirach 26:28). There is also another reason, because trading engages the mind too much with worldly cares, and consequently withdraws it from spiritual cares; wherefore the Apostle says (2 Timothy 2:4): "No man being a soldier to God entangleth himself with secular businesses." **Nevertheless it is lawful for clerics to engage in the first mentioned kind of exchange, which is directed to supply the necessaries of life, either by buying or by selling**.

First let us deal with the gross errors in translation. We are primarily interested in objection 3 and the response to it, so we will leave aside the text of objections 1 and 2 and their responses. The reader however may wish to consider them in the light of what we say.

We have put in bold the words and phrases that we mean to draw attention to. What we say here has already been said in our previous books especially "Economic Science and Saint Thomas Aquinas" and "Ethics Today and Saint Thomas Aquinas". But it is repeated here so as one may appreciate what St. Thomas says about clerics in the answer to objection 3.

The grossest mistranslation is of the Latin word *negotiando*, which is but one grammatical form of the word *negotiatio* (mistranslated as trade), and as is *negotiator* (even more grossly mistranslated as tradesman). St. Thomas has carefully explained its meaning in article 1 and made very clear he is applying it not to ordinary trading or the natural mode of exchange (CMC) but to the non-natural kind (MCM). It is impossible to understand his meaning without knowing the distinction of the two kinds of exchange, which the translator (and all moderns) are completely clueless about. So the text as translated is at best meaningless and at worst deceitful.

Now it is important to note that St. Thomas is not condemning outright the second mode of exchange. For he has argued that though the practice has of itself a certain turpitude having no natural end it might be ordered voluntarily to a natural end (the satisfaction of genuine need or rational want) and thus be rendered even virtuous (as someone might make a profit this way in order to help the poor).

Nonetheless, and this is the point at issue St. Thomas states that it ought not be engaged in by clerics, not because it is intrinsically immoral but because it has *species mali,* by which he means it is attended by many evils, as it is in itself being directed towards worldly gain (money profit) and is open to many vices such as active deceit or failing to disclose hidden defects in order to make a sale. It might be noted that the latter is not necessarily against human positive law (as in the legal principle of contract caveat emptor). But the last sentence of the response to objection 3 (in bold) makes the distinction of the two kinds of exchange and the application of his warning to clerics abundantly clear, saying **it is lawful for clerics to engage in the first mentioned kind of exchange [CMC], which is directed to supply the necessaries of life, either by buying or by selling**.

Now what do we find in the social encyclicals? No explicit reference as far as we can tell to the distinction between the two modes of exchange in modern commerce (the second often unnatural) even in the earlier encyclicals, let alone the ones subsequent to Vatican II. Still more striking is a failure to draw notice to St. Thomas's (the Common Doctor's) warning to clerics to avoid a most common practice in "investing" money in the modern market economy.

Apart from these particular serious moral dangers, without a knowledge of the distinction between the two modes of exchange, clearly made in the *Summa*, it is not possible to have a clear idea of what Capitalism means and how it affects the lives of not just the laity but also the highest levels of the hierarchy in their efforts to administer their "finances".

It is not suggested that this absence is an essential fault in the social encyclicals for it is more a matter for the laity to apply natural moral laws to civic or political circumstances. But without this rational support, supplied by Aquinas himself, the encyclicals must lose a great deal of their incisiveness in addressing the politico-economic ills of the modern era.

There is some fault, however, one would expect, in the moral theologians not paying the requisite attention to the relevant parts of the work of St. Thomas. As things stand there does not seem to be much prospect that this situation will change.

Here we will end our survey of the social encyclicals and hope the reader will have some insight into the importance of restoring to the exposition of the social doctrine of the Church the full theological wisdom of Aquinas; but especially as it is focused on what is also the natural order of practical wisdom and justice the principles of which can even be drawn, as Aquinas did, from the *Ethics* and *Politics* of Aristotle.

Appendix A

A Taste For Sweet Decay

In his book "The Well and the Shallows" G. K. Chesterton has a chapter entitled "Sex and Property". In it he says: *But even the stink of decaying heathenism has not been so bad as the stink of decaying Christianity. The corruption of the best ...*

He was referring to public sexual immorality as it manifested itself in the ancient world and as it was in his time beginning to manifest itself in the modern world. Gross and obscene as the pagan practices may have been, Chesterton sees reason to compare them favorably with the modern. Thus he says: *In one way all this ancient sin was infinitely superior, immeasurably superior, to the modern sin.*

What is this way in which, despite its decadence, the ancient was superior to the modern worship of sexual pleasure? The answer follows on immediately: The ancient sexual perversity, as all historians agree, was connected to *the cult of Fruitfulness...* Hence, Chesterton observes; *It was at least on the side of Nature. It was at least on the side of Life.* The modern "sexual revolution", however, has completely severed the natural connection of sexual pleasure with life. *It has been left to the last Christians, or rather to the first Christians fully committed to blaspheming and denying Christianity, to invent a new kind of worship of Sex, which is not even a worship of Life. It has been left to the very latest Modernists to proclaim an erotic religion which at once exalts lust and forbids fertility.*

He goes on to add: *this unnatural separation, between sex and fruitfulness ... even the Pagans would have thought a perversion.* Today, this perversion even to the dissolute Pagans has become so widely accepted and practiced that it is claimed to be as "natural" as sexual intercourse which is apt, barring natural impediments, to produce offspring, and any moral denunciation of it is beginning to be treated as perverse, even by legislators. One can only contemplate with dismay how this socially "moral" turnaround must end.

Chesterton noticed *this unnatural separation* that characterizes the modern attitude to sex in the early part of the twentieth century. The subsequent years between then and now have seen the gradual re-education of society's attitude to sex so that its divorce from any natural connection with the continuation of human life is made as complete as possible. The introduction of the contraceptive pill played a decisive part in this disconnection process.

The educators in de-perversion having done their job, in relatively recent times social sexual practices have followed suit till we have reached the stage where "sex" between consenting adults, of whatever degree of depravity, is not only looked upon as "normal", but is also given social respectability and legal recognition.

This, however, is not an isolated phenomenon. As the title of his article indicates, Chesterton sees that something analogous has happened in relation to our attitude to property or wealth.

Put shortly, it is that our desire for wealth too has been separated from its natural end. In moral terms this means that, just as the propagandists for the new sexual morality have exalted pure lust as the rationale for engaging in sexual relations, so have the proponents of the new economic morality elevated pure greed or avarice to be the primary motive for engaging in wealth-getting.

How can this occur? Obviously, at root there is moral fault. But there is no moral fault or sin without a corresponding mental error. This latter is what we are mainly concerned to analyze here. Chesterton thus says: *In both departments [sex and property] there is precisely the same fallacy; which it is quite possible to state precisely. The reason why our contemporary countrymen do not understand what we mean by Property is that they only think of it in the sense of Money ... in the sense of something which is immediately consumed, enjoyed and expended; something which gives momentary pleasure and disappears.*

That is to say we have ignored the proper purpose of wealth, to satisfy our natural needs and rational wants, and gone for the pleasure that accompanies the possession of property, as if this could satisfy by itself. Now there is nothing wrong in enjoying one's God-given wealth, provided it is being used for what it is created for, namely, to satisfy our desires for material goods within reason, or in accordance with nature. This pleasure in possession of wealth is epitomized in the possession of money, as it can stand for all wealth. But what happens is that money, being a pure means, disconnects us even further from the natural end of wealth. So we can be deceived into seeking to have money for its own sake, or simply for the pleasure attached to having much wealth.

Chesterton thus continues the analogy: *Now the notion of narrowing property merely to 'enjoying' money is exactly like the notion of narrowing love merely to 'enjoying' sex. In both cases an incidental, isolated, servile and even secretive pleasure is substituted for participation in a great creative process; even in the everlasting Creation of the world.*

Pleasure, as Aristotle noted, is not something bad but good. But it does not and cannot stand alone; it complements some naturally good act. It is not, therefore, properly an end in itself. If we try to possess it without respecting the natural end of the act to which it belongs it vanishes as something without substance, without any support. To pursue pleasure for its own sake is to pursue a delusion, and to achieve not pleasure but misery, which accompanies the unnatural disorder put in the place of the natural order of things. The sweet smell of natural goodness turns quickly into the stink of decadence, though for a time the person concerned may "enjoy" the sickly odor of decay.

What the pleasure of possession thrives and survives in is the achievement of the natural and creative ends of wealth and production. *They do not understand that we mean by Property something that includes that pleasure incidentally; but begins and ends with something far more grand and worthy and creative.*

Chesterton then makes an interesting observation about Communism and Capitalism. The modern mistake regarding sex and property is not peculiar to the capitalist West. For, it is an attitude that has its roots in the decline of Christian civilization and the rise of the modern secularist world.

The same basic attitude towards enjoying money is noted by Chesterton to be just as much present in the communist society as in the capitalist. *From the first, it is admitted, that the whole system was directed towards encouraging or driving the worker to spend his wages; to have nothing left on the next pay day; to enjoy everything and consume everything and efface everything.* That is to say Consumerism was a matter of deliberate policy.

Indeed, many would think that Chesterton goes too far in saying that Communism ironically took to its logical extreme, and implemented by force, what is inherent in the psychology of Capitalism about the pursuit of pleasure and money, but is there left, at least in theory, to the initiative of individuals to realize. *The two sinister things [the mistaken modern beliefs about sex and property] can be seen side by side in the system of Bolshevist Russia; for Communism is the only complete and logical working model of Capitalism. The sins are there a system which are everywhere else a sort of repeated blunder.*

But perhaps Chesterton was more perceptive than most. Certainly, Capitalism in the West, hardly able to resist the temptation to regard the sudden and unexpected demise of Communism as confirmation of the truth of its liberalist ideology, seems to be drifting more and more towards the same sort of totalitarianism, as if driven by an inexorable internal logic.

The psychology of sex, despite the apparent difference in its political "management", is also noted by Chesterton to be something common to both the modern West and East. *But it will be noted that exactly the same spirit and tone pervades the manner of dealing with the other matter. Sex also is to come to the slave merely as a pleasure; that it may never be a power. He is to know as little as possible, or at least to think as little as possible, of the pleasure as anything else except a pleasure; to think or know nothing of where it comes from or where it will go to, when once the soiled object has passed through his own hands. He is not to trouble about its origin in the purposes of God or its sequel in the posterity of man. In every department he is not a possessor, but only a consumer;*

There is no difficulty in recognizing this as also a description of the self-made slave of sex in the Western world. Chesterton thus sums up with a hint of what all this has led to – the culture of death instead of life:

Thus there is an exact parallel between the two modern moral, or immoral, ideas of social reform. The world has forgotten simultaneously that the making of a Farm is something much larger than the making of a profit, or even a product, in the sense of liking the taste of beetroot sugar; and that the founding of a Family is something much larger than sex in the limited sense of current literature; which was anticipated in one bleak and blinding flash in a single line of George Meredith; "And eat our pot of honey on the grave."

Appendix B

Examination of
Cardinal Ratzinger's Notion of Person

Introduction

I have thought it useful, if not indeed necessary, to deal with a specific work published in 1990, by Cardinal Ratzinger, as he then was, on the fundamental topic of the notion of person. This will enable us to assess the then Cardinal Ratzinger's thought on the philosophical aspect of this issue (if it is to be examined as further illuminated under the light of Faith).

No one would deny that Cardinal Ratzinger as a theologian was one of the leading theologians of his day, if not the leading one. Nor does one wish to argue that he did not retain a complete faithfulness to Catholic orthodoxy in what he wrote. Outside of being pope he is one of those privileged brilliant theological minds who are orthodox as it were by instinct. This has enabled him to discourse freely and openly on all sorts of difficult issues of the day, with seeming ease and sureness of touch. Moreover, it has meant that he could approach every subject with a freshness and originality that is remarkable.

It must be said, however, that the good cardinal's original approach at times has led him to venture to improve upon not only St. Thomas, but even St. Augustine. And the weakness alluded to in the theologian delving into matters of philosophy or Metaphysics becomes apparent in his treatment of certain fundamental philosophical or metaphysical aspects of questions arising in Sacred Theology. This, I believe, is the case with his article "Concerning the Notion of the Person in Theology" (1990).

The notion of the person that he propounds has all sorts of philosophical problems. It is not so much what he has to say about the notion of person in God that is problematic but how he tries to extend that notion to persons other than God. And it is precisely in this regard that he alleges that the treatments of St. Thomas and St. Augustine are mistaken. It will be evident, however, that here we have a theologian importing theological considerations into the resolution of purely philosophical questions (for the question of person in creatures is properly a metaphysical one).

It is, of course, one of the most difficult of metaphysical questions. One would not ordinarily be emboldened to contest the good cardinal's position were it not for the fact that in doing so one is defending the position not only of St. Thomas but also of St. Augustine.

His approach is also affected to some extent, we contend, by the strength of his desire to clear away what he describes as the "encrustations" that had come to cover up, as it were, the kernel of the faith. "This impulse is the constant of my life". The desire itself is, of course, something to be praised. It is in line with the Council's effort to show the world the living beauty of the faith anew.

Another image he has used is that of cleaning away from a beautiful old painting all the accumulated dirt and discoloration of the years. As is obvious, that is a delicate operation and a risky one if one is not very careful and expert in the job of "restoration". One would not question his expertise as a theologian but, nonetheless, one's enthusiasm for such a job, and love of what is being revealed afresh, can sometimes mean that one may unwittingly rub out a line or two of the original.

This is not a risk so far as "major lines" are concerned, such as pertain to the substance of the faith, or matters that have been clearly defined by the Magisterium. But it rather relates to "minor lines" of theological/ philosophical matters that belong to common or traditional positions taken in theology and philosophy by the Fathers and Doctors of the Church, especially in the cases of St. Augustine and St. Thomas. We think we find a case of this in the article on the notion of the person. He has thought himself to have discovered a notion of the person, as applied to man, which has been overlooked in the past but is now able to be seen clearly (though later in his article he is somewhat ambivalent about this claim).

It seems he is fortified in asserting this by a view of the intrinsic historical character of theology, so that it requires time for concepts to be more properly defined, with the implication too that further and better "definition" may even be allowed for in the future. But, as St. Thomas notes, though this is generally true of theological truths, it does not mean that doctrines or dogmas are not definitively determined along the way. This is clear enough with regard to definitions by the Magisterium. But it may be applied proportionally at the lower level of theological development of doctrine. Everything discussed by the theologians over the years is not still open for debate. One is not free to question now, for instance, what was commonly held by the Fathers of the Church. Similarly, it seems very bold indeed to dismiss a position of such fundamental importance, even if it is in relation to a question of philosophy, that has the double authority of St. Augustine and St. Thomas behind it. Our endeavour will be to show that it is the good cardinal who is mistaken on this point, not the Common Doctor or the Doctor of Grace.

An occupational hazard of the theologian, who perforce has to enter into the field of philosophy in order to deal satisfactorily with some theological problems, is that his treatment can be "coloured" by his very theological starting point. Many a false philosophical solution has been engendered in this way. Indeed, if St. Thomas is not the only theologian who managed to completely master this tendency to "theologise" purely philosophical problems he is the model for all who wish to avoid this hazard.

What errors St. Thomas felt obliged to correct in other theologians before him, even in such a great theologian as St. Augustine, generally came from an "excess of spirituality" in their thinking. In more general terms, it involved the intellectual error of "making the best the enemy of the good". It is manifest in philosophy in the work of Plato and the Platonists.

This article is presented by way of a critique by way of considering the text of Cardinal Ratzinger's article passage by passage sequentialy where the capital "T" refers to the text of his article in bold and "C" to our commentary.

T: Relativity toward the other constitutes the human person. The human person is the event or being of relativity.

C: Relativity toward the other **does not constitute** the human person. The human person **is not** the event or being of relativity. Relativity toward the other constitutes the **divine** person. An event is not a "being" but "of a being" when being is taken in its full sense which is clearly intended here.[4] A divine person only can in that sense be said to be a being of relativity. Person, outside of God, is necessarily an absolute before it is relative to other; in spiritual creatures "person" signifies absolutely.

T: **The concept of person, as well as the idea that stands behind this concept, is a product of Christian theology. In other words, it grew in the first place out of the interplay between human thought and the data of Christian faith and so entered intellectual history. The concept of the person is thus, to speak with Gilson, one of the contributions to human thought made possible and provided by Christian faith. It did not simply grow out of mere human philosophizing, but out of the interplay between philosophy and the antecedent given of faith, especially Scripture.**

C: The concept of person, as well as the idea that stands behind this concept, **is not** a product of Christian theology. Boethius's classical definition of person is purely Aristotelian. The word

---

[4] Such is the prejudice against the notion of substance in this question that Ratzinger will endeavour to conceive of personhood as a pure event, i.e. as an "act" without substantial support. There is possibly some association suggested here with the notion of God as pure act. But that itself would be to confuse the notion of act as applying in God and in creation. In God existence and operation are not really distinct. In creatures they necessarily are, and personhood is something applying to (substantial) existence before (accidental) action.

may not have been used by Aristotle but the notion is there. "Individual substance" is dealt with in both his Logic and Metaphysics; "of rational nature" is simply one kind of individual substance. It is the concept of **divine** person which "grew in the first place out of the interplay between human thought and the data of Christian faith and so entered intellectual history". This necessarily involved a refinement of the notion of person as it includes the divine. But, as St. Thomas notes, it does not alter the common notion of person which applies to both, just as "animal" means the same abstracted from "rational" and "irrational", but takes on an additional significance when specified. What is mistaken here is the nature of abstraction in our use of names. The notion of "an individual substance of rational nature" applies as much (evenmore so) to the Holy Spirit as to a spiritual creature.

What is meant by "the idea that stands behind this concept"? Idea is only another name for concept. This suggests a confusion of the concept with the word ("person") - which is somewhat confirmed in the subsequent treatment of the question.

T: **More specifically, the concept of person arose from two questions that have from the very beginning urged themselves upon Christian thought as central: namely, the question, "What is God?" (i.e., the God whom we encounter in Scripture); and, "Who is Christ?"**

C: The concept of **divine** person so arose.

T: **In order to answer these fundamental questions that arose as soon as faith began to reflect, Christian thought made use of the philosophically insignificant or entirely unused concept *"prosopon" = "persona."* It thereby gave to this word a**

new meaning and opened up a new dimension of human thought. Although this thought has distanced itself far from its origin and developed beyond it, it nevertheless lives, in a hidden way, from this origin. In my judgment one cannot, therefore, know what "person" most truly means without fathoming this origin.

C: The discussion of the etymology of the name of anything has only peripheral significance in understanding it. As St. Thomas points out time and time again: "Not the same is that wherefrom a word is taken and that whereunto it is imposed to signify". The example he uses is the latin word for stone, *lapis,* which is apparently derived from *laesio pedis* meaning something that hurts one's foot. It is a start to understanding what a stone signifies but it does not distinguish it from my foot striking another's.

The discovery by us of this etymology or linguistic history of the word hardly "opened up a new dimension of human thought" so far as the significance imposed upon the word is concerned. Similarly, the notion from which the word "person" is taken is of minor import in determining its full significance or meaning.

Too much intelligible weight is thus given to this historical exercise and it only proves to be a distraction in examining the difference between the notion of person as generally applied and as specially applied to the divinity.

T: For this reason please forgive me because, although I was asked to talk as a systematic theologian about the dogmatic concept of the person, I will not present the latest ideas of

modern theologians. Instead, I will attempt to go back to the origin, to the source and ground from which the idea of "person" was born and without which it could not exist. The outline flows from what was said above. We will simply take a closer look at the two origins of the concept of person, its origin in the question of God and its origin in the question of Christ.

C: Based upon the assumption that the meaning of a word can be better understood by exploring its origin (etymology) the author embarks upon an elaborate exercise in linguistic history.

He had been asked to tell his audience what "person" means, its notion, ("that whereunto it is imposed to signify"); he provides a narrative of how the word itself came to be used for the notion ("that wherefrom a word is taken").

"I was asked to talk as a systematic theologian about the dogmatic concept of the person, I will not present the latest ideas of modern theologians." Apparently, an examination of the meaning of the notion itself consists in considering "the latest ideas of modern theologians".

This mistaken approach seems to come from an exaggerated sense of the importance of history in dealing with theological questions. History is important and indeed fundamental in theology but only as coming strictly from the Scriptures and the Christian tradition, not generally to do with every philosophical or linguistic matter that comes up. History in such questions of objective understanding has its place; but it is supplementary and preparatory, not primary or fundamental.

In any case the etymological history of "person" embarked upon here is not of the notion but of the word. Moreover, it does not go to the question of the difference between the notion as applied to spiritual creatures generally and as applied to the divine creator.

T: *I. The concept of person in the doctrine of God*

A. *The origin of the concept of person*

The first figure we meet is that of the great Western theologian Tertullian. Tertullian shaped Latin into a theological language and, with the almost incredible sureness of a genius, he knew how to develop a theological terminology that remained unsurpassable in later centuries, because already on the first attempt it gave form permanently to valid formulae of Christian thought. Thus it was Tertullian who gave to the West its formula for expressing the Christian idea of God. God is *"una substantia-tres personae,"* one being in three persons. It was here that the word "person" entered intellectual history for the first time with its full weight.

C: Notice that the main heading limits the discussion to the concept of person in God. The sub-heading is therefore at least ambiguous.

"It was here that the word "person" entered intellectual history for the first time with its full weight." "with its full weight" is, in its own terms, ambiguous and, in the evident intent of the article, wrong. Meant to apply to the common concept of person it is equivalent to saying that the meaning of "animal", signifying the genus only, reaches its full weight in man.

T: "The answer to the question of the origin of the concept "person" is that it originated in "prosopographic exegesis.""

C: Certainly sounds impressive. But all it means that the word "person" comes out of Greek drama. The impressiveness comes from the notion, not from the "exegesis", for the etymology of "person" is more interesting than that of "stone" (as one would expect). The association with drama obviously makes the telling of the history more dramatic.

T: "The ancient scholars noticed that in order to give dramatic life to events, the great poets of Antiquity did not simply narrate these events, but allowed persons to make their appearance and to speak. For example, they placed words in the mouths of divine figures and the drama progresses through these words."

C: Hardly a discovery of modern times by Carl Anderson. The poets also placed words in the mouths of human figures. But all this has little relevance to the philosophy and theology of the person.

T: "The literary scholar uncovers these roles; he shows that the persons have been created as "roles" in order to give dramatic life to events (in fact, the word *"prosopon,"* later translated by *"persona,"* originally means simply "role," the mask of the actor)."

C: One does not have to be a literary scholar, or a prosopographic exegete, to work this out. The literary scholar is of little help to the metaphysican and the theologian in determining that whereunto the word person is imposed to signify, i.e. its metaphysical and theological meaning. This is all done here, apparently, to show how theology (and "ontology") is benefited greatly by historical analysis.

T: In their reading of Scripture, the Christian writers came upon something quite similar. They found that, here too, events progress in dialogue. They found, above all, the peculiar fact that God speaks in the plural or speaks with himself (e.g., "Let us make man in our image and likeness," or God's statement in Genesis 3, "Adam has become like one of *us*," or Psalm 110, "The Lord said to my Lord" which the Greek Fathers take to be a conversation between God and his Son). The Fathers approach this fact, namely, that God is introduced in the plural as speaking with himself, by means of prosopographic exegesis which thereby takes on a new meaning.

C: "God speaks in the plural or speaks with himself". "Himself" is ambiguous. If God as absolutely one in being is intended he does not speak with himself, no more than you or I do; but if God as a person is referred to then he does, in the sense that the Father speaks with the Son and Holy Spirit, just as I speak to another person. But that does not imply that I could do the same with my real being. In the drama the divine speech would equate with the same absolutely one being (real person – another etymology for person is *per se unum*) taking on three masks (fictional persons). This hardly helps with understanding how there can be three real persons in one real being. It rather negates its possibility. An exercise in literary lore is not designed to throw any light on philosophical and theological problems. One does not have to bring in *dramatis personae* to account for ordinary dialogue. A creaturely speaking by oneself is a monologue.

T: I will cite merely one text by Justin to clarify this process. "When you hear that the prophets make statements as if a person were speaking *(hos apo prosopou)*, then do not suppose that they were spoken immediately by those filled with the spirit (i.e., the prophets) but rather by the Logos who moves them." Justin thus says that the dialogical roles introduced by the prophets are not mere literary devices. The "role" truly exists; it is the *prosopon*, the face, the person of the Logos who truly speaks here and *joins* in dialogue with the prophet. It is quite clear here how the data of Christian faith transform and renew a pre-given ancient schema used in interpreting texts. The literary artistic device of letting roles appear to enliven the narrative with their dialogue reveals to the theologians *the one* who plays the true role here, the *Logos*, the *prosopon*, the person of the Word which is no longer merely role, but person.

C: No clarification needed. The *Logos* is behind the "mask" of the prophet to be sure. But in the drama it is the mask which serves as a person, not the actor. With prophesy God is the real actor, what lies behind the "person" (prophet). On the stage the dialogue is between two fictional persons (both masks); with God the dialogue is between two (or more) real persons. This helps (by contrast) in understanding conversations with God (*Logos*). But how does the literary device help understand the Trinity, i.e. God speaking with Himself? If the same actor wants to speak to another he puts on another mask.

T: About fifty years later, when Tertullian wrote his works, he was able to go back to an extensive tradition of such Christian prosopographic exegesis in which the word *prosopon* =

persona had already found its full claim to reality. Two examples must suffice. In *Adversus Praxean*, Tertullian writes, "How can a person who stands by himself say, 'Let us make man in our image and likeness/ when he ought to have said, 'Let *me* make man in my image and likeness,' as someone who is single and alone for himself. If he were only one and single, then God deceived and tricked also in what follows when he says, 'Behold, Adam has become like one of us,' which he said in the plural. But he did not stand alone, because there stood with him the Son, his Word, and a third person, the Spirit in the Word. This is why he spoke in the plural, 'Let *us* make' and '*our*' and '*us*.'"

C:The examples quoted provide no hint of any Christian prosopographic exegesis, but simply point to Scriptural proof of a Trinity of persons in the Godhead. The literary/historical exposition is a side-issue.

T: One sees how the phenomenon of intra-divine dialogue gives birth here to the idea of the person who is person in an authentic sense. Tertullian similarly says in his interpretation of "The Lord said to my Lord" (Psalm 110:1), "Take note how even the Spirit as the third person speaks of the Father and of the Son, 'The Lord said to my Lord, sit at my right hand until I put your enemies at your feet.' Likewise through Isaiah, 'The Lord says these words to my Lord Christ.' ... In these few texts the distinction within the Trinity is clearly set before our eyes. For himself exists the one who speaks, namely, the Spirit; further the Father *to* whom he speaks, and finally the Son *of whom* he speaks."

C: The intra-divine dialogue only establishes the existence of a trinity of persons in God. A prosopographic exegesis might have some slight relevance to the idea of person in God, but it is of no help in understanding the multitude of persons in God. Does it suggest that God is presented as three persons (masks) and that it is his unity as the one God (who would qualify as a person according to the common notion) which is hidden, or that there are three real persons hidden behind the one person (mask), playing the same role? It is in terms of the latter that the problem is presented. It is the one God which we can see (understand); it is the trinity of persons which we do not immediately see. The attempt to use the exegesis in regard to the divine reality causes more confusion than anything else.

T: I do not wish to enter into the historical details of these texts. I will merely summarize what results from them for the issue of the idea "person." First, the concept "person" grew out of reading the Bible, as something needed for its interpretation. It is a product of reading the Bible.

C: The concept "person" **as such did not grow** out of reading the Bible. It was the concept of person as divine that did. But here we have again a sign that there is a confusion of concept and word. It is words, not concepts, which need inverted commas when referred to specifically (and it is the word "person" which has an etymology).

T: Secondly, it grew out of the idea of dialogue, more specifically, it grew as an explanation of the phenomenon of the God who speaks dialogically. The Bible with its phenomenon of the

God who speaks, the God who is *in* dialogue, stimulated the concept "person."

C: The concept of person did not grow out of the idea of dialogue. It is the other way round. Dialogue only makes sense between persons. Dialogue is a sign/proof of the existence of persons. We can identify the presence of a person from hearing him speak (even if not seen). But it does not follow that our idea of person as such grew out of hearing people speaking to one another. There are ways of identifying human persons without entering into dialogue with them. Is the unborn child not a person? In the divine community communication is inseparable from the Trinity and in a real sense constitutive of their personhood. But that is special to the divine character of person; this special intrinsic character (of relativity) is not to be imported into the individuality of created spirits. Communication (just as relativity) comes consequently to human persons, who are separate substances (per se beings) before they are related to others.

T: **To summarize we can say: The idea of person expresses in its origin the idea of dialogue and the idea of God as the dialogical being. It refers to God as the being that lives in the word and consists of the word as "I" and "you" and "we." In the light of this knowledge of God, the true nature of humanity became clear in a new way.**

C: The knowledge of the Trinity does throw new light on the nature of all things and especially ourselves. But it is at the level of faculties and actions rather than substance or essence. For relativity supposes duality at least and, outside of God, cannot be identified with substance (which is absolutely one or nothing).

Hence creaturely relation has to be "accidental" (though this means only non-substantial; it does not mean, as some think, flimsy or superficial – it can be permanent and quite deep rooted).

T: *B. Person as relation*

The first stage of the struggle for the Christian concept of God has been sketched above. I want to add a brief look at the second main stage, in which the concept of "person" reached its full maturity. About two hundred years later, at the turn of the fifth century, Christian theology reached the point of being able to express in articulated concepts what is meant in the thesis: God is a being in three persons. In this context, theologians argued, person must be understood as *relation*. According to Augustine and late patristic theology, the three persons that exist in God are in their nature relations. They are, therefore, not substances that stand next to each other, but they are real existing relations ..., and nothing besides.

C: "They are ... not substances that stand next to each other". Neither are they, but they are substance and individual substance of "rational nature" at that. The sentence is ambiguous. For in saying they are not separate substances, which is true, it seems to be also saying that they are not substantial, which is false. They each share the one individual substance as an absolute being. Each divine person, besides being his own person, is also God, absolute being.

"and nothing besides". This is quite wrong in its intent to exclude substantiality from the notion of a divine person – a case of falling into the ambiguity adverted to. St. Thomas says quite clearly that, although the persons in the Godhead are ultimately differentiated by a relation, the notion of substance also belongs to that of divine person.[5] Indeed, he says that the words we use in relation to God cannot bring out the reality and inevitably fall short of expressing the divine nature and divine personhood. In one sense the expression can be saved: that in God substance and relation are not really different absolutely speaking: it is only the persons who are really different (relatively).

T: **In its nature, the person exists only *as* relation. Put more concretely, the first person does not generate in the sense that the act of generating a Son is added to the already complete person, but the person is the deed of generating, of giving itself, of streaming itself forth. The person is identical with this act of self-donation.**

C: "In its nature, the person exists only *as* relation". This contains another latent ambiguity. Each divine person is really distinct from the others only by opposition of relation. But the intent is evidently to exclude any notion of substance in the notion of person. The divine person does **not exist** only as relation. He exists as a substance as well, the divine substance. It is like saying that man exists only as rational thereby insinuating that he is not animal.

T: **One could thus define the first person as self-donation in fruitful knowledge and love; it is not the one who gives himself, in whom the act of self-donation is found, but it is this**

---

[5] Cf. I, 29, a.4 and in particular ad 1: " This word 'person' is said in respect to itself, not to another, forasmuch as it signifies person not as such, but by way of a substance – which is a hypostasis."

self-donation, pure reality of act. An idea that appeared again in our century in modern physics is here anticipated: that there is pure act-being. We know that in our century the attempt has been made to reduce matter to a wave, to a pure act of streaming. What may be a questionable idea in the context of physics was asserted by theology in the fourth and fifth century about the persons in God, namely, that they are <u>nothing but</u> the act of relativity toward each other. In God, person is the pure relativity of being turned toward the other; it does not lie on the level of substance - the substance is *one* - but on the level of dialogical reality, of relativity toward the other. (underline added)

C: Here the exclusion of substance from the notion of person is further emphasised. An analogy is made with the wave-particle theory of modern physics but so as to reduce it to a pure wave theory. But the point of this physical theory is that matter is both wave and particle, if seemingly impossible to reconcile. The attempt to conceive of matter as a pure wave is like trying to think of the smile of a cat without the cat. The connection between wave and particle is of course essential. But one cannot think of anything material without it being a material substance (particle). Similarly one cannot think of a divine person as not a divine substance, even though what distinguishes him from another divine person is purely relative.

T: In this matter Augustine could attempt, at least in outline, to show the interplay between threeness and unity by saying, for example: *in Deo nihil secundum accidens dicitur, sed secundum substantiam aut secundum relationem* (in God there

is nothing accidental, but only substance and relation). Relation is here recognized as a third specific fundamental category between substance and accident, the two great categorical forms of thought in Antiquity. Again we encounter the Christian newness of the personalistic idea in all its sharpness and clarity. The contribution offered by faith to human thought becomes especially clear and palpable here. It was faith that gave birth to this idea of *pure act*, of pure relativity, which does not lie on the level of substance and does not touch or divide substance; and it was faith that thereby brought the personal phenomenon into view.

C: Relation **is not** here recognized as a third specific fundamental category between substance and accident, the two great categorical forms of thought in Antiquity. It is just that relation as we know it (in creation) is accidental (necessarily). But in God it is substantial (necessarily), for the relations are identified with the divine substance. The three divine persons are the one God. To try to conceive person in creatures as purely relative, and not of substance, as is done below, would be to make such persons accidental beings.

There is a deficient notion of pure act used here. Pure act applies to God as substance, and to each divine person only in so far as they are God in substance (pure being per se). The notion of person does not divide substance in God. But it "touches" substance in the sense that it supposes it. By referring to "the personal phenomenon" the author tries to express the existence and notion of person without supposing substance; but he thereby falls in with the modern scientific error of denying substance. It was **not** faith that thereby brought the personal phenomenon into view, but what brought the **divine** personal "phenomenon" into view.

T: We stand here at the point in which the speculative penetration of Scripture, the assimilation of faith by humanity's own thought, seems to have reached its highest point; and yet we can notice with astonishment that the way back into Scripture opens precisely here. For Scripture has clearly brought out precisely *this* phenomenon of pure relativity as the nature of the person. The clearest case is Johannine theology. In Johannine theology we find, for example, the formula, "The Son cannot do anything of himself" (5:19). However, the same Christ who says this says, "I and the Father are one" (10:30). This means, precisely because he has nothing of himself alone, because he does not place himself as a delimited substance next to the Father, but exists *in* total relativity toward him, and constitutes nothing but relativity toward him that does not delimit a precinct of what is merely and properly its own - precisely because of this they are one.

C: All these quotes do not support the position that the divine persons are not substantial but that they are not separate substances. The Father is really distinct from the Son purely relatively; in all absolute respects, however, he is the same in substance (God) as the Son. What can being one and doing as one mean if not as God, the divine substance.

"he [the Son] has nothing of himself alone" simply means that the Son is one in substance with the Father. But he has sonship as his own. They are not one in person. Why the reluctance to speak in terms of substance?

T: This structure is in turn transferred - and here we have the transition to anthropology - to the disciples when Christ says, "Without me you can do nothing" (15:5). At the same time he prays "that they may be one as we are one" (17:11). It is thus part of the existence even of the disciples that man does not posit the reservation of what is merely and properly his own, does not strive to form the substance of the closed self, but enters into pure relativity toward the other and toward God. It is in this way that he truly comes to himself and into the fullness of his own, because he enters into unity with the one to whom he is related.

C: The turn to anthropology is where the author goes too far. The relations between creatures and with the creator, in the order of nature or creation, are not to be compared with the relations within the Godhead. The human person is not so constituted purely relatively, and cannot be so. He has to be first a substance separate from God. That is what creation involves. Then relation comes into play. People are put off by it being referred to as accidental, as if that meant "insubstantial" in the modern sense. But the creature's relationship with God, even in the natural order, is something deep within its being and inseparable from it.

In the order of grace, however, the spiritual creature is drawn into the divine being and life and is ordained to approach, as far as possible without becoming God, having that unity within God which is had by the divine persons.

"Without me you can do nothing" can be understood in the order of nature only. For that can mean only that without Christ as God I am nothing and can do nothing. It does not mean that I am not a substance separate from Christ (or that Christ's human nature is not a substance really distinct from the divine nature). "that they may be one as we are one" seems rather to refer to the order of grace, as explained above.

T: I believe a profound illumination of God as well as man occurs here, the decisive illumination of what person must mean in terms of Scripture: *not a* substance that closes itself in itself, but the phenomenon of complete relativity, which is, of course, realized in its entirety only in the one who is God, but which indicates the direction of all personal being. The point is thus reached here at which - as we shall see below - there is a transition from the doctrine of God into Christology and into anthropology.

C: Here the author backs away somewhat from what he has been saying about the notion of person as such. For, he distinguishes between person as divine and person as human. Nonetheless, he wishes to keep primary the notion of person as pure relativity, "what person [as such] must mean in terms of Scripture". It is just that it is perfectly realised only in God and imperfectly so in us. That compares with retaining the notion of rationality in the concept of animal but granting that it is perfectly "realised" only in the case of man. The problem lies in the notion of substance as something which is closed in on itself. That only applies to material substance, because of the exclusive character of matter. Pure spirit, as is the human soul, is not so "closed"; it is "naturally" open to grace. One does not have to endow it with grace to account for this openness (as de Lubac seems to think). This mistake about spiritual nature is common to many theologians today, probably from the influence of de Lubac. The same problem is had with the notion of nature, when speaking of "pure" human nature.

T: **One could go much further in following out this line of the idea of relation and of relativity in John, and in showing that it is *the* dominant theme of his theology, at any rate of his Christology. I want to mention only two examples. John picks up the theology of mission found in the Synoptics and in the Judaism of antiquity in which the idea is already formulated that the emissary, inasmuch as he is an emissary, is not important in himself, but stands for the sender and is one with the sender. John extends this Jewish idea of mission, which is at first a merely functional idea, by depicting Christ as *the* emissary who is in his entire nature "the one sent." The Jewish principle, "The emissary of a person is like that person" now takes on a completely new and deepened significance, because Jesus has absolutely nothing besides being the emissary, but is in his nature "the one sent." He is like the one who sent him precisely because he stands in complete relativity of existence toward the one who sent him. The content of the Johannine concept "the one sent" could be described as the absorption of being in "being from someone and toward someone." The content of Jesus' existence is "being from someone and toward someone," the absolute openness of existence without any reservation of what is merely and properly one's own. And again**

the idea is extended to Christian existence of which it is said, "As the Father has sent me, so I am sending you" (20:21).

C: Christ in his human nature may be said to be constituted as "the one sent" from the Father for our salvation. But the problem with that is that so conceived he is not a human person. This relativity (missionness) does not give rise to any notion of a distinct person (which in regard to Christ pre-exists this sending in time, being eternal and divine). That is to say this relativity supposes the existence of a person. Similarly, though in a different way, his sending of his disciples does not give rise to their personhood, but supposes it. The author has got carried away here with the idea of person being constituted by relativity (expressed in mission).

Moreover, the sending of Christ (in his humanity) presupposes the pre-existence of the person sending (the Father). It is not the same as eternal generation, which does account for the distinct personhood of the Son, and which is solely within the Godhead. This example does not support the author's thesis that personhood as such is constituted by relativity. Such a role of relativity is confined to the divine persons. Outside of that relativity presupposes absoluteness (of substance). It is not only in the moral order that we need to avoid relativism. One needs to be careful here not to fall into a kind of relativism in regard to spiritual creation.

T: The other example is the doctrine of the Logos, the concept of the *Word* which is applied to Jesus. Once again, John picks up a schema of theological thought that was extremely widespread in the Greek and Jewish world. Of course, he

thereby adopts a whole series of contents that are already developed therein and he applies them to Christ. However, there was a new element he introduced into the concept of the Logos. In important respects, what was decisive for him was not so much the idea of an eternal rationality - as among the Greeks, or whatever other speculation there may have been; what was decisive was much rather the relativity of existence which lies in the concept of the *Logos*.

C: "the relativity of existence which lies in the concept of the *Logos*" applies to the *Logos* conceived as divine. But there is already a usage of *logos* that is philosophical, translated in Latin as *ratio*, and in English as *reason*, from which the theological notion is taken. This shows that the notion is not purely relative, for it signifies the real object of knowledge. That is to say the *ratio* (*logos*) takes its nature from the thing known. This also applies to the Son. Though he is constituted as a distinct person by opposition of relation he is not pure relativity. For, he is absolute God. Indeed that is the basis of his person, for he is the Son <u>of God</u>, distinctively constituted as God by being the Word of God (the Father). The author has taken the ultimate difference in regard to the notion of divine person and forgotten that that is not all in any definite idea of things. One does not define man as pure rationality.

"In important respects, what was decisive for him was not so much the idea of an eternal rationality". Rationality is "decisive" for the spiritual creature; it is not so for the divine person because beyond the ultimate absolute differentiation of being absolute being or pure act God is further to be differentiated relatively. In the case of the Son or Word of God this relativity has the character of Reason; but it always supposes the real thing or absolute being that belongs to it (shared with the other two divine persons).

Without revelation we would be able to identify God as personal – for he would fit Boethius's definition. God is not one person only because from the inexhaustible abundance of the divine being issues three persons not one. That makes relativity, not absoluteness ultimately "constitutive" in terms of our understanding of a divine person, but it does not tell the whole story about them for this relativity is based in the absoluteness of being God. One should not take the ultimate *differentia specifica* as totally constituting the real thing understood.

This second example, therefore, does not support the author's thesis.

T: Although this is in the first place only a statement about the Trinity, it is at the same time the fundamental statement about what is at stake in the concept of person.

C: Not so: it is only about the person as divine. Moreover, a word makes no sense unless it signifies some **thing** (primarily some thing absolutely). This applies also in the case of the divine Word where the thing spoken is the absolute being of God, which the Son as a distinct person is along with the Father and the Holy Spirit.

T: Let us summarize:

One final remark on this point. As already indicated, Augustine explicitly transposed this theological affirmation into anthropology by attempting to understand the human person

as an image of the Trinity in terms of this idea of God. Unfortunately, however, he committed a decisive mistake here to which we will come back later. In his interpretation, he projected the divine persons into the interior life of the human person and affirmed that intra-psychic processes correspond to these persons. The person as a whole, by contrast, corresponds to the divine substance. As a result, the trinitarian concept of person was no longer transferred to the human person in all its immediate impact. However, at present we can merely hint at this point; it will become clearer below.

C: Augustine **did not** commit a mistake in limiting the grounding of the notion of person in relativity to the divinity. This is clear from our comments above. This will be dealt with further below.

T: *II. The concept of person in Christology*

The second origin of the concept of person lies in Christology. In order to find its way through difficult problems, theology again used the word *persona* and thus gave the human mind a new task. Theology answered the riddle, "Who and what is this Christ?" by means of the formula, "He has two natures and one person, a divine and a human nature, but only a divine person."

C: This is a poorly worded sentence: one has a nature but is a person.

T: The first misunderstanding is to take the statement, "Christ has only one person, namely, a divine person," as a subtraction from the wholeness of Jesus' humanity.

C: If the sentence were correctly formulated there would be no problem accepting his human nature as complete; as every human person has a complete human nature. Why have a nature which is incomplete?

T: one sees what tremendous effort and intellectual transformation lay behind the working out of this concept of person, which was quite foreign in its inner disposition to the Greek and the Latin mind.

C: The concept of person was not foreign to the Greek and Latin mind. The lack of a word for it specifically does not mean the lack of an understanding of its meaning, which as stated above is implicit in having the notion: "individual substance of rational nature". Aristotle had a clear idea of all these elements of the notion. A person is simply an individual in the spiritual order.

T: It is not conceived in substantialist, but, as we shall soon see, in existential terms.

C: See discussion below. But it is to be remembered that Aristotle is not Plato. His essences, natures and substances are all rooted in really individual existing ones. It is only the abstract notions which are universal. But even these are taken from and referable back to existing reality.

T: In this light, Boethius's concept of person, which prevailed in Western philosophy, must be criticized as entirely insufficient.

C: This is an unwarranted assertion derived from a failure to understand the existential force of individual substance in Aristotelian Metaphysics. Boethius's definition remains valid for the common notion of person which applies to all created persons and is even applicable to divine persons in so far as they are (the one) divine substance. Too much is being made of the *differentia specifica* which distinguishes divine personhood – it is then tried to be made the common notion of person.

T: Remaining on the level of the Greek mind, Boethius defined "person" as naturae rationalis individua substantia, as the individual substance of a rational nature.

C: It is not clear whether the fault here is in the translation. But the Latin is not rendered by "individual substance of a rational nature", but by "individual substance of rational nature" – a nice but significant difference in meaning: "of a rational nature" could signify some other individual.

T: One sees that the concept of person stands entirely on the level of substance.

C: So it does for all created persons, if one focuses on "entirely".

T: This cannot clarify anything about the Trinity or about Christology; it is an affirmation that remains on the level of the Greek mind which thinks in substantialist terms.

C: Neither it can, for it leaves out what is specific to divine personhood, namely, relation. But this difference is additional to the common notion which is "substantialist". So even the common "substantialist" notion is verified in the divine persons; but the "relativist" is not verified in the non-divine. The author has things back to front.

T: By contrast, at the beginning ot the Middle Ages, Richard of St. Victor found a concept of the person derived from within Christianity when he defined person as *spiritualis naturae incommunicabilis existentia,* as the incommunicably proper

existence of spiritual nature *[unmittelbar eigene Existenz]*. This definition correctly sees that in its theological meaning "person" does not lie on the level of essence, but of existence. Richard thereby gave the impetus for a philosophy of existence which had, as such, not been made the subject of philosophy at all in Antiquity.

C: Here the author shifts the discussion away from relation to the act of existence, in order to refute the reliance of the Boethian definition upon essence and substance. First of all, we should note the equation of substance with essence, which is not Aristotle's position at all. For it is insinuated that substance stands for second substance, not first substance. The former is universal and non-existential, whereas the latter is individual and decidedly existential. So the criticism is misplaced

T: In Antiquity philosophy was limited entirely to the level of essence.

C: This statement is false so far as Aristotle is concerned, as explained above. Nor did St. Thomas take Aristotle's philosophy as being essentialist. That if anything applied to Plato's.

T: Scholastic theology developed categories of existence out of this contribution given by Christian faith to the human mind. Its defect was that it limited these categories to Christology and to the doctrine of the Trinity and did not make them fruitful in the whole extent of spiritual reality.

C: The scholastics brought in the category of existence to deal with the problem of Christ's divine personality only. But the category of existence, though it helps to deal with this problem, is not limited to the nature of divine existence. It is only relativity which is limited to the divine in explaining what is distinctive about divine personhood. Existence does have some relevance to the problem of understanding the common notion of person (see below), which cannot leave out existence, for individual substances are existing substances. This aspect receives more emphasis with St. Thomas's development of the centrality of *esse*. But in creatures *esse* does not exist or make sense without *essentia*.

T: This seems to me also the limit of St. Thomas in the matter, namely, that within theology he operates, with Richard of St. Victor, on the level of existence, but treats the whole thing as a theological exception, as it were.

C: As noted, the introduction of existence into the consideration of the common notion of person does not affect the absolute uniqueness of the constitution of the person in the deity. The author puts it as amounting to treating the personhood of the divine persons as "a theological exception". God's nature is indeed theologically exceptional; so too must be the kind of personhood in the deity.

T: In philosophy, however, he remains faithful to the different approach of pre-Christian philosophy. The contribution of Christian faith to the whole of human thought is not realized; it remains at first detached from it as a theological exception, although it is precisely the *meaning* of this new element to call into question the *whole* of human thought and to set it on a new course.

C: In philosophy one would expect that that one remained faithful to philosophy, Christian or pre-Christian. The author is treating this as a fault in St. Thomas, as also in St. Augustine and

Boethius. But it is he who is mistaking the significance of the new element, relativity, which only applies to the understanding of person in the Godhead. Philosophy knows nothing of this specific difference in the common notion of person, nor can it. This fault comes from first defining person in theology and then trying to extend it to philosophy, much the same fault as St. Thomas points out, of noting a specific difference (e.g. rationality) and then inserting it into the genus (e.g. animality)

T: **This brings us to the second misunderstanding that has not allowed the effects of Christology to work themselves out fully. The second great misunderstanding is to see Christ as the simply unique ontological exception which must be treated as such.**

C: We will see what the author makes of this below. But it is hardly a misunderstanding to treat Christ as "the simply unique ontological exception". Who else is a divine person with a human nature? But it seems some treat Christ as something other than human as commonly understood. If so, that is unfortunate, for Christ is not exceptional in that sense.

T: **This exception is an object of highly interesting ontological speculation, but it must remain separate in its box as an exception to the rule and must not be permitted to mix with the rest of human thought. I believe it is useful here to remind ourselves of a methodological insight developed by Teilhard de Chardin in a completely different field. He raises the question of the nature of life, "Is it only an accident, on a tiny planet in the midst of the great cosmos, or is it symptomatic for the direction of reality as a whole?" He uses the discovery of radium** as an example to address this question. "How should one understand the new element? As an anomaly, an aberrant form of matter? ... As a curiosity or as the beginning for a new physics?" Modern physics, Teilhard continues, "would not have come to be if physicists had insisted on understanding radioactivity as an anomaly." Something methodologically decisive for all human thinking becomes visible here. The seeming exception is in reality very often the symptom that shows us the insufficiency of our previous schema of order, which helps us to break open this schema and to conquer a new realm of reality. The exception shows us that we have built our closets too small, as it were, and that we must break them open and go on in order to see the whole.

C: The matter here gets mixed up further; not only the philosophical with the theological but also the (modern) science of nature with philosophy, when he illustrates what he means by reference to the ideas of Teilhard de Chardin. For, it seems from this example that we have to be prepared for a whole new vision of human nature upon knowing the human nature of Christ. What we thought was exceptional about Christ's human nature, precisely as human, now has to be thought of as the norm. The point of the illustration is that we need to be open to further elucidation of our concepts (not beyond Christ's human nature, however).

But Teilhard's example is applicable only to the science of nature, because such scientific knowledge is essentially/ materially incomplete. The illustration is not apt for application to philosophy, even to the philosophy of nature, as if our concepts of form and matter were open to revision in the light of modern discoveries in nuclear physics. The author himself has alerted us time and again to the limited nature of reason as it is applied in modern science.

One can allow that to know Christ is to have a much deeper insight into human nature itself. But it does not mean that our previous understanding of the fundamental principles of human nature or nature was flawed. Is Christ in his humanity not a rational animal? Is he not a union of spiritual soul and material body? Certainly, for us, being in a state of grace changes dramatically our state of life. But, it does not change our nature as such – we are still human, and completely so.

Moreover, for other reasons Teilhard de Chardin's example of the change in our understanding of matter by the discovery of radium is not apt. We have the least understanding of the nature of matter, whilst our understanding of our own nature, with its spiritual dimension, is more certain. It is in the nature of scientific theories, but not of fundamental philosophical knowledge, to be essentially reformable. Metaphysical truths are liable to development but not so that our basic concepts are essentially changed.

The positing of this "great misunderstanding" does not therefore have any purpose, except to prepare us for a revolution in our thinking about the notion of the person being newly proposed.

T: This is the meaning of Christology from its origin: what is disclosed in Christ, whom faith certainly presents as unique, is not only a speculative exception; what is disclosed in truth is

what the riddle of the human person really intends. Scripture expresses this point by calling Christ the last Adam or "the second Adam." It thereby characterizes him as the true fulfillment of the idea of the human person, in which the direction of meaning of this being comes fully to light for the first time.

C: How can Christ be characterised as the true fulfillment of the idea of a <u>human</u> person when he is not one?

T: If it is true, however, that Christ is not the ontological exception, if from his exceptional position he is, on the contrary, the fulfillment of the entire human being, then the Christological concept of person is an indication for theology of how person is to be understood as such. In fact, this concept of person, or simply the dimension that has become visible here, has always acted as a spark in intellectual history and it has propelled development, even when it had long come to a standstill in theology.

C: The Christological concept of person can only be that of a divine person. So, the argument must run: since Christ in his humanity is the light for our understanding of human nature as such, then the understanding of human personhood is to be measured by reference to divine personhood. There seems to be something missing here. Would it not rather be more logical to measure human personhood by reference to Christ's human personhood, which he does not have? The lack of a new person arising in Christ as human is indeed the root of the problem. It is the same whether we adhere to the definition of Boethius or the new thesis of constitution by relativity. For does not Christ as human have everything of substance and relativity that any created human person does? How the advocates of substantiality address this is discussed below.

T: After these two fundamental misunderstandings have been rejected, the question remains, What does the formula mean positively, "Christ has two natures in one person?" I must admit right away that a theological response has not yet completely matured.

C: Perhaps not, but St. Thomas's answer is the best we have. The author's puzzlement is no doubt from the added difficulty of attempting to apply the notion of divine person universally.

T: In the great struggles of the first six centuries, theology worked out what the person is not, but it did not clarify with the same definiteness what the word means positively. For this reason I can only provide some hints that point out the direction in which reflection should probably continue.

C: All of a sudden the author becomes hesitant, backing away from his previous apparently firmly held position, as in saying before: "It took centuries for this statement ["one being in three persons"] to be intellectually penetrated and digested, until it was no longer a mere statement, but truly a means of reaching into the mystery, teaching us, not, of course, to comprehend it, but somehow to grasp it". More to the point, at the very beginning of the article it is flatly asserted: "Relativity toward the other constitutes the human person. The human person is the event or being of relativity." Besides, he has been severely critical of the positions of St. Augustine and St. Thomas on the question. It is nonetheless a commendable retreat from such a strong criticism of the two greatest theologians who have written on the question.

T: I believe two points can be made, a) It is the nature of spirit to put itself in relation, the capacity to see itself and the other. Hedwig Conrad-Martius speaks of the retroscendence of the spirit: the spirit is not merely there; it goes back upon itself, as it were; it knows about itself; it constitutes a doubled existence which not only *is,* but *knows* about itself, *has* itself. The difference between matter and spirit would, accordingly, consist in this, that matter is what is *"das auf sich Geworfene"* (that which is thrown upon itself), while the spirit is *"das sich selbst Entwerfende"* (that which throws itself forth, guides itself or designs itself) which is not only there, but is itself in transcending itself, in looking toward the other and in looking back upon itself.

C: This hint is not original. It amounts simply to a discourse upon the nature of spirit or intellectual substance; that it "returns upon itself". It is one of the familiar proofs for the spirituality of the human intellect. It contrasts the spiritual substance with the material substance (this has been adverted to above). The latter is self-enclosed, its form bound by the limitations of matter; the former is free of such limitation and exclusiveness and open to receive all forms other than itself, with a consequent ability to love in an unlimited way.

The author is using it to support his initial thesis about personhood being rooted in relativity. But it provides no support for this. Cognitive and conative relativity is rooted in an absolute, spiritual substance in the created order and also in the uncreated divine. This openness inherent in spiritual substance does not give any support to the author's thesis, as neither does it support de Lubac's notion of human nature (de Lubac seems to mistake the meaning of created spiritual nature, equating it with the closed character of material or physical nature). The spiritual creature is "naturally" open to divine grace but it is another sort of openness than that ordinarily understood by "natural", it is not in any way active but totally passive or "obediential". To use it to support a divine element (of relativity) in the understanding of person as known in creation is the same "crossing" of the divine with the human, prompted by the positive or factual constitution of spiritual created reality in grace.

T: However this may be in detail - we need not investigate it here - openness, relatedness to the whole, lies in the essence of the spirit. And precisely in this, namely, that it not only is, but reaches beyond itself, it comes to itself. In transcending itself it *has* itself; by being with the other it first becomes itself, it comes to itself. Expressed differently again: being with the other is its form of being with itself. One is reminded of a fundamental theological axiom that is applicable here in a peculiar manner, namely Christ's saying, "Only the one who loses himself can find himself" (cf. Mt. 10:36).

C: This elaborates on the character of openness which belongs to all spiritual creatures (including the spiritual soul) though, as seems mandatory in much Catholic theology today (from philosophical Romanticism), the article slips into the language of contradiction, as in: "In transcending itself it *has* itself; by being with the other it first becomes itself, it comes to itself." (underline added). This is acceptable if taken metaphorically, or in the literary form of paradox, but not literally, or in strict analogy (the possible equivocal use of "coming to itself" is dealt with below). It is the sort of language, it seems, that the German/Romantic mind, or rather imagination, loves to indulge in.

Alluding to the Scriptures in this context is ambiguous. The Scriptures are full of parable and paradox. Provided one observes this linguistic mode such seemingly contradictory oppositions are able to be used. But in the modern philosophical mode of speaking (which modern theology, through Heidegger, slips into at times) this oppositional manner of speaking is quite absurd. A person is the same as himself before he is other than himself. It is not by being with something or someone else that one first becomes oneself. One might not be able to be perfectly what one is meant to be without others (especially God) but how can something become itself if it is not itself to start with? How can one be with the other if it is not already with itself? How can *be with* come before *be*?

T: This fundamental law of human existence, which Mt. 10:36 understands in the context of salvation, objectively characterizes the nature of the spirit which comes to itself and actualizes its own fullness only by going away from itself, by going to what is other than itself. We must go one step further. The spirit is that being which is able to think about, not only itself and being in general, but the wholly other, the transcendent God. This is perhaps the mark that truly distinguishes the human spirit from other forms of consciousness found in animals, namely, that the human spirit can reflect on the wholly other, the concept of God. We may accordingly say: The other through which the spirit comes to itself is finally that

**wholly other for I which we use the stammering word "God."
If this is true, then what was said above can be further clarified
in the horizon of faith and we may say: If the human person is
all the more with itself, and is itself, the more it is able to reach
beyond itself, the more it is with the other, then the person is
all the more itself the more it is with the wholly other, with
God.**

**In other words, the spirit comes to itself in the other, it be-
comes completely itself the more it is with the other, with God.**

C: Here is evident the equivocation in the meaning of "itself"
which is the cause of the problem. "Coming to itself" is equated
with coming to one's perfection, actualising one's own fullness
(rather like in the expression of someone coming to himself,
meaning coming to consciousness). But one has a life and existence, a self, even before he comes to himself in this way. The em-
bryo is already itself before it has any actualisation of its human
capabilities, let alone full actualisation.

In knowers other than God one's perfection, especially in
man, is achieved by "becoming other than oneself" and indeed
this is the way of becoming perfectly oneself. But one should
carefully explain that this is another meaning of coming to oneself. That process which follows upon one's generation or creation is simply an expression of the nature of knowledge – it is the
acquiring of a higher form of life, of self-perfection.

It is supremely verified in "becoming God" (by participation)
but that is a perfection that lies beyond the natural powers of
human nature, or of any creature. This "otherness" or relativity
in our nature is not proof, as it is insinuated, of our perfection as

a creature being only achievable in the possession of God in the beatific vision – that that is the only way in which one becomes oneself. If it were so, we would have a proof from reason of a supernatural truth, dependent entirely upon the positive will of God.

It is a case of the smudging of the boundary between philosophy and literature. What it risks, however, is the blurring of the lines between a realist philosophy/theology and an idealist one

T: And again, formulated the other way around, because this idea seems important to me: relativity toward the other constitutes the human person. The human person is the event or being of relativity. The more the person's relativity aims totally and directly at its final goal, at transcendence, the more the person is itself.

C: This is the conclusion which the language of the "other" seeks to come to. But the conclusion which was expressed at the very beginning is frankly erroneous, as pointed out there. The author, after hesitating, has come back to this assertion. This "hint" seems to have convinced him of the rightness of his original thought.

T: b) In this light we may venture a second approach: According to the testimony of faith, in Christ there are two natures and one person, that of the *Logos*. This means, however, that in him, being with the other is realized radically. Relativity toward the other is always the pre-given foundation to all consciousness as that which carries his existence. But such total being-with-the-other does not cancel his being-with-himself, but brings it fully to itself.

C: Now the author reverts to qualifying what he had said above, saying: "such total being-with-the-other does not cancel his being-with-himself, but brings it fully to itself". Such otherness to which one is fundamentally directed, then, does not come <u>first</u>, it supposes being with oneself. If he had said this in the first place there would be no problem with what he says.

This use of metaphysical language, however, to explain a process of psychological development in knowers gets one into a terrible tangle. The author evidently feels this and oscillates between asserting what he thinks is clear enough and hesitating when it comes to applying it. The problem is, of course, that the metaphysical language has been twisted out of shape by modern German philosophy. It is evident that modern theologians suffer badly here from their lack of a proper education in Thomistic psychology.

T: Of course, one will admit that the chosen terminology, *"una persona-duae naturae"* remains accidental and is not without problems. But the decisive thing that emerges from it for the concept of the person and for the understanding of human beings is, in my judgment, still completely clear. In Christ, in the man who is completely with God, human existence is not canceled, but comes to its highest possibility, which consists in transcending itself into the absolute and in the integration of its own relativity into the absoluteness of divine love.

C: It is concluded that "the chosen terminology, *"una persona-duae naturae"* remains accidental and is not without problems." How can the terminology be accidental? It is the concept that we are dealing with. It will remain of course always a problem for us here below. The terminology has been fashioned on a basis of Greek philosophical understanding of nature and person, most definitively expounded in Aristotle's Metaphysics. St. Thomas has dealt with all the difficulties that the Incarnation involves for our reason and provided as good a solution as seems possible. But modern theologians have tried to do without St. Thomas's genial adaptation of this Greek philosophical insight to the analysis of human nature and divine personhood. Hence, the very terminology, now long settled, remains a problem for them. Having only a familiarity with Greek metaphysics through the modern distorted lenses of Hegel and Heidegger this is not surprising.

T: As a consequence, a dynamic definition of the human person flows from Christ, the new Adam. Christ is the directional arrow, as it were, that indicates what being human tends toward, although, as long as history is still on the way, this goal is never fully reached. At the same time it is clear that such a definition of being human manifests the historicity of the human person. If person is the relativity toward the eternal, then this relativity implies "being on the way" in the manner of human history.

C: Now the author comes back again to his original certainty about the relativist definition of human person. It is presented as referring to the human person as such (which is where he has gone wrong), but it can only apply to the human person as graced. Such a person is necessarily a "wayfarer" on the way to the vision of God. So this directedness is a defining aspect of his graced nature. But even here, as with Christ himself, he is something absolute (being per se – an individual substance) before he is something relative. The relativity really expresses his finality, not his substantial form. Call it part of his full definition if you like, but you cannot leave out the intrinsic or formal causality, which in this case is a divine "quality" (grace) in the soul which is already "the seed of glory". This is a relativity but it is not purely so. Grace is an "ontological" quality, something positive, not merely relative. It is essentially related to God himself (or the Trinity themselves) but it is not without "substance"; it is a participation in the divine substance.

True enough, as a creature with a spiritual soul, man is already, in the order of nature, open to receiving grace, and glory. But this openness is not an actual orientation to same. It remains simply a receptivity to an actualisation should the agent will to grant it. Once granted, of course, as grace, it is inconceivable that there should be any other ultimate or perfect end but glory. De Lubac's mistake here demands in his eyes that there should be two grants involved, for the gift of grace is seen as equivalent to the original gift of nature in creation. But nature is a principle of a natural end, and so, though a gift itself, its end is not another gift but a natural consequence (subject to virtue) of the gift of nature. So, if we are created in grace, then glory is the "natural" end of that gift (subject also to free acceptance), not another gift that might be withheld from one dying in God's grace. That would be to accuse God of arbitrariness.

T: c) In closing, a third idea. In my judgment Christology has a further significance for the understanding of the concept of "person" in its theological sense. It adds the idea of "we" to

the idea of "I" and "you." Christ, whom Scripture calls the final Adam, that is, the definitive human being, appears in the testimonies of faith as the all-encompassing space in which the "we" of human beings gathers on the way to the Father. He is not only an example that is followed, but he is the integrating space in which the "we" of human beings gathers itself toward the "you" of God. Something emerges here that has not been sufficiently seen in modern philosophy, not even in Christian philosophy. In Christianity there is not simply a dialogical principle in the modern sense of a pure "I-thou" relationship, neither on the part of the human person that has its place in the historical "we" that bears it; nor is there such a mere dialogical principle on God's part who is, in turn, no simple "I," but the "we" of Father, Son, and Spirit. On both sides there is neither the pure "I," nor the pure "you," but on both sides the "I" is integrated into the greater "we." Precisely this final point, namely, that not even God can be seen as the pure and simple "I" toward which the human person tends, is a fundamental aspect of the theological concept of the person. It explicitly negates the divine monarchy in the sense of antiquity.

C: Here, at the end, the lack of an adequate grasp of Metaphysics in regard to the analysis of human psychology plays havoc somewhat with what the author wishes to express. Now the notion of a trinity of persons is made to enter into the very notion of person. It is fair enough if one is speaking of the human person in a state of grace. But it is quite wrong to import it into the very notion of person as applied to creatures.

T: It expressly refuses to define God as the pure monarchia and numerical unity. The Christian concept of God has as a

matter of principle given the same dignity to multiplicity as to unity. While antiquity considered multiplicity the corruption of unity, Christian faith, which is a trinitarian faith, considers multiplicity as belonging to unity with the same dignity.

C: The metaphysical mistakes here are, firstly, the confusion of numerical or quantitative unity with transcendental unity. Aristotle did not attribute to God a numerical unity in the strict sense, for God is spiritual, not material. God is to be thought of also by Christians as the one ruler of the universe, for the trinity of persons has no effect whatsoever on the (transcendental) unity of God. There is no multiplicity of being in God. If there were the Trinity would not be a problem. God is absolutely one in being.

Antiquity did not consider multiplicity as the corruption of unity. Potency for existence, or essence, accounts for the multiplicity of created spirits which are not just incorrupt but also incorruptible. Multiplicity as such is not to be confused with the numerical multiplicity which holds only for material beings. Multiplicity as such, therefore, is not a principle of corruption, nor did the best of the ancients think so. Even in material things or bodies matter is not essentially a principle of corruption but only accidentally so. A new body can only be generated through the corruption of an existing one. Evidently the author had not studied carefully enough St. Thomas's commentary on Aristotle's Metaphysics.

T: This trinitarian "we," the fact that even God exists only as a "we," prepares at the same time the space of the human "we." The Christian's relation to God is not simply, as Ferdinand Ebner claims somewhat one-sidedly, "I and Thou," but,

as the liturgy prays for us every day, *"per Christum in Spiritu Sancto ad Patrem"* (Through Christ in the Holy Spirit to the Father). Christ, the one, is here the "we" into which Love, namely the Holy Spirit, gathers us and which means simultaneously being bound to each other and being directed toward the common "you" of the one Father.

The bracketing from Christian piety of the reality of the "we" that emerges in the three-fold formula "through Christ in the Holy Spirit to the Father," and that binds us into the "we" of God and into the "we" of our fellow human beings, happened as a consequence of the anthropological turn in Augustine's doctrine of the Trinity and was one of the most momentous developments of the Western Church. In fundamental ways it influenced both the concept of the Church and the understanding of the person which was now pushed off into the individualistically narrowed "I and you" that finally loses the "you" in this narrowing.

C: The human community exists as a "we" but it is not a person in the sense intended. The one human person, such as I am, does not exist as a "we". Such a multiplication of persons only exists in the one God. The author is drawing out implications of his position but the position, that it is relativity which constitutes the person as such and therefore the human person, is itself flawed.

T: It was indeed a result of Augustine's doctrine of the Trinity that the persons of God were closed wholly into God's interior."

C: This relates to what the author previously said: "Augustine explicitly transposed this theological affirmation into anthropology by attempting to understand the human person as an image of the Trinity in terms of this idea of God. Unfortunately, however, he committed **a decisive mistake** here to which we will come back later. In his interpretation, he projected the divine persons into the interior life of the human person and affirmed that intrapsychic processes correspond to these persons. **The person as a whole, by contrast, corresponds to the divine substance.** As a result, the trinitarian concept of person was no longer transferred to the human person in all its immediate impact. However, at present we can merely hint at this point; it will become clearer below." (emphasis added). The mistake is the author's not Augustine's.

T: **Toward the outside, God became a simple "I," and the whole dimension of "we" lost its place in theology." The individualized "I" and "you" narrows itself more and more until finally, for example in Kant's transcendental philosophy, the "you" is no longer found. In Feuerbach (and thus in a place where one would least suspect it) this levelling of "I" and "you" into a single transcendental consciousness gave way to the breakthrough to personal reality. It thus gave the impetus to reflect more deeply on the origin of our own being which faith recognizes as once and for all disclosed in the word of Jesus the Christ.**

C: The mistake of St. Augustine is now related to the rise of individualism in modern society – because he failed to apply the notion of community that applies in the Trinity to the very notion of human person. But this is what is called drawing a long bow, and a very long bow at that. Individualism is a political ideology that arose at the dawn of the modern age approximately a thousand years after Augustine. The community individualism denies to human persons is a natural one (Aristotle: "man is by nature social"), not a trinitarian one.

Augustine's mistake is traced through to Kant and, then the bow is stretched to its limit; Feuerbach is credited with restoring somewhat the notion of community as something of persons.

We may relate this back to what the author had to say about St. Thomas: "By contrast, at the beginning of the Middle Ages, Richard of St. Victor found a concept of the person derived from within Christianity when he defined person as *spiritualis naturae incommunicabilis existentia,* as the incommunicably proper existence of spiritual nature *[unmittelbar eigene Existenz].* This definition correctly sees that in its theological meaning "person" does not lie on the level of essence, but of existence. Richard thereby gave the impetus for a philosophy of existence which had, as such, not been made the subject of philosophy at all in Antiquity. In Antiquity philosophy was limited entirely to the level of essence. Scholastic theology developed categories of existence out of this contribution given by Christian faith to the human mind. Its defect was that it limited these categories to Christology and to the doctrine of the Trinity and did not make them fruitful in the whole extent of spiritual reality. This seems to me also the limit of St. Thomas in the matter, namely, that within theology he operates, with Richard of St. Victor, on the level of existence, but treats the whole thing as a theological exception, as it were. In philosophy, however, he remains faithful to the different approach of pre-Christian philosophy. The contribution of Christian faith to the whole of human thought is not realized; it remains at first detached from it as a theological exception, although it is precisely the *meaning* of this new element to call into question the *whole* of human thought and to set it on a new course."

We have already commented upon this. Just a few final comments, then, are made here. The problem of Christ not being a human person does call for some further clarifications of the philosophical notion of person. It seems that on Boethius's definition that he should be. "Individual substance", therefore, cannot be enough to constitute personhood if one thinks at the level of essence. For Christ's human nature is an individual substance in that sense. But even to Aristotle individual substance denoted an actually existing one. It is not quite true as alleged that "In Antiquity philosophy was limited entirely to the level of essence". That is something that has come into modern theology from Suarez, and then taken in a conceptualist way. It is not in Aristotle and St. Thomas merely brought out the implicit existential/realist character of a common sense (sense-based) philosophy which was Aristotle's.

Even so a problem remains. For it seems necessary to admit that Christ had a distinct human existence as well as a divine one. The connotation needed in the case of the common notion of person is that this existence must be totally independent, or "incommunicable". One can say that this was assumed in the classical definition. But it was not possible to distinguish it from individuality prior to the consideration of the Christ's individual humanity.

This notion of incommunicability (note Richard of St. Victor's notion of *incommunicabilis existentia*) is what is developed in subsequent scholastic theology. It is even more opposed to the author's thesis here that person fully considered signifies communication or communicability. However, all this has nothing to do with the development of the political ideology of individualism in modern times. This proposition is as fanciful as that of de Lubac associating modern secularism with the Thomist conception of the union of grace and nature to be found in Garrigou-Lagrange. Both accusations are a matter of conflating theological and philosophical influences.